DISCIPLINING THE SOUL, REFINING THE CHARACTER, AND CURING THE SICKNESSES OF THE HEART

Kitāb riyāḍat al-nafs wa-tahdhīb al-akhlāq wa-muʿālajat amrāḍ al-qalb

BREAKING THE TWO DESIRES

Kitāb kasr al-shahwatayn

Books XXII and XXIII of the
Revival of the Religious Sciences
Iḥyāʾ ʿUlūm al-Dīn

D1612014

KA 0354757 4

OTHER TITLES IN THE ISLAMIC TEXTS SOCIETY
AL-GHAZĀLĪ SERIES

FROM THE *Iḥyāʾ ʿulūm al-dīn*

Al-Ghazālī on Invocations & Supplications

Al-Ghazālī on the Manners Relating to Eating

Al-Ghazālī on Patience and Thankfulness

Al-Ghazālī on Love, Longing, Intimacy & Contentment

Al-Ghazālī on the Remembrance of Death & the Afterlife

OTHER WORKS

Al-Ghazālī on the Ninety-Nine Beautiful Names of God
(*al-Maqṣad al-asnā fī sharḥ asmāʾ Allāh al-ḥusnā*)

Al-Ghazālī Letter to a Disciple
(*Ayyuhāʾl-walad*)

AL-GHAZĀLĪ ON DISCIPLINING THE SOUL · *Kitāb Riyāḍat al-nafs* & on BREAKING THE TWO DESIRES *Kitāb Kasr al-shahwatayn*

BOOKS XXII and XXIII of THE REVIVAL OF THE RELIGIOUS SCIENCES *Iḥyā' ᶜulūm al-dīn* · translated with an INTRODUCTION and NOTES by T. J. WINTER

THE ISLAMIC TEXTS SOCIETY
CAMBRIDGE 1995

UNIVERSITY OF WINCHESTER
LIBRARY

Copyright © The Islamic Texts Society 1995

First published in 1995 by
The Islamic Texts Society
Miller's House
Kings Mill Lane
Great Shelford
Cambridge CB22 5EN, U.K.

Reprint 1997, 2001, 2003, 2005, 2007, 2009,
2011, 2012

British Library Cataloguing-in-Publication Data.
A catalogue record for this book is
available from the British Library.

ISBN 978 0946621 42 2 cloth
ISBN 978 0946621 43 9 paper

All rights reserved. No part of this publication may be produced,
installed in retrieval systems, or transmitted in any form
or by any means, electronic, mechanical, photocopying,
recording, or otherwise, without the prior written
permission of the publishers.

Cover design copyright © The Islamic Texts Society

UNIVERSITY OF WINCHESTER

PREFACE

Visitors to the Prophet's tomb in Medina are sometimes beguiled from their prayers by a large calligraphic device fixed directly above the entrance. Those who have time to decipher it find a line of verse which announces the presence of 'A great Prophet, whose created nature was the character which the Merciful has magnified in the Master of Books.'[A] This is the epitaph which Islam has chosen for its founder: a celebration not of his conquests, his divine knowledge, or his eschatological glory, but his *akhlāq*: his noble traits of character.

Given the importance which the Muslim tradition, and Sufism in particular, attaches to 'nobility of character', it is unsurprising that Ghazālī (d.505/1111), who, among his other accomplishments, was surely 'the greatest ethical thinker of Islam,'[B] should have addressed the subject at length in his *Revival of the Religious Sciences*. The present translation makes available to Arabicless readers for the first time[C] two sections of the *Revival* which are especially characteristic of his ethics. Book 22 deals with the diagnosis and cure of bad character, which is seen as a spiritual cataract over the inner eye by which man may see God, while Book 23 takes a closer look at two of the most familiar such vices: gluttony and uncontrolled lust.

[A] In Arabic: *Nabīy[un] ʿaẓīm[un] khalquhu 'l-khuluqu 'l-ladhī/lahu ʿaẓẓama 'r-Raḥmānu fī sayyidi 'l-kutbi*. The line is from the *Madḥa nabawīya balīgha*, a eulogy of the Prophet by the South Arabian saint ʿAbd Allāh al-Ḥaddād (d. 1132 AH/1720 AD). It contains an echo of a famous prayer ascribed to the Prophet: 'O Lord God; Thou hast made good my creation, therefore make good my character also!' and refers to the Qur'ānic verse in which he is told, *Assuredly, thou art of a tremendous character*. Cf. below, p. 7.

[B] Horten, *Die Philosophie des Islam*, 227.

[C] If we exclude the abridged and rather mutilated translation of the entire *Revival* by Maulana Fazlu'l-Karim. There is also a French epitome of the *Iḥyā'* by G.H. Bousquet.

Throughout the two works we are reminded of the Prophet's dictum that 'the best of affairs is the middle course'. Ghazālī's spiritual technology, with characteristically Muslim moderation, aims not at destroying the natural impulses of the soul, but at bringing them into an equilibrium which will allow the mystic to approach God without distraction. Reading his words, we should hope that the outlook which this bespeaks will not be forgotten by contemporary Muslims, who, while eager to shake off the deadening influence of secularity, at times seem given to excesses unworthy of their patrimony.

Generations prior to our own took for granted the need for this inward labour. We, however, should remind ourselves of its function before we can hope to understand Ghazālī's concerns, or indeed most of the concerns of pre-modern ethical literature. With his customary passion, Ananda Coomaraswamy has written of the serious difficulties we face in recovering this perspective:

> Our modern civilization is essentially individualistic and self-assertive, even our educational systems being more and more designed to foster 'self-expression' and 'self-realization' [...] On the other hand, in the words of Eckhart, 'Holy scripture cries aloud for freedom from self'. In this unanimous and universal teaching, which affirms an absolute liberty and autonomy, spatial and temporal, attainable as well here and now as anywhere else, this treasured 'personality' of ours is at once a prison and a fallacy.[A]

The following editions of the *Revival* have been used in preparing the translation: (1) the Amīrīya edition of 1289 AH, as reprinted at the margin of al-Zabīdī's commentary, *Itḥāf al-sādat al-muttaqīn* (Cairo: al-Maymanīya, 1311 AH, referred to as A); (2) the text reproduced in the *Itḥāf* itself, irregularities in which are sometimes pointed out by the commentator (Z); (3) the al-

[A] '*Ākimcañña*: Self-Naughting', in *Coomaraswamy*, II. 88-9.

Maktaba al-Azharīya edition of 1317 AH (MA). Attention is drawn to significant discrepancies only; obvious typographic errors are omitted.

Square brackets have been employed for explanatory material added to the text, and also for the Arabic equivalent of certain locutions for which no satisfactory equivalent exists in English. Qur'ānic material, for which I have drawn heavily on Pickthall's *Meaning of the Glorious Koran*, is in italics and is numerated in accordance with the King Fu'ād Edition, while references to the *ḥadīth* literature follow the system used in Wensinck's *Concordance*, with the more recondite Traditions being identified according to the volume and page numbers of the printed editions of those works listed in the Bibliography. Where such material has not been identified in printed works the reader has been referred to the *takhrīj* of al-Zabīdī and the *zawā'id* literature. Roughly following the system of al-ʿIrāqī, all Traditions have been divided into three groups: those included by al-Bukhārī and Muslim, for which no reference to other sources has been made, those covered by the other collections used by Wensinck, for which other sources are mentioned but rarely, and thirdly, the less important texts; this for the sake of clarity. Non-*ḥadīth* sources used by Ghazālī have also been identified as far as is practicable, since the work can only be fully understood by reference to its antecedents. The pagination in references to the *Iḥyā'* is that of the Cairo edition of Muṣṭafā al-Ḥalabī (1347 AH) as being perhaps more widely available than the three texts listed above.

CONTENTS

Preface v · Abbreviations xiii
Introduction xv · Notes to Introduction lxxii

THE BOOK OF DISCIPLINING THE SOUL, REFINING THE CHARACTER, AND CURING THE SICKNESSES OF THE HEART

[PROLOGUE 3]

An Exposition of the Merit which is in having Good Character, and a Condemnation of Bad Character 7
An Exposition of the True Nature of Good and Bad Character 15
An Exposition of the Susceptibility of the Traits of Character to Change through Discipline 24
A General Exposition of the Means by which Good Character may be Acquired 31
An Exposition Detailing the Method Used in Refining the Character 39
An Exposition of the Symptoms by which the Diseases of the Heart may be Recognised, and the Signs which Indicate a Return to Health 46
An Exposition of the Way in which a Man may Discover the Faults in his Soul 51
An Exposition of Evidence Handed Down from Men of Spiritual Insight and Provided in the Law to the Effect that the Way to Cure the Diseases of the Heart

is by Renouncing one's Desires, and that the Stuff of such Diseases is Following Desires 55
An Exposition of the Signs of Good Character 67
An Exposition of the Way in which Young Children should be Disciplined, and the Manner of their Upbringing and the Improvement of their Characters 75
An Exposition of the Requirements of Aspirancy, the Preliminaries to Spiritual Struggle, and the Progressive Induction of the Aspirant in Treading the Path of Discipline 83

THE BOOK OF BREAKING THE TWO DESIRES

[PROLOGUE 105]

An Exposition of the Merit of Hunger and a Condemnation of Satiety 108
An Exposition of the Benefits of Hunger, and the Evils of Satiety 117
An Exposition of the Method by which Discipline is Used to Break the Greed of the Stomach 133
An Exposition of the Variance in the Rule and Merit of Hunger in Accordance with the Circumstances of Men 154
An Exposition of the Ostentation which may Proceed from the Renunciation of Desirable Foods and from Eating Frugally 161
A Discourse on Sexual Desire 165
An Exposition of the Aspirant's Obligations Regarding the Renunciation or Contraction of Marriage 171
An Exposition of the Merit of him who Counters the Desire of the Sex and the Eye 183

Contents

Notes 193
APPENDIX I: Persons cited in text 209
APPENDIX II: Translations of the *Revival* into European languages 225
APPENDIX III: The Wonders of the Heart 233
Bibliography 245
Index to Qur'ānic Quotations 265
General Index 269

ABBREVIATIONS

Bryson	:	Plessner (ed.), *Der Oikonomikoc ...*
Bidāya	:	Ibn Kat͟hīr, *al-Bidāya wa'l-nihāya*
BSOAS	:	*Bulletin of the School of Oriental and African Studies*
EI	:	*Encyclopaedia of Islam* (First edition)
EI[2]	:	*Encyclopaedia of Islam* (Second edition)
Fihrist	:	Ibn al-Nadīm, *K. al-Fihrist*
Fuṣūl al-madanī	:	al-Fārābī, *Fuṣūl al-madanī*
GAL	:	Brockelmann, *Geschichte ...*
GALS	:	Brockelmann, *Geschichte ...(Supplement)*
GAS	:	Sezgin, *Geschichte ...*
G͟hāya	:	Ibn al-Jazarī, *G͟hāyat al-nihāya*
Hannād	:	Ibn al-Sarī, *K. al-Zuhd*
Hujwīrī	:	Nicholson (tr.), *Kas͟hf al-maḥjūb*
IC	:	*Islamic Culture*
IQ	:	*Islamic Quarterly*
Iṣāba	:	Ibn Ḥajar, *al-Iṣāba ...*
Istīʿāb	:	Ibn ʿAbd al-Barr, *al-Istīʿāb ...*
JAOS	:	*Journal of the American Oriental Society*
JESHO	:	*Journal of the Economic and Social History of the Orient*
JRAS	:	*Journal of the Royal Asiatic Society*
Kās͟hif	:	D͟hahabī, *al-Kās͟hif ...*
Lumaʿ	:	Sarrāj, *K. al-Lumaʿ*
Maʿārif	:	Ibn Qutayba, *al-Maʿārif*
Mas͟hāhīr	:	Ibn Ḥibbān, *Mas͟hāhīr ʿulamā' al-amṣār*
Ma't͟hūr,	:	Daylamī, *al-Firdaws bi-ma't͟hūr ...*
MIDEO	:	*Mélanges de l'Institut Dominicain d'Études Orientales*
MW	:	*The Muslim World*
Miskawayh	:	Miskawayh, *Tahd͟hīb al-ak͟hlāq*
Muʿāraḍa	:	Tustarī, *K. al-Muʿāraḍa*
Munqid͟h	:	G͟hazālī, *al-Munqid͟h min al-ḍalāl*
Q.	:	*al-Qur'ān al-Karīm*
Qūt	:	Makkī, *Qūt al-qulūb*
Ṣifat al-ṣafwa	:	Ibn al-Jawzī, *Ṣifat al-ṣafwa*
SEI	:	*Shorter Encyclopaedia of Islam*
SI	:	*Studia Islamica*

Tābi^cīn	:	Dāraquṭnī, *Dhikr asmā' al-Tābi^cīn*
Tahdhīb al-Tahdhīb	:	Ibn Ḥajar, *Tahdhīb al-Tahdhīb*
Tārīkh Baghdād	:	al-Khaṭīb al-Baghdādī, *Tārīkh Baghdād*
Wakī^c	:	Ibn al-Jarrāḥ, *K. al-Zuhd*
ZDMG	:	*Zeitschrift der Deutschen Morgenländischen Gesellschaft*

INTRODUCTION

I. PRELIMINARY REMARKS

TO SOME extent, the history of Muslim mystical literature mirrors the two stages of technique and experience which are its subject. Although there is evidence to suggest that a direct experience of the Divine was a conditioning fact of much early Muslim piety, the sober articulation of this encounter was not attempted for several hundred years. An orthodoxy had to coalesce from countless different strands before it could withstand the shock of an Islamic monism; and even when the impact came, climaxing with the elegant and uncompromising *gnosis* of men like Ibn al-ʿArabī and al-Jīlī, the consequent friction was intense. Only the preceding centuries of moderate, devotional mysticism legitimised Sufism sufficiently for this to occur at all.

Part of Ghazālī's significance lies in his historical situation at the isthmus (*barzakh*) between these two traditions. Authentically at home both in the idiom of ascesis, with its fasts and meditations on death, and in the controlled ecstasy of a metaphysic of encounter which had absorbed the best of Neoplatonism, he is the Janus of Muslim thought.[1] It is from this, rather than from any unique originality, that his prestige derives: he defined an equilibrium between letter and spirit which, despite the continuing vitality of both extremes, was to determine the tenor of Muslim religious life from his day on.

Ghazālī was a polymath who excelled in most of the traditional Islamic disciplines.[2] His was the distinction of refuting those aspects of Greek philosophy which were thought to contradict truths received in the Islamic scriptures.[3] His also were some of the most serious works of Aristotelian logic,[4] of Islamic jurisprudence,[5] theology,[6] the definitive rebuttal of the

Ismāʿīlī sect,[7] and four influential textbooks of law according to the S͟hāfiʿī rite.[8] But many would argue that his most characteristic and impressive contribution to the evolution of Islam lay in the realm of spiritual method. His was a life of introspection, doubt, and unmistakeable sincerity, which bestowed on him a gift for recognising inward purity and the techniques by which man may achieve it. He was distressed by what he saw as the excessive formalism of the day, in which brilliant scholars expounded texts of the greatest complexity, but with intentions tainted by vainglory. In his most interesting work, the *Revival of the Religious Sciences*, one senses a conviction that the righteous élite had been corroded, expressed with an urgency which can only have been intensified by the political vagaries of the period and the fragile position of the doctrine and law school to which he belonged.[9] Deliverance could only come through a rekindling of that sincerity and sanctity for which the early generations of Islam had been celebrated, by means of passing through the refiner's fire of self-naughting. The resulting clarity of soul not only resulted in personal integrity, it opened the way for the supernal light to flood in from above. This methodology, he discovered, lay in that mystical tradition which since about the third century of Islam had been known as Sufism.

To outline the history of Muslim mysticism is not our purpose in this introduction; many excellent accounts are available elsewhere.[10] Instead we shall content ourselves with exploring those trends which were directly formative of G͟hazālī's influential system of ethics and psychomachy.

It is now a commonplace—but one which bears repeating—that from the time when Louis Massignon's work on Sufi terminology appeared, if not before, most Western scholars have acquiesced in Sufism's own claim to an Islamic scriptural provenance. In his *Essai sur les origines du lexique technique de la mystique musulmane*, first published in 1922, the French orientalist, informed both by a mastery of the texts and by his own ecumenical vision, showed that the manner in which the classical derivation of Sufi lexis from the Qur'ān and *ḥadīth*, far from being an exercise in *mauvais foi* or an attempt to hoodwink the orthodox, was both historically and methodologically authentic. Against the traditional Orientalist dismissal of the Muslim source texts as outpourings of an arid legalism, and the claim that the richness of medieval Muslim spirituality must perforce be the product of foreign influence, he argued convincingly that it was the Prophet's intense and sustained experience of God, supported by his moral excellence, which provided the ultimate reference for Sufism. The Qur'ānic citations which often introduce each chapter in the classical Sufi texts are not justifications, but archetypes and commands.[11]

II. SELF-NAUGHTING IN THE ISLAMIC SCRIPTURES

According to the Islamic revelation, the quarry of the religious life cannot be visible here on earth. *No vision can attain Him,* says the Qur'ān, *but He attains all vision.*[12] When Moses asks to see God on Sinai, he is told: *Never shall you see Me.*[13] And yet *wheresoever you turn, lo, there is the face of God*:[14] the Maker may be veiled, but His works, His evidentiary signs, are made strikingly palpable to all men:

> *In the creation of the heavens and the earth, and the succession of night and day, are signs for people of understanding* [albāb]. *Those who remember God while standing, sitting, and on their sides, and who meditate on the creation of the heaven and the earth. 'Our Lord! You have not created this in vain. Glorious are You! So ward off from us the punishment of hell!'*[15]

> *Do they not see the camels, how they are created?*
> *And the sky, how it is raised?*
> *The hills, and how they are set up;*
> *The earth, how it is spread out?*[16]

The natural world contains the *vestigia Dei* which inform man of the Divine attributes and suggest a proper response. God is, for instance, the Resurrector:

Does man think that he will be left to no purpose?
Was he not a drop of gushing fluid?
Then He made him a clot, and shaped him and fashioned,
And created the pair, male and female;
Is not such a one able to quicken the dead?[17]

Man recognises these attributes with his *lubb*[18] (plural *albāb*), a word whose resonances include 'core' or 'seed', and denote an intuitive rather than a purely discursive cognition. The resulting state of secure conviction (*īmān*) is opposed to *kufr*, which has the sense of the 'covering up' of God's existence and signs, and is translated as 'unbelief' only for want of an adequate English term.[19]

The revelation of God in nature is complemented by His revelation in the Qur'ānic text itself. This too is self-authenticating:

Had it been from any but God they would have found many discrepancies therein.[20]

Again it is the *lubb* which perceives its divine authorship:

A Book which We have revealed unto you, full of blessing, that they may reflect upon its signs, and that men of understanding [albāb] *may remember.*[21]

It is not merely by defective reasoning that the Qur'ān is rejected, but through God's covering-over of the faculty of intuition:

We have set veils over their hearts, lest they understand it, and a barrier in their ears.[22]

To be able to respond to God's language in both its modalities, the heart (*qalb*) of man[23] thus needs His grace (*raḥma*) and providential guidance (*hudā*); and although *He singles out for His grace whom He will,* and *guides whom He will,* man may render himself more deserving of this gift by cultivating a policy of inward strife against his *hawā*, the instinctive, animal propensity to immediate gratification, which is the domain and instrument of Satan.[24]

Hawā is the cause of *ḍalāl*, going astray, which may lead not only to moral depravity, but to the greatest sin of all: polytheism (*shirk*). The Prophet is told:

> *Who is further astray than the one who follows his own* hawā *without guidance from God?*[25]

> *Obey not him whose heart We have made heedless of Our remembrance, who follows his own* hawā.[26]

> *Say: 'I am forbidden to worship those whom you call upon besides God.' Say: 'I will not follow your* ahwā' [pl. of hawā], *for then I would go astray, and would not be one of those who are guided'.*[27]

> *Have you seen him who takes his* hawā *to be his god?*[28]

The lower soul, or 'self' [*nafs*], is the enemy:

> *He who purifies it has succeeded,*
> *and he who stunts it has failed.*[29]

After his temptation by Potiphar's wife, Joseph declares:

> *Truly the* nafs *incites constantly to evil, save when my Lord has mercy.*[30]

It is not only God's mercy which saves man from his lower impulses, however; he is able to earn this mercy through effort and discipline.

> *Those who strive for Our sake, We shall surely guide to Our paths.*[31]

Whoso transgresses, and prefers the life of this world, for him Hellfire shall be the place of resort.

And whoever fears the standing before his Lord, and forbids his nafs *its* hawā, *for him Heaven shall be the place of resort.*[32]

The world [*dunyā*] for which the *nafs* yearns is not a pleasant thing; it is *the comfort of illusion*[33] and *nought but game and play.*[34] Its baseness and short duration are contrasted constantly with the *ākhira*, literally 'the other', which refers to the life to come. Man, who *has been shown the two paths,*[35] must choose the latter over the former, by means of a self-control and discipline enabled by God's grace.

The methods of this 'greater *jihād*' (as the *jihād* against the lower soul is termed in a famous saying ascribed to the Prophet),[36] are outlined in several places in the Qur'ān. There is the virtue of *tawakkul*, reliance upon God; there is *tawba*, the turning to Him in repentance, together with *khawf* and *rajā'*: fear of God's chastisement and hope for His reward. By cultivating these virtues man attains to grace, and hence to Paradise, the eternal realm of beauty and perfection.

The Qur'ān also speaks of what may be regarded as more 'secular' virtues, which must characterise the practitioners of its message. Generosity, courage, loyalty, truthfulness and patience receive the greatest emphasis.[37] It holds up a range of exemplars from the past as ideals for the moral life: Abraham, for instance, is *mild, imploring and penitent.*[38] The sage Luqmān counsels his son thus:

Do not turn your cheek in scorn towards people, nor walk with arrogance upon the earth. God loves not the arrogant boaster. Be modest in your bearing, and subdue your voice.[39]

And the Prophet Muḥammad is told:

It was by the grace of God that you were gentle with them. Had you been stern and fierce of heart they would have dispersed from round about you. So pardon them, and ask forgiveness for them, and consult with them in affairs.[40]

Your Lord decrees that you worship none save Him, and be kind to parents. Should one or both of them attain to old age with you, then do not say 'Fie!' to them, or repel them, but speak to them with gracious words. Lower to them the wing of humility through mercy, and say, My Lord! Have mercy upon them, as they did care for me when I was small.[41]

Other passages condemn backbiting, lying, extravagance and hypocrisy, and praise justice, sexual restraint, forgiveness and moderation, building up a comprehensive system of practical ethics which was firmly to underpin the ideals of subsequent Muslim society and thought.

The word *akhlāq*, which later became the standard term for 'ethics', occurs only once in the Qur'ān, in its singular form *khuluq*, which here bears the apparent meaning of 'character' or 'character trait'. In a celebrated verse, the Prophet is told: *Truly, yours is a tremendous trait of character*.[42] Yet in the *ḥadīths*, the vast body of sayings and episodes attributed to the Prophet, it is employed very extensively, as the first section of the present translation will show. Perhaps the best-known account is that Tradition according to which the Prophet said, 'I was sent only to perfect the noble qualities of character' (*innamā buʿithtu li-utammima makārim al-akhlāq*).[43] Many other *ḥadīths* commend improving the character:

O Lord God! Thou hast made good my creation; therefore make good my character also![44]

A bondsman [of God] may attain through his good character high and noble degrees in the Afterlife, even though he be feeble in his worship.[45]

The *ḥadīths* also stress the importance of the related duty of self-discipline:

> Heaven is surrounded by unpleasant things, while Hell is surrounded by desires.[46]

> If you see a man who has been given renunciation (*zuhd*) of the world, and goodly speech, then draw close to him, for he has been taught wisdom.[47]

The Prophet expounded an attitude of responsible austerity, based on the Qur'an, in which extremes of worldliness and of asceticism were eschewed. He placed great emphasis on integrity of conduct, and there are many *ḥadīth*s which depict his own personal excellence, which undoubtedly go a long way towards explaining the devotion and loyalty which he evinced in his followers.

> God will not show mercy to him who does not show mercy to others.[48]

> A man does not believe until he likes for his brother what he likes for himself.[49]

> All creatures are God's children, and those dearest to God are the ones who treat His children most kindly.[50]

III. EARLY ISLAMIC PSYCHOMACHY

Faced with this large body of moral guidance, which was not systematised until the advent of a sophisticated legal theory,[51] the primitive Muslim community soon diverged into various broad traditions of interpretation, each with its own devotional and ethical priorities. Apart from the spectrum which recognised religiosity and self-interest as its two poles, there were subtler ranges of emphasis: on fear as opposed to hope, isolation as opposed to living with the trials of human company, on the rejection or acceptance of positions of juridical authority.

The otherworldly impulse which is the essence of every great religion was given added impetus by the horror felt in pious circles at the often secular and corrupt administration of the Umayyad dynasty. Many forms of early Islamic piety were inspired by a rejection of Umayyad rule, either in the form of armed dissent, as in the case of the Shīʿī and the Khārijī sects, or in the guise of a severe, world-denying asceticism. This latter tendency, which looked for inspiration to the example of certain of the Companions of the Prophet,[52] and of the subsequent generation (the so-called 'Followers'[53]), verged at times on a penitential self-contempt which seems closer to primitive Christianity than to the austere but essentially moderate example of the Prophet.

Massignon's verdict about the Islamic credentials of Sufism should not obscure the fact that in the early formative period — we have in mind here the first and second centuries of Islam— substantial and verifiable Christian influence upon certain forms of Muslim piety did take place. Although it is true that Islamic and Christian understandings of the moral good and the path to self-purification did in any case overlap to a large extent, specifically Christian attitudes to 'the world, the flesh, the devil' are identifiable in the hagiographies of several Muslim figures of this period. In apparent contrast to the teaching of the Prophet, who regularly fasted and hungered, but who forbade his Companions to fast on every day,[54] the Iraqi ascetic Mālik ibn Dīnār (d. 131/748) refused to eat even so basic a commodity as dates, dismissing them as a luxury.[55] Ibrāhīm ibn Adham (second/eighth century), who lived for a while in seclusion at a Basra mosque, would eat only once every three days.[56] And Sahl al-Tustarī, perhaps the best known of all Muslim ascetics, and of whom various encounters with Christian anchorites are recorded,[57] is said to have eaten only once every fifteen or even twenty-five days.[58] Even more notably, in the realm of sexuality, al-Dārānī's remark that 'Whoever marries has inclined towards the world'[59] is more reminiscent of the 'Virginity renders mortals like unto angels' of St John Chrysostom[60] than the 'Marry and multiply'[61] of the

Arabian Prophet. Muslim attitudes to Christians in the Umayyad period were often respectful, even companionable, and it seems certain that the attitude of radical repudiation of the world which characterised much early Christian piety did to a certain extent infiltrate Muslim ideals.[62]

Towards the middle of the second Islamic century (mid-eighth century AD), this rigorous asceticism began to be tempered by a rediscovery of the transformative, often passionate love of God and confidence in His mercy. This attitude found a degree of scriptural warrant: the Qur'ān had proclaimed that *Those who have faith, have more love of God*;[63] while a popular prayer attributed to the Prophet ran: 'O Lord God! Grant me love of Thee, and love of those who love Thee, and love of that which brings me nearer to the love of Thee! And render Thy love dearer to me than cool water!'[64] The Baghdad mystic Bis͟hr al-Ḥāfī (d. *c* 227/841), revising earlier stresses on the dread of meeting a wrathful God,[65] declared, 'Only a doubter resents death; for a lover will always love meeting his beloved, whatever the circumstance.'[66] Even more influential was Yaḥyā ibn Muʿādh, the preacher from the Persian city of Rayy, whose teaching of hope in God, with a consequentially benign attitude to the things of this world—he was famous for his public banquets—was an example accepted by a number of later mystics.[67]

These two alternatives, of fear of God and hope in His mercy, were, in early Muslim piety, closely associated with differing understandings of 'the world'.[68] In the austere milieu of the first century, this was an enemy, bewailed and condemned in innumerable sermons and pious counsels. For instance, al-Ḥasan al-Baṣrī, precursor of the Sufis at Basra: 'The world is a place of departure, not of permanence. Adam was expelled from Heaven into it only as a punishment. So beware of it, for the sole provision which one may take from it is not having taken from it, while the only prosperity which is to be had in it is poverty. Beware of this treacherous, faithless, deceitful abode!'[69] Yet whereas in Christianity the religious life had demanded a categorical rejection of the world as 'fallen', Islam, unencumbered by a doctrine of original sin, and inspired by the Qur'ānic image of the world as created for human usufruct as well as temptation, was, in the course of its second and third centuries, able to evolve a relatively more cheerful attitude, often holding that the 'world' was morally neutral and that the worth or hazard of any participation in it was determined by the extent of an agent's conformity to the revealed Law, and his inner purposes. To cite Ibn Muʿā<u>dh</u> again: 'How could I refrain from loving the world, wherein God has given me livelihood and nourishment, whereby I am able to preserve my earthly life, the life in and by which I can achieve that obedience to God which guides me to the next world?'[70] Rarely is the world (*dunyā*) condemned *tout court* in Sufi tracts; instead, it is the *ḥubb al-dunyā*, 'love of the world', against which the spiritual wayfarer must continually secure himself.[71]

These polarities, both of fear or hope towards God, and of rejection or celebration of the world, had become well-developed traditions by the fourth Muslim century when the first Sufi compendia were compiled. These in most cases represent a mature piety which sought to reap the benefits of both possibilities. But from the viewpoint of practical method, the problem remained as to which path the devotee should tread: that of grieving self-discipline through fasts and night vigils, or the way of thankfully enjoying God's blessings. The frequency of the debate over the relative worth of fear and hope, or renunciation and consumption, suggests that Sufi initiates were not always sure how to combine the two in practice.

The resolution of this tension was sought in multiple ways. One of these, which found support in the teaching of the Prophet himself, stressed an awareness of the importance of right intention in religious acts. Muslim spirituality had always been sensitive to this: 'Actions depend on their intentions', a *ḥadī<u>th</u>* famously affirms, 'and every man is credited only with that which he has intended'.[72] Al-Ḥasan al-Baṣrī declared, 'Men are consigned everlastingly to heaven or to hellfire only by virtue of their intentions.'[73] One early Sufi recounts how he was once late for attendance at his mosque, and, realising that for years he had taken unconscious pride in praying in the front row, forced himself to repeat all the prayers that had thus been polluted by ostentation.[74] There hence developed a recognition that acts of self-mortification could achieve the reverse of their intended effect by opening doors into an unwitting vanity which might damage the heart far more deeply than any indulgence in worldly pleasure. This recognition, and the consequent practice of meticulously scrutinising the conscience, found its best expression in the writings of the early Baghdad mystic al-Ḥārith al-Muḥāsibī (d. 247/857).[75]

Muḥāsibī, more than any other writer, is Ghazālī's precursor, and his influence is especially apparent in the realm of ethics and self-discipline.[76] His lengthy disquisitions on 'self-delusion' (*ghurūr*), that vice of the soul which contaminates spiritual works with vainglory, commend the practice of *muḥāsaba*, 'self-examination,' from which Muḥāsibī's name is itself said to derive.[77] 'Before each of your acts,' he urged, 'ask "Why?" and "For whom?". Should it be for God, then continue, while should it be for anyone else, then cease, and blame your soul for having pointed you towards the impulses of passion.'[78] Without *muḥāsaba*, ascetic piety is liable to redound against its practitioners: 'How many a one who was diligent in the performance of outward acts of service has become fuel for the flames of Hell and his acts of service have become as dust strewn abroad [...] Though there were to come to you a revelation that you were praised by the Lord of the Throne, yet it would behove you to cleave to fear and godliness.'[79]

Another development in Sufism also served to resolve the tension of opposites indicated above. This was the evolution of a mystical typology of 'stations' (*maqāmāt*), first attempted, we are told, by Muḥāsibī's contemporary, Dhu'l-Nūn of Egypt (d. 245/859). According to him, the spiritual wayfarer passes in turn through the *maqāmāt* of faith, fear, reverence, obedience, hope, love, passion, and intimacy with God.[80] In this fashion, attitudes which seem to be opposed can be integrated into the spiritual life in the form of stages in a progressive ascent to God. Although the sequence of these 'stations' was not defined with much consistency in classical Sufism, it is generally the case that the *maqām* of fear is ranked below that of hope, above which are conditions of love (*shawq*) and joyful contentment (*riḍā*) with God's will.[81] Each of these stations engenders a particular attitude to the world, and requires a particular type of spiritual method in order to overcome the receding passional self. As the mystic's experience of God grows brighter and more permanent, the devil's hold on him loosens, until techniques of abstinence which had been essential at the outset can progressively be dispensed with, to be replaced with the increasing use of tools such as *murāqaba* (vigilant meditation) and *muḥāsaba*.

The third method by which a correct attitude to 'fear and hope' was sought lay in the quest for a golden mean between the two. Much of early Muslim religious history can be interpreted as the story of tensions resolving themselves through median positions which in time were regarded as constituting 'orthodoxy'. The Ashʿarī doctrinal school, which ultimately became a prevalent orthodoxy, is a compromise between the literalism of the Ḥanbalite traditionalists, and the rationalism of the Muʿtazilī sect.[82] In the same way, 'Sunnī' ideas of political legitimacy represent a compromise between the conflicting notions held by the Shīʿa, who believed that a descendant of ʿAlī should be 'Commander of the Faithful', and the more egalitarian Khārijīs, who stressed piety alone.[83] This collective instinct was also at work within Sufism, and ensured that the temper of dread was not contradicted by hope, but came to be moderated and balanced by it, so that the two, complementing each other, became the 'wings by which the believer may fly'.[84] Asceticism (*zuhd*) was now defined not as a practice but an outlook; not as the simple renunciation of the world, but as an indifference to its temptations. '*Zuhd*,' as al-Junayd simply remarked, 'is for the heart to be empty of what the hand is empty of'.[85]

Attaining this degree of detachment from the world, however, could only come about through the hard test of self-discipline (*riyāḍa*). 'Slaughter the soul with the knives of contravening its desire', the Sufis urged.[86] For the soul (*nafs*), when unweaned, is 'constantly enjoining evil' (*ammāra bi'l-sū'*), as the Qur'ān describes it; it is the subtle, unfixable abode of *hawā*, the condition of desire, and of *shahwa*, the desire itself.[87] These cravings are multifarious and untiring: for wealth, fame, power, physical gratification—everything, in short, that draws man away from God and towards the lower possibilities of the human condition. All of these attributes must be purged from the heart, and replaced by their praiseworthy opposites. The *nafs*, conventionally translated as 'soul',[88] and which corresponds to what is known in Latin and Greek as *anima* and *psyche*, as the lower, instinctive, mortal self of man, stands opposed to the *rūḥ* (*spiritus, pneuma*), the imperishable Spirit, which, as the Qur'ān tells the Prophet to announce, is *of the command of my Lord, and of knowledge you have been vouchsafed but little.*[89] Of the soul, much can be said; of the Spirit, little that has meaning to minds still in the grip of their passional natures. Ghazālī, for one, wishes there to be no doubt that his *Iḥyā'* explores only the sciences of the soul, and will not venture to speak of higher, more metaphysical realities.[90]

When the believer conforms to God's will, the 'soul which constantly enjoins evil' is tamed, and, over time, grows enfeebled. Unseated from its dominant place in the heart, it gives way to the 'soul which blames' (*al-nafs al-lawwāma*)—another Qur'ānic term—which came to denote the active conscience stricken by guilt and self-reproach whenever God's commands are violated and the lower soul wins a skirmish with the rational mind.[91] After much inward labour, the *nafs muṭma'inna*, the 'soul at peace', should predominate.[92] These three conditions of the soul are not to be thought of as distinct stages, but rather as different aspects or potentials within the soul, which are all present simultaneously, some being latent and others active. Their relative strength is contingent upon four factors: man's inborn disposition, which may be good or evil, angelic or animal; his upbringing; his self-discipline in adulthood, and, finally, God's grace. It is the 'soul at peace' which is worthy of divine acceptance; in a celebrated passage in the Qur'ān, God exclaims: *O thou soul at peace! Return to thy Lord, pleasing and well-pleased! Enter thou among My bondsmen! Enter thou My garden!*[93]

The lower soul is often likened to an animal, such as a dog or donkey.[94] Whereas in early Muslim piety it was often believed, perhaps under Christian influence, that this creature should be put to death, later generations (from about the year 200 onwards), developed the teaching that it could not be killed, but should instead be trained and disciplined. Thus even the stubbornest horse can become a well-trained steed, a necessary aid on the spiritual path.[95]

Although the actual methods followed in self-discipline varied considerably, most of the early ascetics stressed four practices: 'solitude, silence, hunger, and sleeplessness.'[96] Solitude (*ʿuzla*), even if pursued only on occasion, distances the seeker from worldly distractions. 'Shun people as you would shun a lion', was common advice.[97] While there is little evidence that early Sufis often lived out their lives in complete eremitic isolation, many did seek to wander 'alone with their Lord' in deserts, islands or mountains, after which they might return to teach. (The story of Ibrāhīm al-Khawwāṣ wandering on a mountain in Syria, recorded below on pages 61–2, is characteristic.) Reference was often made to the Prophet's annual retreats to a mountain cave outside Mecca, where, following long meditation, he received the divine revelation.[98] A precedent was also found in his recommendation to withdraw in a mosque for the last ten days of Ramaḍān.[99] Unlike the Desert Fathers of the Church, however, the Sufis normally professed a spirituality which confronted the trials of everyday life, and, where possible, sought to ameliorate the lot of others. 'The believer who lives with people, and tolerates the harm they do, is better than he who does not.'[100] The work here translated shows a representative attitude: the isolation which Ghazālī recommends, in conjunction with the remembrance (*dhikr*) of God, and meditation (*fikr*),[101] is clearly meant to be practiced only for short periods: it can be achieved merely by pulling one's shirt over one's head.[102] An entirely solitary life, while attempted by a few, could not ultimately flourish in the soil of an eminently social religion such as Islam.

The second fundamental practice, silence (*ṣamt*), was similarly emphasised: the tongue, 'while small in weight, is a dangerous thing',[103] for had not the Prophet said: 'Whoso is silent, is saved'?[104] Many of the mortal vices, such as backbiting, slander, flattery, lying, and cursing, are occasioned by ill-considered speech. Hence Sufyān al-Thawrī could declare, 'Long silence is the key to worship'.[105] Another remarked, 'A wise man's tongue is located beneath his heart: if he wishes to speak, his words will refer to his heart, and if they serve it, he will speak; otherwise he will hold his peace. The heart of an ignorant man, however, is on the tip of his tongue: his words never refer to his heart, and whatever his tongue desires to utter he will say.'[106] But just as the *nafs* may assert itself by means of speech, it may also be gratified by silence, and this, too, is to be guarded against. For silence can be nothing more than a ploy to convince others of one's own gravamen and piety; likewise, to remain silent in the presence of falsehood is to be nothing more than a 'dumb devil'.[107] The key is to be sought in the heart; as Bishr al-Ḥāfī taught: 'When it would please you to speak, be silent, and when it would please you to be silent, speak!'[108]

The religious benefits of hunger, or at least of the renunciation of food, were recognised from the earliest days of Islam, for fasting (*ṣawm*, *ṣiyām*) was a cardinal duty of the new faith. The fast in the month of Ramaḍān, which requires that one refrain from food, drink, and sexual relations from first light until sundown, is not only an act of worship which brings reward from God, but is a recognised means of self-purification.[109] According to a *ḥadīth*, 'Patient endurance (*ṣabr*) is half of faith, and fasting is half of patient endurance.'[110] In addition to this obligatory annual fast, other days may be observed as fasts: Mondays and Thursdays, for instance, or the middle three days of each lunar month.[111] Many early ascetics also observed the 'Fast of David', eating and fasting on alternate days.[112] But uninterrupted fasting (*ṣawm al-dahr*) was generally condemned, following the teaching of the Prophet.[113]

During the first century, a semi-independent virtue was made of hunger (*jūᶜ*), which could be attained externally to the canonical form of fasting simply by reducing one's intake of food.[114] Some accounts of the early ascetics' love of hunger have already been given above, and many more will be encountered in the translation which follows. But hunger and fasting are not ends in themselves, as acts of mortification with no higher efficacy. For, as Hujwīrī put it, 'fasting is really abstinence, and this includes the whole method of Sufism'.[115] According to Tustarī, 'When God created the world, He set sin and ignorance in satiety, and knowledge and wisdom in hunger.'[116] Bishr al-Ḥāfī said, 'Hunger purifies the heart, kills caprice (*hawā*), and yields subtle knowledge.'[117] As the physical form diminishes and one's regular reliance on the world becomes more tenuous, then the *nafs* is subdued, the unseen world becomes nearer of access, one's need to spend time in earning a living is reduced, and prayer itself becomes easier.[118]

Whether it was possible to live entirely without food was seriously debated in ascetic circles. Hujwīrī tells us of a man he had met who did not eat for eighty consecutive days and nights.[119] More frequently, we find references to fasts of forty days[120] (forty being the conventional 'number of trial and repentance'[121]). Here, however, it is a question of men who are nourished by Divine grace, for such feats are declared impossible by the physicians: the foodless man, who, like the angels, is free of passion, is nourished from the same transcendant source. This may not be a permanent condition, however. As the conversion to God becomes more complete, hunger as a technique diminishes in significance. Sahl al-Tustarī himself, whose feats of abstinence have already been noted, was able in the end to eat 'without any particular limit, or any fixed time'[122]—for his *nafs* had been definitively subdued.[123]

The last of the four famous techniques of vanquishing the *nafs*, sleeplessness (*sahr*), is less frequently spoken of. It is touched upon by G͟hazālī, who explains that 'sleep hardens and deadens the heart, unless, that is, one sleeps only in that amount which is needful, when it will conduce to the unveiling of the secrets of the Unseen.'[124] Sleep is a waste of time if done to excess; one should strive to spend the pre-dawn hours in prayer, the highest activity, rather than sleep, which is the lowest. Of S͟hāh al-Kirmānī (third/ninth century), it is related that 'for forty years he never slept; then he fell asleep and dreamed of God. "O Lord!" he cried, "I was seeking Thee in nightly vigils, but I have found Thee in sleep". God answered: "O S͟hāh, you have found Me by means of those nightly vigils: if you had not sought Me there, you would not have found Me here".'[125]

IV. ETHICS AND SELF-TRANSCENDENCE

These four principles of the spiritual path were, in a sense, selfish, being directed only to the reform of the individual soul. They were complemented, however, by an attention to the moral and social virtues of Islam, which they were believed to improve. Great stress was laid on goodness of character (*ḥusn al-k͟huluq*), as being both a condition and a product of the religious life. 'Refining (*tahd͟hīb*) the character is one of the methods of self-discipline'.[126] It brought peace to the soul: when D͟hu'l-Nūn was asked which man has the fewest cares in this world, he replied, 'The one with the best character.'[127] For good character is 'to endure harm',[128] and 'harm', proceeding, like all else, ultimately from God, albeit through the medium of miscreants and misfortunes, is a trial, an opportunity for purification both through suffering and through self-restraint. In meeting the vicissitudes of life with equanimity and kindness, a man attains *riḍā*, contentment with the decrees of his Beloved. Hence the definition of al-Wāsiṭī: 'Good character is not to argue with anyone, or to be argued with by anyone, because of one's firm knowledge of God.'[129] To know God is to have an infinite capacity to endure the wickedness of men.

Good character expresses itself in two fundamental virtues: humility (*tawāḍuʿ*), and setting others before oneself (*īthār*). The true Muslim is necessarily humble, alert to the failings of his soul,[130] convinced that every passer-by is his superior in faith.[131] But 'God's bondsman only attains true humility when the lights of divine contemplation begin to shine in his heart, at which time the soul's deceit and self-regard will melt away, and it will become soft, obedient to both God and man.'[132] Those who have attained the greatest proximity to God become the most modest and humble of His creatures. In their humility, they love to serve others, hoping for God's reward and for the delight of renunciation, recalling the Qur'ānic text, *They prefer others over themselves, though theirs be the greater need.*[133] 'Goodness is to do good even to those who have mistreated you,' said Sufyān al-Thawrī.[134] 'It is to do good to all, in the manner of the sun, the wind, and the rain' (al-Ḥasan al-Baṣrī).[135] It extends even to animals: 'Should a man achieve all goodness, and yet mistreat a hen that he owns, he is not truly to be reckoned among those who do good.'[136] And the following celebrated tale shows how humility, generosity and kindness were regarded as the characteristic traits of a saint:

> Maʿrūf al-Karkhī once went down to the Tigris to perform his ablutions, leaving his Qur'ān and his cloak to one side. A woman came along, and stole them. Maʿrūf pursued her, saying, 'Sister! I am Maʿrūf, no harm will come to you. Do

> you have a son who can read?' 'No' she replied. 'Or a husband?' 'No,' she answered again. 'Then give me back the Qur'ān,' he told her, 'and keep the cloak'.[137]

V. 'ACQUIRE THE CHARACTER TRAITS OF GOD!'

By Ghazālī's time, the importance of acquiring noble traits of character was being treated in an increasingly systematic way. It was recognised that the process was supported by the presence of strong faith, and that faith, in turn, was supported by it.[138] As the influence of Plato made itself felt, the Platonic notion of the philosophical life as an attempt to become as similar to God as is possible for mortal beings[139] was increasingly 'in the air'. This was backed up by a *ḥadīth* which enjoined *takhallaqū bi-akhlāq Allāh*—'acquire the character traits of God!'—which seemed to hint that ethics could be a path to reclaiming man's theomorphic nature; and it was this which inspired one of Ghazālī's most original works, the *Highest Aim* (*al-Maqṣad al-Asnā*), in which he lists each of the ninety-nine names of God established by tradition, and explains how man can assume the nature associated with each. In a chapter entitled, 'An Exposition showing that Man's Perfection and Happiness lie in Acquiring the Character Traits of God', he writes that man

> must strive to adopt and acquire what is possible [for him] of these attributes, and adorn himself with their beauties, for thus does man become Lordly [*rabbānī*], that is, close to the Exalted Lord, and become a companion to the Highest Host of angels.[140]

As a modern commentator has pointed out, Ghazālī adopts a precedent (set by Qushayrī and Bayhaqī) of meditating on the moral implications of the Names, as the basis for a more methodical and ambitious spiritual programme of discarding the ugly, and nurturing the beautiful, traits of the soul.[141] It is when man has achieved this that he, like the angels, is fit to receive the divine light. Every divine trait of character, he implies, is innate in man, is part of his primordial disposition (*fiṭra*). *Khuluq* ('character trait') is therefore inseparable from *khalq* ('creation', 'created nature'); and it is thus that man must make use of the 'hidden correspondance' which exists between him and his Maker in order to return to Him by His attributes.[142] This perception was later taken up and made more explicit by Ibn ʿArabī of Murcia, for whom it became a key principle of the spiritual path.[143]

VI. SUFISM AND SEXUALITY

One of the most telling divergences between Islam and Christianity lies in the attitude which each religion has nurtured towards sexuality. Christian and Muslim ascetics may have agreed on the value of hunger as a means of self-discipline, but on the rather more intractable matter of sex, they trod very different paths. Inspired by the vision of a celibate Christ, preoccupied with the notion of original sin and the subsequent curse of concupiscence transmitted to Adam's progeny, which was dwelt on in detail by Augustine, Tertullian and other patristic writers, Christianity produced a remarkable catalogue of exploits against the demon of lust.[144] Many believed that 'virginity was the foundation of the church',[145] or even that virgins alone could reclaim that angelic state by which man becomes worthy of Heaven.[147] By the sixth century, most notably in Eastern Christianity, the Church had settled into a set of moral teachings which expected virginity from all men and women with a higher vocation, tolerating marriage only for less gifted believers. For the body was of the devil, and, as Gregory of Nyssa pointed out, 'if the life which is promised to the just by the Lord after the resurrection is similar to that of angels— and release from marriage is a peculiar characteristic of the angelic nature—he [the virgin] has already received some of the beauties of the promise'.[147]

Islam preached a physical resurrection, and also a physical paradise, with the more spiritualised pleasures being reserved for the righteous and the saints. With a candour which continues to draw reproach from Christian polemicists,[148] it called men and women to a paradise in which every pleasure which brought no harm upon others would necessarily be present, and even enhanced. As the Prophet had taught:

> And in Heaven there is a host of the Large-eyed Houris, who lift up their voices in a sound the like of which has never been heard by any creature, saying, 'We are the eternal ones, and shall never pass away. We are the joyful ones, and shall never grieve. We are the contented ones, and shall never be vexed. Blessed, therefore, is he who shall be ours, and for whom we shall be'.[149]

The Qur'ānic paradise, an exquisite, limitless garden of rivers, fruits, crystalline mansions, and—for the elect—the beatific Vision of God, stood before the eyes of the early Muslims with a constancy that is now hard to imagine. It did much to confirm the Muslim assurance that the world was not 'fallen', that the attractions of the earth reflected, however faintly, the archetypal beauty of Paradise, and that to renounce them could be no more than a provisional strategy, not a necessary state. Just as the age-old Muslim love of gardens—in modern Arabic *junayna*: 'little paradise'—reveals the extent of the Muslim desire to create on earth, albeit distantly, a reminder of the perfection which is to come, so too does the traditional Islamic understanding of sexuality reflect the conviction that something of heaven can be enjoyed here–below. The frequency with which lovemaking is pursued in a botanical setting in Persian and Turkish poetry can be seen as a charming testimony to this.

Further support for an active married life was available in the example and teaching of the Prophet. 'Marriage is my way (*sunna*)', a *ḥadīth* announces, 'and whoever leaves my way is not of me'.[150] When he heard that an ascetically-minded Companion, ᶜAbd Allāh ibn ᶜAmr, was in the habit of praying all night and fasting all day, the Prophet is said to have reproved him with the words, 'Your eye has a right over you, your guests have a right over you, your wife has a right over you.'[151] In reading the *ḥadīth* literature one is struck by a consistently positive and healthy attitude to marriage and sexuality. While transgressions against public morality were dealt with severely, sexual expression in private was generally encouraged, rather than suppressed, by the new religion.

> The Prophet said: 'In the sexual act of each of you there is a charity'. The Companions replied, 'O Messenger of God! When one of us fulfils his sexual desire, will he be rewarded [by God for so doing]?' And he said, 'Do you not think that were he to act upon it unlawfully he would be sinning? Likewise, if he acts upon it lawfully, he will be rewarded.'[152]

It is commonly remarked that attitudes to sexuality can never be studied separately from attitudes to the relative moral worth of the sexes. Where women are seen as deceitful temptresses, sexuality is liable to be scorned by the religious. Conversely, it might be possible to see Islam's benevolence towards sexual expression as a clue to the relatively high esteem in which it held its female believers. It cannot be our purpose here to enter the highly-charged debate about the status of Muslim women. But an understanding of Ghazālī's text will be substantially enhanced if we bear in mind some essential background material, which may, perhaps, be startling to non-specialist readers accustomed to resolutely anti-female images of Islam.[153]

It has rightly been observed that it is the understanding of God in theistic religions, in which man is 'made in God's image',[154] which underpins the understanding of gender differentiation. For traditional Christians, the Deity, as Father, was unmistakeably male. The honour thus accorded the masculine principle was further reinforced by the Incarnation, for which a male vessel had been chosen; while those who administered the sacraments had without exception to be masculine. Islam, by contrast, did not call God 'Father'; neither did it recognise either the Incarnation or a priesthood. The metaphysical assumptions which underlay Islamic civilisation, then, did not in principle exclude the possibility that a high status might be accorded to women, and to female spirituality.

Islamic law, similarly, furnished women with rights which carried with them a considerable degree of esteem. The Qur'ānic legislation which permitted women the right of inheritance—albeit only one-half of a man's[155]—and endowed them with the inalienable right to the ownership of property even after marriage, seems to have strengthened the financial independence which many women were able to exercise.[156] The institution of the facial veil, too, irregularly documented in the first Muslim century, is now accepted to have been of Byzantine rather than Islamic provenance.[157] Writing of the first two centuries of Islam, Margaret Smith provides several instances of this feminine freedom, and notes that

> There is ample evidence, then, that at the beginning of the Islamic era women had much freedom in the choice of their husbands, that marriage was in many cases an equal partnership and that women could, and did, assert their right to an independant life. Social intercourse between women and men was not restricted to close relatives, but women might meet with strangers in society. They went about freely and had the right, as we have seen, to go into the mosques at the time of prayer, to worship in common with the men. Moreover, those who were versed in jurisprudence expressly recognised the right of a wife on marriage to make a condition that there should be no second wife, nor even a concubine, and this right, as we have seen above, was frequently claimed.[158]

A related contrast between Islamic and Christian views of womanhood is supplied by conflicting ideals of female sanctity. Christianity did of course nurture many female saints, but its ideal was almost invariably celibate, drawing inspiration from the virginal immaculateness of Christ's mother. While Islam retained great reverence for Mary, expressed at some length in the Qur'ān,[159] in practice most Muslims chose to adopt Fāṭima, the Prophet's daughter, as their feminine ideal. Fāṭima was at once saint, wife and mother, whose nearness to God seemed to have been confirmed rather than compromised by her biological fulfilment. As the fertile source of the *ahl al-bayt*, the privileged and saintly descendants of the Prophet, she gave to Muslim women a paradigm of fulfilment, and to men a sign that sanctity was not excluded by the normal functions of womanhood.[160]

Further proof of this esteem for women is supplied by an interesting genre of Sufi tales, which depict righteous women either demonstrating superior powers of sexual continence, or confounding the spiritual pride of their male brethren. The following anecdotes are not untypical:

> They relate that a leading man in Basra went to his garden. By chance his eye fell upon the beautiful wife of his gardener. He sent the fellow away on some business and said to the woman: 'Shut the gates'. She replied: 'I have shut them all except one, which I cannot shut.' He asked, 'Which one is that?' 'The gate', said she, 'that is between us and God.' On receiving this answer the man repented and begged to be forgiven.[161]

> Once, when travelling in the desert, I went on ahead of my caravan and espied someone. I hurried to catch up with this person, and found that it was a woman walking slowly with the aid of a staff. Thinking that she was sick, I put my hand in my pocket and produced twenty dirhams. 'Take these,' I said, 'and wait until the caravan catches up with you, and you can pay to join it. Then come to me tonight, and I'll set your affairs in order.' But she waved her hand in the air, and lo! it contained dinars [larger coins], saying, 'You take dirhams from your pocket (*jayb*), but I take dinars from the Unseen (*ghayb*).'[162]

Ghazālī, too, uses stories such as these (see page 188 of the present translation). He even includes a long section in the *Iḥyā'* devoted to stories of pious women.[163] Some of these are shown wandering in the desert seeking solitude with God, while others, like the saintly Shaʿwāna, have their own teaching-circles in which they give spiritual counsel to men and women alike.[164]

This tradition, however, existed side by side with a reservoir of Near Eastern aphorisms and proverbs which portrayed women as licentious, perfidious creatures of the stamp of Potiphar's wife,[165] and many of these stories too found their way into popular Muslim lore.

> A sage wished that his short wife might have been tall. People asked him, 'Why did you not marry a wife of full stature?' 'A woman is an evil thing,' he answered, 'and the less there is of an evil thing the better.'[166]

In general, this kind of sentiment was expressed in more secular literature, such as the *Thousand and one Nights*,[167] rather than in the religious texts with which we are here concerned. For the religious writers, faith was the only value, and, as another of Ghazālī's translators observes,

> In general, though not always, religious faith in women appears to be valued no less highly than religious faith in men; and while divorce and polygamy are, of course, regarded as 'disabilities' of women, some of the passages and anecdotes seem to imply a concept of marriage as a happy and lasting, and perhaps ideally monogamous partnership. A wife ought to be chosen for her piety, and also for her sincere intention to bear and rear children, but not for beauty, wealth or nobility of birth. Pious domesticity in women is regarded as no less pleasing to God than religious scholarship or holy war in men; and an anecdote tells how a man of the Children of Israel acted upon his pious wife's advice in a way which pleased God and was rewarded in this world and the next.[168]

How to address the contradiction? It would be useful, perhaps, to start by recalling that in Ghazālī's immensely varied world, men's opinions and preferences differed no less frequently than they do in ours, and that the presence of contradictory attitudes was often no more than the natural result of human diversity. Yet there are further complications here, such as the fact that although the position established for women in primitive Islam deteriorated, possibly through Christian and classical Greek influence, after the first century and a half,[169] it was the later mystical metaphysicians, of whom Ibn ʿArabī is the most striking example, who were the most inclined to exalt the feminine principle.[170] And what are we to make of the poetic convention of likening the celestial Beloved to Laylā, or some other coy and exquisite woman?[171] Then there is the phenomenon of the considerable involvement of women in *ḥadīth* scholarship, the most prestigious academic discipline in early Islam.[172] Neither can we find a pronouncement in any structured and authoritative Muslim magisterium, for Islam had nothing resembling a 'church' which might define and administer an 'orthodoxy'.[173] The traditional discreetness of Muslim family life also serves to cloud and reduce our awareness of female contributions to religious and social life. To classify medieval Muslim society as enlightened or oppressive would, perhaps, merely serve to impose the values of our generation onto a time and culture whose priorities were radically different to our own. The texts do suggest, however, that many Muslim pietists showed attitudes which we would judge much more 'favourable' to women than the outlook either of the early Church, or of the 'secular' Arab tradition.[174]

Another problem is presented by a further type of edifying story, in which men warn one another about the charms of women to whom they are not married. Ghazālī gives us several of these, such as the following:

> Someone once said, 'The devil says to woman: You are half my army! You are my arrow with which I do not miss! You are my confidante! You are my messenger with whom I achieve my wants!'[175]

This type of story is commonly encountered in the context of *ghaḍḍ al-baṣar*, 'lowering the eyes', a virtue required in the presence of members of the opposite sex:[176]

> Ash^cab once looked at his son, who was gazing intently at a woman. 'My son!' he said. 'That gaze of yours could get her pregnant!'[177]

What is apparently intended is not so much an outright condemnation of sexuality, still less of womanhood—for pious women are also enjoined to guard against temptation from handsome men[178]—but of the woman's sexual presence; or, as one modern writer puts it, of the man's satanic impulse to look, not the woman's inherent wickedness.[179] It is the power of public sexual attraction which Islam fears, not its private marital dimension, or its association with womanhood. It is thus that one may reconcile apparently misogynistic statements with the Prophet's famous remark, 'Three things of this world are made beloved to me: women, and perfume, and my greatest delight is in prayer.'[180]

It is surprising then that despite the 'sex-positive' backdrop of the Islamic dispensation, and Islam's generally constructive view of women, we should find in the second and early third centuries of Islam a nascent movement towards celibacy on the part of some Muslim ascetics. Andrae is probably right in attributing this to Christian influence:

> The Islamic attitude to marriage may be summed up as follows: marriage is an absolute duty for everyone who needs it in order to live chastely, and should be entered into by anyone who can afford it. This being so, it is rather surprising that there have been any celibates at all in Islam. It is a

well-known fact that in Christian monastic piety the first rule of asceticism was to observe strict sexual abstinence. Evil lust, concupiscence, *is* sexual desire. The influence of monastic religion was in fact so powerful, that individual ascetics within Islam not only accepted the doctrine of celibacy in principle but also practiced it. It is true that they were few in number and seem to have been considered eccentrics, odd exceptions to the rule, and were not very highly-regarded. Occasionally such pious eccentrics were brought before the Caliph on charges of heresy, on the grounds of their unwillingness to submit to the Prophet's Sunna.[181]

What impiety could be more heinous than to ignore the duty of marriage, which had been the Prophet's example? Did not the religious scholars teach that marriage does not compromise the ascetic life?[182] But there is no doubt that some men were anxious to evade it. Abū Sulaymān al-Dārānī believed that 'the sweetness of adoration and undisturbed surrender of the heart which the single man can feel the married man can never experience.'[183] More obscurely, we are told that Ibn Khafīf of Shirāz married many times, yet never submitted to passion.[184] Naturally, one may not assume that all celibates were following specifically spiritual impulses in renouncing the flesh, for there have been other Islamic figures, not particularly associated with asceticism or Sufism, who also opted for the bachelor's life, perhaps for reasons of health, or out of a desire for academic freedom, or for more personal reasons.[185] On the whole, classical Islam was consistent in its emphasis on marriage as a virtue, and celibacy as an idiosyncrasy with no justification in scripture.[186]

Sahl al-Tustarī, in the midst of his feats of fasting, saw no reason why he should treat marriage in the same way as food. 'An ignorant bachelor,' he taught in one of his famous gnomic utterances, 'is a devil; a married ignoramus is a beast (*bahīma*); a learned bachelor is God's slave; while a learned married man is an angel.'[187] The angelic condition of the man of God, then, is not only not impeded by marriage, but actually depends upon it.[188]

What many early Sufis did disparage, however, was the kind of amorous passion (*ᶜishq*) which distracts a man from the contemplation and love of God. There is not much support for a condemnation of *ᶜishq* in the *ḥadīth* literature, although a frequently-cited report does have the Prophet say, 'Whoever loves (*ᶜashiq*), is chaste, conceals his passion, and dies, dies as a martyr.'[189] It seems more likely that the condemnation of *ᶜishq* which had become common by Ghazālī's time originated in the Greek heritage, where the attitude to *eros* had been rather supercilious. In an anthology of philosophical adages, the Arabs could read the verdicts of Plato, Aristotle, Galen[190] and others about love, discovering, for instance, that Diogenes regarded *ᶜishq* as 'the disease of an empty, careless heart'.[191] Following in this tradition, al-Kindī and Ibn Sīnā had some hard words to say about profane love,[192] while the Platonising freethinker Muḥammad ibn Zakarīyā al-Rāzī thought that it had been uncommon among the Greek philosophers simply because they had occupied themselves with more worthy activities, such as study.[193] The Christian philosopher Yaḥyā ibn ᶜAdī defines *ᶜishq* as 'among the reprehensible traits, being an extravagant excess of love (*ḥubb*)'.[194] Ghazālī takes up this theme, defining it as 'utter ignorance of the intended purpose of sexual congress,'[195] and he is followed in this by a number of later writers, including Ibn al-Jawzī, whose work *The Condemnation of Passion* is perhaps the most impressive defence of this attitude.[196] The argument was that *ᶜishq* is not only a waste of time and an extravagant misuse of the sexual faculty, but also leads men and women into sins such as adultery, or worse. While the pious Muslim may and should love (*ḥubb*) his spouse, this must never be allowed to turn into an obsession.[197] At all times he is to be the master of his passions.

Following this tradition, Ghazālī believes that although the sex drive is not to be classed with other appetites as inherently bestial and demeaning,[198] nevertheless 'the desire for women

[...] is susceptible to excess, defect, and equilibrium'.[199] And 'excess in the matter of sexual desire, then, causes the intellect to be overcome [...], which is very much to be condemned. Insufficient sexual desire, however, leads to an indifference to women, or to giving them insufficient pleasure, which is also to be condemned.[200] Sexual desire is a praiseworthy thing when it stands in a state of equilibrium, obedient to the intellect and the Law in all its movements.'[201]

Here again we are in the presence of classical Islam's tendency to moderation, of which Ghazālī is among the most convincing theorists. From his treatment it is clear that although extravagances abound in the hagiographies, these serve, finally, to show the reader the benefit of the golden mean, which in this sphere of human experience, as elsewhere, was identified with the way of the Prophet. The tales of extreme abstinence, or of lawful indulgence, whether concerning food or sex, are deployed to shock the reader out of his complacencies; they aim to create an effect, an atmosphere, not establish a rule of life. It is one of Ghazālī's virtues that he makes explicit the contingent nature of the hyperbolic and extravagant *exempla* of which the Sufis were so fond, where in other pious writings this had been obscured, albeit for the best of reasons.

VII. THE INFLUENCE OF PHILOSOPHICAL ETHICS

As we have seen, the early Muslims soon came into productive contact with Oriental Christianity, whose severe and world-denying tendencies were at first influential, but were later attenuated following the advent of a more balanced and mature spirituality. More significant in the long term, however, was the Greek philosophical legacy, which was both older and more intellectually developed. For a thousand years, Greek learning had been pursued in schools in Syria and Egypt, and, although by the time of the Arab conquests it had become somewhat reiterative and degraded, it was only a matter of time before Muslims took note of it, and attempted to reconcile it with Islam, rather as men like Philo and John Philoponus had tried to reconcile Greek thought, as they understood it, with Judaism and Christianity.

Directly or otherwise, this enterprise generated many of the great sectarian controversies of Muslim history. Not only were there wide divergences in the interpretation of the Hellenic legacy, there were many men who believed that as a pagan tradition alien to Islam, it had nothing to offer the community of believers. There was no shortage of religious scholars schooled in the traditional disciplines of *ḥadīth* and Qur'ānic learning to pronounce anathemas against those who drank from such polluted springs. But the Muslim philosophers defended themselves vigorously; believing, in the words of the Basran thinker al-Kindī (d. *c* 256/870) that

> We should not be ashamed to acknowledge truth and to assimilate it from whatever source it comes to us, even if it is brought to us by former generations and foreign peoples. For him who seeks the truth there is nothing of higher value than truth itself; it never cheapens or abases him who searches for it, but ennobles and honours him.[202]

The dispute between the Muᶜtazilite sect, which made use of basically Aristotelian methods of reasoning, and the traditionalists led by such men as Aḥmad ibn Ḥanbal (d.241/855), eventually gave birth to compromise positions such as that of al-Ashᶜarī (d.324/935), whose followers developed a theology which, while making use of Greek reasoning, contrived to exclude philosophy from subjects such as the resurrection and judgement, which, it held, could be known only through the Islamic scriptures.[203]

The process of translating Greek works into Arabic had begun to flourish during the reign of the caliph al-Ma'mūn (198-218/813-33). An institution was founded in Baghdad for the purpose, and within a century the Arabs had at their disposal a very considerable number of the Greek classics.[204] The bulk of Aristotle's works were rendered with remarkable accuracy into Arabic, and more than a hundred of the works of Galen—far more than were ever available in Latin—were likewise translated.[205] Partly through passages cited in Galen, many works of Plato, including the *Timaeus* and the *Laws* became known, at least in summary.[206] But, as we shall see, the Arabs were more familiar with the later interpretations of Plato, particularly in the form of Neoplatonism, which exercised its greatest influence among them through a work misleadingly known as the *Theology of Aristotle* which while universally believed to be by the Stagirite, was in fact an anthology of passages culled largely from the *Enneads* of Plotinus.[207]

This Greek heritage included, of course, discussions of medicine, metaphysics, logic, meteorology and physics. What concerns us here, however, in the context of the present work, is the field of ethics. Gh̲azālī had used Neoplatonic ideas in a few of his esoteric writings,[208] and relied heavily on the Arab Aristotelians in his works on philosophy and logic.[209] What is more striking, perhaps, is that he makes use of Greek wisdom in the context of Islamic religious practice. The author of the *Incoherence of the Philosophers* was not a crude 'fundamentalist', opposed on principle to any possibility of learning from abroad. He was, it is true, resolutely opposed to certain conclusions of the Neoplatonising Aristotelianism of the Arab philosophers. Yet he was not too far removed from the attitude of al-Kindī cited above. After all, had not the Prophet of Islam taught that 'Wisdom is the lost animal of the believer; wherever he finds it, it is he that has the most right to it?'[210]

Gh̲azālī's willingness to profit from non-Muslim thought may also have been supported by his allegiance to the Sh̲āfiʿī legal tradition. In their analysis of the concept of orthodoxy, the Sh̲āfiʿī jurists had shown some flexibility on the vexed question of 'innovation' (*bidʿa*), defined as any amendment or addition introduced into Islamic belief or practice, which was considered by some, particularly the advocates of the Ḥanbalī school of law, to be reprehensible under all circumstances. It was thus that Ibn Ḥanbal himself had felt obliged to condemn al-Muḥāsibī as an 'innovator', who had adulterated Islamic teachings by borrowing certain philosophical ideas.[211] The S͟hāfiʿīs, by contrast, found scriptural sources which enabled them to draw a distinction between 'good' and 'bad' innovations. Al-S͟hāfiʿī himself, from whom the school takes its name, is credited with stating:

> There are two kinds of introduced matters (*muḥdat͟hāt*). One is that which contradicts a text of the Qur'ān, or the *Sunna*, or a report from the early Muslims (*at͟har*), or the consensus (*ijmāʿ*) of the Muslims: this is an 'innovation of misguidance'. The second kind is that which is in itself good and entails no contradiction of any of these authorities: this is a 'non-reprehensible innovation'.[212]

G͟hazālī's openness to certain aspects of Greek thought thus seemed to be potentially authorized, rather than condemned, by his Islamic legal training.

How G͟hazālī learnt his philosophy is not fully understood. In his autobiography, the *Deliverer from Error*, he describes how, having lost his faith in knowledge acquired through the uncritical acceptance of tradition (*taqlīd*)[213], he sought to restore it through investigating the epistemologies claimed by four groups: the theologians (*mutakallimūn*), the philosophers (*falāsifa*), the esoteric Bāṭinites[214] and the Sufis.[215] It seems unlikely that he did investigate them in this order, as his account suggests, for we know that he had been familiar with Sufism from his youth,[216] and when studying the As͟hʿarī theology taught in his city he would also have been aware of its debt to Greek ideas, which were particularly evident in the works of his principal teacher, al-Juwaynī (d.478/1085), who had been responsible for the introduction of a more philosophical approach to epistemology.[217] More than any other sizeable faction, with the exception of the Muᶜtazilite 'rationalists' and the Arab philosophers themselves, the Ash̲ᶜarī tradition in which G̲h̲azālī stood had been open to Greek thought. The channels were usually indirect, and there is little firm evidence to suggest that G̲h̲azālī ever studied Aristotle directly, as he preferred instead to read the Arab philosophers, whose ideas presented the more immediate challenge to the Ash̲ᶜarī position; but their very indirectness made them the more efficient in infiltrating the thought of his school; for it was emotionally easier for a devout Muslim to borrow ideas from a Muslim philosopher, even one with heretical notions about the afterlife, than it was to borrow directly from ancient sources which did not even nod in the direction of Islam.

Disillusioned with the presentation of philosophical ideas by the theologians—G̲h̲azālī tells us—he made a detailed private study of philosophy:

> Having realised that to refute a school of thought before understanding it and penetrating to its essence was like loosing arrows blindly, I applied myself diligently to acquiring [philosophy] from books, simply by reading and without the aid of a teacher. This I did in my spare time, when I was not writing and teaching the Islamic disciplines, and even though I was burdened with the instruction of three hundred students in Baghdad. But in less than two years, simply by studying in those snatched moments, the Sublime God appraised me of all their sciences, and after having comprehended them, I spent about a year thinking about them constantly, reviewing and going over them, searching out their pitfalls and entanglements, until I understood beyond any doubt what they contained by way of deceit and delusion, truth and imagination.[218]

G̲h̲azālī then goes on to present a synopsis of the various branches of philosophy as these were understood by the Arab philosophers Ibn Sīnā (d.428/1037) and (to a lesser extent) al-

Fārābī (d.339/950), noting that some of their doctrines constituted unbelief (*kufr*), others were heretical innovations (*bidʿa*), while others need not be rejected. He identifies six disciplines: mathematics, logic, the natural sciences, theology, politics, and ethics. The first three can be of benefit to religion, or are at least morally neutral. But the science of theology (*al-ilāhīyāt*) 'contains the bulk of their errors', since the philosophers have denied the bodily resurrection, God's knowledge of particulars, and the createdness of the world.[219] Politics, by contrast, 'is about governing the world to secure its benefit, and this they simply took from the scriptures God revealed to the Prophets, and the words of wisdom inherited from them.'[220] As for ethics,

> all that they say comes down to enumerating the attributes and character traits of the soul, stating their types and categories, and the method of treating and disciplining them. This [method] they took only from the writings of the Sufis, who are the mystics (*muta'allihūn*) constantly engaged in the remembrance of God, the combat against passion, and treading the path to God the Exalted by turning away from the world's delights. Through their inner strife, the character traits of the soul were discovered to them, together with its defects and the blemishes of its works, and they spoke of this. The philosophers took their words, and mixed them with their own, hoping that by adorning their words in this way their own falsehood might be spread abroad.[221]

Philosophical ethics, then, are not necessarily to be rejected by the Muslim intellectual. One must be on one's guard, G͟hazālī counsels, against two temptations. Firstly, there is that of writing off Greek thought as being tainted by the infidelity of its authors, for, as he observes, 'only inferior minds judge doctrines by their exponents, rather than vice versa'.[222] Instead, the theologian should be 'zealous to snatch truth from the statements of misguided men, knowing that the [...] moneychanger with confidence in his own perception is not wrong to put his hand into the bag of a forger in order to bring out what is pure gold from among bad and counterfeit coin.'[223]

The second temptation is that the theologian, when he reads philosophical works which include authentic Prophetic material, may be deluded into accepting the fallacies which such books contain. Hence it is necessary to discourage people who do not enjoy the necessary intelligence and learning from reading them, in the manner of the wise snake-handler, who will not perform his craft in front of his son, lest the latter attempt to emulate him and perhaps be bitten.[224]

In accordance with this last principle, G͟hazālī has evidently striven to exclude direct references to the philosophers from his more popular works, including the *Iḥyā'*. This confronts the modern student with serious difficulties when attempting to trace the pedigree of his ideas, particularly those of a metaphysical nature. With ethics, however, the task is a little easier, partly because the large-scale introduction of Greek ethics into Muslim thought had begun rather later than was the case with metaphysics. The text here translated, together with one or two of G͟hazālī's other works, contains long passages whose lineage stretches unmistakeably back to Plato, Aristotle, and, in a lesser degree, to the Stoics and to Galen.

The most distinctive feature of Platonic ethics is the division of the soul into three faculties: rational, irascible, and appetitive,[225] which interact with four cardinal virtues: wisdom, courage, temperance and justice, which exist as unchanging 'forms' independently of their agents.[226] The implication is that by achieving virtue, man not only learns how to deal righteously with other men, but can come into connection with higher reality. Later Platonists drew out the suggestion that the four virtues exist in conjunction with a number of subordinate virtues, and these, while inferior to the intellectual life, are indispensable for the maintenance of good administration and order in society.

Aristotle's moral theory, which develops that of his teacher, is well-known.[227] The wise man will strive for a state of happiness (*eudaimonia*),[228] which, unlike the natural state of the animals, is to be attained through the application of a rule to one's acts. A man must know which rule to follow, and also be capable of constraining his appetites to obey it. But to be able to recognise the rightness of this rule, his character must first be improved, for man is not born with innate good character; it must be inculcated through proper education and training. The natural tendencies in himself may be turned to either good or evil ends, and, when they become a habit, they are called a trait of character (*ethe*). Anger, for instance, is intrinsically neutral, and can, through training, be turned either to righteous indignation against injustice, or into defiance of what is just.

To distinguish virtuous from vicious traits, Aristotle had recourse to a medical analogy. Just as bodily health results from a balance in the humours, and disease from an imbalance, so also when the natural impulses in the soul are encouraged to find an equilibrium, a middle point which ensures its health will ensue. This mean is a fixed state of the soul, acquired through habituation, whose value and exact position are recognised by the mind.[229] The mind, in turn, has been guided in youth by an education drawn up to reflect the ideals of the community.

Although the last great flowering of Greek thought represented by the Neoplatonists did refer to Aristotle's doctrine of the mean, Neoplatonic ethics had a chiefly mystical, rather than practical, objective. Following Plato, Plotinus (AD 205–270) taught that virtue is twofold: the higher soul must be oriented permanently towards the One, through philosophy and meditation, while the lower soul must be subdued and disciplined, lest it interfere with the higher soul's contemplation of the intelligibles. More emphatically than Plato, but less rigidly than Porphyry and many of his Christian rivals, he held that this must be achieved through a process of constant discipline, so that the irrational soul is progressively subdued, although not extinguished altogether.[230]

Another author who adds to our not altogether satisfactory picture of late Greek ethical thought is Galen (AD 129–*c.* 199). More usually associated in the European mind with the world of medicine, Galen was also a prolific author on philosophical themes, following a broadly middle-Platonic line.[231] Galen acknowledged his allegiance to Plato in his use of the tripartite division of the soul into rational, irascible and appetitive faculties, and appears to have been the first to identify these with Aristotle's rational, animal and vegetative souls, a development which was later accepted into Arab philosophy.[232] 'People's characters differ because the appetites of these three souls may be strong or weak, and their relative strength constitutes the individual character.'[233] Character traits are hereditary and innate, being linked to the bodily temperaments, but may in some cases be improved by the regular use of the intelligence, so that through habituation a trait which was previously dormant may become dominant.[234]

When the Greek tradition was made known to the Muslims, it was in the form of this late synthesis, characterised both by a powerful and ethically-based mysticism, and by a conviction that the systems of Plato and Aristotle were fundamentally compatible. Aristotle was seen mainly through the eyes of Porphyry, whose commentary on the *Nicomachean Ethics* was available in an Arabic translation.[235] Arab ethical thought was also enriched by translations from the works of Galen, in particular a summary of his treatise *On Ethics*,[236] and a book entitled *How a man may discover his own vices*.[237]

The Arabs did, however, have direct access to Aristotle. His ethics had been made known to them through the translations of Isḥāq ibn Ḥunayn, whose version of the *Nicomachean Ethics* was rediscovered in a Moroccan mosque library some years ago.[238] Several late Greek epitomes of the *Nicomachean Ethics* were also available in translation.[239]

While much was still untranslated by the third century of Islam, the first Muslim philosopher of note, al-Kindī (d.256/870), was well acquainted with Greek ethics. Although his works *On Ethics* and *Spiritual Physic* are lost,[240] he elsewhere expounds the outlines of a late-Platonic ethical system which includes Stoic and Aristotelian elements, including the doctrine of the mean and the secondary virtues.[241]

Also influenced by Plato was al-Rāzī (d.313/925), known in the West as Rhazes. The author of a commentary on the *Timaeus*, and indebted also to Galen, he wrote a work entitled *Spiritual Physic* (*al-Ṭibb al-Rūḥānī*), which has been translated into English by A.J. Arberry.[242] More than any other philosopher in the Islamic world he seems to have been indifferent to religion, although his austere and largely Platonic understanding of ethics assumes the existence of God, if not the immortality of the soul. There is little evidence that his work exerted an influence over later Muslim writers.[243]

The Neoplatonist tendency is again prominent in the *Epistles* of the Brethren of Purity, a group of Muslim thinkers whose eclecticism extended to the use of Pythagorean, Hermetic, Ismāʿīlī and other ideas.[244] Although their fifty-two epistles range from treatments of minerology and botany to religious law, their evident Muslim commitment and their Neoplatonic interests encouraged them to take a close interest in ethical method, which, like Plotinus, they believed was the key to self-purification and hence to the return to the One. They taught that although all men are born with a natural receptivity to goodness, character traits (*akhlāq*) are affected by four factors: the balance of humours (*akhlāṭ*) in the body, climate, upbringing, and the influence of the stars.[245] The interplay of these factors generates and affects the four principal Platonic virtues, and hence the subsidiary virtues and vices.[246]

When man's character is perfect, he becomes God's viceregent (*khalīfa*) on earth, and his spiritual faculty, transformed through a complex Neoplatonic hierarchy of souls, will penetrate to

God.[247] Porphyry's emphasis on asceticism and an attitude of disdain for the world is here expressed in the Islamic language of *zuhd* (asceticism), which, the Brethren assert, is in fact the highest of all virtues.[248] In the same work a tendency becomes visible which was to be even more marked in the work of Ghazālī, namely, the filtering-out of Greek virtues which seemed to contradict Islamic ideals. For instance, the virtue known as 'greatness of soul' (*kibar al-nafs*), while entirely acceptable in a Greek context, seemed to the Brethren to smack of vainglory, and they debated whether it should be considered a virtue at all.[249] Finally, the Brethren diverged from the mainstream Arab philosophers in stressing the Muslim claim that in view of man's general incapacity to work out his own salvation, God, in His mercy, has sent prophets with laws and moral guidance to assist him.[250]

Another ethical theorist, the Christian philosopher Yaḥyā ibn ᶜAdī (d.364/974), was similarly Platonic in orientation (as one would expect from his devotion to al-Fārābī), although Aristotelian ideas are not wholly absent from his ethical treatise, the *Refinement of Character* (*Tahdhīb al-akhlāq*).[251] He follows Plato's threefold division of the soul,[252] which had already been recognised by the Brethren, and then proceeds to enumerate twenty virtues and twenty vices, most of which are familiar from Plato and Aristotle, but may have been communicated to him through the work of some late intermediary which has since vanished. This is followed by a section in which he lists traits which can be virtues in some men and vices in others, a category which does not appear in Ghazālī and other orthodox Muslim thinkers.[253]

Far more influential was Abū ᶜAlī ibn Sīnā (d. 428/1037), known in the West as Avicenna, who is often and not unjustly regarded as the greatest of the Muslim philosophers. Although he did not write very extensively on ethics,[254] his developed theory of the soul, which he drew from the Greek, and particularly the Aristotelian tradition, provided the basic source of philosophic psychology for both Miskawayh and Ghazālī. Of the three faculties of the soul, which for him are the 'vegetative', 'animal' and 'rational', Ibn Sīnā devotes particular attention to the latter two, and shows how the concupiscent and irascible aspects of the animal soul are the root of the virtues and vices, being governed or neglected by the active faculty of the intellect, which in turn should be in harmony with the intellect's theoretical faculty, or spirit, which is in contact with the world of intelligibles.[255] Partly for this reason, there is a strongly religious dimension to Ibn Sīnā's thought, which manifests itself in a serious consideration of spiritual discipline (*riyāḍa*), whose categories he is clearly borrowing from Sufism, rather as the Brethren of Purity had done.[256] This was later to appeal to G͟hazālī, who, although concerned to avoid the use of philosophical language, developed a psychology which was largely in conformity with this Avicennian system.[257]

Also dependant on Aristotle was the Baghdad philosopher and historian Abū ʿAlī Miskawayh (d.421/1030), who, like Ibn ʿAdī, wrote a work called *The Refinement of Character.*[258] This work, which was destined to become the most influential text of its kind in Arabic, was popular not so much for any great originality as for the author's talent for synthesizing Platonic, Aristotelian and Islamic ideas on the moral life, which he cast in a pleasing Arabic style and adorned with quotations from sources as varied as Homer, Aristotle, Galen, Pythagoras, al-Kindī, al-Ḥasan al-Baṣrī, and the Qur'ān. Drawing on Ibn ʿAdī, al-Kindī[259] and Galen,[260] Miskawayh again explains the three faculties of the soul and the four cardinal virtues,[261] and develops the attempts of earlier philosophers to relate these to numerous subordinate virtues.[262] His Muslim background disposes him against the Aristotelian teaching that the end of virtue is the attainment of happiness in this world, and he is confident that the Neoplatonic interpretation of the acquisition of virtue as having essentially spiritual ends is correct.[263] This suggests, as do certain indications in his work itself, that he was reading the *Nicomachean Ethics* with the lost commentary of Porphyry, together, perhaps, with the *Perfect State* of al-Fārābī.[264] In a section which treats of the upbringing of children, he acknowledges the influence of the neo-Pythagorean philosopher Bryson.[265] Perhaps his most important contribution, however, was his reliance on Aristotle's doctrine of the mean, which, as he showed, could be comfortably squared with the Platonic system.[266] Although, as we have seen, this marriage had been attempted before, it was Miskawayh who expounded the fullest Muslim synthesis of the two ethical systems. It was partly for this reason that his work served as a model, not only for Ghazālī, but for the major works of Muslim philosophically-oriented ethics from his time on.[267]

Also teaching at Baghdad was the Shāfiʿī jurist and judge al-Māwardī (d.450/1058).[268] In his book *Conduct in the World and Religion*, he shows himself prepared to quote extensively from Greek wisdom in order to buttress Islamic morality, although his approach is largely anecdotal and lacks Miskawayh's more systematic approach. In common with several other works of the period,[269] the book is a popular anthology of episodes drawn from both Greek and Islamic sources, and as such it has retained its popularity in the Arab world into the present century. It does, however, also include a programme of self-reform (*tahdhīb*) of a firmly Islamic character, and in its use of such terms as *riyāḍa* and *muḥāsaba* displays an awareness of the Sufi tradition.[270] A debt to Aristotle, too, is visible in Māwardī's frequent references to the principle of the mean, which he expresses in terms of 'moderation' (*tawassuṭ*), a word which would shortly be employed by Ghazālī.[271]

The Arabs could count themselves fortunate in that the differences between the systems of Plato and Aristotle, and also that of the Stoics, had already to a large extent been resolved for them by the later Greek thinkers, some of whom also added a more recognisably religious dimension. Yet the underlying incompatibility between Greek and Semitic thought continued to cause discomfort: namely, the inability of the Greeks to recognise a true concept of duty. For the Greeks, a man's conduct was determined by his character as this has been developed by education and maintained by bodily health; and since only the wealthy aristocracy could expect to enjoy this, it was a notion which supported a conception of a natural elite. The Islamic ideal was rather different: while it is true that some men are born better than others, the Muslim stress on self-discipline aided by a God who is indifferent to man's outer circumstances implied that true virtue may be attained whatever one's station in life.[272] Such contradictions, which had been only imperfectly resolved by earlier thinkers, found in the Shāfiʿī intelligensia men equipped both with sufficient openness of mind to learn from philosophic ethics, and enough Muslim commitment to attempt a resolution. Ghazālī's achievement in the realm of ethics was not the conversion of the ulema to Greek thought, but rather the long-delayed, but very sophisticated, conversion of Plato and Aristotle to Islam.

VIII. SUMMARY OF THE PRESENT WORK

The Book of Disciplining the Soul, Refining the Character, and Curing the Sicknesses of the Heart

Ghazālī opens with some general remarks on the importance of purifying the soul from bad character traits, which are a 'sure path to perdition'.

1 *An Exposition of the Merit which is in having Good Character, and a Condemnation of Bad Character.*

Following his usual practice in the *Iḥyā'*, Ghazālī begins with a collection of passages relevant to his theme, culled from the Qur'ān, the *ḥadīth*, and the dicta of the first Muslims.

2 *An Exposition of the True Nature of Good and Bad Character.*

Ghazālī now suggests that the mainstream ulema of his day have contented themselves with praising and enumerating the virtues, without analysing the true nature (*ḥaqīqa*) of good character. He then proceeds to offer such an analysis,[273] basing himself on the tradition of philosophical ethics, and particularly on Chapter One of Miskawayh's *Refinement of Character*, but without mentioning either the word 'philosophy' or the names of philosophers, lest this alienate some of his readers. Recalling the commonplace Muslim juxtaposition of *k͟halq* (creation, outwardly created form), and *k͟huluq* (inner character trait), he reproduces Miskawayh's verdict, itself drawn from Galen, that 'a trait of character is a firmly established condition [*hay'a*] of the soul, from which actions proceed easily without any need for thinking or forethought.' But he differs from the Greeks in asserting that good deeds are those which are recognised as such not only by the intellect, but by the revealed law (*s͟harᶜ*) as well.

A man is only virtuous when all his traits are pure, and G͟hazālī now introduces the four Platonic virtues (wisdom, courage, temperance and justice), and briefly explains how these are conditioned by the three faculties of the soul (the rational, irascible and appetitive), basing his discussion, with various amendments, on Miskawayh.[274] Each of the four cardinal virtues should be in equilibrium (*iᶜtidāl*), which will result in the generation of a range of secondary virtues. For instance, when the intellect is balanced, it will bring forth the rational virtues, such as 'deliberative excellence'; when unbalanced in the direction of excess (*ifrāṭ*), it yields vices such as cunning and deception, and when unbalanced in the direction of defect (*tafrīṭ*), other vices like stupidity and heedlessness will result. Virtue is defined in Aristotelian terms as a mean equidistant between two extremes,[275] and G͟hazālī finishes the section by explaining that only the Prophet attained complete equilibrium in this regard.[276]

3 *An Exposition of the Susceptibility of the Traits of Character to Change through Discipline.*

Although the Islamic tradition was founded on the belief that character traits can be reformed,[277] a judgement supported by the Qur'ān and, on the basis of Aristotle, by most philosophers,[278] an opinion was apparently current which held that character is innate, and cannot be changed.[279]

Drawing on Miskawayh,[280] Ghazālī briefly summarises the debate on the mutability of character, concluding that this is both possible and necessary. There are some traits which are innate and unchanging, he concedes, but many others which are a proper object of self-scrutiny and control. Miskawayh had presented the Stoic view of mankind as being innately good but subsequently corrupted by society, contrasted it with the contrary view of man's inherent evil, and then cited Galen to show that among men a minority are born virtuous, while the remainder may in most cases be reformed through pious counsels and keeping the company of good men.[281] Miskawayh then cites Aristotle's differentiation between people who are easily reformed and those who are improved only with difficulty or not at all, and this is echoed by Ghazālī, who distinguishes four types of human being in this regard. Ghazālī then shows that the purpose of discipline is not to extirpate anger and desire, but simply to redirect them towards a condition of just balance. Several Qur'ānic passages are adduced to justify this doctrine, together with the famous *ḥadīth*: 'The best of affairs is the middle course'.[282]

Finally, Ghazālī mentions the Shaykh, the spiritual master to whose guidance the aspirant should submit, explaining that the Shaykh must use the strategy of compelling his disciple to aim for the opposite of his vices, not because this is the true end of the spiritual path, but because only this will give him sufficient energy to overcome his ugly traits, and attain to the golden mean.

4 *An Exposition of the Means by which Good Character may be Acquired.*

Some men are born with virtue, while others must acquire it. This can be done through habituation:[283] a miser can become generous by constantly obliging himself to give money to the poor, until such time as this becomes a natural trait in his soul.[284] The other method of acquiring good character is through keeping the company of the righteous. However unlikely it may seem at the outset, perfect virtue yields constant delight, for vice is the inclination towards what is low and mean, while virtue is to resemble the truth and beauty of God. It is thus the proper condition of man.

5 *An Exposition Detailing the Method Used in Refining the Character.*

In this section, G͟hazālī uses a medical metaphor, which was already widely current by his time. Just as the body falls sick when the four humours (*ak͟hlāṭ*) are out of equilibrium,[285] so too does the soul became sick when the four cardinal virtues are imbalanced.[286] Here the principal source is Chapter Six of Miskawayh,[287] who in turn has made use of Galen's medico-philosophical synthesis, which had combined ideas from the psychology of Plato and the medicine of Hippocrates, together with the physics of Aristotle.[288] In the *Nicomachean Ethics*, too, Aristotle had made use of the medical metaphor,[289] and several Arab philosophers used the phrase 'spiritual physic' (*ṭibb rūḥānī*) as the title of a book;[290] al-Fārābī is also interested in the theme.[291] This had appeared also in the more mainstream Islamic tradition: Junayd composed a brief epistle called *The Medicine of Hearts*,[292] while the image of the S͟hayk͟h as a spiritual physician whose prescriptions must be followed is common throughout Sufism.[293]

G͟hazālī then returns to stress the importance of constantly acting contrary to one's desires in order to achieve equilibrium and the consequent liberation of soul, using the image of the student calligrapher, who must force himself to imitate a good hand.[294] He then furnishes some further examples of how the spiritual teacher should help his novices to accomplish this.

6 *An Exposition of the Symptoms by which the Diseases of the Heart may be Recognised, and the Signs which Indicate a Return to Health.*

Here Ghazālī returns to a discussion of the 'heart', the wonders of which had formed the subject of the previous book of the *Revival.* The heart, he reminds us, is the faculty which understands and knows God, and which directs the other faculties and members accordingly. When distracted by worldly interests, it is heedless of God, and this constitutes its 'sickness'. The cure lies in understanding this, and in combating the desires in question, preferably under the direction of a Shaykh. When the heart is cured—by achieving equilibrium—it stands upon what the Qur'ān terms the 'straight path.'[295]

7 *An Exposition of the Way in which a Man may Discover the Faults in his Soul.*

Following on from the previous section, Ghazālī explores another familiar idiom of both the Islamic and the philosophical traditions. The Sufi practice of *muḥāsaba*, self-examination, had been expounded particularly by al-Muḥāsibī, who includes a section on how a man may know his own faults in one of his works.[296] And among the philosophers, Galen, Rāzī and Miskawayh had dealt with the question,[297] suggesting that a man can learn of his faults from a sincere friend, and from the insults of his enemies.[298] Ghazālī here proposes that a man may be informed of his own faults from four sources: the Shaykh, a close friend, his enemies, and a study of the faults of others.[299]

8 *An Exposition of Evidence handed down from Men of Spiritual Insight and Provided in the Law to the effect that the Way to cure the Diseases of the Heart is by Renouncing one's Desires, and that the Stuff of such Diseases is Following Desires.*

Ghazālī begins this section by remarking that even if the reader has not understood the importance of self-discipline on the theoretical level which he has been presenting, the reader can nonetheless benefit by the simpler means of *taqlīd*: following the guidance laid down in the Qur'ān and *ḥadīth*, and imitating the sages and scholars. In other words, he is here presenting the content of the previous sections in a manner more congenial to those unaccustomed to philosophical discourse.

He proceeds to cite some of these texts, which include what is perhaps the most famous *ḥadīth* relating to the theme of self-purification. Speaking to some men who had returned from a campaign, the Prophet said, 'Welcome! You have come from the lesser to the greater *Jihād*!' On being asked what the greater *Jihād* might be, he explained, 'The *Jihād* against the *nafs*'. This *ḥadīth*, although thought to be of doubtful authenticity, is regularly used to stress the importance of the inner struggle, and to characterise it, partly for rhetorical purposes, as being superior even to struggles waged in defence of the Faith. Al-Ḥakīm al-Tirmidhī provides the usual explanation of this:

> God (holy is His name!) has ordained *jihād*, which is of two kinds: fighting the enemy with the [physical] sword, and fighting passion and the self with the sword of renouncing one's own will. As recompense for the former struggle, He has promised Heaven, and for the latter, attainment unto Him. For when a man fights the enemy, and is killed, he finds the path to Heaven and rejoices in its delights; as for he who fights the self and passion until they are dead, he finds the path to the Throne, to the place of Proximity, and then to the sessions of intimate discourse [*majālis al-najwā*]. Regarding the *jihād* against the enemy, God says: *Those who* [...] *strive with their wealth and lives in God's path* [...] *are the triumphant. Their Lord gives them good tidings of mercy from Him, and acceptance, and Gardens where enduring pleasure shall be theirs.*[300] And regarding the *jihād* against the self, He says: *As for those who strive in Us, We surely guide them to Our paths.*[301]

This superiority, Ghazālī's tradition affirms, lies in the fact that the inner *jihād* is more difficult, and is to be fought unceasingly, and that the inevitable reward for success in it is salvation.[302]

9 *An Exposition of the Signs of Good Character.*

One can only identify evil traits within oneself if one is aware of their excellent opposites. These are listed in the Qur'ān and the *ḥadīth*, and exemplified in the lives of the Prophet and the saints, some incidents in which Ghazālī proceeds to cite. Here Ghazālī's position is far from that of Aristotle, who had relied on reason and consensus alone.

10 *An Exposition of the Way in which Young Children should be Disciplined, and the Manner of their Upbringing and the Improvement of their Characters.*

Although the question of educating the young is clearly related to Ghazālī's theme,[303] this section reads as something of an intrusion. It is drawn largely from a chapter of Miskawayh's *Refinement of Character*,[304] with a few amendments designed to bring it into accord with Ghazālī's Sufi perspective. Chief among these is the addition of a long story about the childhood of Sahl al-Tustarī.

Miskawayh tells us that his section is 'mostly copied from the book of Bryson'. This refers to an obscure neo-Pythagorean philosopher of the first century AD, whose work had also been known to Ibn Sīnā.[305] Bryson's work on economics, by which is meant the ordering of the household, is lost in Greek, but Arabic and Hebrew translations have survived, which enable us to identify the origin of Miskawayh's ideas fairly precisely.[306] Miskawayh has filtered out the more offensively un-Islamic practices, such as wine-bibbing,[307] but the Greek background of the work is still visible, for instance, in the recommendation that young boys take regular exercise.

11 *An Exposition of the Requirements of Aspirancy, the Preliminaries to Spiritual Struggle, and the Progressive Induction of the Aspirant in Treading the Path of Discipline.*

This is one of the most interesting sections in the *Iḥyā'*, revealing as it does the outline of Ghazālī's spiritual practice as he must have taught it to his own disciples. Although it is not clear whether it was written primarily for teachers or students,[308] it functions as a kind of summary, recapitulating the discussions of this and the previous book concerning the heart, the ego, the spiritual guide, and mystical experience. Many of the practical aspects of Sufi training seem never to have been set down in writing, which makes this section of particular value.

'Aspirancy' (*irāda*) is, according to a useful definition, 'the desire to come to the Beloved through inner combat (*mujāhada*).'[309] Put differently, it is 'the voluntary quest of the heart for spiritual sustenance'.[310] Its agent is a *murīd*, a word sometimes rendered as 'neophyte',[311] or 'disciple',[312] but in reality denoting any spiritual seeker who has not yet attained the goal.[313] *Irāda* had been used in early Islam to mean 'will'; and although by Muḥāsibī's time it had acquired a rather more specialised connotation among pietists and Sufis, for whom it denoted the sincere will to obey God,[314] it was in the fourth and fifth Islamic centuries (the tenth and eleventh of the Christian calendar) that its later sense of 'spiritual ambition' was developed. To 'will for God' truly was to renounce one's own will for anything else. It was to feel a sense of alienation from the world, and an awakening love and longing for Him.[315] *Irāda* thus supplies the motive behind refining the character.

Once the spiritual wayfarer has set off, numerous distractions and obstacles beset him. Some of these are so dangerous that he must cling to his guide as though he were a blind man walking by a river.[316] The most intransigent are 'money, status, conformism and sin.' Attachment to money is to be shaken off by giving away what one does not truly need.[317] Satisfaction with one's social status can be removed by acts of public humility. Sin is to be avoided by adhering sincerely to the Revealed Law. 'Conformism' or 'imitation' (*taqlīd*), the vice to which G͟hazālī himself had fallen prey before his conversion, is a little more complex; it is the blind acceptance of doctrine on the authority of others, and a consequent fanaticism on its behalf. But as he came to appreciate, this is not a secure path to truth; rather, spiritual 'tasting' (*d͟hawq*) is the only sound epistemology, as he writes elsewhere:

> The meanings of the [divine attributes] are to be known through unveiling (*mukāshafa*) and witnessing (*mus͟hā-hada*), so that their realities become clear to [the mystics] through a proof in which all error is impossible [...] How great a gulf divides this from belief (*iʿtiqād*) taken through conformism from one's parents and teachers, even if this be accompanied by dialectical, theological proofs![318]

Although G͟hazālī remained committed until his death to the As͟hʿarī theological school, in his mystical writings he emphasises that *taqlīd* is a veil, and that 'it is not a condition of aspirancy that one adhere to any particular school of thought (*mad͟hhab*).'[319] This attitude was informed both by his juristic background, which recognised the benefits of divergent opinions,[320] and also the Sufi tradition, which had often held that the Sufis

> regard the differences between the jurists as correct, and do not object to what those who follow other positions hold. For them, every *mujtahid*[321] is correct, and everyone who believes in an Islamic school of doctrine, being supported by [texts from] the Qur'ān and Sunna, and being of those able to derive such doctrines, is adhering to a true doctrine.[322]

Elsewhere in the *Iḥyā'*, G͟hazālī had used the celebrated parable of the blind men and the elephant. Groping around the animal, each constructed a different conception of it; but although each of these men was partially correct, only vision could truly apprehend the elephant in its completeness.[323] Thus, by implication, are the formal theological schools of his day, which argue about issues such as predestination while handicapped by reason, a faculty insufficient to grasp realities which transcend its own nature.

Another obstacle to spiritual progress is provided by the *khawāṭir*, the usually irrelevant thoughts which 'come at random into the mind',[324] and which may destroy the novice's concentration. They can be from God, or a good angel—in which case they are termed *ilhām* ('inspiration')—but more usually they are from the devil, and the egotism of the soul, and are called *waswās* ('whispering'), or *ḥadīth al-nafs* ('discourse of the soul'). Their source is to be known from the action they encourage.[325] Although they are not a sin,[326] the 'soul at peace' is the one that is liberated from these distractions, and it is said that God protected (*ʿiṣma*) His Prophet from them.[327] The Sufis, however, have disagreed as to whether this liberation can ever be complete.[328]

In order to calm the heart and minimise external distractions, the spiritual wayfarer may be advised to enter a retreat (*khalwa*) for up to forty days.[329] Here he will occupy himself with prayer and the remembrance of God, and intensify the struggle against his lower self. The Shaykh will have instructed him to repeat certain brief litanies, and these he should concentrate upon, until he can repeat them without moving his tongue.[330] This is called the 'remembrance of the heart' (*dhikr al-qalb*).[331] When it is perfected, so that no distractions remain, a condition of rapturous love of God ensues,[332] and God may, in His grace and mercy, bestow spiritual unveiling upon the seeker. As Ghazālī writes elsewhere:

> If his aspirancy is true, his ambition pure, and his concentration good, so that his appetites do not pull at

him, and he is not distracted by the *ḥadīth al-nafs* towards the attachments of the world, the gleams of the Truth will shine in his heart. At the outset, this will resemble a brief, inconstant shaft of lightning, which then returns, perhaps after a delay. If it returns, it may be fleeting or firm; and if it is firm (*thābit*), it may or may not endure for some time. States such as these may come upon each other in succession, or only one type may be present. In this regard, the stages of God's saints (*awliyā'*) are as innumerable as their outer attributes and qualities.[333]

The Book of Breaking the Two Desires

In his prologue, Ghazālī summarises the dangers of gluttony and excessive lust, pointing out that they are the 'greatest of the mortal vices'.[334] Satiety encourages lust, which in turn leads to a range of further defects, for fame and wealth are no more than means by which man gratifies his baser cravings, and conduce to enmity, injustice and corruption.

1 *An Exposition of the Merit of Hunger and a Condemnation of Satiety.*

This is a collection of material which recalls the poverty and hunger of the first Muslims. The author's purpose is a strategic one, for later in the book he will explain that hunger is a means, not an end, and that the ideal to be aimed for is moderation.[335]

2 *An Exposition of the Benefits of Hunger and the Evils of Satiety.*

This section is a good example of Ghazālī's methodical approach.[336] He writes that hunger has ten benefits: (I) it purifies the faculties of spiritual perception; (II) it softens the heart and renders it more receptive to divine grace; (III) it is a form of humbling the ego; (IV) it reminds the novice of the sufferings of the poor, and the punishments of hell; (V) it weakens the passional self, and enables one to control the sex drive more easily; (VI) it causes the seeker to need less sleep; (VII) it reduces the time wasted in preparing and eating food; (VIII) it benefits the health; (IX) it saves money; (X) it hence enables one to comply with God's command to help the poor.

3 *An Exposition of the Method by which Discipline is Used to Subjugate the Greed of the Belly.*

The spiritual seeker has four duties in regard to food. (I) He must only eat food that is lawful; (II) he should assess and reduce the frequency of his eating; (III) he should estimate and control the speed with which he eats, and (IV) he should look to the kind of food he is eating, and ensure that he avoids luxury. All of these are to be investigated with a high degree of rigour, and Ghazālī explains in some detail certain methods to be followed.

4 *An Exposition of the Variance in the Rule and Merit of Hunger in Accordance with the Circumstances of Men.*

Ghazālī now returns to the subject of the just mean, recalling the *ḥadīth* that 'the best of affairs is the middle course'. The objective is to attain a position of equal distance from both hunger and satiety, inasmuch as these distract the seeker from the remembrance of God. Yet the path to this equilibrium usually lies through a programme of hunger and fasting, which can only be relaxed when the *nafs* has thereby been subdued.

5 *An Exposition of the True Nature of Good and Bad Character.*

This brief section explains that the practice of self-denial in the matter of food is accompanied by two risks: (I) The novice may eat in secret to preserve his reputation, thereby committing 'hidden polytheism';[337] (II) He may be successful in renouncing his desire for food, but take delight in the fact that he is known to do so. Ghazālī concludes that it is spiritually healthier for both of these people to eat more, and publicly, rather than fall prey to either hypocrisy or conceit.

6 *A Discourse on Sexual Desire.*

Ghazālī now comes to the second of the 'two desires'. A different approach is to be adopted for this, for indulgence in food is a worldly weakness, while sexual gratification is not. In an earlier book of the *Iḥyā'*, he had discussed marriage, and the present section recapitulates some of this discussion. But whereas the *Book of Marriage* had included details on the actual practice and legal conditions of wedlock, together with advice on the rights and proper conduct of both parties, the present section, and the two which follow, are largely confined to a discussion of the appetite itself.

Sexual desire has been created for two beneficial reasons: (I) the perpetuation of the species, and (II) to provide a pleasurable foretaste of the bliss of Paradise. And yet it can also 'destroy both religion and the world if it is not controlled and subjugated, and restored to a state of equilibrium'. There are many indications in the Qur'an and Tradition of the extreme danger of lust, metonymically referred to as 'women'. Again, the golden mean is the ideal: the man of God errs neither towards celibacy nor towards the excess which is amorous passion (*ʿishq*), for the former is unnatural, and the latter a distraction.

7 *An Exposition of the Aspirant's Obligations Regarding the Renunciation or Undertaking of Marriage.*

Marriage, although it is the way of the Prophet, has drawbacks as well as advantages. In particular, beginners on the Path are likely to find married life a distraction, and should therefore be celibate, unless, that is, their desire be so strong that it cannot be weakened through fasting.

Ghazālī then discusses *naẓar*, the vice of ogling attractive women, which is the necessary prelude to unlawful sex. To avoid distraction, and possible mortal sin, the spiritual aspirant should cast down his eyes when women pass by. In keeping with the usual Islamic ethic, men and women who are neither married nor related should only speak with each other 'for purposes of general necessity'. Still worse than looking at strange women is looking at adolescent boys, and Ghazālī, conforming to Muslim values, condemns homosexuality in the strongest terms.[338]

Ghazālī then turns his attention briefly to the conditions of a successful marriage, and cites some tales of Sufis who served their wives in the house or endured their bad temper with a commendable mildness. He closes with some stories which stress the importance which the early Muslims attached to marriage.

8 *An Exposition of the Merit of him who Counters the Desire of his Sex and his Eye.*

In Exposition 6, Ghazālī had explained that one of the dangers of the sex drive is that when it is aroused, the mental faculties are partially suspended. It is thus better not to arouse it, for it is easy to restrain a horse from entering a stable door, but once it has done so, to pull it out again by the tail is extremely difficult. The present section claims our admiration for those who have succeeded in accomplishing this, and shows that it entails abundant reward from God—for it is the most intense of all forms of 'disciplining the *nafs*'.

Notes to Introduction

1 The popularity of his methodologically rigorous harmonisation of scripture and mysticism did much to prepare the ground for the success of Ibn ʿArabī's doctrine, the rapid spread of which has often been seen as enigmatic. Similarly, his critique of philosophic epistemology, whereby he showed that the underlying premises of knowledge are themselves without proof, perhaps facilitated the later emphasis in Islamic civilisation on mystical rather than ratiocinative knowledge. To establish this point more firmly, however, much more research on G͟hazālī's influence on other Islamic thinkers would be required.

2 For his biography, see references listed in Winter, *Remembrance of death*, xxv, note 24.

3 He had summarised the views of the Arab philosophers in his *Maqāṣid al-falāsifa*, a work which in Latin translation found wide currency in Europe.(Badawī, *Mu'allafāt al-G͟hazālī*, 53-62; Alonso, 'Influencia de Algazel en el mundo latino'; Hanley, T. 'St. Thomas' Use of Al-Ghazālī's *Maqāṣid al-Falāsifa*'.) These views he refuted in his *Tahāfut al-falāsifa*, which, although the subject of a famous rejoinder by Ibn Rus͟hd, was widely seen as conclusive. (For the *Tahāfut* see Badawī, *Mu'allafāt*, 63-9; and Van den Bergh's English translation of Ibn Rus͟hd's response, *Tahāfut al-tahāfut*.)

4 *Miʿyār al-ʿilm fī fann al-manṭiq* (Badawī, *Mu'allafāt*, p.71); *Miḥakk al-naẓar fi'l-manṭiq* (Badawī, *Mu'allafāt*, p.73-4).

5 Including *al-Mustaṣfā min ʿilm al-uṣūl* (Badawī, *Mu'allafāt*, pp.216-8); *al-Mank͟hūl fi'l-uṣūl* (Badawī, *Mu'allafāt*, pp.6-16).

6 The best known of these is *al-Iqtiṣād fi'l-iʿtiqād* (Badawī, *Mu'allafāt*, pp.87-8): a brief work, but one which is still very generally read.

7 *Faḍā'iḥ al-Bāṭiniyya*, also known as *al-Mustaẓhirī* (Badawī, *Mu'allafāt*, pp.82-4). There is a study of this work by Ignaz Goldziher: *Streitschrift des Gazālī gegen die Bāṭinijja-Sekte*, which includes a partial edition.

8 *al-Wajīz* (Badawī, *Mu'allafāt*, pp.25-9); *al-Wasīṭ* (Badawī, *Mu'allafāt*, pp.19-24); *al-Basīṭ fi'l-furūʿ* (Badawī, *Mu'allafāt*, pp.17-8); *K͟hulāṣat al-muk͟htaṣar* (Badawī, *Mu'allafāt*, pp.30-1).

9 For the historical and social

background see Bulliet, *The Patricians of Nishapur*; Madelung, *Religious Trends in Early Islamic Iran*; Allard, *Le problème des attributs divins*, 25–47. Ghazālī's worries about contemporary political instability are recorded in his "Mirror for Princes", *al-Tibr al-Masbūk fī naṣīḥat al-mulūk*, tr. F. Bagley as *Ghazālī's Book of Counsel for Kings*, 76–7.

10 General background will be found in the studies of Annemarie Schimmel (*Mystical Dimensions of Islam*), Hellmut Ritter (*Das Meer der Seele*), Marijan Molé (*Les mystiques musulmans*), Louis Massignon (*The Passion of al-Hallāj*). A classic text in English translation is Hujwīrī's *Kashf al-maḥjūb*.

11 Ghazālī, a skilled exponent of the art of quotation, gives Qur'ānic references at almost every juncture in the *Iḥyā'*, which, even more than the Sufi exegetical literature, displays the well-known comprehensiveness of the Islamic scripture. The Qur'ānic vision of the religious life has been exhaustively studied by Isutzu in his *Spiritual-ethical concepts in the Qur'ān*; for Qur'anic ethics cf. also B.A. Dar, 'Ethical Teachings of the Qur'an'; G. Hourani, *Reason and tradition in Islamic ethics*, 23–48; F.Denny, 'Ethics and the Qur'an'.

12 Q. VI:103.

13 Q. VII:143.

14 Q. II:115.

15 Q. III:190–1.

16 Q. LXXXVIII:17–20.

17 Q. LXXV:36–40.

18 Despite its inherent richness, this term was not widely employed by Muslim theorists of the soul, although the occasional exceptions included al-Ḥakīm al-Tirmidhī (*Bayān al-farq*, 70–9) and the Ikhwān al-ṣafā (*Rasā'il*, I. 360).

19 For *īmān* see Isutzu, 184–202; for *kufr* see ibid., 119–177.

20 Q. VI:82.

21 Q. XXXVIII:30.

22 Q. VI:25; XVII:46.

23 For the Qur'ān on the heart, see Massignon, *Passion*, III. 20–2.

24 Cf. Isutzu, 140; Jurjānī, *Taʿrīfāt*, 278.

25 Q. XXVIII:50.

26 Q. XVIII:29.

27 Q. VI:51. Cf. Isutzu, 139.

28 Q. XXV:45.

29 Q. XCI:9–10.

30 Q. XII:53.

31 Q. XXIX:69.

32 Q. LXXIX:37–41.

33 Q. III:185.

34 Q. VI:32.

35 Q. XC:10.

36 See Renard, 'al-Jihad al-Akbar: Notes on a Theme in Islamic Spirituality,' also above, LXIII.

37 This is the list compiled by Isutzu, pp.75–104.

38 Q. XI:75.

39 Q. XXXI:18–9.

40 Q. III:159.

41 Q. XVII:24.

42 Q. LXVIII:4. (*Wa-innaka la-*

UNIVERSITY OF WINCHESTER LIBRARY

ʿalā khuluq[in] *ʿaẓīm*.) See below, pp. 7, 70.

43 See below, p 7.

44 See below, p. 9.

45 See below, p. 12; for other *ḥadīths* of this nature see Qushayrī, *Risāla*, 393.

46 Muslim, Janna, 1; cf. Muḥāsibī, *Muʿātaba*, 32.

47 Qushayrī, *Risāla*, 324; Muḥāsibī, *Qaṣd*, 88.

48 Tabrīzī, *Mishkāt* (tr. Robson), 1031.

49 Ibid., 1033.

50 Ibid., 1039. Cf. also the fine *ḥadīth* translated by Sherif, *Ghazali's Theory of Virtue*, 101.

51 For our purposes this may be assumed to have commenced with al-Shāfiʿī (d. 204/820), who established and elaborated the doctrine that every moral principle should be supported by a Qur'ānic or *ḥadīth* text. (Cf. Khadduri, *al-Shāfiʿī's Risāla*, for a translation of Shāfiʿī's manifesto on this issue.) The early Islamic jurists commonly recognised five moral categories, into which every action could be classed: mandatory (*wājib*, or *farḍ*), recommended (*mandūb*, or *mustaḥabb*), neutral (*mubāḥ*), disliked (*makrūh*), and forbidden (*ḥarām*); for which see Kamali, *Principles of Islamic Jurisprudence*, 324-335. Van den Bergh has advanced the theory that this division is of Stoic origin (*Averroes' Tahafut*, II. 117), and this has been developed by Jadaane (*L'influence du stoïcisme sur la pensée musulmane*, 184-6). The link remains unproven, however; and it would seem more probable that the Muslim jurists, who did not lack originality in other spheres, developed this rather obvious and in many ways indispensable division from their own resources.

52 Such as ʿAbd Allāh ibn ʿAmr ibn al-ʿĀṣ (d. *c* 65/684), Abu'l-Dardā' (d. 32/652), and ʿAbd Allāh ibn ʿUmar (d. 73/693). See also Appendix I.

53 Ar. *tābiʿūn*, such as Bakr ibn ʿAbd Allāh al-Mazanī of Basra (d. 106/724), al-Ḥasan al-Baṣrī (d. 110/728), and Saʿīd ibn al-Musayyib of Medina (d. *c* 93/711). Some others are listed in Appendix I.

54 Cf. 'Your body has a right over you'; cited below, XXXVII.

55 See below, p.146.

56 Andrae, 53.

57 Andrae, 14.

58 Andrae, 53; Suhrawardī, 232; Hujwīrī, 201; Qushayrī, *Risāla*, 373; ʿAṭṭār, *Tadhkira*, I. 253; cf. below, 114.

59 *Iḥyā'*, II. 31 (*K. Ādāb al-nikāḥ*, bāb 1, āfa 3).

60 Cited in Fuchs, *Sexual Desire and Love*, 99.

61 Nasā'ī, Nikāḥ, II; Ibn Mājah, Nikāḥ, 8; Ibn Ḥanbal, *Musnad*, III. 158. Cf. Massignon, *Passion*, III. 164.

62 Andrae, 8-9; Molé, 8-21. For a characteristic example of this type of encounter see Ikhwān al-ṣafā, *Rasā'il*, I. 338-

42. Early Christian attitudes to hunger and fasting are discussed in A. Arbesmann, 'Fasting and Prophecy in Pagan and Christian Antiquity'; H. Musurillo, 'The Problem of Ascetical Fasting in the Greek Patristic Writers'.

63 Q. II:165.

64 *Iḥyā'*, IV. 253 (*K. al Maḥabba*, Bayān shawāhid al-sharᶜ).

65 For some statements by Companions and other early figures on this fear, see *Iḥyā'*, IV. 410-1 (*K. Dhikr al-mawt*, Bab 5, Bayān aqāwīl ...); tr. Winter, *Remembrance of death*, 88-90.

66 *Iḥyā'*, IV. 283 (*K. al-Maḥabba*, al-Qawl fī ᶜalāmāt al-maḥabba).

67 Schimmel, *Mystical Dimensions*, 51-3; Hujwīrī, 122-3; ᶜAṭṭār, *Tadhkira al-awliyā'*, I. 311.

68 For Ghazālī's understanding of these principles, see Sherif, *Ghazali's Theory of Virtue*, 132-38.

69 *Iḥyā'*, IV. 183 (*K. Dhamm al-dunyā*, Bayān al-mawāᶜiẓ).

70 Andrae, 68, quoting from Zakarīyā al-Anṣārī's commentary on Qushayrī's *Risāla*.

71 This is clearly set out in Muḥāsibī, *Qaṣd*, 56-7, in a section entitled 'The Meaning of "World", and a Clarification of what is Praiseworthy of it, and what is Reprehensible.' Even where *dunyā* is used as a derogatory term, it is usually *ḥubb al-dunyā* that is intended, as is clear from Ghazālī's own examination of the subject (*Iḥyā'*, IV. 174- 199, = *K. Dhamm al-dunyā*). Cf. further Andrae, 67-8.

72 Related by Bukhārī and Muslim, this is the first entry in al-Nawawī's celebrated anthology of forty *ḥadīth*.

73 *Iḥyā'*, IV. 312 (*K. al-Niyya*, Bayān faḍīlat al-niyya).

74 Qushayrī, *Risāla*, 293-4.

75 For Muḥāsibī see Van Ess, *Die Gedankenwelt des Ḥārit al-Muḥāsibī*; M. Smith, *An Early Mystic of Baghdad*. Since these books appeared, most of Muḥāsibī's writings have been published, thanks to the devoted labours of ᶜAbd al-Qādir ᶜAṭā of Cairo.

76 In the *Iḥyā'* (III. 229 [*K. Dhamm al-bukhl*, Bayān dhamm al-ghinā ...]), Ghazālī explicitly mentions Muḥāsibī as the greatest Muslim writer on practical religion.

77 Smith, *An Early Mystic*, 6.

78 Muḥāsibī, *Qaṣd*, 40.

79 Muḥāsibī, *Waṣāyā*, cited in Smith, *An Early Mystic*, 148.

80 Abū Nuᶜaym, *Ḥilya*, IX . 59-60, cited in Andrae, 81.

81 For the *maqāmāt* see Schimmel, *Mystical Dimensions*, 109-148.

82 Allard, 37-42; 98-133. As Makdisi has pointed out ('The Sunni Revival'), this acknowledgement of Ashᶜarism as the Islamic orthodoxy was not made by Ghazālī's time, 'orthodoxy' then being most closely identified

with the 'Traditionalists', who opposed the Shīʿa, the Muʿtazila and the Ashʿarīs alike.

83 For more on the concept of moderation see below, 154–6. The collective Muslim self-perception as constituting an *ummat*^{an} *wasaṭ*^{an} (Q. II:143) is further analysed in von Grunebaum, 'Concept and function of reason in Islamic ethics', 1–3.

84 Andrae, 103; Schimmel, *Mystical Dimensions*, 127; Kharrāz, *Lumaʿ*, 62.

85 Qushayrī, *Risāla*, 327.

86 Ibid., 393.

87 Cf. Q. LXXIX:40; Qushayrī, *Risāla*, 394; Smith, *An Early Mystic*, 90–1; van Ess, *Gedankenwelt*, 31–5.

88 The translation is of course unsatisfactory, and leads to many ambiguities (which are, however, not always infertile). But 'soul' seems preferable to 'ego' or 'self' in a text such as the present one, which includes ideas of a philosophical character.

89 Q. XVII:85.

90 Cf. *Iḥyā'*, IV. 422 (tr. Winter, *Remembrance of death*, 126): 'It is not given to any of the divines to reveal the secret of the spirit, even if one were to uncover it.' (Cf. also *Iḥyā'*, III. 3 [*K. ʿAjā'ib al-qalb*, Bayān maʿnā al-nafs, tr. McCarthy, *Freedom and Fulfillment*, 365]; *Iḥyā'*, IV. 213 [*K. al-Tawḥīd wa'l-tawakkul*, Shaṭr 1]; Jabre, *Lexique de Ghazali*, 210–1.) In fact, Ghazālī does discuss the *rūḥ*, for instance in his *Mishkāt al-anwār*, and by letting slip the occasional hint in the *Iḥyā'* apparently designed both to remind the initiated, and to arouse the interest of the gifted but uninitiated reader. For instance, in *Iḥyā'* III. 17 (*K. ʿAjā'ib al-qalb*, Bayān al-farq ...) he describes the early stages of mystical experience.

91 Q. LXXV:2; Smith, *Early Mystic*, 91–2.

92 For the three souls see Hujwīrī, 196–207; Schimmel, *Mystical Dimensions*, 112; Anawati and Gardet, *Mystique*, 206; Gardet, *Pensée*, 177n. Zabīdī (*Itḥāf*, VII. 207–8) lists seven more types.

93 Q. LXXXIX:25–7.

94 For instance, *Iḥyā'*, III. 8 (*K. ʿAjā'ib al-qalb*, Bayān khāṣṣīyat qalb al-insān; tr. McCarthy, *Freedom and Fulfillment*, 375); Miskawayh, *Tahdhīb al-akhlāq*, 51; see also Schimmel, *Mystical Dimensions*, 112–3. Cf. Plato, *Republic*, 589 D–E.

95 See below, p. 156.

96 See below, p.88.

97 Andrae, 57.

98 See, for instance, Guillaume's translation of Ibn Isḥāq's biography of the Prophet, pp.105–6.

99 For this, the rite of *iʿtikāf*, see Jazīrī, *al-Fiqh ʿalā al-madhāhib al-arbaʿa*, 1.582–9.

100 Suhrawardī, *ʿAwārif al-maʿārif*, 175 (tr. Gramlich, *Gaben*, 224).

101 These two principles,

while central to Sufism, are only peripheral to the books translated here, and will therefore not be discussed. Cf. (for dhikr), Nakamura (tr.) *Invocations and supplications*, xx-xxviii; (for *fikr*), Sherif, *Ghazali's Theory of Virtue*, 121-4. There is some reference to dhikr, however, in *Bayān* 11 of the *Disciplining the Soul* (pp.92-94 below), and this will be touched on at pp.LXVII.

102 Below, 91. Elsewhere, Ghazālī explores the arguments for and against withdrawal in a separate 'book' of the *Iḥyā'* (II. 197-217: *K. Ādāb al-ʿuzla*). The advantages and proper conduct associated with the companionship of other men are expounded in *Iḥyā'* II. 138-97 (*K. Ādāb al-ulfa*, which has been partially translated by Muhtar Holland). Cf. also Suhrawardī, 294-307; tr.Gramlich, *Gaben*, 365-80.

103 *Iḥyā'*, III. 92 (*K. Āfāt al-lisān*, prologue).

104 Ibn Ḥanbal, *Musnad*, II. 159; Ibn Abi'l-Dunyā, *Ṣamt*, 38; *Iḥyā'*, III. 93 (*K. Āfāt al-lisān*, Bayān ʿaẓīm ...).

105 Ibn Abi'l-Dunyā, *Ṣamt*, 223.

106 Ibid., 220.

107 Qushayrī, *Risāla*, 334, where the remark is attributed to Abū ʿAlī al-Daqqāq, the shaykh of Qushayrī.

108 Qushayrī, *Risāla*, 336.

109 Cf. Q. 11:183: *Fasting is prescribed for you, as it was prescribed for those who came before you, that you may have piety* (taqwā). For fasting as a meritorious act rewarded by God, there is the famous *ḥadīth*, 'Fasting is Mine, and I shall give reward for it' (Bukhari, Ṣawm, 6; Muslim, Ṣiyām, 160). Cf. Hujwīrī, 36, 321; Suhrawardī, 230 (tr. Gramlich, *Gaben*, 287).

110 Suhrawardī, 230 (Gramlich, *Gaben*, 287).

111 The canonical requirements of fasting are treated in, for instance, Jazīrī, I. 541-89.

112 Schimmel, *Mystical Dimensions*, 115.

113 Hujwīrī, 322; cf. above, XXXVI.

114 For an early text on the benefits of hunger, see Shaqīq al-Balkhī, *Ādāb al-ʿibādāt*, 17-8.

115 Hujwīrī, 321.

116 Qushayrī, *Risāla*, 373.

117 Suhrawardī, 231 (Gramlich, *Gaben*, 288).

118 These and other benefits are expounded below, pp.117-32.

119 Hujwīrī, 323.

120 Qushayrī, *Risāla*, 375.

121 Shaqīq al-Balkhī, *Ādāb al-ʿibādāt*, 18; Suhrawardī, 147-63 (tr. Gramlich, *Gaben*, 193-210); Schimmel, *Mystical Dimensions*, 94.

122 Below, p.158.

123 Such elementary techniques need not wholly be abandoned, for their own significance changes: hunger, for instance, is 'a source of discipline for aspirants (*murīdīn*), of a trial for the penitent, of strength for

ascetics, and of nobility for the gnostics.' (Qushayrī, *Risāla*, 373.)

124 Below, p.90; cf. also p.123-5.

125 Hujwīrī, 138; as cited in Schimmel, 115.

126 ʿAbdallāh Anṣārī, *Manāzil*, p.70.

127 Qushayrī, *Risāla*, 496.

128 Ibid.

129 Ibid., 494; cf. 15 below. See also Kharrāz, *Rasā'il*, 51-2.

130 Suhrawardī, 171 (Gramlich, *Gaben*, 219).

131 Ghazālī, *Iḥyā'*, III. 295 (*K. Dhamm al-kibr*, Bayān faḍīlat al-tawāḍuʿ).

132 Suhrawardī, 174 (Gramlich, *Gaben*, 223).

133 Q. LIX:9.

134 Suhrawardī, 181 (Gramlich, *Gaben*, 231).

135 Suhrawardī, 181 (Gramlich, *Gaben*, 231).

136 Qushayrī, *Risāla*, 495. For more on kindness to animals, see e.g. *Tibr*, tr. Bagley, 17-18; Van den Bergh, *Averroes' Tahafut*, I. xi; also a forthcoming work by Denys Johnson-Davies.

137 Qushayrī, *Risāla*, 497; variant in ʿAṭṭār, *Tadhkira*, I. 269-70.

138 Cf. the *ḥadīth* cited in Mundhirī, *Targhīb*, III. 411: 'The believer with the most perfect faith is he who has the finest character.'

139 Cf. for instance *Republic* 352 A-B, 612 E; Plotinus, *Enneads*, I.ii; Ibn Sīnā, *Ishārāt*, IV. 839 (tr. Goichon, *Livre des directives*, 497-8).

140 Ghazālī, *Maqṣad*, 44, and cf. ibid., 162.

141 Shehadi's introduction to his ed. of the *Maqṣad*, xxviii, note 1; see also Gimaret, *Les noms divins en Islam*, 21-2, 24-5.

142 Cf. *Iḥyā'*, IV. 263 (*K. al-Maḥabba*, Bayān anna'l-mustaḥiqq li'l-maḥabba ...); also Jabre, *Notion de maʿrifa*, 110.

143 Chittick, *Sufi Path of Knowledge*, 283-8. Ibn ʿArabī's debt to Ghazālī's doctrine of the names is acknowledged in a citation in *ibid.*, p.284, which is evidently a reference to the *Maqṣad*.

144 For marriage and sexuality as consequences of original sin, a notion which gained popularity with the teachings of Origen, see Fuchs, 98; Brown, *The Body and Society*, 93-4. Procreation, for many early Christians, was a necessary consequence of the Fall: since man was now mortal, and animal, he had to reproduce himself. Islamic accounts of the Fall, which include the doctrine of God's forgiveness of Adam, may be read in an excellent translation from Ṭabarī's *tafsīr*: Cooper, *The Commentary on the Qur'ān*, 244-61.

145 Epiphanius, cited in Brown, 254.

146 Brown, 245.

147 Gregory of Nyssa, *On Virginity*, cited in Fuchs, 100.

148 Miguel Asín Palacios (d.1944), the Spanish priest who

gave us the finest account of Islamic eschatological beliefs, does not trouble to hide his distaste. Confronted with the information that in Heaven men will consort with their wives *bi-dhakar*[in] *lā yamall, wa-farj*[in] *lā yuḥfā, wa-shahwat*[in] *lā tanqaṭi*ʿ, he betrays a contempt which stands entirely in the tradition of medieval polemicists of the type of Ramon Lull. (*La Escatología Musulmana en la Divina Comedia*, 374n, and passim.) Hans Küng, too, adduces the Prophet's 'sensual lifestyle' as evidence against the authenticity of his mission (Küng, 'Christianity and World Religions', 84). For the early Christian belief in Muslim licentiousness see Brundage, 'Prostitution, Miscegenation and Sexual Purity in the First Crusade', 60; Daniels, *Islam and the West*, 135-61.

149 Ghazālī, *Iḥyā'*, IV. 463 (*K. Dhikr al-mawt*, ṣifat al-ḥūr...); tr. Winter, *Remembrance of death*, 244-6.

150 Ibn Māja, Nikāḥ, 1.

151 Bukhārī, Ṣawm, 55.

152 Muslim, Zakāt, 52; Nawawī, *Arba*ʿ*ūn*, no.25. For this attitude see Goldziher, *Muslim Studies*, II. 357-8.

153 For some recent attempts to challenge Western stereotypes of Muslim women, see Chantal Lobato, 'Femmes afghanes, femmes musulmanes'; Sachiko Murata, 'Masculine-Feminine Complementarity in the Spiritual Psychology of Islam'; Marcel Boisard, *L'Humanisme de l'Islam*, 104-110.

154 Genesis, 1.26-7. Cf. Bayhaqī, *Asmā'*, II. 17. As acknowledged by Ghazālī (*Iḥyā'*, II. 148; cf. Jabre, *Notion de ma*ʿ*rifa*, 86-108, 204-6; Wensinck, *Pensée de Ghazālī*, 39-43).

155 Modern Muslim apologists are at pains to point out that this is offset by the responsibility of earning a living, which is a legal obligation binding upon the husband. Cf. J. Smith, 'The Experience of Muslim Women', 96. The classical Muslim jurists were in disagreement over a number of key questions touching on women's legal status; see for instance Hashim Kamali, 'Divorce and Women's Rights'. But the overall understanding was one of mutual rights, which were seen as standing in a complementary balance, and could if necessary be enforced by appeal to a magistrate. Cf. the following summary by Laoust (of Ibn Taymiyya's position): 'La femme a des droits à la fois sur les biens et sur le corps de son mari. Les premiers sont constitués par la dot, l'un des éléments essentiels du mariage musulman, et par la pension alimentaire (*nafaḳa*). Les seconds sont le droit d'exiger du mari la cohabitation et la jouissance (*suknā, mut*ʿ*a*), dont les conditions minima sont fixées par la Loi. Le mari, de son côté, ne saurait, en aucun cas, avoir le

moindre droit sur les biens de sa femme: il n'a de droit que sur son corps.' (*Essai sur les doctrines sociales et politiques de Taḳī-d-Dīn Aḥmad B. Taimīya*, 427–8.)

156 Few legal documents have survived from the first six or seven centuries of Islam, making it difficult to assess the extent of female participation in commerce and landowning. Ottoman commercial life, however, is abundantly documented in the Istanbul archives, from which it appears that women did have substantial disposable assets. For instance, it has been calculated that in mid-sixteenth century Istanbul, 36.8% of charitable endowments (*awqāf*) were founded by women. For 18th century Aleppo the figure was 36.3%, while for seventeenth and eighteenth century Cairo it lay between 22% and 50%. (G. Baer, 'Women and *waqf*: an analysis of the Istanbul *tahrîr* of 1546', p.10.) See further Jennings, 'Women in Early 17th Century Ottoman Judicial Records—The Sharia Court of Anatolian Kayseri'.

157 Sarah Hutchinson, 'The Ḥijāb', chap.3; cf. J. Smith, 'Experience', 97.

158 M. Smith, *Rābiʿa the Mystic*, 125.

159 Q. XIX:16–30. Mary, of course, is not *theotokos*, but merely the virginal mother of the prophet Jesus.

A valuable study of Mary as understood by Muslims has recently been published by Jane Smith and Yvonne Haddad: 'The Virgin Mary in Islamic Tradition and Commentary', which includes a comparison with Fāṭima on pp.179–81. See also the PhD thesis of Aliah Schleifer, 'A Modified Phenomenological Approach to the Concept and Person of Maryam in Islam'.

160 Rābiʿa al-ʿAdawīya, the best known of all woman Sufis, was, nevertheless, celibate, as the story below, p.178, explains.

161 Hujwīrī, 13.

162 Qushayrī, *Risāla*, 425–6; ʿAṭṭār, *Tadhkira*, I. 257. For some other tales in this genre see *Lumaʿ*, 62; ʿAṭṭār, *Tadhkira*, I. 123 (translated in Schimmel, *Dimensions*, 45); ʿAṭṭār, *Tadhkira*, I. 120–1; Ibn Qutayba, *ʿUyūn*, IV. 85; Ghazālī, *Tibr* (tr. Bagley), 166–7; Kalābādhī, *Taʿarruf*, 10 (tr. Arberry, *The Doctrine*, 11); *Iḥyā'*, IV. 339 l.16 (*K. al-Murāqaba*, Murābaṭa 2); ibid., I. 318 l.6 (*K. Tartīb al-awrād*, Bayān ikhtilāf al-awrād; tr. Cuperly, *Temps et prières*, 161); Andrae, 56, 69; Arberry, *Aspects of Islamic Civilisation*, 316–27.

163 *Iḥyā'*, IV. 353–5 (*K. al-Murāqaba*, Murābaṭa 5).

164 For Shaʿwāna, see Smith, *Rābiʿa*, 145–8.

165 And yet the tale of Potiphar's wife Zulaykhā is given an unusual twist in some Muslim legends, which assert that her love for Joseph was justified, because

she was infatuated by the divine beauty and perfection which he manifested (cf. Schimmel, *The Triumphal Sun*, 179). Other accounts speak of her ultimate repentance; Ghazālī has preserved one of these on p.58 below.

It is interesting to note that with this ambivalent exception, the early Islamic imagination utilised no individual female symbol of temptation and distraction comparable to the Biblical characters of Jezebel (I Kings 21) and Delilah (Judges 16). These temptresses were of course known, but only to antiquarians—and as history, not scripture.

166 Ghazālī, *Tibr* (tr. Bagley), 163.

167 Shahrazād does of course ultimately overcome her spouse's misogyny. For other literary sources on women, see the *ʿUyūn al-akhbār* of Ibn Qutayba, IV. 1-147; Ibn ʿAbd Rabbihi, *al-ʿIqd al-Farīd* (relevant sections conveniently extracted in *Ṭabā'iʿ al-nisā'*, ed. Muḥammad Salīm); and al-Sarrāj's *Maṣāriʿ al-ʿushshāq*, which, despite the Ḥanbalite leanings of its author, also stands within this tradition.

168 Bagley, XLIX.

169 F. Rosenthal, 'Sources', 14: 'The basic theme of the greater freedom of women in early Islam is historically quite true'; cf. also Margaret Smith (*Rābiʿa*, 125, cited above). See also Bürgel, 'Love, Lust and Longing: Eroticism in Early Islam', 108-9, where various examples of Christian (and also Persian) misogyny infiltrating Islam are cited, which, according to Bürgel, 'do not reflect the Koranic attitude on women'.

A characteristic collection of Greek warnings about the fair sex, attributed to Socrates, was available to the Arabs in Mubashshir ibn Fātik, *Mukhtār al-ḥikam*, 114-5.

170 Ibn ʿArabī, *Fuṣūṣ al-ḥikam*, 214ff; *Futūḥāt*, III. 114-20; Schimmel, 'Eros in Sufi Literature and Life', 129-30. Ibn ʿArabī even permits women to act as prayer leaders for male congregations, on the basis of the Prophet's teaching that women as well as men have attained perfection, and of the absence of any scriptural prohibition. (*Futūḥāt*, I. 562-3.)

171 Cf. for instance the following commentary by a modern Muslim: 'The Divine Essence is often addressed by the Sufis as Layla, a woman's name which has the meaning of night. In this highest sense, night is the symbol of Absolute Reality in its 'feminine' aspect of Infinitude. The blue-black night sky with its stars reflects the 'womb' of Infinite Totality in which the supreme archetypes of all existing things are mysteriously contained in Oneness'. (Martin Lings, *Symbol and Archetype*, 40.)

172 Documented by P. Salazar in her thesis. It appears that women accounted for approximately one-

sixth of the *ḥadīth* scholars and narrators of the early period, which would presuppose both public instruction, and a high regard on the part of male scholars for the integrity and ability of the women concerned. The phenomenon has been remarked upon by Goldziher, *Muslim Studies,* II. 366–8, who notes that it tailed off after the first Muslim millennium. 'When reading the great biographical work of Ibn Ḥajar al-ʿAsqalānī on the scholars of the eighth [Muslim] century we may marvel at the number of women to whom the author has to dedicate articles' (ibid., II. 367). Salazar draws attention to the rich source material available in Kaḥḥāla's *Aʿlām al-nisā'*, a modern biographical dictionary of prominent Muslim women. Further background material on female academic life in Islam can be found in Tritton, *Materials on Muslim Education in the Middle Ages*, 140–3; Siddiqi, *Ḥadīth Literature,* Appendix I.

173 Although in theory the doctrine of *ijmāʿ*, the consensus of competent scholars, could define an 'orthodox' doctrine (which might have pronounced finally on the worth and function of women), the conditions laid down for the establishment of a valid *ijmāʿ* were in fact so rigorous as to render the mechanism a largely theoretical one. Cf. Kamali, *Principles of Islamic Jurisprudence*, 168–96.

174 Such is the conclusion of, for instance, Saadia Chishti in her 'Female Spirituality in Islam'.

175 Below, p.167.

176 For *ghaḍḍ al-baṣar* see below, 172–5; F. Yakan, *al-Islām wa'l-jins*, 88–9.

177 Ibn Qutayba, *ʿUyūn*, IV. 84.

178 See below, p.174.

179 Hutchinson, chap. 4. Cf. also Ibn ʿArabī, *Futūḥāt*, I. 463: '"women" are an expression and metaphor (*ʿibāra wa-kināya*) for "desires".'

180 Nasā'ī, ʿIshrat al-nisā', I; Ibn Ḥanbal, *Musnad*, III.128.

181 Andrae, 42.

182 Cf. Qāḍī ʿIyāḍ, *Shifā'*, I. 191: '*lam yarahu al-ʿulamā' mimmā yaqdaḥu fi'l-zuhd*'.

183 Schimmel, *Mystical Dimensions*, 36, citing the *Iḥyā'*.

184 Hujwīrī, 247. For more on the celibate tendency, see Bellamy, 'Sex and Society in Islamic Popular Literature', 30–4.

185 Al-Nawawī and Ibn Taymīya were among these learned bachelors. See Abū Ghudda, *al-ʿUlamā' al-ʿUzzāb*; Pouzet, *Une Herméneutique de la tradition islamique*, 3. Renunciation of marriage did not, of course, imply either a belief that it was inherently damaging to spirituality, or that the temptation of sexuality was the principal reason why some preferred the celibate life. Hujwīrī thought that many adopted celibacy because 'in our time it is

impossible for anyone to have a suitable wife, whose wants are not excessive' (Hujwīrī, 363).

186 Several major Islamic theologians even wrote erotic treatises, clearly not regarding this as incommensurate with their dignity. For instance: (i) al-Suyūṭī (d.911/1505), author of almost a thousand works on virtually every aspect of Islam, wrote several books of this nature, including *Shaqā'iq al-uṭrunj fī daqā'iq al-ghunj*, *Nuzhat al-ʿumr fi'l-tafḍīl bayn al-bīḍ wa'l-sūd wa'l-sumr*, and others (cf. Khazandār and Shaybānī, *Dalīl makhṭūṭāt al-Suyūṭī*, nos.857–865). One such text has been translated into French by René Khawam as *Nuits de noces, ou comment humer le doux breuvage de la magie licite.* (ii) The Ottoman Shaykh al-Islām, Kamāl Pāshā-zāde (d.940/1534), renowned for his historical and theological works, also translated into Turkish what is possibly one of the most popular Muslim erotic texts: *ʿAwdat al-Shaykh ilā ṣibāh fi'l-quwwa ʿala'l-bāh* by al-Tīfāshī, of which an English translation exists. Cf. Parmaksızoğlu, 'Kemal Paşa-Zâde', 565. (iii) The prominent Shāfiʿī jurist Ibn Jamāʿa was the author of *Nuzhat al-albāb fīmā lā yūjad fi'l-kitāb* (Kaḥḥāla, *Muʿjam al-mu'allifīn*, v. 257).

For a list of classical Muslim erotic texts see Tāshköprüzāde, *Miftāḥ*, I. 287–8.

Another leading jurist and Sufi who wrote on the spiritual benefits of sexuality was ʿAbd al-Wahhāb al-Shaʿrānī of Cairo: see V. Vacca, *Il Libro dei Doni*, pp.74–6, and index, s.v.'donne'. One might mention as further confirmation of Islam's recognition of the value of non-procreative sexuality the general acceptance among the jurists of most forms of contraception (for which see B. Musallam, *Sex and society in Islam*).

187 Tustarī, *Muʿāraḍa*, 48. According to the Qāḍī ʿIyāḍ (*Shifā'*, I. 191) he gave the following explanation of this: 'Since women were made beloved to the Master of the Messengers, how can one renounce them [*yuzhad fīhinn*]?'

Sahl's ascetic rule is recalled in the life of a more recent mystic, Ibn ʿAjība of Morocco, who, during a programme of intense self-abnegation which included sweeping the marketplace, carrying ordure, and wearing garments so old that the original fabric could not be seen for patches, also married several wives. (Michon, *Le soufi marocain Aḥmad ibn ʿAjība*, 49, 73.) One might note that Ibn ʿAjība was an assiduous student of Ghazālī's writings.

188 According to Nawawī, 'all appetites harden the heart, with the exception of sexual desire, which softens it.' (*Sharḥ al-Arbaʿīn*, 65 [to *ḥadīth* 25]; tr. Pouzet, 167.)

189 *Tārīkh Baghdād*, v. 156; XI. 297; *Tahdhīb al-Tahdhīb*, IV. 273; Dhahabī, *Mīzān*, II. 250. For this

see Massignon, *Passion*, I. 357n; also Bell, 'Al-Sarrāj's *Maṣāriʿ al-ʿushshāq*'; idem, *Love Theory in early Hanbalite Islam*, 26 and passim.

190 Galen is cited in Ibn Fātik, 294: "*ʿIshq* is an action of the soul [*nafs*], and is latent in the brain, the heart and the liver. The brain contains three faculties: the imagination, which lies at the front of the brain, thought, which is located in the centre, and memory, which lies at its back. No-one is perfectly 'passionate' [*ʿāshiq*] unless, when he is away from his beloved, his imagination, thought and memory of the beloved do not cease, so that all parts of the soul are preoccupied with the beloved.' The implication is clear: amorous passion is a reprehensible distraction.

191 Ibid., 77; repeated without attribution below, 169. This ancient condemnation of *ʿishq* has survived in a modern Turkish religious text: Nevzat Akaltun, *Islam Fıkhı ve Hukukuna Ait 1099 Fetva*, p.235, where it is duly ascribed to Diogenes—and quoted approvingly.

192 al-Kindī, *Fī ḥudūd al-ashyā'*, 176; Ibn Sīnā, *Ishārāt*, IV. 827 (tr. Goichon, *Directives*, 492); Goichon, *Introduction à Avicenne*, 61.

193 Rāzī, *Ṭibb Rūḥānī*, 35ff, cited in Mohaghegh, 'Notes on the "Spiritual Physic" of al-Rāzī', 12-3. It appears that Plotinus and Proclus never married, while Porphyry only married in later life—in order to care for the widow of a friend; cf. Wallis, *Neoplatonism*, 9-10. For Plato's early position see, e.g., *Republic*, 329 C, 573 B-C.

194 Ibn ʿAdī, *Tahdhīb al-akhlāq*, 12. For Aristotle on lust and love see *Nicomachean Ethics*, VII.xiv.1-2; Fortenbaugh, *Aristotle on Emotion*, 87; Walzer, *Greek into Arabic*, 48-59. For the *falāsifa*'s view of sexuality generally, see Rosenthal, 'Sources', 8-10.

195 Below, 168.

196 The *Dhamm al-hawā* has been carefully studied by Bell, *Love Theory*, 11-45.

197 Cf. for instance al-Rāghib al-Iṣfahānī, *Dharīʿa*, 210-1; also below, 169.

198 Cf. Schuon, *Sufism: Veil and Quintessence*, 69: the Sufis 'see no need to expose themselves needlessly to the torment of the sexual instinct and to the distracting preoccupation which it involves. Some will object that this way of looking at things opens the door to every form of concupiscence, especially to the sin of gluttony, for if there is no limit to sexuality, there can be none to other satisfactions of the senses; this is false, for eating too much makes one ill, degrades one and makes one ugly, which is not the case as regards the conjugal life of healthy people, and in this inequality is the proof that the two items are not comparable, except,

precisely, when they are both reduced to animality.'

199 Below, p.167.

200 The recommendation to ensure the wife's sexual satisfaction (*taqḍī ḥājatahā*) is commonplace in the literature (cf. Ibn Qutayba, *ʿUyūn*, IV. 96), for the Prophet would discourage a man from 'lying with a woman, and satisfying his need from her before she had satisfied her need from him' (*Iḥyā'*, II. 46 [*K. Ādāb al-nikāḥ*, bāb 3]). Various methods by which this may be accomplished are described by Ghazālī's commentator al-Zabīdī (*Itḥāf*, v. 371).

201 Below, p.169.

202 al-Kindī, *Fi'l-falsafa al-ūlā*, in *Rasā'il al-Kindī*, I. 103, as translated by Walzer, *Greek into Arabic*, 12.

203 Readers unfamiliar with the doctrines of the Muʿtazila will find a convenient summary in Watt, *Islamic Philosophy and Theology*, 46-55. For the Ashʿarīs see ibid., 64-8, and the references there cited.

204 For the translation process see Bergsträsser, *Ḥunain ibn Isḥāq und seine Schule*; Steinschneider, *Die arabischen Übersetzungen aus dem Greischischen*; Walzer, *Greek into Arabic*; Peters, *Aristotle and the Arabs*, 58-67; idem, *Aristoteles Orientalis*.

205 Walzer, 'Djālīnūs', *EI*², II. 402-3. For Galen in the Islamic world see Temkin, *Galenism*, 69-80; Bergsträsser, *Ḥunain ibn Isḥāq, Über die syrischen und arabischen Galen-Übersetzungen*; idem, *Neue Materialen zu Ḥunain ibn Isḥāq's Galen-Bibliographie*; Walzer, *Greek into Arabic*, 142-63.

206 F. Rosenthal, 'On the knowledge of Plato's Philosophy in the Islamic World'; M. Fakhri, 'The Platonism of Miskawayh', 39n1; R. Walzer, 'Aflāṭūn', *EI*², I. 234-6.

207 Ed. Badawī, in *Plotinus apud arabes*. For this work see Zimmermann, 'The Origins of the so-called *Theology of Aristotle*'; Kraus, *Plotin chez les Arabes*, 267n, 290ff.

208 The best known of these is the *Mishkāt al-anwār*. Cf. the translation by Temple Gairdner; and Montgomery Watt, 'A Forgery in al-Ghazālī's *Mishkāt*?'

209 See notes 3 and 4 above.

210 Tirmidhī, ʿIlm, 19; Ibn Mājah, Zuhd, 15. Cited in the introduction to Ibn Fātik's *Mukhtār al-ḥikam*, 2, in order to justify the use of Greek wisdom by Muslims.

211 Ibn Kathīr, *Bidāya*, x. 330.

212 Ibn ʿAsākir (d.571/1174), *Tabyīn*, 97.

213 For this term see note c on p.85 below.

214 For details of this esoteric Shīʿa sect, which claimed that knowledge was to be had only from the teachings of an infallible Imam, see Watt, *Islamic Philosophy*, 124-8; Ivanow, *A Guide to Ismaili Literature*.

215 *al-Munqidh min al-ḍalāl*

(Arabic), 10, 1

216 Jabre, 'Vie', 80–1.

217 Gardet and Anawati, *Théologie musulmane*, 72–3. Juwaynī's best known work, the *K. al-Irshād*, reveals this tendency clearly.

218 *Munqidh*, 18.

219 ibid., 23–4 (Arabic). These objections were expounded exhaustively in Ghazālī's *Tahāfut*.

220 *Munqidh*, 24.

221 ibid.

222 ibid., 25.

223 ibid.

224 ibid., 27.

225 Plato, *Republic*, 435 A; 504 A.

226 Ibid., 427 E ff; 536. For Plato's ethics generally, see Gould, *The Development of Plato's Ethics*.

227 For some more detailed and nuanced accounts, see Gauthier, *La Morale d'Aristote*; Jaeger, *Aristotle*, tr. Robinson, pp.228–58; Hardie, *Aristotle's ethical theory*.

228 Defined as an end 'which we wish for its own sake, while we wish the others only for the sake of this.' *Nicomachean Ethics*, I.ii. 1; cf. the Arabic translation of Isḥāq ibn Ḥunayn (ed. Badawī), p.54. Cf. also Kenny, 'Aristotle on Happiness'. The *summum bonum* was to a greater or lesser extent recast by the Islamic thinkers to apply to otherworldly salvation; cf. Ibn Sīnā, *Ishārāt*, IV. 782 (tr. Goichon, *Directives*, 479); Khan, 'Miskawayh's conception of *sa'āda*'.

229 For more on the doctrine of the mean, see *Nicomachean Ethics*, II.ii; Hardie, 'Aristotle's Doctrine that Virtue is a 'Mean''; cf. Plato, *Republic*, 558 D—559 D.

230 Wallis, *Neoplatonism*, 8–11, 84–6.

231 His ethical thought is also influenced by the position of Posidonius of Rhodes (first century BC). Cf. Walzer, *Greek into Arabic*, 149.

232 Cf. Fakhri, 'The Platonism of Miskawayh', 45.

233 Tr. in Walzer, 156.

234 Walzer, 159.

235 This is now lost. See Walzer, art. 'Akhlāḳ', *EI*[2], I. 327; idem, *Greek into Arabic*, 240.

236 Ed. Kraus, 'The Book of Ethics by Galen', and translated by J. Mattock. Cf. Walzer, *Greek into Arabic*, 142–74. Cf. also below, 17A.

237 'Akhlāḳ', 327.

238 Arberry, 'The Nicomachean Ethics in Arabic'; Dunlop, 'The Nicomachean Ethics in Arabic'; idem, 'Observations on the Medieval Arabic Version of Aristotle's *Nicomachean Ethics*'; Lyons, 'A Greek Ethical Treatise'; Berman, 'A Note on the Added Seventh Book of the Nicomachean Ethics in Arabic'. The text of Isḥāq ibn Ḥunayn's translation has been edited by Badawī and published in 1979.

239 'Akhlāḳ', 327; Lyons, 'A Greek Ethical Treatise'.

240 'Akhlāḳ', 327–8. The only specifically ethical work of his which seems to have survived is his *al-Ḥīla li-dafʿ al-aḥzān*, which has been studied by Walzer and Ritter.

241 al-Kindī, *Fī ḥudūd al-ashyā'*, 178–9.

242 Ed. Kraus, 15–96; tr. Arberry, *The Spiritual Physick of Rhazes*.

243 Cf. 'Akhlāḳ', 328; Arberry's introduction, 1–17.

244 See for instance I. Netton, *Muslim Neoplatonists*; Y. Marquet, art. 'Ikhwān al-ṣafā', in *EI*², III. 1071–6; I. al-Fārūqī, 'On the Ethics of the Brethren of Purity.'

245 *Rasā'il*, I. 299. To be born under Jupiter, for instance, is to be disposed to asceticism and gentleness. (ibid., I. 307.)

246 Ibid., I. 310. It is not clear when the connection between the principal and derivative virtues originated, although it was accepted by the Stoics. Cf. Walzer, *Greek into Arabic*, 240.

247 *Rasā'il Ikhwān al-ṣafā*, I. 306, 311, 361.

248 Ibid., I. 356–8.

249 Ibid., I. 353; cf. *Nicomachean Ethics*, IV.iii.1–35. *Kibar al-nafs* was acknowledged, however, in Ghazālī's list of the secondary virtues; see below, 21.

250 *Rasā'il Ikhwān al-ṣafā*, I. 335.

251 For Ibn ʿAdī see Platti, *Yaḥya ibn ʿAdī, théologien chrétien et philosophe arabe*, 1–32; Endress, *The Works of Yaḥyā ibn ʿAdī* and references there given.

252 Ibn ʿAdī, ed. in Takrītī, *Yaḥyā ibn ʿAdī*, 73.

253 Ibid., 101–4. An example is *zuhd*, which is a virtue in scholars but a vice in kings.

254 His principal works devoted to ethics are *Fi'l-akhlāq wa'l-infiʿālāt al-nafsānīya*, and *Fī ʿilm al-akhlāq*; together with sections of his larger works.

255 *al-Nafs*, in Rahman, *Avicenna's De Anima*, 39–51.

256 For his religious thought, particularly well expressed in the final book of the *Ishārāt*, see Gardet, *La pensée religieuse d'Avicenne*.

257 For the reliance of his ethical system on Ibn Sīnā, see Sherif, 24–8; Skellie, xx–xxii; xxx.

258 The text has been edited and annotated by C. Zurayk. For Miskawayh see Arkoun, *L'Humanisme arabe*; Walzer, *Greek into Arabic*, 220–35; Fakhri, 'The Platonism of Miskawayh and its implications for his ethics.'

259 The first chapter of the *Tahdhīb* is, according to Walzer, probably based on al-Kindī ('Akhlāḳ', 328).

260 Walzer, *Greek into Arabic*, 147n2.

261 *Tahdhīb*, 15–6.

262 al-Takrītī, 263; Walzer, *Greek into Arabic*, 224.

263 Cf. *Tahdhīb*, 13, 41, where he explains that the purpose of refining the character is to attain to

the status of *khalīfa*, and to attain eternal life in the Muslim paradise. For the Neoplatonic influence on Miskawayh (specifically Porphyry), see Fakhri, 'The Platonism', 53-4; for the Stoic element in his thought, see Jadaane, 90, where it is affirmed that he reproduces certain passages from Epictetus.

264 'Akhlāk', 225-6.

265 *Tahdhīb*, 55; cf. p.LXIV below.

266 Ibid., 24-6.

267 Pre-eminently Naṣīr al-Dīn al-Ṭūsī (d.672/1274) and al-Dawwānī (d.908/1502).

268 C. Brockelmann, art. 'al-Māwardī', in *EI*², III. 416; Arkoun, *Essais*, 251-282.

269 Such as the *Mukhtār al-ḥikam* of Ibn Fātik, and the *K. al-Saʿāda wa'l-isʿād* of al-ʿĀmirī.

270 Arkoun, *Essais*, 266-8.

271 Ibid., 262.

272 However, while Aristotle holds that our virtue generally depends on ourselves (*Nicomachean Ethics*, III.v.1-2), he does not entirely discount the possibility that the achievement of *eudaimonia* may be helped by God. Cf. ibid., I. ix.2.

273 There are two other works ascribed to Ghazālī which bear substantially on his ethics. (i) *Mīzān al-ʿamal* (Badawī, *Mu'allafāt*, pp.79-81; French translation by Hikmat Hachem), the thought of which is generally in harmony with the philosophical ethics expounded in the *Iḥyā'*, with the exception of its conception of justice, which is presented as a term for all the virtues combined (Abul Quasem, 'Al-Ghazālī's Theory of Good Character', 238n), and its breakdown of some of the subsidiary virtues (Sherif, 178). For these and other reasons (cf. Watt, 'The Authenticity of the Works Ascribed to Al-Ghazālī', 39; idem, *Muslim Intellectual*, 67-8, 150; but see Sherif, 170-6), the book may be wholly or partly spurious. (ii) *Maʿārij al-quds fī madārij maʿrifat al-nafs* (Badawī, *Mu'allafāt*, pp.244-8; tr. Schammas, 'The Ascent of the Divine') is not mentioned in any of Ghazālī's other works, and is questioned by Watt ('Authenticity', 30), and Vajda ('Le ma'āriǧ al-quds', 470-3), and dismissed as inauthentic by Tritton ('*Maʿārij al-Quds*'). In view of this controversy, it has seemed preferable to avoid any reference to these two works in the present consideration of Ghazālī's ethics.

274 *Tahdhīb al-akhlāq*, 19-24. Cf. Sherif, 38-73, whose detailed discussion of Ghazālī's deployment of the subsidiary virtues renders further discussion here unnecessary.

275 Watt's judgement, that Ghazālī 'turned to a complete rejection of the criterion of the mean as a scientific basis for ethics' (*Muslim Intellectual*, 68) is hard to account for.

276 Earlier in the *Iḥyā'*, Ghazālī has provided an entire

book to show the Prophet as a moral ideal. (*Iḥyā'*, II. 312–46, = *K. Ādāb al-maʿīsha wa-akhlāq al-nubuwwa.*)

277 For instance, Māwardī, 444–6, and Ibn Qutayba, *ʿUyūn*, II. 5–6, explain in traditional Muslim terms that *akhlāq* are susceptible of change.

278 Cf. Fārābī, *al-Tanbīh ʿalā sabīl al-saʿāda*, 7–9; Miskawayh, *Tahdhīb al-akhlāq*, 33.

279 Cf. Jadaane, 180.

280 *Tahdhīb al-akhlāq*, chapter 2.

281 *Tahdhīb al-akhlāq*, 32–3. For his debt to the Stoics, see Jadaane, 189–95.

282 Below, p.29. For the philosophical deployment of this *ḥadīth* see Bürgel, '*Adab* und *iʿtidāl* in ar-Ruhāwī's *Adab aṭ-ṭabīb*,' 100.

283 Cf. *Nicomachean Ethics*, II.i.1.

284 Cf. ibid., IV.i.12–14.

285 Man derives nourishment as follows: he inhales air, drinks water, eats transformations of earth, and all these contain particles of fire. Foods which derive from water contain phlegm, those from air contain blood, those from fire contain yellow bile, and those from the earth, black bile. (ʿAlī al-Ṭabarī, *Firdaws al-ḥikma*, cited in F. Rosenthal, *Classical heritage*, 187). The influence of *akhlāṭ* on *akhlāq* was known in the mainstream Islamic tradition by the time of Ibn Qutayba (*ʿUyūn*, II. 62).

286 For parallels and influences between the medical and ethical concepts of *iʿtidāl*, see Bürgel's article; also Goldziher, *Muslim Studies*, II. 360–2; Gauthier, *Antécédents gréco-arabes de la psychophysique*.

287 For Miskawayh's understanding of this image see Arkoun, *Humanisme arabe*, 307–14; Sunar, *Ibn Miskeveyh*, 158–71.

288 Arkoun, *Humanisme arabe*, 247; Walzer, *Greek into Arabic*, 142–63. A work called *Why a Good Physician must be a Philosopher* is attributed to Galen (Arkoun, 307; Dols, 27).

289 Cf. the article of Jaeger, 'Aristotle's Use of Medicine as Model of Method in his Ethics'.

290 Most famously Muḥammad al-Rāzī; but also al-Kindī (Mohaghegh, 7). Ibn al-Jawzī (d.597/1201), too, wrote a book with this title.

291 *Fuṣūl al-madanī*, 103–5, 117–8.

292 Abdel Kader, 60; *GAS* I. 648.

293 Muḥāsibī, *Qaṣd*, 87; Ghazālī, *Ayyuhā*, 137, *Iḥyā'*, I. 28 (*K. al-ʿIlm*, bāb 3); Ibn ʿArabī, *Futūḥāt*, II. 251–2; cf. Obermann, *Der Philosophische und Religiöse Subjectivismus Ghazālīs*, 169.

294 The comparison with the process of habituation in learning the arts had been studied by Aristotle, *Nicomachean Ethics*, II.iv.3.

295 Jurjānī (*Taʿrīfāt*, 19) also identifies the *straight path* with following the middle course

(*tawassuṭ*); it is not clear when this identification originated.

296 Muḥāsibī, *Ādāb al-nufūs*, 80–5.

297 'Akhlāḳ', 327; Zureik's note to Miskawayh, *Tahdhīb*, 224–5; cf. Rāzī, *Ṭibb Rūḥānī*, 33–5, and Miskawayh, *Tahdhīb*, 189, where the debt to Galen is acknowledged.

298 Miskawayh, 190, refers to Galen's work *Good men profit by their enemies* in this connection.

299 This latter technique is cited by Miskawayh (*Tahdhīb*, 190), who attributes it to al-Kindī. Cf. Jadaane, *Stoicisme*, 221.

300 Q.IX:20–1.

301 Q. XXIX:69. The entire quote is from al-Ḥakīm al-Tirmidhī, *Masā'il*, 119.

302 Cf. Chittick, 'The Theological Roots of Peace and War According to Islam'.

303 For elementary education in classical Islam see Tritton, *Materials*, 1–26.

304 *Tahdhīb al-akhlāq*, 55–64.

305 Ibn Sīnā, *Aqsām al-ᶜulūm*, in *Tisᶜ rasā'il*, 73f, who distinguishes three practical sciences: ethics, as taught in the *Nicomachean Ethics*, economics, as in Bryson, and politics, as in Plato and Aristotle. Cf. E. Rosenthal, *Studia*, 48n.

306 These translations have been edited in Plessner, *Der Oikonomikoc des Neupythagoreers 'Bryson'*. In the present translation of this Exposition, markers have been inserted to show Ghazālī's more literal borrowings from Miskawayh, and thence from Bryson.

307 This reappears, however, in Ṭūsī's *Nasirean Ethics* (Wickens), 176–7.

308 Other passages in this Book have suggested that Ghazālī is writing for spiritual instructors (cf. for instance p.160 below); here, however, the principal source is the final chapter in Qushayrī's *Risāla*, entitled 'Advice for Aspirants'. The question of identifying Ghazālī's intended readership is a complex one, and will have to be left for a subsequent, more detailed discussion in an introductory volume to the present series.

309 Ibn ᶜAjība, *Miᶜrāj al-tashawwuf* (tr. Michon, *Le Soufi marocain*, 203).

310 Jurjānī, *Taᶜrīfāt*, 15.

311 E.g. by Bercher, 'Extrait', 318.

312 Eg by Arberry, *K.al-Ṣidq*, 1.

313 For the 'beginner' Ghazālī prefers the term *mubtadi'*; cf. Jabre, *Lexique*, 20–1.

314 Muḥāsibī, *Ādāb al-nufūs*, 143ff.

315 Ibid., 435. For more on *irāda* see ᶜAzzām, '*al-Irāda*'; ᶜAbd Allāh Anṣārī, *Manāzil*, p.112; Qushayrī, *Risāla*, (11) 433–9; idem, *ᶜIbārāt al-ṣūfīya*, 56–7; for Ibn Sīnā's mystical use of the term see *Ishārāt*, IV. 818–9 (tr. Goichon, *Livre des directives*, 491); Gardet,

Pensée, 177.

316 For a deeper characterisation of the spiritual guide, see Ghazālī's treatise *Ayyuhā al-walad*, p.129: 'The Shaykh who is fit to be a deputy [*nā'ib*] to God's Emissary (may God's blessings and peace be upon him), must be learned (although not every learned man is fit for successorship [*khilāfa*]), and I shall clarify and summarise for you some of his distinguishing signs, lest everyone and anyone lay claim to being a [spiritual] guide. Whoever turns away from the love of the world and of worldly status, and has in his turn followed a Shaykh possessed of insight [*baṣīra*], who is attached to a chain of discipleship extending back to the Master of the Messengers (may God bless him and grant him peace), and has well disciplined his soul by eating, speaking and sleeping little, and praying, giving and fasting much, who through following his insightful Shaykh has made the good traits of character his way, such as patience, prayer and gratitude, reliance, certainty, generosity, peace of soul, mildness and modesty, knowledge, truthfulness, shame, loyalty, dignity, quietness and measuredness; such a one is among the lights of the Prophet, may God bless him and grant him peace, and is worthy to be followed.'

317 Cf. Qushayrī, *Risāla*, 736, where this act is regarded as the first step towards divesting oneself of worldliness.

318 Ghazālī, *Maqṣad*, 43. Cf. *Iḥyā'*, I. 13 (*K. al-ʿIlm*, bāb 2, Bayān al-ʿilm alladhī huwa farḍ ʿayn); also note C on p.85 below.

319 Below, 86-7. Ghazālī was anticipated in this by Qushayrī (*Risāla*, 734).

320 Cf. C. Chehata, 'L'ikhtilāf et la conception musulmane du droit'. The jurist's dictum that 'the divergences among scholars are a source of grace' could be happily repeated by the apparently antinomian Abū Yazīd (cited by Sahlajī in Badawī, *Shaṭaḥāt*, 169).

321 A jurist competent to derive rulings directly from the sources of law.

322 Kalābādhī, 56. Al-Shaʿrānī, too, (d.973/1564), the great Cairene Sufi and jurist, thanked God for not having been a fanatic for any belief (Arberry, *Sufism*, 124).

323 *Iḥyā'*, IV. 6 (*K. al-Tawba*, Bayān wujūb al-tawba). Cf. T. Rhys Davids, 'Does Al-Ghazzali Use an Indian Metaphor?' also F. Meier, 'The Problem of Nature in the Esoteric Monism of Islam', 166-70, where a translation is included. Ghazālī seems to have been the first Muslim to use the image, which can be traced back to a Pali text of the second century BC.

324 Lane, 765.

325 Qushayrī, *Risāla*, 263-5; Makkī, *Qūt*, I. 129; Tustarī, *Muʿāraḍa*, 20; Muḥāsibī, *Qaṣd*, 92-

3, 95; Ibn ʿAyād, *Mafākhir*, 71–2, 185–7; Massignon, *Passion*, I. 92–3, III. 23n; Jabre, *Lexique*, 61, 274–5; Kably, 'Satan dans l'Iḥyā', 12–14, 36. Kalābādhī (p.62) distinguishes four types of *khawāṭir*, which may be from God, from the angels, from the *nafs*, or from the devil.

326 Muḥāsibī, *Qaṣd*, 95.

327 Qāḍī ʿIyāḍ, II. 275.

328 *Iḥyā'*, III. 38–9 (*K. ʿAjā'ib al-qalb*, Bayān anna'l-wasāwis ...); summarised below, 242.

329 This concept is considerably expanded in a separate Book of the *Iḥyā'*: *K. Ādāb al-ʿuzla* (II, book I).

330 This follows the Central Asian tradition of mystical practice. Cf. for instance Qushayrī, *Tartīb al-sulūk*, 65.

331 For this concept see Anawati and Gardet, *Mystique musulmane*, 221–6.

332 Although this is not mentioned in the book here translated, Ghazālī stresses it elsewhere, especially in the book consecrated to divine love in the *Iḥyā'*: *K. al-Maḥabba wa'l-shawq wa'l-uns wa'l-riḍā*.

333 *Iḥyā'*, III. 17 (*K. ʿAjā'ib al-qalb*, Bayān al-farq bayn al-ilhām wa'l-taʿallum ...).

334 Cf. Tustarī: 'The two desires are the lowest of the attributes of human nature.' (*Muʿāraḍa*, 15.) Also Miskawayh, *Tahdhīb*, 10.

335 This moderate attitude to the subject became commonplace in later Sufism. Cf. Ibn ʿArabī, *Futūḥāt*, II. 249, where he criticises some shaykhs for contravening the *Sharīʿa* by imposing excessive fasts on their disciples. As he remarks, 'For the Sufis, renouncing hunger does not mean satiety'. Cf. also Kharrāz, *Lumaʿ*, 417ff; also the popular verse in al-Būṣīrī's *Burda*: 'You must fear insinuations from both hunger and satiety, for many a hunger is worse than bloatedness.' (*Wa'-khsha'l-dasā'is*[a] *min jūʿ*[in] *wa-min shabaʿ*[in]*/ fa-rubba makhmaṣat*[in] *sharr*[un] *min al-tukham*[i].)

336 It recalls the list given by the Ikhwān al-ṣafā, *Rasā'il*, I. 358–9, although this is unlikely to be the source.

337 See note A on p.161 below.

338 See note A on p.175 below.

THE BOOK OF DISCIPLINING THE SOUL REFINING THE CHARACTER & CURING THE SICKNESSES OF THE HEART

Kitāb riyāḍat al-nafs
wa-tahdhīb al-akhlāq
wa-muʿālajat amrāḍ al-qalb

BOOK XXII OF THE REVIVAL OF THE RELIGIOUS SCIENCES

Iḥyāʾ ʿUlūm al-Dīn

THE BOOK OF DISCIPLINING THE SOUL, REFINING THE CHARACTER, AND CURING THE SICKNESSES OF THE HEART

Being the Second Book of the Quarter of Mortal Vices

[PROLOGUE]

In the Name of God, Most Compassionate and Merciful

PRAISED BE GOD, Who has disposed all matters through His arrangement thereof, Who has equitably composed His creation[1] and given it excellent form, Who has adorned the aspect of man by granting him good stature and proportion, safeguarding him from increase and decline in his aspect and measurements; Who has assigned the improvement of character to the effort and labour of His bondsmen, urging them thereto by inspiring in them fear and trepidation. For the elect among them has He made this improvement easy, by His providence and facilitation, blessing them with the easing of the difficulties and hardships[2] which lie therein.

AND MAY BLESSINGS AND SALUTATIONS BE INVOKED upon Muḥammad, the Bondsman of God, His Prophet, loved one and chosen one, who was His bearer of good tidings and His warner, from the lines of whose brow the radiance of Prophethood shone forth, through whose signs and announcements the reality of the True God was discerned;[3] upon him, and upon his Family and Companions, who rendered the countenance of Islam clean of the darkness and shadows of unbelief, who uprooted falsehood, and were not polluted by it in any wise or to the very smallest degree.[A]

To proceed. Goodness of character was the attribute of the Master of the Messengers, and was ever the most righteous action of the Truthful Saints [*ṣiddīqūn*][B]; in truth, it constitutes half the Faith, and is the fruit of the austerities of the pious and the self-discipline of the people of constant worship. Bad character is a mortal poison and a sure path to perdition and humiliating disgrace, open vices and foul practices which set a

[A] Ghazali here ends his prologue, which, in keeping with the almost universal custom of his time, he has composed in formal rhyming prose. Elsewhere in the *Iḥyā'*, he alternates between two other styles: a highly rhetorical idiom designed to arouse the heedless, and a functional, unaffected prose used for the exposition of doctrine and practices.

[B] Ar. *ṣiddīq*: a term denoting complete sincerity, trust, and truthfulness. It is of Qur'ānic ancestry (cf. Q.XII:46, where Pharoah describes Joseph as *ṣiddīq*, referring to his veracity), and also appears in the *Sunna* in an alternate sense, as the celebrated epithet of Abū Bakr, the 'Sincere Believer'. For Ghazālī, heir to a tradition which had built on these archetypal usages, the expression is to be particularly applied to gnostic saints of the highest degree. Man's acknowledgement of God's Unity (*tawḥīd*), he tells us, exists on four levels. Firstly, there is the 'outer husk': where one professes *tawḥīd* with the tongue but without true faith. Above this is the 'inner husk', which is the level of faith experienced by ordinary believers. Thirdly, one may attain to the 'kernel', the illuminative apprehension of the truth of God through 'unveiling' (*mukāshafa*). And finally, a few individuals enjoy the 'oil of the kernel', and 'see only One in existence' (*lā yarawna fi'l-wujūd illā wāḥid*[an]). Such a person is a *ṣiddīq* (*Iḥyā'*, IV. 212 [*K. al-Tawḥīd*, Bayān ḥaqīqat al-tawḥīd]), and his genuineness in this station is confirmed by his continuing faithful attachment to the revealed law (*Iḥyā'*, IV. 136 [*K. al-Khawf*, Bayān ḥaqīqat al-khawf]). For more on this term, which we will encounter several times in the present work, see Bayḍāwī, 717; Massignon, *Passion*, I. 217; Jabre, *Lexique*, 138–9.

distance between man and the proximity of the Lord of the Worlds, and induce him to follow the path of Satan the accursed,[4] which matters are the gates opening into *God's stoked-up fire, which rises over men's hearts*,[5] just as fair characteristics form gates opening from the heart into the delights of Heaven's gardens, and the presence of the Most Compassionate. Foul characteristics are the very sicknesses of hearts and the diseases of souls, constituting an illness which deprives man of everlasting life, which thing stands no comparison with an illness which causes the loss of the corporeal life alone. For however carefully the physicians may establish the canons by which the body is cured, the ailments with which they deal lead only to the loss of this transient life: it is therefore a matter of greater priority to lay down the canons by which the illnesses of hearts are treated, such as conduce to the loss of the life eternal[6]. To learn this form of medicine is incumbent upon all men of sense, since there is not a single heart which is free of diseases which, were they to be neglected, would redouble in strength, leading to disorders still more frequent and powerful. A bondsman[A] thus needs to meditate in such a way as to learn the origins and causes of these sicknesses, and then to roll up his sleeves to treat them and set them aright. It is this treatment which God (Exalted is He!) indicates when He says, *Successful is he that purifies it*,[7][B] and this neglect to which He refers when He says, *Thwarted is he that stunts it.*[8]

In this Book we shall indicate a number of sicknesses[9] of the heart, and provide a general discourse on how these are to be treated, without giving details of cures for specific ailments, since these will be set forth in the remaining Books of this Quarter. Our present purpose is to review in an overall fashion how the traits of character may be refined, and to provide a preparatory method for this. In the course of this discussion we

[A] ʿ*abd*, i.e. of God; any of His human creatures.

[B] The pronoun refers to the soul.

shall make use of the symbol of the treatment of the body, in order to render the matter more easily understood. This shall be made clear through an Exposition of the Merit which is in having Good Character, which shall be followed by an Exposition of the True Nature of Good Character, an Exposition of the Susceptibility of the Traits of Character to Change through Discipline, an Exposition of the Means by which Good Character may be Acquired, an Exposition Detailing[10] the Method used in Refining the Character and Disciplining the Soul, an Exposition of the Symptoms by which a Disease of the Heart may be Recognised, an Exposition of the Way by which a Man may Discover the Faults in his Soul, an Exposition of Textual Evidence Showing that the Sole Way to cure the Heart is by Renouncing one's Desires, an Exposition of the Signs of Good Character, an Exposition of the Way in which Young Children should be Disciplined, and an Exposition of the Requirements of Aspirancy and the Preliminaries to [Spiritual] Struggle. These constitute eleven Sections, which, God willing, shall gather together the objectives of this book.[11]

[22.1]

An Exposition of the Merit which is in having Good Character, and a Condemnation of Bad Character

GOD (Exalted is He!) said to His Prophet and loved one, in praise of him, and in order to make manifest His blessing upon him, *Assuredly, thou art of a tremendous character.*[12A]

And ʿĀ'isha (may God be pleased with her) said, 'The character of the Emissary of God (may God bless him and grant him peace) was the Qur'ān'.[13B]

A man once asked the Emissary of God (may God bless him and grant him peace) about good character, and he recited[14] His statement (Exalted is He!): *Hold to forgiveness, and enjoin kindness, and turn aside from the ignorant ones.*[15] Then he said (may God bless him and grant him peace),[16] 'It is that you should seek reconciliation with those who avoid you, give to those who withhold from you, and forgive those who deal with you unjustly'.[17]

And he said (may God bless him and grant him peace), 'I was sent only[18] to perfect the noble qualities of character'.[19]

And he said (may God bless him and grant him peace), 'The heaviest things to be placed in the Scales[C] shall be the fear of God[20] and good character'.[21]

[A] According to Bayḍāwī (p.751), this refers to his forbearance under the Qurayshite persecution. For various Sufi interpretations of the verse see Suhrawardī, 166–7 (tr. Gramlich, *Gaben*, 214–5); Massignon, *Passion*, III. 204–5.

[B] This simply means that 'the medium was the message', to borrow a modern proverb: he was the perfect exemplar of the virtues expounded in the Book.

[C] *al-Mīzān*, the scales in which good and evil deeds will be weighed against each other on the Day of Judgement. See *Iḥyā'*, IV. 444; tr. Winter, *Remembrance of Death*, 195–7.

A man once came to the Emissary of God (may God bless him and grant him peace) from before him, and asked, 'O Emissary of God! What is religion?' 'Good character', he replied. Then he came to him from his right hand side, and asked, 'What is religion?' 'Good character', he replied again. Then the man approached from his left, and asked, 'What is religion?' to be told, 'Good character'. He then came to him from behind, and asked, 'What is religion?' 'Have you not grasped it?' the Prophet replied. 'It is that you do not become angry'.[22] [A]

It was once asked, 'O Emissary of God! What is inauspiciousness [*shu'm*]?' And he replied, 'Bad character'.[23]

A man said to the Emissary of God (may God bless him and grant him peace), 'Give me some advice'. 'Fear God,' he replied, 'wherever you may be.' 'Give me more', he said. 'Follow a sin with a good deed,' he replied, 'and you will erase it'. 'Give me more', the man said, and he replied, 'When you deal with people, do so with goodness of character'.[24]

He was asked (may God bless him and grant him peace) which was the best of deeds, and replied, 'To have a good character'.[25]

He said (may God bless him and grant him peace), 'Never shall God make good the character [*khuluq*] and created form [*khalq*][B] of a man and then allow him to be devoured by Hell'.[26]

Said al-Fuḍayl, 'The Emissary of God (may God bless him and grant him peace) was once told that a certain woman fasted all day and prayed all night, but was possessed of a bad character, so that she injured her neighbours with her words. 'There is no good in her,' he said, 'she is of Hell's people'.[27]

Said Abu'l-Dardā', 'I once heard God's Emissary (may God bless him and grant him peace) say, "The very first thing to be

[A] The point of the anecdote, somewhat obscured in translation, is to demonstrate the importance of good character, and its complete exemplification by the Prophet.

[B] This common juxtaposition is explored below, p. 16.

weighed in the Scales shall be good character and generosity. When God created faith, it said, 'O Lord God! Strengthen me!' and He strengthened it with good character and generosity. And when He created disbelief, it said, 'O Lord God! Strengthen me!' and He strengthened it with avarice and bad character'.[28]

And he said (may God bless him and grant him peace), 'Verily, God has chosen this religion for Himself. Thus nothing is appropriate for your religion except generosity and good character. Ornament, therefore, your religion with them'.[29]

He said (may God bless him and grant him peace), 'Goodness of character is God's greatest creation'.[30]

He was once asked, 'O Emissary of God! Which believer is the best in faith?' and he replied, 'He who is best in character'.[31]

And he said (may God bless him and grant him peace), 'You will not be able to suffice all people with your wealth; suffice them therefore with a cheerful face and a goodly character'.[32]

He also said (may God bless him and grant him peace), 'Bad character corrupts one's works just as vinegar corrupts honey'.[33]

It is related on the authority of Jarīr ibn ʿAbd Allāh that he said (may God bless him and grant him peace), 'You are a man whose form God has made excellent; therefore make excellent your character also'.[34]

Said al-Barāʾ ibn ʿĀzib, 'The Emissary of God (may God bless him and grant him peace) was of all men the most beautiful of face and the most noble of character'.[35]

Said Abū Masʿūd al-Badrī,[36] 'The Emissary of God (may God bless him and grant him peace) used to say during his prayers, "O Lord God! Thou hast made good my creation [*khalqī*], therefore make good my character [*khuluqī*]!"'[37]

Said ʿAbd Allāh ibn ʿUmar[38], 'The Emissary of God (may God bless him and grant him peace) used frequently to pray: "O Lord God! I ask Thee for health, contentment with my lot, and good character."'[39]

It is related on the authority of Abū Hurayra (may God be

pleased with him) that the Prophet (may God bless him and grant him peace) said, 'The honour of a Muslim is his religion, his lineage is his good character, and his virtue[A] is his intellect [ʿ*aql*].'[40]

Said Usāma ibn S͟harīk, 'I once witnessed the bedouins asking the Prophet (may God bless him and grant him peace), "What is the best thing that a bondsman can be given?" And he replied, "Good character".'[41]

And he said (may God bless him and grant him peace), 'The most beloved of you to me on the Day of Arising, and the ones who shall sit closest to me, will be the best of you in character'.[42]

Said Ibn ʿAbbās, 'The Emissary of God (may God bless him and grant him peace) once said, "There are three things which, when they are all absent from a man, should lead you to take no account of his works: a piety which restrains him from disobedience to God, a clemency which prevents him from harming the foolish, and a [noble] character with which he lives among men".'[43]

One of his supplications (may God bless him and grant him peace) when beginning the Prayer [*ṣalāt*] was, 'O Lord God! Guide me to the better traits of character, for assuredly, no-one guides to the better traits of character but Thee. And preserve me from the bad traits of character, for assuredly, no-one may preserve me from them but Thee.'[44]

Said Anas, 'One day, when we were with the Emissary of God (may God bless him and grant him peace), he said, "Good character melts away sin just as the sun melts ice".'[45]

And he said (may God bless him and grant him peace), 'Good character is part of man's saving felicity [*sa*ʿ*āda*]'.[46]

[A] Ar. *muruwwa*, a trait much extolled in the pre-Islamic poetry, and which was perpetuated in Islamic culture with some modification and diminution of emphasis. *Muruwwa* is derived from *mar'*, 'man', and hence has a connotation akin to the Latin 'virtus'. See Bravmann, *Spiritual background*, 1-7, which is a correction of the view of Goldziher, *Muslim Studies*, I. 11-44; see also Isutzu, *Spiritual-ethical concepts*, 75. The present *ḥadīt͟h* is typical of a genre in which the Prophet is seen challenging the tribal and egotistic values of the pre-Islamic period.

And he said (may God bless him and grant him peace), 'Good character is auspiciousness [*yumn*]'.[47]

He said (may God bless him and grant him peace) to Abū Dharr, 'O Abū Dharr! There is no intelligence like foresight, and no lineage like good character'.[48]

It is related on the authority of Anas that Umm Ḥabība once said to the Emissary of God (may God bless him and grant him peace), 'O Emissary of God! What if a woman had had two husbands in this world,[A] and she died, and they died also, and all were received into Heaven: whose wife would she then be?' And he replied, 'The wife of him whose character was best when in the world. O Umm Ḥabība! Good character brings all that is good in this world and the next.'[49][B]

And he said (may God bless him and grant him peace), 'The rightly-guided Muslim attains the degree of him who fasts and prays at length merely through his good character and noble nature'.[C][50] And in another version [we read], 'the degree of him who is thirsty during the midday heat [through fasting]'.[51]

Said ʿAbd al-Raḥmān ibn Samura, 'We were once with God's Emissary (may God bless him and grant him peace) when he said, "Yesterday I beheld a remarkable thing. I saw a man from my nation crouching on his knees, being divided from God by a veil. Then his good character came, and brought him into God's presence".'[D][52]

[A] Not concurrently, of course, as polyandry is forbidden by the *Sharīʿa*.

[B] In Paradise, women who had had more than one husband will be wed to the last man they had married, or to the best, or simply to the one they had preferred. Cf. Smith and Haddad, *Death and Resurrection*, 165.

[C] According to one early theorist of Sufism, this *ḥadīth* means that good character perfects faith with the virtues of thankfulness and patience (*al-shukr wa'l-ṣabr*), which are the virtues engendered by prayer and fasting. It is not implied, he says, that fasting and prayer may be dispensed with. (Al-Ḥakīm al-Tirmidhī, *Nawādir*, 321.)

[D] Because good character erodes the passional self, which comprises the veil. This *ḥadīth* may refer either to a dream, or to a Prophetic vision of some future scene at the Judgement. (Ibid.)

Said Anas, 'The Emissary of God (may God bless him and grant him peace) said, "A bondsman may attain through his good character high and noble degrees in the Afterlife, even though he be feeble in his worship".'[53]

It is related that ᶜUmar (may God be pleased with him) once asked permission to enter of the Prophet (may God bless him and grant him peace), who had with him some women[A] of Quraysh who were talking to him in voices loud enough to drown out his own. When ᶜUmar asked leave to enter they rushed behind a screen. And when he entered, God's Emissary (may God bless him and grant him peace) was laughing, so that he asked, 'What has made you laugh, may my father and mother be your ransom?' And the Prophet replied, 'I was surprised at those women who were with me, and who, when they heard your voice, rushed behind the screen!' 'It would be more proper for them to hold *you* in awe, O Emissary of God,' ᶜUmar declared. Then he went over to them and said, 'You enemies of your own selves! Are you awed by me and not by God's Emissary (may God bless him and grant him peace)?' And they replied, 'Yes! You are sterner and harsher[B] than him'. And the Prophet said (may God bless him and grant him peace), 'O Ibn al-Khaṭṭāb! By Him in Whose hand lies my soul, never does Satan meet you in one valley without turning off into another!'[54]

And he said (may God bless him and grant him peace), 'Bad character is an unpardonable sin, and assuming the worst is a transgression which produces[55][evil]'.[56]

And he said (may God bless him and grant him peace), 'Through his bad character a man can sink to the lowest tier of Hell.'[57]

[A] Certain of his wives.

[B] 'The use of the elative here is inappropriate,' Zabīdī remarks. 'What is intended is that the Prophet (may God bless him and grant him peace) was free of all sternness and harshness'.

The Narratives[A]

Luqmān the Wise once asked his father, 'Father, what is the finest single trait in a man?' 'Religion', he replied. Then he asked, 'And what are the finest two traits?' 'Religion and wealth,' said he. 'And the finest three?' 'Religion, wealth and modesty[B].' 'And if they should be four?' 'Religion, wealth, modesty and good character'. 'And if they should be five?' And he replied, 'Religion, wealth, modesty, good character and generosity'. 'And if they should be six?' 'O my son', he replied, 'When these five traits come together in a man, then he is pious and pure, one of God's saints, and is quit of Satan'.

Al-Ḥasan said, 'A man of bad character punishes his own soul'.[C]

Anas ibn Mālik said, 'A bondsman can reach the very highest rank in Heaven through his good character, without being a man of much worship, and can reach the lowest region of the Inferno through his bad character, even though he should worship abundantly'.

Said Yaḥyā ibn Muʿādh, 'In an expansive character lie the treasures of provision'.[58][D]

Said Wahb ibn Munabbih, 'The man of bad character is like a piece of broken pottery, which can neither be patched up nor returned to clay'.

[A] Ar. *āthār*: used in the *Iḥyā'* to denote reports concerning the early Muslims which do not directly involve the Prophet.

[B] Ar. *ḥayā'*: shyness, shame, diffidence, embarrassment. For its mystical interpretation, see particularly Anṣārī, *Manāzil*, 92–4.

[C] Because of the ambivalence of the word *nafs*, this may equally well be rendered: 'A man of bad character punishes himself'.

[D] Ar. *fī saʿat al-akhlāq kunūz al-arzāq*; a reasonably well-known proverb. The sense is that God provides generously for the man who is by nature generous.

Said al-Fuḍayl, 'The company of an irreligious man of good character is preferable to me to that of an ill-natured man much given to worship'.[59]

Ibn al-Mubārak was once accompanied on a journey by a man of bad character, and treated him with forbearance and politeness. When they parted [Ibn al-Mubārak] wept. Upon being asked why he did so, he replied, 'I weep out of compassion for him:[60] I have left him, but his character is still with him, and has not departed from his company'.

Said al-Junayd, 'Four things lift a man up to the highest degrees, even should his knowledge and works be insubstantial: forbearance, modesty, generosity and good character. By these things faith is made complete.'

Said al-Kattānī, 'Sufism is good character, so anyone who improves your character has improved your Sufism also'.[61]

Said ʿUmar (may God be pleased with him), 'Deal with the [common] people on the basis of good character, and differ from them with your deeds'.

Said Yaḥyā ibn Muʿādh, 'Bad character is a sin in the presence of which abundant good deeds are of no avail, while good character is a virtue in the presence of which many sins can do no harm'.

Ibn ʿAbbās was asked, 'What is nobility [*karam*]?' and he replied, 'That which God has mentioned in His mighty[62] Book: *Assuredly, the most noble of you in God's sight are the most pious*'.[63] And he was asked, 'What is good lineage?' and replied, 'The man with the best character has the best lineage'.

It has been said that 'every building has a foundation, and the foundation of Islam[64] is good character'.

Said Ibn[65] ʿAṭā', 'Those who have reached high degrees have done so only through good character, the perfection of which has been attained solely by the Chosen One (may God bless him and grant him peace). The nearest of all creatures to God are those who follow in his footsteps through [assuming the traits of] his noble character.'

[22.2]

An Exposition of the True Nature of Good and Bad[1] Character

KNOW that people have discoursed upon the true nature of good character, and upon what it constitutes, but have in fact treated only the fruit which it bears, and not its reality. They have not even grasped the entirety of its fruit, of which everyone has mentioned that which occurred to him and came to his mind; never have they directed their attention towards providing a definition for it or a discussion of its nature which takes all of its fruits into account in a detailed and comprehensive fashion.

There is, for example, the saying of al-Ḥasan that 'Good character is a cheerful face, magnanimity, and doing no harm'.

And al-Wāsiṭī has said, 'It is that one should not argue with anyone or be argued with by anyone, because of one's firm knowledge of God (Exalted is He!)'.[2]

S̲h̲āh al-Kirmānī said, 'It is to do no harm, and to endure harm instead'.[3]

Someone said, 'It is that one should be friendly to people but remain a stranger in their midst'.[A4]

Al-Wāsiṭī once said, 'It is to please people secretly and in public'.

Said Abū ʿUt̲h̲mān, 'It is to be content [*riḍā*] with [the will of] God'.

When Sahl al-Tustarī was asked about [good] character, he replied, 'Its least degree is tolerance, seeking no reward, com-

[A] The phrasing is designed to recall the famous *ḥadīt̲h̲* which runs, 'be in the world as though you were a stranger or a wayfarer' (Buk̲h̲ārī, Riqāq, 3).

passion and pity for the wrongdoer, and asking God's pardon for him'.

And he once said, 'It is that you do not direct accusations at your Lord concerning your sustenance, and that you trust in Him, being confident that He shall provide that which He has guaranteed you. It is that you obey Him and do not transgress against Him in any of your affairs, both in that which is between you and Him, and that which takes place between you and mankind'.

And ᶜAlī (may God ennoble his face) said, 'Good character consists in three traits: avoiding that which is forbidden, seeking that which is permitted, and being generous to one's family'.[A]

Said al-Ḥusayn ibn Manṣūr [al-Ḥallāj], 'It is that you should be unaffected by the harshness of mankind after having beheld the Truth'.[5]

Said Abū Saᶜīd[6] al-Kharrāz, 'It is that you should have no concern [*himma*] but for God'.[7]

There are many statements of this nature, but they all treat of the fruit of good character, not its essence; neither do they succeed even in encompassing all of these fruits. Since to unveil its true nature is more important than to cite various sayings on the matter, we shall proceed with our discourse as follows.

'Creation' [*khalq*] and 'character' [*khuluq*] are two expressions which may be used together. We say, for example, that 'So-and-so is good in his creation and in his character', meaning that both his outward and inward aspects are good. 'Creation' refers to the external, and 'character' to the internal, form. Now, man is composed of a body which perceives with ocular vision [*baṣar*], and a spirit [*rūḥ*] and a soul [*nafs*] which perceive with inner sight [*baṣīra*]. Each of these things has an aspect and a form which is either ugly or beautiful. Furthermore, the soul which perceives with inner sight is of greater worth than the body which sees with ocular vision, which is why God has stressed its importance

[A] Or, 'one's wife'.

by ascribing it to Himself in His statement, *I shall create a man from clay; and when I have fashioned him, and have breathed into him something of My spirit, then fall ye down before him in prostration!*[8] In this text He states that the body is ascribed to clay, but that the spirit is ascribed to the Lord of the Worlds;[9] 'spirit' and 'soul' in this context referring to the selfsame thing.

A trait of character, then, is a firmly established condition [*hay'a*] of the soul, from which actions proceed easily without any need for thinking or forethought.[A] If this condition is disposed towards the production of beautiful and praiseworthy deeds, as these are acknowledged by the Law [*al-shar*ᶜ] and the intellect, it is termed a 'good character trait'; if, however, ugly acts proceed from it, the condition is known as a 'bad character trait'. We describe this condition as 'firmly established' [*rāsikha*] because the character of a man who gives some of his wealth rarely and under transient circumstances[10] cannot be described as generous, since this attribute has not become firmly estab-

[A] This definition, with certain slight variants, is commonplace in Islamic discussions of ethics. Its source is an ethical treatise by Galen, lost in Greek, but whose Arabic summary has been published by P. Kraus ('The Book of Ethics by Galen', which includes this passage on p.25), and translated by J. Mattock ('A Translation of the Arabic Epitome of Galen's Book Περὶ Ἠθῶν'; passage on p.236). Walzer (*Greek into Arabic*, 147), traces the principle back further, to other Middle Platonist thinkers of the time of Augustus. The wording chosen by Ghazālī leaves little doubt that he came across this definition through the medium of Miskawayh's *Tahdhīb al-akhlāq*, 31. The same definition is cited by Ibn ᶜAdī (*Tahdhīb*, 70), Fakhr al-Dīn al-Rāzī (*Jāmi*ᶜ *al-*ᶜ*ulūm*, 201, cited in Maᶜṣūmī, 39-40); Naṣīr al-Dīn Ṭūsī (*Akhlāq*, tr. Wickens, 74); and, in the later period, Ibn ᶜAjība (*Mi*ᶜ*rāj*, tr. Michon, 211), and ᶜAbd Allāh al-Ḥaddād (tr. Badawī, *The Book of Assistance*, 114). It may probably be assumed that the latter two sources (from Morocco and the Ḥadramawt respectively) received it from Ghazālī, while the earlier writers found it in Miskawayh. Jurjānī (*Ta*ᶜ*rīfāt*, 106) makes not only this statement but Ghazālī's entire paragraph serve as his definition of *khuluq*. See further F. Rosenthal, *Classical Heritage*, 85; Arkoun, *Contribution*, 251; Obermann, 162; for Galen's tract see Walzer, *Greek into Arabic*, 142-74; for his influence on the Islamic world generally see above, Introduction, LIII.

lished and fixed in his soul: as we specified, such acts must proceed from a man easily and without thinking, since the man who, with forethought and an effort, makes a show of generosity or remaining silent when angry is not to be called generous, or mild of character.

Four things are thus involved. Firstly, there is the doing of something beautiful or ugly; secondly, the ability to act; thirdly, cognition of the act; and fourthly, a condition of the soul by which it inclines to one side or the other, and which renders the beautiful or the ugly thing easy to do. Therefore, character is not the same as action: there are many people of generous character who do not make donations from their wealth, either because they have none, or by reason of some other obstacle, just as there are people whose character is avaricious but who distribute their wealth for some motive or other, or out of ostentation and in the interests of their reputation.[11] Neither is it the same as ability, since this does not differ whether it is ascribed to withholding or giving, or to the two opposite traits: every man has been created to be by disposition [*fiṭra*][A] capable of withholding and giving, yet this does not necessarily bring about an avaricious or a generous character. Nor yet is it the same as one's cognition of the act,[12] for cognition pertains to the beautiful and the ugly in the same way. Instead it is to be identified with the fourth sense, namely, the condition through which the soul prepares itself for the issuing of 'giving' or 'withholding'. Character, therefore, is a term for the condition and inner aspect of the soul.

[A] A well-known *ḥadīth* states that 'Every child is born with the *fiṭra*; it is only his parents who make of him a Jew, a Christian or a Zoroastrian.' (Bukhārī, Janā'iz, 92.) The *fiṭra* may be translated as man's 'primordial disposition': his inborn purity of soul, which is corrupted by the world. The radical discord between this concept and the Christian doctrine of original sin lies behind many of the divergences between Muslim and Christian spirituality and anthropology. See Ṭabarī, *Tafsīr,* XXI. 24; D.B. Macdonald, art. 'Fiṭra' in *EI²*, II. 931–2; Jabre, *Lexique*, 222–3; also below, pp. 26, 81.

Just as one's external appearance can never be beautiful when the eyes are beautiful but not the nose, the mouth[13] and the cheek—for all [the features] must be beautiful if one's outward aspect is to be beautiful also—so too there exist things, four in number, which must all be beautiful if one is to be possessed of a beautiful character, which will obtain when these four things are settled, balanced, and in the correct proportion to each other. These are the rational faculty, the irascible faculty, the appetitive faculty,[A] and the faculty which effects a just equilibrium between these three things.

The rational faculty is sound and good when it is easily able to discriminate, that is, to distinguish honesty from lies in speech, truth from falsehood in questions of belief, and beauty from ugliness in actions. When this faculty is sound it bears fruit in the form of Wisdom, which is the chief of the good traits of character, and regarding which God has said, *And whosoever is granted wisdom has truly been granted abundant good.*[B14] Regarding the irascible faculty, this is sound when its movements lie within[15] the bounds required by Wisdom. Likewise, the appetitive faculty is sound and good when it is under the command of Wisdom, by which I mean the command of the Law[16] and the intellect. As for the faculty to effect a just equilibrium, it is this which sets desire and anger under the command of the intellect and the Law. For the intellect has the status[17] of a guiding counsellor, while the faculty for just equilibrium is the [actualising] power, and has the

[A] Respectively, *quwwat al-ʿilm, quwwat al-ghaḍab, quwwat al-shahwa.* This is Plato's trichotomy of the soul, which occurs throughout the Muslim philosophical tradition: it was used, for instance, by Rāzī (see Mohaghegh, 'Notes on the "Spiritual Physick" of al-Rāzī', 10), and appears in the diatribe by Galen mentioned above, and also in Miskawayh (*Tahdhīb*, 15); see also above, Introduction, p.LIII.

[B] Islam's *ḥikma* means 'wisdom' in the traditional sense, i.e. 'the kind of understanding which allows one to hit the mark, attaining perfection'. *Aḥkama shayʾan* means 'to do something well'. Cf. *Nicomachean Ethics*, VI.vii, where 'wisdom' allows Phidias to be a perfect sculptor. Ghazālī is here following Miskawayh, *Tahdhīb*, 18.

status[18] of something which carries out its orders. The same command is carried out by the irascible faculty, which is like a hunting dog which needs to be trained before its unleashing and restraint can conform to orders rather than to the outbursts of the soul's desire. In turn, desire is like a horse which one rides during the chase, and which is sometimes tractable and well-disciplined, and sometimes endeavours to bolt. Therefore, the man in whom these characteristics are sound and balanced is possessed of a good character under all circumstances.[19] The man in whom some of them are balanced and not others is good of character in respect of his balanced traits alone, in the manner of a man only some of whose facial features[20] are handsome. The irascible faculty, when sound and balanced, is called 'Courage' [*s̲hujāʿa*]; similarly, the appetitive faculty, when sound and balanced, is known as 'Temperance' [*ʿiffa*]. Should the former faculty lose its balance and incline towards excess it is called 'recklessness' [*tahawwur*], while should it incline towards weakness and insufficiency it is termed 'cowardice' [*jubn*] and 'languor' [*k̲hūr*].[21] Should the appetitive faculty move to the point of excess it is called 'cupidity' [*s̲harah*], while if it should incline to defect it is known as 'indifference' [*jumūd*]. The mean is the praiseworthy thing, and it is this which constitutes virtue, while the two extremes are blameworthy vices.

The faculty for just equilibrium, however, when in disorder, has no extremes of excess and defect; rather it has one opposite,[22] which is tyranny [*jūr*]. As for Wisdom, exceeding the bounds in its regard by using it for corrupt ends is called 'swindling'[23] and 'fraud',[24A] while its insufficient application is termed 'stupidity' [*balah*]. Again, it is the mean to which the word 'Wisdom' is applied.

Therefore the fundamental good traits of character are four in number: Wisdom, Courage, Temperance and Justice. By

[A] Ar. *jurbuza*. For this unusual word, which is of Persian origin and may recall an earlier generation of Greek-Syriac translations, see D. Dunlop, 'The Manuscript Taimur Pasha 290 Ak̲hlāq and the Summa Alexandrinorum', 254.

'Wisdom' we mean a condition of the soul by which it distinguishes true from false in all volitional acts, by 'Justice' a condition and potency in the soul by which it controls the expansion and contraction of anger and desire as directed by Wisdom. By 'Courage' we refer to the subjection of the irascible faculty to the intellect, while by 'Temperance' we have in mind the disciplining of the appetitive faculty by the intellect and the Law. It is from the equilibrium of these four principles that all the good traits of character proceed,[25] since when the intellect is balanced it will bring forth discretion [*ḥusn al-tadbīr*] and excellence of discernment [*jawdat al-dhihn*],[26] penetration of thought [*thaqābat al-ra'y*] and correctness of conjecture [*iṣābat al-ẓann*], and an understanding of the subtle implications of actions and the hidden defects of the soul. When unbalanced in the direction of excess, then cunning,[27] swindling,[28] deception and slyness result, and when in that of defect, then stupidity [*balah*], inexperience [*ghimāra*], foolishness [*ḥamq*], heedlessness[29] and insanity are the consequences. By inexperience I mean an insufficient experience which is nonetheless combined with sound understanding: a man may be inexperienced in one matter and not in another. The difference between stupidity and insanity is that the intention of the stupid man is sound, only his means of realising it are defective, since he is not possessed of a correct understanding of how to follow the way leading to his goal; the madman, on the other hand, chooses that which should not be chosen, so that the basis of his decisions and preferences is flawed.

As for the trait of Courage, this gives rise to nobility [*karam*], intrepidity [*najda*], manliness [*shahāma*], greatness of soul,[30] endurance [*iḥtimāl*], clemency [*ḥilm*], steadfastness [*thabāt*], the suppression of rage [*kaẓm al-ghayẓ*], dignity [*waqār*], affection[31] and other such praiseworthy qualities. When unbalanced on the side of excess, which is recklessness, it leads to arrogance [*ṣalaf*], conceit [*badhkh*], quickness to anger [*istishāṭa*], pride [*takabbur*] and vainglory [*ʿujb*], and when on the side of defect, to ignominy [*mahāna*], self-abasement [*dhilla*], cowardice [*jazaʿ*], meanness [*khasāsa*], lack of resolution [*ṣighar al-nafs*], and holding oneself back from doing that which is right and obligatory. As for the quality of Temperance, this gives rise to generosity [*sakhā'*], modesty [*ḥayā'*],[A] patience [*ṣabr*], tolerance [*musāmaḥa*], contentedness with one's lot [*qināʿa*], scrupulousness,[B] wit,[32] helping others [*musāʿada*], cheerfulness [*ẓarf*] and absence of craving [*qillat al-ṭamaʿ*]. When it deviates towards excess or defect, greed [*ḥirṣ*], cupidity [*sharah*] and obscenity [*waqāḥa*] result, as do spite [*khubth*], extravagance [*tabdhīr*], stinginess [*taqṣīr*], ostentation [*riyā'*], immorality [*hutka*], obscenity [*majāna*], triviality [*ʿabath*], flattery [*malq*], envy [*ḥasad*], malice [*shamāta*], self-abasement before the rich, disdain for the poor, and so forth.

The fundamental noble traits of character are therefore these four virtues, namely Wisdom, Courage, Temperance and Justice; and all the other traits constitute branches of these things. A perfectly just equilibrium in these four has been attained by no-one but the Emissary of God (may God bless him and grant him peace); other people are of divergent degrees of proximity and distance from them. Thus a man is close to God (Exalted is He!) in proportion to his closeness to His Emissary (may God bless him and grant him peace).[C] He who combines within himself all of these traits is worthy to be a powerful king among men whom all creatures submit to and follow in all their deeds. In like wise, he who is divested of all these qualities and acquires their oppo-

[A] Here we have an example of conflict between Greek and Islamic ideals. Modesty was not recognised as a virtue by Aristotle (*Nicomachean Ethics*, IV.IX.1-8, translated as *ḥayā'* by Ibn Ḥunayn [*Akhlāq*, 170]), but had been stressed by the Prophet: 'Modesty comes from faith' (Bukhārī and Muslim), and included by Miskawayh (*Tahdhīb*, 20).

[B] Ar. *waraʿ*: normally a religious term for careful adherence to the revealed Law (see below, 133A). In this context, however, it denotes something closer to the definition given by Miskawayh (*Tahdhīb*, 21) as 'adhering to becoming acts which involve the soul's perfection.'

[C] Because, as Zabīdī puts it (VII. 331), 'one who is close to one who is close, is close himself'.

sites deserves to be exiled from all lands and all peoples, for he has become close to the accursed and banished devil, and should be banished even as he was banished, just as the former is close to the king, who is close [to God], and who should therefore be emulated and drawn close to. For the Emissary of God (may God bless him and grant him peace) was 'sent only to perfect the noble qualities of character', as he himself said.[A] The Qur'ān has referred to these qualities when describing the moral qualities of the believers: God (Exalted is He!) has said, *The believers are only those who have faith in God and His Emissary, and do not then doubt, and who strive with their wealth and their selves in the path of God. Such are the sincere.*[33] Therefore, faith in God and His Emissary which is free from doubt is powerful certainty, which is the fruit of the intellect and the utmost limit of Wisdom. Striving with one's wealth is generosity, which comes from controlling the appetitive faculty, while striving with one's self is Courage, which proceeds from the use of the irascible faculty under the control of the intellect and with just moderation.[B] And in describing the Companions, God (Exalted is He!) has said, *Severe against the unbelievers, compassionate amongst themselves,*[34] indicating that severity and compassion both have their place: perfection is not to be found through severity or compassion in every situation.

Thus, then, [is concluded] the exposition of the meaning of 'character', and how it may be good or ugly, and of its pillars, consequences and ramifications.

[A] For this *ḥadīth* see above, p.7.

[B] Ghazālī thus finds Plato's four cardinal virtues implied in this verse.

[22.3]

An Exposition of the Susceptibility of the Traits of Character to Change through Discipline

KNOW that the man who is dominated[1] by sloth will consider unpleasant any spiritual struggle and discipline, or any purifying of the soul and refinement of the character. Because of his deficiency and remissness, and the foulness of his inward nature, his soul will not permit him to undertake such a thing;[A] therefore he will claim that the traits of a man's character cannot conceivably be altered, and that human nature is immutable. He will adduce two things in support of this claim. Firstly, he will say that character [*khuluq*] is the form of the inward in the same way that the created form [*khalq*] of man is the form of the outward. No-one is able to alter his external appearance: a short man cannot make himself tall, neither can an ugly man render himself handsome, and *vice versa*; and thus is the case with inward ugliness. Secondly, he will assert that goodness of character proceeds from suppressing[2] one's desire and anger, and that he has tested this by means of a long inward struggle which demonstrated to him that these things are part of one's character and nature, which can never be separated from the human creature, so that busying oneself with such struggling is profitless and a waste of time. What is required is to bar the heart from inclining to the fleeting fortunes [of this world], and this is impossible.

[A] Or: 'His soul will not permit him to acknowledge that this is the consequence of his deficiency and remissness, and the foulness of his inward nature...'

[To such an objection] we would say: Were the traits of character not susceptible to change there would be no value in counsels, sermons and discipline, and the Prophet (may God bless him and grant him peace) would not have said, 'Improve your characters!'[3] How could such a denial with respect to the human creature be made? It is possible to improve the character even of an animal: a falcon[4] can be transformed from savagery to tameness,[A] a dog from mere greed for food to good behaviour and self-restraint, a horse from defiance to docility and obedience,[5] and all of these things constitute a change in character.

In order to unveil the nature of this subject more fully we would say that existent things are divided into [firstly], those on the root and branches of which man and his volition have no effect, such as heaven, the earth[6] and the stars, and even the outside and inside of the parts of the body, and the other organs of living things: in short, everything which is already complete in its existence and its perfection; and [secondly], those things which exist in an incomplete form but which are possessed of the ability to be perfected when the condition for this, which may be connected to the volition of man, is met. For a seed is not an apple tree or a date-palm: it has merely been created in such a way as to permit it to become one when it is properly nurtured; and even when nurtured, a date-stone can never become an apple tree. Therefore, just as a seed is affected by human choice, so that it is susceptible of acquiring some qualities and not others, so also anger and desire, which we cannot suppress and dominate entirely so as to destroy every trace of them, can be rendered, should we so wish, obedient and docile by means of self-discipline and struggle. And this we have been commanded to do, for it constitutes the means of our salvation and our coming to God.

Of course, temperaments vary: some accept this thing rapidly, while others do not. There are two reasons for this disparity.

[A] This image is used by al-Ḥakīm al-Tirmidhī, *Riyāḍa*, 86.

Firstly, there is the power of the instinct [*gharīza*] which lies at the root of one's temperament, together with the length of time for which it has been present: the capacities for desire, anger and pride[7] are [all] present in the human creature; however the most difficult to deal with and the least susceptible to change is that of desire, which is the oldest capacity in man. For it is the first thing to be created in a child, to be followed, perhaps after seven years, by anger, and, finally, the power of discretion. The second reason is that a trait of character may be reinforced as a result of acting frequently in accordance with it and obeying it, and considering it to be fine and satisfactory. In this regard, people are of four degrees.

Firstly, there is the man who is innocent and without discernment, who cannot tell truth from falsehood, or beautiful from foul actions, but who rather remains with the disposition [*fiṭra*] with which he was created, being devoid of any doctrines, and whose desire was never aroused through the pursuit of pleasures. Such a man will respond very rapidly to treatment, and only needs the instruction of a guide and an internal motivation which spurs him on to the spiritual struggle, through which thing his character will be reformed in the shortest possible time.

Secondly, there is the man who recognises ugly acts for what they are, but is not in the habit of acting righteously, for his evil actions have been made to seem fine to him and he commits them under the influence of his desires, which, having won control of him, deflect him from his better judgement. Despite this, however, he knows that he is not acting as he should. The condition of this man is more intractable than that of the first, and he has a far heavier task to perform: he must first uproot[8] the habitual inclination to corruption which has become rooted firmly in his soul, and secondly sow therein the quality of habituation to righteousness. Nevertheless, he is in general susceptible to the effects of self-discipline, should he undertake this in a serious, determined and resolute fashion.

Thirdly, a man may consider ugly traits of character to be obligatory and preferable, and to be right and beautiful, having been brought up in this way. The treatment of such a man is almost impossible, and his reform can be hoped for only in the the rarest of cases, because the sources of misguidance in his case are so many.

Fourthly, there is the man who has been reared to believe in and to work corruption. He believes that merit lies in abundant iniquity and murder, and boasts of this in the belief that this raises his status. This is the most difficult degree, in which connection it has been said that 'Improving an old man is hardship itself,[9] while reforming a wolf is torture'.

Thus the first of these [four men] is simply ignorant, while the second is ignorant and misguided, the third is ignorant, misguided and corrupt, while the fourth is ignorant, misguided, corrupt and evil.[A]

The other illusory notion which is adduced is the statement that anger, desire, worldliness and the other traits of this kind cannot be torn from the human creature for as long as he lives. This is also an error, into which a faction has fallen which imagines that the purpose of spiritual struggle is the complete suppression and effacement of these attributes. Such a view is absurd, for desire has been created for a purpose, and is an indispensable part of human nature: should the desire for food cease man would die; should the desire for sexual intercourse cease man would die out; and should man feel no anger he would not be able to defend himself from those things which threaten his life. When the basis of desire remains, the love of property must necessarily remain also, which encourages one to guard it. What is required is not the total extirpation of these things, but rather

[A] Some implications of this fourfold categorisation for Muslim conceptions of human freedom are drawn out in a recent work by the Moroccan writer Abdallah Laraoui, who is concerned to challenge Orientalist presentations of Islam as fatalistic. (*Islam et modernité*, 52–3.)

the restoration of their balance and moderation, which is the middle point between excess and defect. With regard to the trait of anger, what is needed is sound ardour, which lies in the avoidance of both recklessness and cowardice, and generally to be strong in oneself but nevertheless under the control of the intellect. It is for this reason that God (Exalted is He!) has said, *Severe against the unbelievers, compassionate amongst themselves,*[10] describing the believers as 'severe': severity can only arise from anger, and were there to be no anger, there could be no *Jihād* against the unbelievers.[11] And how could one intend to uproot anger and desire entirely when the Prophets themselves were not divested of them? God's Emissary (may God bless him and grant him peace) once said, 'I am only a man, and, like other men, I become angry'.[12] People used to say things he disliked in his presence (may God bless him and grant him peace), and he would become so angry that his cheeks would be flushed, although he would never say anything but the truth, from which anger never caused him to diverge.[13] And God (Exalted is He!) said, *And those that suppress their rage, and are forgiving toward people*[14] rather than 'those that have no rage'.

Restoring rage and anger to a position of moderation, whereat they do not overcome and subdue the intellect but instead submit to its control and authority, is therefore a possibility, and it is this to which we refer when we speak of 'reforming the character'. A man may be so dominated by desire that his intellect is unable to restrain his desire from evildoing, yet he may, by means of self-discipline, restore it to the position of moderation. The possibility of this is demonstrated by experience and observation in such a way as to leave no room for doubt. The proof that it is this moderation which is required in the traits of character rather than one of the two extremes lies in the fact that generosity is a trait which the Law deems praiseworthy,[15] and constitutes a middle point between the two extremes of avarice and extravagance. God (Exalted is He!) has praised this moderation by saying *And those who, when they spend, are neither extravagant nor grudging; and there is ever a middle point between the two.*[16] And He has said (Exalted is He!), *Let not thy hand be chained to thy neck, nor open it completely.*[17A] Likewise is the case with the desire for food: moderation should prevail, rather than greed or indifference. God (Exalted is He!) has said, *Eat and drink, but be not extravagant, for God loves not the extravagant.*[18] And in the matter of anger He has said *Severe against the unbelievers, compassionate amongst themselves.*[19] The Prophet (may God bless him and grant him peace) said, 'The best of affairs is the middle course'.[20]

There is a secret and an explanation to this. For felicity[B] is predicated on the salvation of the heart from the vicissitudes of this world. God (Exalted is He!) has said, *Save him who comes to God with a sound heart.*[21C] Avarice is one of these vicissitudes, and so is extravagance:[22] the heart should be safely between the two;[23] that is, not attentive to money, nor zealous either to spend or withhold it. For the heart of the man who is zealous to spend or to withhold is distracted by these two inclinations: his heart cannot be whole until he is purified of both. Since this cannot come about in this world, we ask for the state which most closely resembles their absence, and that which is farthest from both extremes, which is the mean. Just as tepid water is neither hot nor cold, but exists in a middle state between the two, and is, as it were, free of both qualities, so too does generosity lie between extravagance and avarice, and courage between cowardice and recklessness, and temperance between cupidity and indifference; and such is the case with all the other traits of character. It is the extreme, then, of any matter, which is reprehensible.

This, then, is what is required, and it is a thing very possible to achieve. Certainly, the guiding Shaykh must make all anger ugly to the aspirant, and all withholding of wealth, and should not

[A] The verse is a reference to charity. Cf. the gloss of Bayḍāwī on this text: 'Generosity is the mean between the two'. (Bayḍāwī, 374.)

[B] Ar. *saʿāda*: see above, p. LXXXVI.

[C] A 'sound heart', according to Bayḍāwī (p.491), is one free of unbelief, sin and blemishes.

allow him any concessions in this regard, for were he to make the slightest concession [the aspirant] would use this as an excuse to retain his avarice and anger, imagining that he possessed only the permitted amount. If, however, he were to try with all his might to pull these traits out by the roots, he would prove able only to destroy its strength and restore it to moderation. Therefore the correct course of action is for him to intend to uproot it, which will permit him to change it to the required level. This secret, however, should not be revealed to the aspirant, for a foolish man might be deceived by it, and think that his anger and his withholding of his money were just.

[22.4]
A General Exposition of the Means by which Good Character may be Acquired

YOU have come to know that goodness of character proceeds from an equilibrium in the rational faculty brought about through sound wisdom, and in the irascible and appetitive faculties through their submission to the intellect and the Law. This equilibrium may come about in two ways.

One of these is through Divine grace, and completeness of innate disposition [*kamāl fiṭrī*], whereby a man is born and created with a sound intellect and a good character, and is preserved from the powers of desire and anger, which are created in him moderate and submissive to the intellect and the Law. Thus he becomes learned without an instructor, and disciplined without being subject to any discipline, in the manner of Jesus, the son of Mary,[A] and John, the son of Zacharias, and all the other prophets (may the blessings of God be upon them all). Yet it is not to be deemed improbable that certain things should exist in a man's nature and disposition which can be obtained through acquisition: some children are created truthful, generous and courageous, while in others the opposite characteristics have been set, so that [in this case] good qualities can only be acquired through habituation and associating with those who possess them,[1] and also through education.

The second is the acquisition of these traits of character by

[A] For this special virtue in Jesus see below, p. 54.

means of spiritual struggle and exercise. By this I mean the constraining of the soul to perform the actions which necessarily proceed from the trait[2] desired. For example, a man who wishes to acquire the quality of generosity must oblige himself to do generous things; that is, to give of what he owns, and must continue in this wise, affecting this thing and struggling with his soul until his nature conforms to it and it becomes easy, at which point he will have become a generous person. Similarly in the case of the man dominated by arrogance who wishes to inculcate in his soul the quality of modesty: he should persist for a lengthy period in imitating the behaviour of the modest and struggling against his soul until such behaviour becomes one of his traits and part of his nature, at which time it will come easily. Every one of the qualities which the Law deems praiseworthy is acquired by these means, the end point of which is that the act should be pleasurable. For the generous man is he that takes pleasure in giving money, not he who gives it reluctantly; and in the same way, the modest man is he who finds modesty delightful.

The religious traits of character cannot take firm root in the soul until it has grown accustomed to every good habit, renounced every evil one,[3] and persevered in this in the wise of one who feels a love for and takes pleasure in beautiful deeds, and loathes and is hurt by ugly ones. As God's Emissary (may God bless him and grant him peace) said: 'Prayer has been made my delight'.[4] As long as worship and the renunciation of forbidden things are felt to be unpleasant and burdensome their performance will be defective, and cannot bring one to full felicity. Certainly, to struggle to persevere with them is a good thing, but only in comparison with abandoning them, not in comparison with doing them willingly. It is in this context that God (Exalted is He!) has said, *Seek help in perseverance and in prayer, and truly it is hard save for the humble-minded.*[5] And His Emissary (may God bless him and grant him peace) has said, 'Worship God with pleasure, and if you cannot, then with perseverance, for perseverance in something which you dislike contains much good'.[6] Neither is it sufficient to obtain the felicity consequent upon good character that obedience to God should be found delightful and disobedience unpleasant at some times and not others; rather this should be constant and remain with one throughout one's life, so that the longer a man's life extends, the more solid and complete will be his virtue. This is why the Prophet (may God bless him and grant him peace) replied, when asked about felicity: 'It is a long life in the obedience of God'.[7] This is also why the Prophets and the Saints disliked death, for 'this world is the sowing-ground of the next'.[A] The more acts of worship one performs through living a long life, the greater will be the reward, the purer and clearer the soul, and the stronger and more deeply-rooted the good traits of character. For the sole purpose of acts of worship is to influence the heart, and this influence will only grow strong when they are persistently repeated.

The purpose of such traits of character is to cut the love of this world away from the soul and to set firmly therein the love of God (Exalted is He!), so that one would love nothing so much as the meeting with Him. Such a man will then employ his wealth only in ways which will bring him to Him; likewise with his anger and desire, since these will be under his command, and weighed up in the scales of the intellect and the Law so that he is contented and happy with them. It is wrong to deem it unlikely that one's delight might be in prayer and that one's worship might become delectable, for everyday life draws even more wondrous things from the soul: we see[8] kings and the voluptuous rich in constant misery, and the bankrupt gambler so overcome with delight and joy during his gambling that one might well discount the possiblity of man's gaining any pleasure without this practice, even after it had taken away his wealth, ruined his home and left him quite penniless, for he will still love and enjoy it by reason of his soul's long familiarity with it. Similarly with the man whose hobby is

[A] For this proverb, sometimes held to be a *ḥadīth*, see Sakhāwī, 351; for Ghazālī's extensive use of it see Lazarus-Yafeh, 312-4.

pigeons, who may stand all day in the hot sun without feeling any pain due to the pleasure he takes in his birds, and their movements, flight and soaring around in the sky.[A] And there is the sly criminal who boasts of the blows and stabs he receives, and of his steadfastness under the whip, and who goes up to the cross or the gibbet[9] bragging about his endurance of these [punishments], considering this to be a source of pride: he may be torn limb from limb in an attempt to make him confess to his crime or to that committed by another man with his knowledge, and persevere in his denial,[10] and pay no heed to the punishments because of his joy at what he considers to be his courage and virility. Despite the torment provided by his circumstances, he is delighted by them and finds them a source of pride. And there is no condition more ugly and despicable than that of an effeminate man, who imitates women by plucking out his hair, tattooing his face, and keeping their company, so that you see him rejoicing in his state and boasting of the perfection of his effeminacy to other such men.[B] Even the cuppers and sweepers can be seen boasting to one another just as much as the kings and scholars. All of this is the result of habit and persisting in one course for a long period and seeing the same thing in one's acquaintances.

Since the soul commonly takes pleasure even in vain things and inclines towards ugliness,[11] how could it not take pleasure in the Truth were it to be restored to it for a while and made to[12] persevere therein? The soul's inclination to these disgusting

[A] A sport popular in medieval Islamic culture; see for instance Ibn Abi'l-Dunyā, *Dhamm al-malāhī*, ed. ʿAṭā, 50–1, ed. Robson, 59; Sakhāwī, 530–1; F. Rosenthal, 'Child psychology in Islam,' 4. Ghazālī is assuming that his readers regard it as a rather frivolous and undignified pursuit; as is suggested by the above sources. According to one early jurist, the testimony of pigeon trainers cannot be accepted in court, for the same reason (Ziadeh, 'Integrity (ʿ*Adālah*) in Classical Islamic Law', 82). The hobby did, however, find practical application in the carrier pigeon trade; it is interesting to note in passing that the use of carrier pigeons was first introduced to Europe by knights returned from the Crusades: cf. Holmes, 'Life among the Europeans in Palestine and Syria', 31.

[B] For this vice see note A on p.175 below.

things is unnatural, and resembles an inclination to the eating of mud; yet even this may gain control over some people and become a habit.[A] As for the inclination to wisdom and the love, knowledge and worship of God, this resembles the inclination towards food and drink. It is the expression of the heart's nature, and is a divine command, while an inclination to the demands of one's desires is in itself something strange, and is not part of its nature. The heart's food is wisdom, knowledge and the love of God (Exalted is He!), and it only diverges from the demands of its nature when afflicted by some disease, just as the stomach may be afflicted by an illness which prevents it from desiring the food and drink which give it life. Thus every man's heart which inclines to anything but the love of God (Exalted is He!) is afflicted by a disease in proportion to this inclination, unless he love a thing because it helps him to love God and to practice his religion—which is not the symptom of an illness.

From the foregoing you have come to know beyond all doubt that good traits of character may be acquired through self-discipline, by means of imitating, at the outset, the actions which result from such traits so that they may ultimately become part of one's nature. This is one of the wonders of the relationship between the heart and the members [*jawāriḥ*], by which I mean the soul and the body: the effect of every attribute which appears in the heart must emanate onto the members, so that these move only in conformity to it; similarly, every act performed by the members has an effect which makes its way up[13] to the heart, thereby constituting a form of circular movement. To understand this thing a metaphor may be employed, as follows.

A man who wishes his soul to acquire the attribute of skilful calligraphy[B] so that he becomes a calligrapher by nature and dis-

[A] As remarked in the same context by Aristotle, *Nicomachean Ethics*, VII.v.3.

[B] The reference to *kitāba* may instead be to the simple act of writing, together with such ancillary skills as were required of the secretarial class. Ghazālī seems to have drawn this illustration of the process of habituation from al-Fārābī (*Fuṣūl*, 109).

UNIVERSITY OF WINCHESTER
LIBRARY

position must do with the member which is the hand those things which the calligrapher does, and devote himself assiduously to this for a long period, during which he imitates the calligrapher by copying his fine script. He continues to persevere in this until it becomes a firmly-rooted attribute in his soul, and, at last, he comes to write naturally with a beautiful hand, whereas he had earlier done so only artificially. It was fine calligraphy itself which rendered his own calligraphy fine, at first through a difficult simulation, the effect of which nevertheless rose to his heart[14] and then descended again from the heart to the member in question to enable him to write well naturally. The case of a man who wishes to become a sage of the soul[A] is similar: he is obliged to do the things which such sages do, namely, a constant application to sagacity, until this attribute becomes attached to his heart and he becomes a sage of the soul.

The case of the man who wishes to become generous, continent, clement and unassuming is identical: he must perform by simulation the actions associated with these qualities until they become part of his habitual nature. This is the only treatment available. And just as the one who wishes to become a sage of the soul does not despair of achieving his goal when he has wasted one night, but will not reach it if he does so repeatedly for many nights, similarly he who desires to purify and perfect his soul and to adorn it with good qualities[15] will neither achieve his goal by worshipping for one day nor be barred from it because for one day he

[A] Ar. *faqīh al-nafs*. A characteristically Ghazālian term applied to a sincere expert in the religious art of reforming souls. This, or its cognate expression *faqīh al-dīn* ('sage of religion') is contrasted with the *faqīh al-dunyā*, the "worldly jurist", who knows the formal requirements of liturgy and law, and yet has no appreciation of their true spiritual function. Ghazālī chose the root *f.q.h* to remind people of the original sense of 'understanding', which had become obscured as the word *fiqh* became increasingly applied to legal casuistry. Cf. *Iḥyā'*, IV. 342–3 (*K. al-Murāqaba*, Bayān ḥaqīqat al-murāqaba); I. 28–9 (*K. al-ʿIlm*, bāb 3, Bayān mā buddil min alfāẓ al-ʿulamā'). The word *fuqahā'* had, however, already been used, e.g. by Tustarī (*Muʿāraḍa*, 4–5), to denote people learned in spiritual matters.

sinned. This is the purport of our [credal] statement that one mortal sin does not necessarily lead to eternal damnation.[A] However, one day of idleness will invite [the student] to the next, and then, little by little, to others, until his soul takes pleasure in laziness and abandons studying altogether so that the merit which attaches to being a sage passes him by. Similarly, one venial sin leads to another, until the basis for salvation is lost through the destruction of the basis of faith at the moment of death. And just as the effect of a single night on the acquisition of the status of sage of the soul is not felt,[16] since this is something which appears little by little, like the growth and increasing height of the body; similarly the effect of one act of devotion on the purification and cleansing of the soul is not immediately perceptible. Nonetheless, one should not undervalue even a small amount of devotion, for a large quantity, which is made up of individual small acts, has an effect, so that each one of them must exercise an influence. There is not a single act of devotion but that it has an effect, even though it be concealed, and it must therefore necessarily entail some reward, since reward is in proportion to its effect; and this is the case with sin also. How many sages there are who deem the wasting of a day and a night a paltry thing, and continue to do so, procrastinating day after day until at last their natures depart from the acquisition of understanding: likewise is it with the man who underestimates small sins, and procrastinates and delays his repentance day after day,[17] until such time as death suddenly seizes him, or the darkness of his sins so builds up in his heart that he is unable to repent (for a little ever invites one to abundance), and his heart becomes loaded with the chains of desires, from which he is unable to release himself. This is what is meant by the 'closing of the gate of

[A] This is the orthodox Ash<u>ʿ</u>arī position, which contrasts with that of the Khawārij and Muʿtazila, who taught that the commission of a mortal sin necessarily entails eternal punishment. (Ashʿarī, *Maqālāt*, 124; Laqqānī, 147; Ghazālī, *Iḥyā'*, I. 104 [*K. Qawāʿid al-ʿaqā'id*, faṣl 4, mabḥath 3; tr. Faris, *Foundations*, 105].)

repentance',[A] and by God's statement (Exalted is He!): *And We have set a barrier before them and a barrier behind them* [to the end of] the verse.[18] [B] And in the same wise, ʿAlī (may God ennoble his face) said, 'Faith appears in the heart as a white gleam.[19] As faith grows, so does its whiteness, until, when the bondsman's faith is complete, the whiteness covers his entire heart. And hypocrisy appears as a black speck, the blackness of which grows in proportion to it, until, when the hypocrisy becomes complete, the heart becomes entirely black.'[20]

You have therefore come to know that good character proceeds sometimes from one's nature and innate disposition [*fiṭra*], sometimes from accustoming oneself to beautiful deeds, and sometimes from seeing and keeping the company of people who perform them, who are the companions of charity and the brethren of righteousness. For one nature can purloin[21] both good and evil from another.[C] The man in whom all three aspects are manifest, so that he is virtuous by nature, by habituation and by education, is possessed of the supreme virtue; similarly, he who is by nature ignoble, and chances to fall in with bad company from which he learns, and for whom the means of evildoing are readily available so that he grows accustomed to wickedness, is the most distant of men from God (Exalted is He!). Between these two degrees there are people of disparate participation in these three aspects, each of whom is possessed of a degree of proximity or remoteness in accordance with his quality and state. *Whoso works an atom's weight of good shall see it, and whoso works an atom's weight of ill shall see it also.*[22] *And God wronged them not; rather did they wrong themselves.*[23]

[A] Although repentance until the last moment of life is possible for every individual, it is said that the 'gate of repentance is closed' when the heart is so overgrown with corruption and heedlessness that repentance is very improbable. Cf. Zabīdī, VII. 341.

[B] The verse continues: *and have covered them so that they see not.*

[C] Zabīdī (VII. 342) reminds us here of the popular proverb *al-ṭabʿ al-salīm sarrāq*: 'a sound nature is a thief', meaning that it acquires the traits of the people with whom it associates.

[22.5]

An Exposition Detailing the Method Used in Refining the Character

YOU have learnt from the foregoing that an equilibrium of the traits of character[1] causes the soul to be healthy, while any deviation from this equilibrium constitutes a sickness and a disorder within it, just as an equilibrium of the humours of the body leads to its health, and an imbalance entails its sickness. Let us therefore take the human body as our metaphor, and proceed with our discourse as follows.

The soul, in being divested of ugly traits and qualities and given virtuous and beautiful ones, is like a body, which may be cured through the removal of diseases and the restoration of health. Just as the basic constitution is usually in equilibrium, which a transforming disorder afflicts[2] through the effects of food, air and other circumstances, so also every child is born in equilibrium and with a sound innate disposition: it is only his parents who make of him a Jew, a Christian or a Zoroastrian;[A] that is, it is through familiarity and education that ugly customs are acquired. And just as the body is not initially created complete, but rather moves towards completion and strength through its growth (provided by nourishment) and upbringing, so too the soul is created deficient, with its completion and perfection being present in a latent form, and will only become perfected through training [*tarbiya*],[3] the refinement of the character, and being nourished with knowledge. Just as when the body is healthy the physician should establish the canon

[A] See above, p.18A.

which will maintain this health; and when it is ill he should restore it to health: similarly, when your soul is pure, clean and of good character you should strive to keep it in this way and strengthen and purify it yet further, and when it is not, you should struggle to make it so. And just as a disorder which changes the body's equilibrium and brings about its sickness may only be treated through its opposite (if it proceeds from heat then through something cooling, and *vice versa*); similarly, the ugliness which is the heart's sickness can only be treated with its own opposite, so that the disease of ignorance is treated by education, that of avarice by giving money away, that of pride by self-effacement, and that of greed by forcibly restraining oneself from the things one craves. The curing of a sick body requires that one endure the bitter taste of the medicine and persevere in renouncing certain things one desires; and in like fashion, in the treatment of the heart's sickness one must endure the bitterness of struggle and steadfastness—this is even more the case, in truth, since one can escape a bodily illness through death, whereas the sickness of the heart (and we seek refuge with God!) is a sickness[4] which abides even after death, and for all eternity.

A cooling medicine will not be sufficient to effect the cure of a disorder caused by heat unless it be administered in a certain measure, which will vary according to the severity or mildness of the complaint and the length of time for which it has been present. It is essential that there be a standard measure for this by which the efficient amount to be given may be known, since if the wrong quantity is administered the disorder will be exacerbated. The opposites with which the traits of character are treated must also be provided with a standard measure: just as the quantity of medicine used is taken in accordance with the sickness, so that the physician will not give any treatment until he knows whether the disease is caused by heat or cold, and has ascertained the degree to which the temperature is high or low, and will only then turn to the conditions of the body and the weather, the profession, age and other circumstances of the patient, and will then, in accordance with all this, begin his treatment; so also the guiding Shaykh, who is the physician of his aspirants' souls and the treater of the hearts of those who wish for guidance, should not impose any specific duties and forms of self-discipline upon them until he has learnt about their characters and ascertained the diseases from which they suffer.

Were a physician to treat all of his patients with a single medicine he would kill most of them; and so it is with the Shaykh, who, were he to charge all his aspirants with one kind of exercise, would destroy them and kill their hearts. Rather, attention should be paid to the illness of each aspirant, his circumstances, his age, his constitution, and the capacity of his body[5] to perform such exercises, which should be prescribed on this basis. If the aspirant is a beginner, and is ignorant of the provisions of the Law, he should first be taught about ritual purity and prayer, and the external acts of worship. If he is occupied in gaining money from forbidden sources or is regularly perpetrating some wrongdoing, he should be asked first to forsake this. And when he is made outwardly[6] beautiful through acts of worship, and his members have been purified from external transgressions, the Shaykh should look, through the evidence provided by his states, to what lies within him in order to ascertain his character and the diseases of his heart. At this point, should he perceive that he has wealth in excess of his needs he should take it from him and give it in charity in order to empty his heart of it and to prevent him from being distracted. Should he perceive that frivolity, pride and self-esteem have taken hold of him he should instruct him to go to the marketplace and beg, since self-esteem and love of authority can only be broken by humiliation, of which begging is the most intense form. He will require him to persist in this for a period until his pride and self-esteem are destroyed, for pride, and also frivolity, are among the illnesses which lead to destruction.

Should the Shaykh see that the body and dress of the aspirant are usually clean, and that his heart inclines to this and is pleased with it, he will give him a job as a latrine attendant and cleaner, and instruct him to sweep filthy places, and to remain in the kitchen and places where there is smoke until the attachment he has to cleanliness departs. For someone who cleans and adorns his clothes, and makes requests for clean[7] patched garments [*muraqqaʿāt*][A] and coloured prayer-carpets is no different from a bride who spends the entire day decorating herself. There is no difference at all between a man who worships himself and one who worships an idol: inasmuch as one worships anything other than God one is veiled from Him. Therefore, anyone who pays attention to anything in his dress, apart from its being from a legitimate source and ritually pure, in a way which turns his heart towards it, is occupied with his own self.

It is one of the subtle aspects of discipline that if an aspirant does not permit himself to renounce frivolity or some other trait at all, and will not allow himself its opposite all at once, he should move from one blameworthy trait of character to another which is less harmful, in the manner of a man who washes off blood with urine, and then rinses off the urine with water, if water would not have removed the blood; and like a schoolboy who loves to play with balls and sticks and suchlike things, and then is progressively drawn from such play by being encouraged to improve his appearance and to wear fine clothes, and then from this by being encouraged to seek

[A] The distinctive wear of Sufis in many medieval Islamic societies. (Cf. Hujwīrī, 45–57; Anawati and Gardet, 37.) On the spiritual veil which lies in distraction by appearances, Ghazālī writes elsewhere of those who, lured by the vice of spiritual illusion (*ghurūr*), 'renounce silk and other fine stuffs, and ask instead for expensive patched garments [...] and dyed carpets [...] and think that they are Sufis simply because of the colour of their dress and the fact that it is patched, forgetting that the Sufis only wear patched garments because their clothes are threadbare'. (*Iḥyā'*, III. 348 [*K. Dhamm al-ghurūr*, ṣinf 3].)

influence and authority, and then by being encouraged to long for the Afterlife. The case of the man whose soul does not permit him to abandon his illusion all at once is similar: let him move on to a lesser form of this vice. And so it is with the remaining traits.

Should the Shaykh see that the aspirant is usually under the influence of greed for food, he should oblige him to fast and to reduce the amount he eats. Next, he should instruct him to prepare delicious meals and serve them to others without tasting them himself, until his soul becomes stronger and he becomes used to forbearance, whereupon his greed will have been subjugated. And should he see that the aspirant is a young man longing to be married, but cannot afford to do so,[8] he should instruct him to fast. Should this not do away with his sexual desire, he should tell him to break his fast with water and no bread or *vice versa* on alternate evenings, and forbid him to eat meat or any other thing with his bread, until his soul is reduced to submission and his sexual desire broken. For at the beginning of aspirancy there is no cure more effective than hunger.

If he sees that his is a predominantly irascible disposition he should oblige him always to be gentle and quiet, and should make him serve and keep the company of an ill-mannered man in order that he might train his soul to tolerate him. One of the Sufis habituated his soul to mildness and freed himself from excessive anger by hiring a man to insult him in public: he forced himself to be forbearing and to suppress his anger, continuing in this way until his nature became characterised by a proverbial gentleness.[A] Another of them felt the presence of

[A] Ghazālī's direct or indirect source for this section seems to have been an ethical tract now conserved at the Qarawiyyīn Library in Fez, which has been attributed to Nicolaus of Laodicea, an obscure Aristotelian with mild neo-Platonic interests who lived at the time of Julian the Apostate. (M.C. Lyons, 'A Greek Ethical Treatise'.) The person hired in this particular story was a woman called طالطوس من اهل طاغيس. (Ed. Badawi, in appendix I to his edition of the Arabic *Nicomachean Ethics*, p.414.)

cowardice and faint-heartedness in his soul, and, wishing to acquire the trait of bravery, made it his practice to put to sea in the wintertime when the swell was at its roughest.[A] The ascetics of India treat laziness in worship by standing up all night on pillars.[B] And one of the Shaykhs at the outset of his own aspirancy, finding that his soul was lazy during his night devotions, for this reason forced himself to stand on his head all night so that his soul would willingly accept standing on his feet. Another treated his love of wealth by selling all that he owned and throwing the proceeds into the sea, fearing that if he gave it to other people he would be afflicted by self-satisfaction and a desire to be seen doing this.[C]

These examples should teach you the way to treat hearts. It is not our intention to mention the medicine for each sickness, for this will be done in the remaining Books; rather what we intend to do here is to draw the reader's attention to the fact that the general technique consists in doing the opposite of everything

[A] It appears that this particular anecdote was originally—and perhaps oddly—attributed to Dionysios. ('Nicolaus', ed. Badawī, 413; see Lyons, 'A Greek Ethical Treatise', 46.) It is also told in Miskawayh's *Tahdhīb*.

[B] Cited by 'Nicolaus' (ed. Badawī, 414; tr. Lyons, 46).

[C] Cf. 'Nicolaus' (ed. Badawi, 414; tr. Lyons, 46): 'An example of that was the man who sold all that he owned and threw the purchase money into the sea—Crates was his name. After that he cried, "Crates frees himself!"' Hujwīrī (*Kashf al-maḥjūb*, tr. Nicholson, 228) believes that the protagonist of the story was the eccentric Baghdad mystic al-Shiblī. Ibn al-Jawzī, although unaware of its pedigree, has doubts about the ethical value of the tale; these are, however, credibly dispelled by Zabīdī (*Itḥāf*, I. 37-8), who explains that such lessons are not cited as general principles of conduct, but merely illustrate ways in which the religious obligation of attaining *tawakkul*, true reliance upon God, may for certain individuals under the guidance of a Shaykh sometimes take precedence over those usages of religion which, while recommended, are not obligatory. Cf. also Kably, 'Satan dans l'Iḥyā'', 36-7, where Ibn al-Jawzī's remarks are similarly dismissed.

that the soul inclines to and craves. God (Exalted is He!) has summed up all of these things in His statement: *And whoever fears the standing before his Lord, and forbids his soul its whim, for him Heaven shall be the place of resort.*[9]

The important principle in the spiritual struggle is to carry out what one has determined upon: if one determines to renounce a desire, then the means to pursue it will be made easier; this is a trial and a test from God, and one should therefore have fortitude and perseverance. If one habituates oneself to violating one's own resolution the soul will come to take pleasure in this and will be corrupted. Should it happen that a man does violate his resolution, he should compel his soul to accept a punishment for this, as we have already mentioned in [the section on] the chastisement of the soul in the *Book of Self-Examination and Vigilance*:[A] if he does not intimidate it through the presence of a punishment it will defeat him and make the following of the desire seem good, and this will corrupt his self-discipline entirely.

[A] *Iḥyā'*, IV. 346–8 (*K. al-Murāqaba*, Murābaṭa 4), a list of incidents which includes the well-known story in which Junayd forces himself to bathe fully-clothed in cold water as a punishment for his *nafs*, which had demanded that he delay the required ablutions for his prayers until hot water became available.

[22.6]

An Exposition of the Symptoms by which the Diseases of the Heart may be Recognised, and the Signs which Indicate a Return to Health

KNOW that each member of the body has been created to discharge a particular function, and that it falls ill when it is no longer able to perform it, or else does so in a disturbed fashion: the hand ails when it can no longer strike, and the eye when it can no longer see. Thus it is with the heart, which falls ill when it becomes incapable of performing the activity proper to it and for which it was created, which is the acquisition of knowledge, wisdom, and gnosis,[A] and the love of God and of His worship, and taking delight in remembering[1] Him, preferring these things to every other desire, and using all one's other desires and members for the sake of His remembrance. God (Exalted is He!) has said: *I created jinn and mankind only to worship Me.*[2]

Thus every part is possessed of a benign function,[3] that of the heart being the acquisition of wisdom and gnosis

[A] Ar. *maʿrifa*. Readers accustomed to Christian terminology should recall that this word, conventionally and conveniently translated as 'gnosis', really denotes a direct experience of God attained through humility and seriousness, which is far removed from the 'self-importance of the Gnostic, as well as his naive rejoicing in fantastic speculation' (the comment of the Lutheran scholar Tor Andrae: *Garden of Myrtles*, 79). Cf. Gardet and Anawati, *Introduction à la théologie musulmane*, 230, 342; Goichon (tr.), *Livre des directives et remarques*, 475-6, 486.

[*ma*ʿ*rifa*],which is the specific property of the human soul which distinguishes man from the animals: for he is superior to them not with regard to his capacity for eating, mating, seeing and so forth, but rather with regard to his gnosis of the true nature of things, and their origin, and their Originator, Who is God (Great and Glorious is He!). For should he know all things but God it would be as though he knew nothing at all. The sign of the gnosis of Him is love, for whosoever knows Him loves Him also; and the sign of this love is that one should prefer none of the things of this world over Him. As God (Exalted is He!) has said, *Say: If your fathers, and your sons, and your brothers, and your wives, and your tribe, and the wealth you have acquired and the trade you fear may not prosper, and the dwellings you desire, are dearer to you than God and His Messenger and striving in His way, then wait until God brings His command to pass.*[A] Therefore, whosoever possesses a thing which is more dear to him than God is harbouring a sickness in his heart, just as a man who, loving to eat mud, and having lost his desire for bread and water, must needs suffer a sickness in his belly. These are the symptoms of the disease, by which we learn that every heart—saving only those which God has rescued—is sick. Yet there are some diseases which exist unbeknown to those they afflict, and the disease of the heart is one of these, which is why the man who suffers from it is heedless. Even if he becomes aware of it, he finds it difficult to persevere in the bitter medicine of opposing his desires, which is akin to the spirit's extraction during the agonies of death; or, should he indeed find in himself the strength needed for such perseverence, he may be unable to find a physician of insight to treat him. For the physicians, who are the scholars [ʿ*ulamā'*], have also been overpowered by this disorder; and treatment will but rarely be sought from a physician who is himself unwell. It is for this reason that the malaise has become so taxing and chronic, and that this science has become obliterated, so that some

[A] The 'command' refers to the Day of Judgement.

people have been led to deny altogether the existence of the medicine—and even the disease—which are proper to hearts. Instead, men have given themselves over to worldliness and to activities which in outward appearance are acts of worship, but inwardly are no more than customs and acts, performed when others are watching.

So much for the symptom of the underlying disorder.

As for the sign which indicates a return to health following upon treatment, this is perceived by scrutinising the particular sickness which is being addressed. If one is treating the fatal disease of avarice, which sets man at a far distance from God, then [it will be found that] the only method of doing so is to encourage the patient to give and spend his money. This should not be done, however, to the point where he squanders it, for this also would be an illness, resembling the case of a man who treats coldness with heat until the heat, which is also a disorder, comes to predominate. What is required is the establishment of an equilibrium between 'grudgingness' and 'prodigality', so that one remains in the centre and at the greatest possible distance from the two extremes. Should you wish to determine where this middle point lies, then consider the action which results necessarily from the blameworthy trait: if it is easier and more pleasurable for you than its opposite, then that trait is predominant in your case. For instance: should you find the acquisition and retention of money easier and more enjoyable than giving it to those who may justly receive it, then you should know that avarice is a dominant characteristic in you, and you must constantly give until such time as giving to a undeserving recipient[5] becomes easier and more enjoyable than to withhold it legitimately, at which time prodigality will have assumed the dominant place. Then return to the practice of withholding your wealth, and constantly watch over your soul and draw inferences about your character from the evidence of what deeds it finds easy and which ones hard, until the connection between your heart and money is broken, and you incline neither towards giving it nor withholding it, since it has become as water to you, so that when you give or withhold it you do so for a needful purpose, and so that giving your money does not seem preferable to you than its retention. Every heart which becomes like this has *come to God* with a sound aspect in this regard.[A] However, it must be sound in respect of the other traits of character also, so that it retains not a single tie with anything connected with the world, whereupon the soul will be enabled to leave this world unattached to it, paying it no heed, and no longer yearning for the things which it contains. At this point it will return to its Lord, at peace, *content in His good pleasure*, having entered among God's bondsmen[B] who are close to His presence, such as are *the Prophets, the Saints, the Martyrs and the Righteous; the best of company are they!*[6]

The authentic mean between the two extremes is exceedingly obscure, being thinner than an hair and sharper than a sword.[C] Assuredly, the man who keeps to the Straight Path [*al-ṣirāṭ al-mustaqīm*] in this world shall cross the Traverse [*al-ṣirāṭ*] in the next; yet it is a rare thing for a man to be free of all deviation from this Straight Path (by which I refer to the mean), and any inclination either to one side of it or the other, which thing would cause his heart to be attached to that side and thereby to suffer chastisement of some sort by passing through Hell, even if only at the speed of a lightning-bolt.[D] For God (Exalted is He!) has said, *There is not one of you that shall not come to it. This is a fixed ordinance of thy Lord. Then*

[A] Cf. Q.XXVI:88,89: *The day when wealth and sons avail not, save him who comes to God with a sound heart.*

[B] Cf. Q.LXXXIX:28–30: *O thou soul at peace! Return unto thy Lord, content in His good pleasure! Enter among My bondsmen! Enter thou My Garden!*

[C] The Traverse (*ṣirāṭ*), which spans Hell and across which all mankind must pass on the Day of Judgement, is thus described in several Traditions, for example Ibn Ḥanbal, *Musnad*, VI. 110. Ghazālī outlines the doctrine at *Iḥyā'*, IV. 447 (*K. Dhikr al-mawt*, Ṣifat al-ṣirāṭ; tr. Winter, *Remembrance of death*, 205–10).

[D] Another characteristic of the Traverse is that the righteous will pass over it in this way. (*Iḥyā'*, IV. 447; tr. Winter, 208.)

shall We save those that were Godfearing,[7A] that is, those that were close to rather than distant from the *Straight Path*. It is because of the difficulty of preserving rectitude [*istiqāma*] that every one of God's bondsmen is required to pray *Guide us to the Straight Path* seventeen times each day, the recitation of the Opening *Sūra* being an obligatory part of every *rakʿa*.[B] It is related that a man once saw the Emissary of God (may God bless him and grant him peace) in a dream. 'O Emissary of God!' he said, 'Why did you declare that "Hūd" had turned your hair grey?' And he replied, 'Because of the statement of God (Exalted is He!), *Practise rectitude as you have been commanded*.'[8C] Thus the treading of the *Straight Path* with due rectitude is something extremely obscure; nevertheless the bondsman, should he be unable to do this properly, must at least strive to keep in its vicinity. Whosoever wishes for salvation can only win it by means of righteous acts, which proceed solely from good traits of character. Therefore let every bondsman look to and reckon his attributes and qualities, and devote his energies to treating them one after the other.

And we ask God, the Generous, to render us among the devout.[9]

[A] Most Muslim theologians, on the basis of this verse, hold that all mankind shall enter Hell, which, for the righteous, will comprise a kind of purgatory for their minor sins, after which they are to be received into Heaven through the Prophet's intercession. The Prophets and Saints, although also destined to visit the infernal regions, will not be tormented there. Cf. Winter, *Remembrance of death*, 59, note A.

[B] In the Shāfiʿī school of law to which Ghazālī subscribed, this is one of the eleven obligatory components (*arkān*) of the canonical prayer. (Ghazālī, *Wajīz*, 42.)

[C] The verse is in the *Sūra* of 'Hūd'.

[22.7]

An Exposition of the Way in which a Man may Discover the Faults in his Soul

KNOW that when God (Exalted is He!) wishes His bondsman well, He grants him insight into the faults which lie in his soul. The faults of a man of perfect insight[1] are never hidden from him, and whosoever knows his faults is in a position to treat them. Most people, however, are ignorant of the faults of their souls, and might see the mote in their brother's eye but not the beam which lies in their own.[A] There are four ways by which the man who would know the faults of his soul may do so.

Firstly, he should sit before a Shaykh who has insight into these faults and hidden weaknesses, and put him in authority over his soul, and follow the instructions he gives in connection with his struggle therewith, as is the place of the aspirant with his Shaykh; this latter will ascertain these faults, and explain to him the method by which they should be treated. However, such a man is hardly to be found in this age.

[A] There is an unmistakeable echo here of Matthew VII.3. For the use of this idiom by Ghazālī and other Muslim writers see Asín, *Espiritualidad*, I. 189n; Goldziher, 'Matth. VII. 5 in der muhammedanischen Literatur'. There is no reason to suppose that Ghazālī has been using the Gospels directly at this point rather than his Muslim sources. The following all cite this image: Abū Nuʿaym, *Ḥilya*, IV. 99; Quḍāʿī, I. 356; Ibn al-Mubārak, *Zuhd*, 70; Ibn Abī Shayba, XIV. 38; and Goldziher finds it also in al-Mubarrad's *Kāmil*. For the Muslim use of New Testament idioms see Arnaldez, *Jésus fils de Marie prophète de l'Islam*; Jomier, 'Jésus tel que Ghazālī le présente dans 'al-Ihyā'', and Jomier's list of other works on the subject in note 3 to his page 77.

Secondly, he may seek out a true, perceptive and religious friend, and appoint him to be the overseer of his soul, so that he notes his circumstances and deeds, and brings to his attention the inner and external faults, acts and traits which he finds dislikeable in him. This was the practice of the wise men[2] and the great leaders of the Faith: ʿUmar (may God be pleased with him) used to say, 'May God grant His mercy to a man who shows me my faults'. And he used to ask Salmān about his faults when they met, saying, 'What things have you heard about me that you find dislikeable?' Salmān pleaded to be excused answering this, but when he insisted, replied, 'I have heard that you once ate two kinds of food at one meal, and that you have two sets of clothing, one to wear at night and the other for the day'. 'Have you heard anything else?' he enquired, and he said that he had not. 'These two things,' he said, 'I now renounce'.[3] He used also to question Ḥudhayfa, saying, 'You were the confidant of God's Emissary (may God bless him and grant him peace) in the matter of the Hypocrites.[A] Can you see any of the signs of hypocrisy in me?' In this way used he to accuse himself, despite his great worth and exalted position, for the greater a man's intelligence and position the less impressed will he be with himself and the more often will he engage in self-accusation.

This too, however, is rarely to be found. Few indeed are the friends who do not resort to flattery, but tell one about one's faults instead, and who harbour no envy. Among your friends you must needs have one who is jealous, or who has an ulterior motive, who deems something a fault when it is not, or a flatterer who conceals some of your defects from you. It was for this reason that

[A] Ḥudhayfa is remembered as the *ṣāḥib sirr al-Nabī*, the 'repository of the Prophet's secret', partly because he was told of certain events which would usher in the end of time, and in part because he was aware of the identity of a number of hypocrites within the ranks of the Muslim community at Medina. (Cf. Ghazālī, *Iḥyā'*, IV. 214 [*K. al-Tawḥīd wa'l-tawakkul*, Shaṭr I]; Massignon, *Essai*, 161; Ibn ʿArabī, *Futūḥāt*, cited by Chittick, *The Sufi Path of Knowledge*, 270.)

Dāūd al-Ṭā'ī renounced all human company, and said, when asked why, 'What can I do with people who hide my faults from me?' It was ever the desire of religious people to discover their faults through being told of them by others; however, things have come to such a pass with us that the most hateful of all people are those who counsel us and draw our attention to our defects. This is almost expressive of a weakness in our faith, for bad traits of character are vipers and stinging scorpions, and were someone to tell us that under our clothes there lurked a scorpion we would account this a great favour, and be delighted, and would occupy ourselves with removing and killing the scorpion in question. Yet the injury and pain it could cause to the body would last no more than a day, while ugly traits of character cause an injury in the very core of one's heart, which, it may be feared,[4] will endure even after death and for evermore, or for thousands of years.[A] Nevertheless, we are not delighted when someone calls these things to our notice, nor do we busy ourselves with removing them; instead we repay the one who thus counsels us in kind, and say, 'What about you? You also do this, that and the other,' so that resentment towards him distracts us from gaining any profit by his advice. This is a kind of hardness in the heart produced by many sins,[5] which in turn are the consequence of weak faith. Therefore we ask God (Exalted is He!) that through His grace and generosity He should inspire us with right guidance, show us the faults of our souls, occupy us with treating them, and guide us to thank those who reveal such weaknesses to us.

The third way is to learn of the faults of one's soul by listening to the statements of one's enemies, for a hostile eye brings out defects: it may happen that a man gains more from an enemy and a foe who reminds him of his faults than from a dissimulating friend who praises and speaks highly of him, and hides from him his faults. Although human nature is inclined to disbelieve an

[A] Until such time as God relents towards the sinner, and delivers him from hellfire.

enemy and to interpret his statements as the fruit of envy, still, the man of insight, whose faults must necessarily be noised abroad in the statements of his foes, will not fail to derive some benefit.

The fourth way is to mingle with people, and to attribute to oneself every blameworthy thing which one sees in them. For 'the believers are mirrors one to another',[6] and recognise their own faults in the faults of others, knowing that temperaments are similar in the following of desire, and that every attribute in a man must be shared by his associate to some degree; thus one will come to scrutinise one's own soul and cleanse it of everything one finds blameworthy in others. This constitutes the highest degree of self-discipline. Were all people only to renounce the things they dislike in others they would not need anyone to discipline them. Jesus (upon whom be peace) was once asked, 'Who taught you?' 'I was taught by no-one,' he replied. 'I perceived the ignorance of the ignorant man, and avoided it'.[A][7]

All of the above are devices which may be resorted to by those who have no gnostic Shaykh, who is intelligent, insightful into the faults of the soul, and compassionate, who gives one counsel in the affairs of religion, and who, having completed the refinement of his own soul, occupies himself with counselling and refining the souls of other bondsmen of God. Whosoever finds such a man has found his physician, and should stay with him, for it is he who will deliver him from his sickness and from the destruction which lies before him.

[A] This attribute forms part of Islam's image of the Prophet Jesus. See Jomier, 'Jésus', 49.

[22.8]

An Exposition of Evidence handed down from Men of Spiritual Insight and Provided in the Law to the effect that the Way to cure the Diseases of the Heart is by Renouncing one's Desires, and that the Stuff of such Diseases is Following Desires

KNOW that should you contemplate what we have said above with an eye ready to draw lessons, your inner sight will be opened, and the diseases and remedies of hearts will be unveiled to you through the light of knowledge and certitude. If, however, you are not capable of this, you should nevertheless not fail to believe and have faith, through learning and the imitation of those who deserve to be imitated. For faith and knowledge are two degrees, and the latter occurs after the advent of faith, and comes subsequently to it. God (Exalted is He!) has said, *God exalts those among you that have faith, and those that have knowledge, to high ranks.*[1] Thus whosoever believes that the path to God (Great and Glorious is He!) lies in resisting his desires, but has not grasped the cause and secret of this, is among those that have faith; while he who learns the profundities[2] and secrets of these desires becomes one of *those that have knowledge. And God has promised the best to both.*[3] [A] The texts of the Qur'ān, the

[A] *The best* refers to Paradise.

Sunna and the statements of the scholars which demand that one credit this thing are innumerable. God (Exalted is He!) has spoken of he who *restrains his soul from its whims; for him Heaven is the place of resort.*[4] And He has said (Exalted is He!), *They are those whose hearts God hath proven unto piety,*[5] [the meaning of which] is said to be: 'He divested them of love for their desires'.[A]

The Emissary of God (may God bless him and grant him peace) said, 'The believer is beset with five afflictions: a believer who envies him, a hypocrite who hates him, an unbeliever who makes war on him, a devil who misguides him, and a soul which struggles against him'.[6] He thus explained that the soul is an enemy which struggles with one, and which must be fought.

It is said that God (Exalted is He!) revealed to David: 'O David! Warn and caution your companions about indulging in desires,[B] for hearts which are attached to wordly desires are veiled from Me'.[7]

And Jesus (upon whom be peace) said, 'Blessed is he who renounces a present desire for the sake of something promised which he has not beheld.'[8] [C]

And our Prophet (may God bless him and grant him peace) said to some people who had just returned from the *Jihād*: 'Welcome! You have come from the lesser to the greater *Jihād*'. 'O Emissary of God!' he was asked. 'And what is the greater *Jihād*?' 'The *jihād* against the soul,' he replied.[9]

And he said (may God bless him and grant him peace), 'The real *mujāhid* is he that wars with himself for the sake of God (Great and Glorious is He!).'[10]

And he said (may God bless him and grant him peace), 'Refrain from harming your own soul, and follow not its whims

[A] Cf. Qushayrī, *Laṭā'if*, III. 438: 'He proved their hearts unto piety by divesting them of the love of their desires, so that they eschewed evil traits and observed decency of conduct.'

[B] An alternative translation might be: 'Beware of those of your companions who indulge in desires.'

[C] i.e. Heaven.

into the disobedience of God, lest it dispute with you on the Day of Arising so that one part of you curses another, unless God (Exalted is He!) grant you His forgiveness and protection'.[11]

Said Sufyān al-Thawrī, 'Never have I dealt with anything more difficult than my soul, which sometimes helps me, and sometimes opposes me'.[12]

Abu'l-ʿAbbās al-Mawṣilī used to say to his soul, 'O soul! Neither do you revel in the world with the sons of kings, nor do you struggle for the Afterlife with the ascetics. It is as though you had imprisoned me between Heaven and Hell. O soul! Are you not ashamed?'

Al-Ḥasan said, 'An unruly riding-beast is in no greater need of a strong bridle than is your soul'.

Said Yaḥyā ibn Muʿādh al-Rāzī, 'Fight your soul with the swords of self-discipline. These are four: eating little, sleeping briefly, speaking only when necessary, and tolerating all the wrongs done to you by men. For eating little slays desire, sleeping briefly purifies your aspirations, speaking little saves you from afflictions, and tolerating wrongs will bring you to the goal—for the hardest thing for a man is to be mild when snubbed and to tolerate the wrongs which are done against him. And when the wish to indulge your desires and sin stirs in your soul, and the delight of superfluous discourse is aroused, you should draw the sword of eating little from the scabbard of the midnight prayer and sleeping briefly, and[13] smite them with the fists of obscurity and silence until they cease to oppress you and avenge themselves upon you, and you become safe from[14] their vicissitudes to the end of your days,[15] having cleansed them of the darkness of the soul's desires so that you escape from their hazardous afflictions. At this you will become a subtle spiritual body, and a radiance without weight,[16] and shall roam in the field of goodness, travelling[17] the paths of obedience to God like a swift horse in the field, and a king taking his recreation in a garden.'

He also said, 'Man has three enemies: the world, the devil, and the soul. Be on your guard against the world through renunciation, against the devil by disobeying him, and against the soul by abandoning desire'.

A sage once said, 'The man who is ruled by his soul is a prisoner-of-war in the well[A][18] of his desires, and is incarcerated in the gaol of his whims, which govern and lead him wherever they wish by means of a halter which lies in their hand,[19] so that his heart is denied all benefit.'

Said Jaʿfar ibn Muḥammad,[20] 'The scholars and the sages all concur that pleasure cannot be gained save through the renunciation of pleasure'.[B]

Said Abū Yaḥyā[21] al-Warrāq, 'Whosoever gratifies his members by indulging in desire has planted the tree of regret in his heart.'

Said Wahb,[22] 'Everything more than bread is desire'.[23]

Said Wuhayb ibn al-Ward, 'Whosoever inclines toward the desires of this world should prepare himself for humiliation.'

It is related that after Joseph (upon whom be peace) had been set in charge of *the storehouses of the land*,[24] and during a state procession in which he rode with some twelve thousand of the nobles of his kingdom,[25] Potiphar's wife, who was seated on a nearby eminence, said, 'Glory be to Him Who enslaves kings who disobey Him,[26] and makes slaves into kings when they obey Him![27] O Joseph! It is greed and desire which make slaves from kings, which is the reward of the iniquitous,[28] while steadfastness and piety bring kings forth from slaves'. And Joseph replied, as God (Exalted is He!) has said,[29] '*Whosoever has piety and steadfastness; God shall not cause the reward of those who do good to be lost*'.[30]

Said al-Junayd, 'Last night, finding myself unable to sleep, I arose and began my litany [*wird*].[C] However, I failed to find therein the sweetness to which I had been accustomed. I wanted to

[A] The Arabic word is *jubb*, which recalls the well into which the Prophet Joseph was cast by his brothers.

[B] The pleasures of this world as against the next.

[C] The most common term for a sequence of devotional phrases and

sleep, but could not; I sat, but I could not abide this, so I went outside. And there I saw a man lying in the roadway, wrapped in a cloak. When he perceived me he said, "O Abu'l-Qāsim! Why so long in coming?" "O sir!" said I. "Without a time fixed beforehand?" "A time was fixed," he replied. "I asked God, Who moves all hearts, to move your heart towards me." "Thus did He do," I said, "so what would you have of me?" He asked, "When does the heart's ailment become its cure?" "When the soul is contradicted by its own whims",[A] I replied. And, addressing his soul, he said, "Listen! Seven times have I given you this answer, yet you refused to hear it from anyone except al-Junayd! Now you have done so!" At this, being still unknown to me, he went his way.'[31]

Yazīd al-Ruqāshī said, 'Keep cold water away from me in this world, that perhaps I may not be denied it in the next!'

A man once enquired of ᶜUmar ibn ᶜAbd al-ᶜAzīz, 'When should I speak?' And he replied, 'Whenever you wish to remain silent'. 'And when should I be silent?' the man asked, and ᶜUmar replied, 'Whenever you wish to speak'.[32] [B]

Said ᶜAlī (may God ennoble his face), 'Whosoever desires Heaven will forget the desires of this world'.

Mālik ibn Dīnār used to roam the marketplace, and, whenever he saw something that he desired, would say to his soul, 'Be patient, for I swear by God that I only deny it you because of the esteem in which I hold you'.

---

prayers, typically culled from the Qur'ān, which are to be recited at specific times as directed by a Shaykh.

[A] That is, it is only when the soul's faculty of persistent insinuation is refined into an impulse to virtue rather than to vice and self-indulgence that it becomes an ally, rather than an obstruction, on the path to God. Cf. the famous *ḥadīth*: 'not one of you believes until his inclination [*hawāhu*] is in accordance with what I have brought.' (Baghawī, *Sharḥ al-sunna*, cited in Nawawī, *Arbaᶜīn*, no.41; Tabrīzī, *Mishkāt*, tr. Robson, I. 45.)

[B] Controlling the urge to assert oneself through speech is an important part of Ghazālī's programme, forming the subject of an entire 'book' of the *Iḥyā'* (III. book 4: *K. Āfāt al-lisān*).

Since the scholars and sages are thus agreed that there is no path to felicity in the Afterlife except the denial of the soul's whims and desires, to believe in this thing is therefore an obligation. The details concerning which desires should be renounced can be discerned[33] from what we have set out above. The essence and secret of self-discipline is this: that the soul should not take pleasure in anything which will not be present in the grave—apart from that quantity which cannot be dispensed with. In matters of food, marriage, clothing,[34] accommodation, and every other thing which one needs, one should restrict oneself to what is necessary and indispensable, for should the soul take pleasure in any of these things it will grow familiar with it, and, upon death, will wish to return to the world on its account; and no-one wishes to return to this world save him who has no share in the next. The only road to salvation in this regard is for the heart to be occupied with the knowledge, love, meditation upon and devotion to[35] God, the strength for which can be derived from Him alone,[36] and for one to restrict oneself to such worldly things as will set aside the obstacles to remembrance and meditation.

The man who is unable to do this rightly should come as close to it as he can. There are four classes of people in this regard. Firstly, there is the man whose heart is so engrossed in the remembrance of God that he pays no heed to the world, apart from the bare necessities of life: he is one of the Truthful Saints [*ṣiddīqūn*]. It is only by dint of long discipline and patient abstinence from one's desires that one can attain to this rank. Secondly, there is the man whose heart is engrossed in the world, and who remembers God only mechanically, doing so with his tongue rather than his heart: such a man will be destroyed. Thirdly, it may be that a man is occupied with both religion and with the things of this world, with the former being predominant over his heart. This man, while he must necessarily come to Hell, shall be delivered from it rapidly, in proportion to the preponderance of God's remembrance in his heart.[A] Fourthly, there is the man whose heart, although occupied with both, is nevertheless dominated by the world. He will remain in Hell for a long period, but must, however, ultimately emerge from it because of the power of the remembrance of God which, despite the preponderance of worldly concerns, had established itself in his innermost heart. O Lord God! We seek refuge in Thee from disgrace, for truly Thou art the place of refuge![37]

The following objection may be raised: since the enjoyment of permitted things is itself permitted, these cannot be a cause of remoteness from God. This, however, is a feeble notion, for 'the love of this world is the source of every sin'[38] and invalidates every good deed.[39] For a permitted thing which is in excess of what one needs is also a thing of this world and a source of remoteness from God, as will be discussed later in the *Book of the Condemnation of the World.*[B]

Ibrāhīm al-Khawwāṣ said, 'When I was once on Mount al-Likām,[C] I beheld a pomegranate tree, and conceived a desire to eat from it. I took one pomegranate and split it open, but found it sour, so I left it and continued on my way. In due course I saw a man lying on the ground with hornets swarming over him. "Peace be upon you!" I said, and he replied, "And upon you be peace, Ibrāhīm!" "How did you know my name?" I demanded, and he said, "He who knows God knows all things". "I see that He has granted you a spiritual state", said I; "why then do you

[A] According to the Ashʿarite doctrine, sinful monotheists will remain in Hell only for as long as is necessary to punish them for their erstwhile transgressions, after which, by the Prophet's intercession, they will be received into Paradise. Cf. *Iḥyā'*, IV. 466-9 (*K. Dhikr al-mawt*, shaṭr 2, saʿat raḥmat Allāh; tr. Winter, *Remembrance of death*, 254-60).

[B] *Iḥyā'*, vol.III, book 6 (III. 173-200). A part of this important book has been translated by A. Uthman; see Appendix II.

[C] A mountain overlooking Antioch, where there had been a hermitage since the time of Ibn Adham, frequented by ascetics and mendicants. See Vadet, *Traité d'amour mystique*, 4; Ibn al-Jawzī, *Ṣifat al-ṣafwa*, II. 308-14.

not ask Him to protect you from those hornets?" But he replied, "I see that you too have a state in God's sight. Why then do you not ask Him to protect you from your desire for pomegranates? For the sting of pomegranates is felt in the Afterlife, while that of hornets is felt in this world alone". At this, I left him, and went on my way.'[40]

Said al-Sarī, 'For forty years my soul has been asking me to dip my bread into some treacle, yet I have not done so.'[41]

Thus it is that one can never reform the heart so that it follows the path of the Afterlife until one has prevented the soul from taking pleasure in what is permitted. For the soul, if allowed some permitted things, will then desire others which are forbidden. In this way the man who wishes to keep his tongue free from backbiting and chatter should remain silent in all things save the remembrance of God and[42] the duties of religion, until such time as his desire for speech dies, for then he will speak only in ways that are proper, so that both his silence and his speaking become forms of worship. Similarly, for as long as the eye is accustomed to looking at all that is beautiful it will not restrain itself from looking upon that which is forbidden to it. And so it is with the other desires, since the faculty with which one desires the permissible is the same as that with which one desires the prohibited; desire is one thing, and the bondsman of God is required to restrain it from forbidden things. If the soul is not accustomed to being confined to the essentials, its desires will gain control.

This constitutes one of the hazards which inhere in licit things. Behind them lies a greater hazard, which is that the soul might take pleasure in its enjoyment of this world, and incline towards it and find contentment therein because of its exuberance and vanity, until it becomes intoxicated[43] after the fashion of a drunkard who never wakes from his inebriation. This rejoicing in the world is a deadly poison which runs in a man's veins, driving from the heart all fear and sadness,[44] and all remembrance of death and of the terrors of the Day of Arising. Thus does it constitute the death of the heart.

God (Exalted is He!) has said, *They desire the life of the world, and feel secure therein;*[45] *And they rejoice in the life of the world, whereas the life of the world is but a [brief] comfort as compared with the Afterlife.*[46] And He has said, *Know that the life of the world is but play and idle talk, pageantry, and boasting among you, and rivalry in wealth and children* [to the end of] the verse.[47] [A] All of this constitutes a condemnation of the world; and we ask God for His safekeeping.[48]

The resolute Sufis have tested their hearts during states of rejoicing in the world, and have found them to be hard, wanton,[49] and slow to be affected by the remembrance of God and the Last Day; they have also tested them in the state of sadness, and found them to be soft, delicate, pure, and receptive to the effects of His remembrance. In this way have they learnt that salvation lies in constant sadness, and in distance from the sources of arrogance and joy. Then they weaned their souls from the things they found delightful, and habituated them resolutely to the renunciation of their desires, whether for permitted or forbidden things, knowing that they would be called to account for the former, punished for the latter, and reproached for that which was ambiguous[50] (reproach being itself a form of punishment, for whosoever is questioned during the Reckoning on the plains of the Arising has been punished).[B] In this way they saved[51] their souls from their torment, and, being delivered from the imprisonment[52] and slavery of their desires, and having acquired intimate familiarity with the remembrance of God and obedience to Him, gained freedom and abiding power in this world and the next. They had treated their souls as though they were falcons to be trained and transformed from a state of sav-

[A] The verse continues: *as is vegetation after rain, the growth of which is pleasing to the husbandman, but afterwards it dries up and you see it turn yellow; then it becomes straw. And in the Afterlife there is grievous punishment, and forgiveness from God and His good pleasure; whereas the life of the world is but the comfort of illusion.*

[B] An echo of a *ḥadīth*: 'Whosoever is questioned during the Reckoning has been punished [thereby]'. (Bukhārī, ʿIlm, 35; Muslim, Janna, 79.)

agery and wildness to one of obedience and discipline. For a falcon should first be shut up and hooded in a dark chamber until it forgets its freely-roving nature and how it used to fly in the air hither and yon, and then should be tamed by being offered meat until it becomes familiar with its owner, and so docile that wherever it may be when it hears his voice, it returns to him when called. The soul is similar: it does not become tame before its Lord or enjoy His remembrance until it is weaned from its habits, firstly through enduring isolation and retreat, in order to keep the hearing and the sight from familiar things, and, secondly, through acquiring the habit of praise, remembrance and prayer while still in a state of retreat, until it becomes dominated by familiarity with God's remembrance rather than with the world and its desires. This is a heavy burden for the aspirant at the outset, but ultimately becomes a source of pleasure, in the manner of a small boy who finds being weaned from the breast a hardship, and cries bitterly and with anguish, and is repelled by the food which is set before him as a substitute for his milk. However, if he is then denied any milk at all, he finds his abstinence from food extremely exhausting, and, when hunger overmasters him, he eats. Although this is an effort at first, in due course it becomes second nature to him, so that were he to be returned to the breast he would leave it alone and dislike its milk, having acquired a familiarity with food. Similarly, a riding-beast initially shies away from saddle and bridle, and will not be ridden, and has to be forced to endure these things, and must be restrained with chains and ropes from the roaming at will[53] which had been its custom. Later it becomes so familiar with these things that when it is left untethered it stands quite still.[A]

The disciplining of the soul is similar to that of birds and riding-beasts. It is first denied exuberance, arrogance[54] and taking pleasure in the delights of the world and in everything which it

[A] This image is used in a more elaborate form by al-Ḥakīm al-Tirmidhī (*Amthāl*, 184-6).

must leave at the time of death, having been told, 'Love whatsoever you will, for you shall surely leave it',[55] so that when it realises that the man who loves a thing which he must lose will certainly suffer,[56] it occupies itself with the love of that which it shall never lose, which is the remembrance of God, which shall accompany him into his grave and never depart from him. All of this is achieved by means of endurance, which lasts but a few days, since this life is short in comparison with the length of the life to come, and there is not a single intelligent man who is not happy to endure the hardships of travel and of learning a trade, and so forth, for one month, in order to enjoy himself for a year, or for the rest of his life. When compared with eternity, it is as though all of one's lifetime is less than one month of one's life; thus one must struggle and endure. For 'in the morning people praise the one who travelled by night, when the blindnesses of slumber depart from them', as ʿAlī (may God be pleased with him) said.[57]

The method of discipline and struggle varies from one person to the next, in accordance with their circumstances. The basic principle, however, is that all should renounce those things of the world which are found to be pleasurable. The man who rejoices in wealth or fame, or an audience receptive to his sermons, or in a high position in the judiciary or the government, or in the great number of his pupils, should firstly renounce this thing in which he takes such pleasure and delight. For if, when he is denied any of these things and is told that his reward in the Afterlife is undiminished by this denial, he dislikes this and finds it painful, then he is one of those who *desire the life of the world and feel secure therein,*[58] and this will be a cause of his destruction. Then, when he has renounced these sources of joy, let him remove himself from the company of others and remain by himself, and keep watch over his heart until it occupies itself with nothing but the remembrance of God and meditation upon Him. Let him lie in wait for any desire or insinuation which might appear in his soul until he extirpates the stuff of which these are made; for every insinuation has a cause,[59] and will not depart until that cause is destroyed. Let him persevere in this for the remainder of his life, for the *Jihād* can only end at death.

[22.9]
An Exposition of the Signs of Good Character[1]

KNOW that every man is [at first] ignorant of the faults which lie in his soul. When he comes to struggle with it, even in the least degree, until he has abandoned the grosser transgressions, he may think to himself that he has refined his soul and made good his character, and may now dispense with any further struggle. It is therefore essential to explain what are the signs of good character, since good character is equivalent to faith, and bad character to hypocrisy. God (Exalted is He!) has in His Book made mention of the traits which characterise believers and hypocrites, which are all the fruits of good or bad character. We shall now set forth some of these texts so that you may come to know the sign by which good character is to be recognised.

God (Exalted is He!) has said, *The faithful have triumphed: who are humble in their prayers, who shun vain talk, are payers of the Tithe, who guard their private parts—save from their wives or those whom their right hands possess (for then they are not blameworthy); but whosoever desires what is beyond that, such are the transgressors. And who observe their pledge and their covenant, and who pay heed to their Prayers; such are the inheritors.*[A] [2]

And He has said, *Those who repent, who worship, who praise, who fast, who bow, who prostrate, who enjoin what is right and forbid what is wrong, and who keep the limits ordained by God. And give good tidings to the believers!*[3]

[A] Of Paradise.

And He has said (Great and Glorious is He!), *Those whose hearts feel fear when God is mentioned, and who, when the signs of God are recited to them, grow in faith, and who trust in their Lord; those who establish the Prayer and spend of that which We have bestowed upon them. Such are the true believers.*[4]

Similarly, He has said (Exalted is He!), *The bondsmen of the All-Merciful are they who walk gently upon the earth, and who, when the foolish address them, answer: Peace,*[5] to the end of the *Sūra*.

The man who is uncertain what his condition might be should measure himself against these verses. The presence of all of[6] these attributes betokens a good character, while their complete absence is the sign of a bad one,[7] and the presence of only some indicates a character that is good in parts, and should encourage a man to busy himself with acquiring that which is lacking and preserving that which he possesses already. When describing the believer, the Emissary of God (may God bless him and grant him peace) attributed to him many traits, and referred to their totality as 'the good traits of character' [*maḥāsin al-akhlāq*]. He said, 'The believer loves for his brother that which he loves for himself'.[8] And he said (may God bless him and grant him peace), 'Whosoever believes in God and the Last Day should honour his guest',[9] and 'Whosoever believes in God and the Last Day should honour his neighbour',[10] and, 'Whosoever believes in God and the Last Day should say something good, or remain silent'.[11] He declared that the qualities of believers are the best of qualities: 'The believer with the most perfect faith is he with the finest character'.[12] And he said (may God bless him and grant him peace), 'If you see a believer who is quiet and dignified, then draw near to him, for he has been vouchsafed wisdom'.[13] And he said (may God bless him and grant him peace), 'The man who is made joyful by his good deeds and melancholy by his transgressions is a believer'.[14] And he said (may God bless him and grant him peace), 'It is not permissible for a believer to look at his brother in a manner that hurts him'.[15] And he said (may God bless him and grant him peace), 'A

Muslim should not frighten another Muslim'.[16] And he said (may God bless him and grant him peace), 'When two people sit together they are under a trust established by God; therefore let neither of them speak about his brother afterwards in a way which he would dislike'.[17]

A man once summed up the signs of good character by saying, 'It is to be abundantly modest, to avoid harming others, to be righteous, truthful in speech, and of little discourse; it is to do many things and slip up infrequently, to avoid excess, to be loyal, friendly, dignified, patient, grateful, satisfied,[18] forbearing, charitable, chaste[19] and pitying; and not to curse or to insult people, or to backbite or slander them, and to avoid hastiness, hatred, meanness, and jealousy; to be cheerful and kind, to love [good] and hate [evil] for the sake of God, to be well-pleased with Him and to be angry for His sake. Such is the man of good character'.

The Emissary of God (may God bless him and grant him peace) was once asked about the distinguishing marks of the believer and the hypocrite. He replied, 'The believer's concern is for prayer, fasting and worship, while the hypocrite, like an animal, is concerned with food and drink'.[20]

Ḥātim al-Aṣamm said, 'The believer is occupied with meditation and perseverance,[21] while the hypocrite is occupied with greed and his hopes. The believer has despaired of everyone but God, while the hypocrite has set his hopes in everyone save Him. The believer feels safe from everyone except God, while the hypocrite fears not Him, but all others. The believer sets his religion before money, while the hypocrite sets money before his religion. The believer does good, and weeps,[A] while the hypocrite does evil, and laughs. The believer loves solitude and isolation, while the hypocrite loves company and assemblies. The believer sows, and fears that his crop will be spoilt, while the hypocrite uproots his crop, and hopes to harvest it. The believer orders and prohibits for the sake of [good] government,[22] and

[A] For fear his good deeds will not be accepted.

succeeds in setting things right,[A] while the hypocrite orders and prohibits for the sake of power, and causes corruption.'

The finest thing through which good character can be put to the test is steadfastness in the face of suffering, and enduring the harshness of others, for whosoever complains of the bad character of another man has revealed the badness of his own character, since good character is to endure that which offends. God's Emissary (may God bless him and grant him peace) was once walking with Anas when one of the nomads came up to him and pulled violently at his thickly-edged Najrānī[B] cloak. Anas said, 'I looked at the neck of God's Emissary (may God bless him and grant him peace) and saw that the cloak's edge had left a mark there, so roughly had it been pulled. Then the nomad said, "O Muḥammad! Give me some of God's money which you have!" And the Emissary of God (may God bless him and grant him peace) turned to face him, and laughed, and ordered that he be given some money'.[23] And when Quraysh assailed him with injuries and blows, he said, 'O Lord God! Forgive my people, for truly they do not know'. (It is said that this was on the day of Uḥud.)[C] [24] It was for this reason that God (Exalted is He!) said, *Assuredly, thou art of a tremendous character.*[25]

It is told that Ibrāhīm ibn Adham went out one day into the desert. There he met a soldier, who asked him, 'Are you a slave?' and he told him that he was. 'Where is the inhabited country?' the soldier asked, and Ibrāhīm pointed to a cemetery. 'I meant the inhabited country!' the soldier said, but Ibrāhīm replied, 'The cemetery is such'. At this the soldier lost his temper and struck Ibrāhīm's head with his goad, cracking his skull. Then he took him back with him to the town, where he was met by his companions, who asked him what had happened. And when the

[A] Among the common people.

[B] Najrān, a city of the Yemen now in Saudi Arabia.

[C] Uḥud: site of a battle fought in the year 3 AH between the Muslims and the idolators of Mecca, to the temporary advantage of the latter.

soldier told them, they said, 'But this is Ibrāhīm ibn Adham!' At this the soldier dismounted, and kissed his hands and feet, and tendered his apologies. Later on, Ibrāhīm was asked why he had called himself a slave. 'He did not ask me whose slave I was,' he answered, 'he merely asked me if I was one, and I said yes, for I am a slave of God. And when he struck my head I asked God to admit him into Heaven'. 'But he did you an injustice!,' someone said. 'How could you pray for such a thing?' And he replied, 'I knew that I would be rewarded [for my forbearance], and did not want to come by something good because of him, while he gained something evil because of me'.[26]

Abū ʿUthmān al-Ḥīrī once received an invitation from a man who wished to put him to the test. When he arrived at the latter's house, he said, 'You cannot enter now',[27] so Abū ʿUthmān went away. But before he had gone any great distance, the man called him again, and said, 'O Shaykh! Come back',[28] and Abū ʿUthmān did so. Then he called him a third time, and said, 'Return to what you should be doing at this time', but when he reached his door again, he repeated what he had first said. He went away, and returned a fourth time, only to receive the same rebuttal. The man continued to do this again and again, with Abū ʿUthmān responding in the same fashion each time. At last, he bent down [and kissed Abū ʿUthmān's] feet, and said, 'O Shaykh! I only wanted to test you! How fine is your character!' But he only replied, 'The actions you saw me do were no more than the character traits of a dog, for a dog, when ordered not to do something, simply refrains'.[29]

It is related that Abū ʿUthmān was once riding in the street when a pot of ashes was thrown down upon him. He dismounted, and prostrated himself to God in gratitude,[30] and then brushed the ashes from his clothes without saying a word. 'Shall you not rebuke them?' he was asked, but he replied, 'A man who deserves hellfire but receives only ashes cannot fairly be angry'.[31]

It is related that ʿAlī ibn Mūsā al-Riḍā was of a swarthy complexion, his mother having been a negress. Near the door of his house at Nīsābūr there was a public bath, which the attendant would ensure was empty whenever he wanted to use it. One day when he was in this bathhouse the attendant shut the door and went away to run some errands. A rustic then went up to the door of the bathhouse, opened it, entered, and undressed. When he saw ʿAlī ibn Mūsā al-Riḍā he thought that he was a bath attendant, and asked him to bring him some water. ʿAlī ibn Mūsā rose, and followed the man's every instruction. When the attendant returned, and saw the rustic's clothes and heard him speaking to ʿAlī ibn Mūsā, he was terrified, and fled, leaving them where they were. And when Ibn Mūsā emerged, and asked about the attendant, he was told that he had been so frightened by what had happened that he had run away. 'He should not have fled,' Ibn Mūsā remarked. 'The fault lies only with the man who slept with a black slavegirl'.[A]

It is related that Abū ʿAbd Allāh al-Khayyāṭ had a shop in which he would sit, and a Zoroastrian client who made use of his tailoring services. Whenever he made something for this Zoroastrian, the latter would pay him with bad coins, which Abū ʿAbd Allāh would take, without either saying anything to him or refusing them. Now, it so fell out that one day Abū ʿAbd Allāh had left his shop on some task, and the Zoroastrian came, and, not finding him,[32] paid his apprentice instead—with a bad coin—for something which had been sewn for him. The apprentice looked at it, saw that it was bad, and gave it back. When Abū ʿAbd Allāh returned he told him what had occurred. 'You have done wrong!' Abū ʿAbd Allāh told him. 'That Zoroastrian has been dealing with me in this fashion for some while,[33] and I have been patient with him, taking his coins and throwing them into a well so that no other Muslim might be taken in by them'.[34][B]

[A] Ibn Mūsā's mother was a freed Nubian slave. (Shībī, *Ṣila*, 219–20.) The anecdote is unsurprisingly omitted from al-Fayḍ al-Kāshānī's Shīʿī abridgement of the *Iḥyā'*.

[B] The Sufis had much to say on the morally correct means of disposing of forged currency; see *Qūt*, II. 268–9.

Yūsuf ibn Asbāṭ said, 'Good character has ten signs: reluctance to argue, fairness, never hoping for slips in others, looking for a charitable interpretation of other people's misdeeds, finding excuses for them, tolerating the harm they do to one, blaming oneself, knowing one's own faults and not those of others, meeting young and old alike with a cheerful face, and speaking kindly to those who are superior or more humble than oneself'.

Sahl was once asked about good character, and said, 'Its least degree is to tolerate the wrong done to you, and not to seek compensation. It is to have compassion and pity for the one who wrongs you, and to ask God to forgive him'.

Al-Aḥnaf ibn Qays was asked from whom he had learnt forbearance.[35] 'From Qays ibn ʿĀṣim', he replied. 'How forbearing[36] was he?' he was then asked, and he answered, 'Once, when he was sitting in his house, a slave-girl of his came with a large skewer of roast meat. This fell from her hand and landed on and killed his baby. The slave-girl was horrified, but he said, "Do not be afraid. You are free to go: I give you your freedom, hoping for a reward from God".'[37]

Whenever children pelted Uways al-Qaranī with stones he would say to them, 'Brothers! If you must throw stones at me, then do so with little ones, so that my legs do not bleed, for when they do so I cannot perform the Prayer'.[A] [38]

A man once insulted al-Aḥnaf ibn Qays, and followed him about, yet he held his peace.[39] When they drew near to his home district al-Aḥnaf stopped, and said, 'If you have something more to say then say it now, lest some of the foolish men of the district hear you and do you some harm'.[40]

It is related that ʿAlī (may God ennoble his face) once called a slave-boy to him. When he failed to respond he called him a second time, and then a third, yet he still did not respond. So he

[A] Not because he was seriously injured, but because the presence of more than a small quantity of blood on one's body or garments renders the canonical prayer invalid. (Ghazālī, *Wajīz*, I. 7.)

arose and went to him, and found him lying down. 'Did you not hear me?' he asked. 'Yes I did,' he replied. 'So why did you not respond?' 'I knew that you would not punish me,' he said, 'so I was lazy'. 'Depart from me,' he said, 'for I have freed you for the sake of God'.[41]

A woman once said to Mālik ibn Dīnār, 'You hypocrite!' And he said, 'Woman, you have found my name which everyone else in Basra has mislaid!'[42]

Yaḥyā ibn Ziyād al-Ḥārithī had an ill-mannered slave-boy. 'Why do you keep him?' people asked. 'He is teaching me forbearance,' was his reply.[43]

These souls were made humble through discipline, so that their qualities reached an equilibrium and their inner aspects were cleansed of all dishonesty, rancour and ill-will. This in turn bore fruit in the form of contentment with all that God (Exalted is He!) has decreed, which is the highest form of good character, since the man who dislikes the actions of God is discontented with Him, an attitude which is the most ignoble of all traits. The signs mentioned above appeared in the external aspects of these men; whosoever does not find in himself these same tokens should not be pleased with himself and think that he is possessed of good character; rather should he occupy himself with self-discipline and struggle until he attains this degree, which is an exalted one, attained solely by the Ones Brought Nigh [*al-muqarrabūn*] and the Truthful Saints [*al-ṣiddīqūn*].

[22.10]

An Exposition of the Way in which Young Children should be Disciplined, and the Manner of their Upbringing and the Improvement of their Characters

KNOW that the way in which young children are disciplined is one of the most important of all matters.[1] A child is a trust in the care of his parents, for his pure heart is a precious uncut jewel devoid of any form or carving, which will accept being cut into any shape, and will be disposed according to the guidance it receives from others. If it is habituated to and instructed in goodness then this will be its practice when it grows up, and it will attain to felicity in this world and the next; its parents too, and all its teachers and preceptors,[2] will share in its reward. Similarly, should it be habituated to evil and neglected as though it were an animal, then misery and perdition will be its lot, and the responsibility for this will be borne by its guardian and supervisor. For God (Exalted is He!) has said, *Ward off from yourselves and your families a Fire.*[3] A father may strive to protect his son from fire in this world, but yet it is of far greater urgency that he protect him from the fires which exist in the Afterlife. This he should do by giving him discipline, teaching him and refining his character, and by preserving him from bad company, and by not suffering him to acquire the custom of self-indulgence, or to love finery and luxury, in the quest for which he might well squander his life when older and thus perish forever. Rather should he watch over him diligently from his earliest days, and permit none but a woman of virtue and religion to nurse and raise him; her diet should be of permitted things, for there is no blessing [*baraka*] in milk which originates in forbidden food, which, should a child be nourished on it, will knead his native disposition in such a way as to incline his temperament to wrongdoing.

When the signs of discretion appear in him he should again be watched over carefully. The first of these is the rudiments of shame, for when he begins to feel diffident and is ashamed of certain things so that he abandons them, the light of the intellect has dawned in him, whereby he sees that certain things are ugly, and different from others, and begins to be ashamed of some things and not others.[A] This is a gift to him from God (Exalted is He!), and a good foretoken that his traits will be balanced, his heart pure, and his intellect sound when he enters upon adulthood.

The child who has developed the capacity for shame should never be neglected; rather this and his discretion should be used as aids in his education. The first trait to take control of him will be greed for food; he is to be disciplined in this regard, so that, for instance, he picks up food only with his right hand, says 'In the name of God' when raising it, eats from that which is nearest to him, and does not start eating before others.[B] ⌜He should not stare at his food or at the other people present, neither should he bolt it, but should chew it properly; he should not eat one mouthful after another without pause, he should not get food on his hand or his clothes, and he should acquire the habit of sometimes eating nothing but bread so that he does not think that the presence of other kinds of food is inevitable.⌝[4] He should be made to dislike eating large quantities by being told that this is

[A] According to Galen, the expressions of shame appear in the third year of life. (Rosenthal, *Classical Heritage*, 89.)

[B] These practices being in conformity with the Prophetic *Sunna*.

the practice of animals, and by seeing other children reproached for overeating or praised for being well-mannered and moderate. He should be made to enjoy giving the best food to others, and encouraged to pay little heed to what he eats and to be contented with its coarser varieties.

⌜He should be encouraged to like white rather than coloured or silk garments, and made firmly to believe that these latter are proper to women and to effeminate men, and that [true] men disdain them.⌝[5] This should be repeatedly emphasised to him so that he dislikes and criticises the wearing by any child he sees of silken or coloured clothes. He should be protected from children who are accustomed to luxury and comfort, and to wearing expensive garments, and from mixing with all who would speak to him of such things and thereby make them seem fine in his eyes. For the child who is neglected in the early years of his growth will usually grow up to be ill-natured, dishonest, envious, obstinate, inclined to theft, backbiting, and excessive chatter and laughter, and slyness and immorality, from all of which things he can be protected through a sound upbringing.

Next he should be busy at school learning the Qur'ān, the Traditions, and tales of devout men, so that love for the righteous may take root in his heart.[6] ⌜He should be preserved from those varieties of poetry which treat of lovers and passion,[A] and from the company of such men of letters as claim that these things are part of an elegant and sophisticated nature, for this would implant the seeds of corruption in his heart. Whenever a good trait or action manifests itself in the child he should be admired and rewarded with something which gives him joy, and should be praised in front of others; likewise, when once in a while he does something bad it is best to pretend not to notice and not to bring it to the attention of others (but never to reveal to him that it is something which others might be bold enough

[A] Ṭūsī (tr. Wickens, *Nasirean Ethics*, 168) names the poetry of Abū Nuwās and Imru'l-Qays as prime examples.

to do), particularly if the child himself has diligently endeavoured to hide his action, for the exposure of such deeds may cause him to grow emboldened, until he no longer cares when they are made public. Should he repeat the action, he should be privately reproached and made to feel that it was a very serious thing,⌝[7] and be told, 'Beware of doing anything like this again,[8] or I shall tell others and you will be disgraced in front of them!'. He should not be spoken to at length every time, for this would accustom him to being blamed for his misdeeds, and destroy the effectiveness such words have upon his heart. A father should rather preserve the awe[9] in which the child holds his speech by reproaching him only sometimes: similarly the mother, when reproving him, should frighten him by [threatening to mention the matter to] his father. ⌜He should not be permitted to sleep by day, for this conduces to laziness, and should always be allowed to sleep at night, but not on a soft bed, which would prevent his members from growing tough.⌝[10] His body should not be allowed to grow fat,[11] for this would make it hard for him to renounce self-indulgence; instead he should be habituated to rough bedding, clothing and food.

⌜He should also be prevented from doing anything secretly, for he will conceal things only when he believes them to be ugly, and if he is left to continue these practices he will grow used to doing ugly things.⌝[12] ⌜He should acquire the habit of walking, moving about and taking exercise for part of the day so that he is not overcome by idleness, and should be taught not to uncover his limbs or walk fast, and not to dangle his arms but to keep them close to his trunk.⌝[13] ⌜He must be forbidden to boast to his fellows about any of his parents' possessions, whether these be money or property, or about anything he eats or wears, or about his tablet and pencase, and should become used to being modest, generous and mild in his speech to all with whom he associates.⌝[14] He should be prevented from accepting anything from other boys, if he is from a wealthy and powerful family, and be taught that it is honourable to give, and base and blameworthy to take; while if his parents are poor he should be taught that greed and taking from others is a disgraceful and humiliating practice fit only for dogs, which wag their tails hoping for a morsel.

⌜Children should always be made to deem the love of gold and silver an unsightly thing, and should be warned in this regard even more vigorously than they are warned about snakes and scorpions, for the vice which consists in such a love is more dangerous to them (and to adults also) than poison.⌝[15]

⌜A child should be put in the practice of not spitting, yawning or wiping his nose in the presence of others, and taught not to turn his back to anyone, or to cross his legs, or lean his chin and support his head on his hand, for these practices indicate the presence of sloth.⌝[16] He should be taught how to sit, and be forbidden to speak excessively, it being explained to him that this is a sign of impudence and the custom of children from low families. ⌜Making oaths of any sort, whether true or false, should be forbidden him, so that he never acquires this habit as a child. He should be put in the habit of never speaking before anyone else, and of speaking only in response to questions and in proportion to them, and of listening properly whenever an older person is speaking,⌝[17] and rising [when he enters], and making a place for him and sitting facing him. He should be forbidden to speak loosely, or to curse or insult anyone, or to mingle with those who do such things, for these habits will inevitably be acquired should he fall in with bad company, the preservation from which is the very root and foundation of the education of children. ⌜If his teacher strikes him he should not cry out and sob, or seek anyone's intercession, but should rather bear his punishment, and be told that to do so is a mark of courage and manhood, while to cry is the practice of slaves and women.⌝[18]

After school, ⌜he should be allowed to play in a fashion which gives him some rest after his hard work in class, although he should not be allowed to grow exhausted.⌝[19] To prevent a child from playing, and to fatigue him with constant lessons, will cause his heart to die and harm his intelligence, and make life so hateful to him that he will cast around for some means of escape.

⌜He should be taught to obey his parents and his teacher, and all people who are older than himself, whether relations or not, and to look upon them with respect and admiration⌝[20] and not to play in their presence. As he reaches the age of discretion he should not be excused the ritual ablutions and the Prayer, and should be told to fast for a few days during Ramadan, and should be prevented from wearing gold, silk or embroidered clothes. He should be taught about the limits[A] laid down by the Law, and put in fear of theft and unlawful gain, and also of lying, treachery, deceit,[21] and all the other traits which tend to predominate among children. If he is brought up in this way, then as he approaches adulthood he will come to understand the reasons which underlie these things, and will be told that food is a means of maintaining health, and that its sole purpose is to enable man to gain strength for the worship of God (Great and Glorious is He!), and that this world is without reality, since it will not endure, and that death must bring its pleasures to an end, and that it is a place through which we pass but in which we cannot abide, unlike the Afterlife, in which we must abide and through which we cannot pass,[22] for death awaits us at every moment, and that therefore the intelligent and insightful man will lay up provisions in this world for his journey into the next so as to gain a high degree in the sight of God and abundant bliss in the Gardens of Heaven. If his upbringing was sound, then when he attains to maturity these ideas will have a powerful and wholesome effect which will leave an impress on his heart like an inscription on stone; had it been otherwise, so that the child had grown accustomed to play, boastfulness, rudeness and insolence, and greed for food, clothes and finery, his heart will shrink from accepting truth in

[A] Ar. *ḥudūd*, which may equally be rendered 'canonical punishments'.

the manner of a field where crops wither because of its dry soil.

It is the beginning which should be supervised carefully, for a child is a creature whose essence is receptive to both good and evil: it is only its parents who cause it to be disposed to one or the other. As the Prophet said, 'Every child is born with the sound natural disposition [*fiṭra*]: it is only his parents who make of him a Jew, a Christian or a Zoroastrian'.[23]

Sahl ibn ᶜAbd Allāh al-Tustarī said, 'When I was [only] three years old I used to say the midnight prayer, having watched my maternal uncle Muḥammad ibn Suwār doing this. One day he said to me, 'Do you not remember God, your Creator?' and I asked, 'How should I remember Him?' 'When you put on your bedclothes, say in your heart three times, without moving your tongue, "God is with me. God beholds me. God watches over me". This I did for several nights, telling him what I had done. Then he instructed me to say the same words seven times each night, which I did, and then eleven times, upon which I felt a sweetness growing in my heart. When a year had passed, my uncle said to me, "Keep doing what I have told you until you enter your grave, for it will help you in this world and the next". I continued to do it for several years,[24] finding a sweetness within myself, until my uncle said, "Sahl! If God is with somebody, and beholds him and watches over him, can he then disobey Him? You should never do so".

'Now, it was a habit of mine to keep my own company, and when they sent me to school I said, "I am afraid that my concentration will be lost". But they made it a condition upon the schoolmaster that I should be with him and study for a certain period each day, and would then come back home. And so I went to school, where I memorised the Qur'ān by the time I was six or seven years old. It was my practice to fast every day, my only nourishment for twelve years being from barley-bread. When I was thirteen I came across a question [which I could not answer], and asked my family to send me to Basra to search for the answer to it there.[A] When I arrived, I asked the scholars of that city regarding it, but not one of them was able to provide me with a satisfactory response. I journeyed therefore to ʿAbbādān,[B] where I met a man named Abū Ḥabīb Ḥamza ibn Abī ʿAbd Allāh al-ʿAbbādānī, who was able to answer my question. I then stayed with him for a while, benefiting from his discourse and taking on some of his good manners, and then went back to Tustar.[C] Now I restricted myself in the matter of food to buying for one dirham a measure[D] of barley, which I would cause to be ground and baked, and of which I would eat one ounce [*ūqiya*] before dawn, without any salt or other food, so that that one dirham sufficed me for a whole year. Then I resolved to fast for three days at a stretch, and then break my fast, and then for five days, and then seven, and at last twenty-five days. This I did for twenty years. Then I went out, and wandered in the earth for several more years, and then returned to Tustar, where I prayed all night for as long as God willed.'[25] Said Aḥmad, 'I never saw him eat salt until he went to meet his Lord'.[26]

[A] The question, according to Ibn al-ʿArabī (cited in Böwering, *Mystical Vision*, 48, and Chittick, *Sufi Path of Knowledge*, 407), was whether the heart itself could prostrate. Qus͟hayrī interprets the story as an indication that mysticism solves the problems that theology is unable to answer. (Böwering, loc. cit.)

[B] 'ʿAbbādān, then situated on an island between the estuaries of the Tigris and the Dugail (=Qārūn) River, was the site of a retreat (*ribāṭ*) which was founded by the disciples of al-Ḥasan al-Baṣrī (d.110/728)' (Böwering, 47). It was frequented by important figures of both exoteric and esoteric Islam.

[C] The home town of Sahl was located in K͟hūzestān in south-western Iran. Cf. J.H. Kramers, art. 'Tustar', in *EI*, IV. 393–5.

[D] Ar. *faraq*, a large measure of grain, variously defined. (Cf. Lane, 2385.)

[22.11]
An Exposition of the Requirements of Aspirancy, the Preliminaries to Spiritual Struggle, and the Progressive Induction of the Aspirant in Treading the Path of Discipline

BE IT known unto you that the man who has in all certainty beheld the *harvest of the Afterlife* with his heart must needs aspire to [*murīd*] it,[A] and must long for it and follow its ways, despising thereby the pleasures and delights which this world contains. For the man who has a bauble will lose all desire for it when he spies a precious gem, and will long to make an exchange. Lack of desire for the *harvest of the Afterlife* and the meeting with God (Exalted is He!) is the outcome of a lack of faith in God and in the Last Day. Now, I do not mean by 'faith' the 'discourse of the soul'[B] and the movement made by the tongue when pronouncing the Two Testimonies[C] in a way which

[A] According to the Qur'ān (XLII:20), *Whoever aspires to* [yurid] *the harvest of the Afterlife, We give him increase in its harvest; and whoso aspires to the harvest of the world, We give him thereof, and in the Afterlife he shall have no portion.* Ghazālī was not the first Sufi to find a Qur'ānic derivation for the term *murīd*, which we translate as 'aspirant'. Qushayrī (*Risāla*, [II.]433) tells us that it originates in the verse *Do not repel those who call upon their Lord morning and night, aspiring to* [yurīdūna] *His Face* (VI:52).

[B] Ar. *ḥadīth al-nafs*: the undirected flow of consciousness inside the soul. See Introduction, p.LXVII.

[C] These being 'I testify that there is no deity save God', and 'I testify that

is devoid of any sincerity or single-heartedness, for this would be equivalent to believing that the gem were better than the bauble while knowing its name alone, and not its reality. Such a believer will not renounce[1] the bauble, having grown accustomed to it, and will harbour no passionate yearning for the gem.

The obstacle which bars us from attaining to God is therefore our lack of wayfaring [*sulūk*], and this in turn proceeds from a lack of aspirancy;[A] this being the result of an absence of faith, which is in turn the consequence of a lack of guides[2] and of people who might remind one, and who know about God (Exalted is He!) and will lead one along the path to Him, who give men to realise the baseness and impermanence[3] of this world and the great import and everlasting duration of the next. Mankind is in a state of heedlessness, having plunged into the desires of this world and fallen deep into slumber, and there is not a single scholar of the Faith who is working to arouse it from this plight. Should anyone happen to awake he will find himself incapable of following the Path because of his ignorance: when he questions the scholars about it he finds them to be far removed from it and disposed instead towards their own whims.[B] Thus it is that weakness in aspirancy, ignorance of the Path, and the self-interested discourses pronounced by the scholars, are the causes of the present absence of wayfarers on the Path of God (Exalted is He!). If the objective be veiled, the guide absent, worldly desire predomi-

---

Muḥammad is the Emissary of God'. The classical theologians held that the mere pronouncement of these words suffice to make a man a Muslim, and that, if accompanied by faith, they must lead him ineluctably to salvation. (Bayhaqī, *Iʿtiqād*, 19-21; Ghazālī, *Iḥyā'*, I. 103-11 [*K. Qawāʿid al-ʿaqā'id*, faṣl 4; tr. Faris, *Foundations*, 99-135]; Nader, *Système philosophique des Mu'tazila*, 302-5.)

[A] Ar. *irāda*. Apologies are offered to defenders of correct English for this neologism, which seems inescapable. For some definitions see our Introduction, p.LXV.

[B] The Imām is here repeating his familiar disenchantment with the exponents of the formal learning of his day, whom he bitterly censured for their indifference to matters of the spirit. For instance, in the *Bidāya* (p.78) he

nant and the seeker heedless, then attaining unto Him is an impossibility and the Paths must needs fall into desuetude.[4] But should it happen that a man awake, either of his own accord or by virtue of the activity of another, and aspire to [*irāda*] the commerce[A] and *harvest of the Afterlife*, he should be aware that there are diverse requirements which must be observed at the outset of aspirancy, and that there exists a place of refuge and a fortress within which he must defend himself if he is to be safe from those highwaymen who would obstruct him, and likewise that there are duties which he must perform while on his journey without cease.

The requirements of aspirancy which must be observed pertain to the lifting of the veil and the barrier which lies between one and the Truth.[B] For mankind has been deprived of the Truth by reason of a successive establishment of veils and the presence of a barrier on the Path. God (Exalted is He!) has said, *And We have set a barrier before them and a barrier behind them, and have covered them so that they cannot see.*[5] Now, the 'barrier' which lies between the aspirant and the Truth is constituted of four things: wealth, status [*jāh*], imitation,[C] and sin. The veil of wealth can be lifted only by divesting oneself of it so that no

---

teaches that 'whoever associates with the jurists [*mutafaqqiha*] of the age will have a nature overmastered by disputation and ostentatious argument, and will find silence hard to bear, since the evil scholars [*ʿulamā' al-sū'*] have made him believe that merit lies in these things, and that the ability to argue and debate is the praiseworthy thing. Flee from them, therefore, as you would flee from a lion, and know that ostentatious argument brings contempt from both God and mankind.'

[A] A not uncommon Qur'ānic image which describes man's salvific 'transaction' with his Creator: *God has purchased from the believers their wealth and their souls, that Heaven might be theirs* (Q. IX:111; cf. also Q. XXXV:29; LXI:10; II:16).

[B] Ar. *al-Ḥaqq*, which also bears the meaning of 'reality', and 'God'.

[C] Ar. *taqlīd*, here used in the sense of adherence to a school of thought through imitation of others rather than through experience or intellectual conviction. Elsewhere Ghazālī tells us that a righteous man may be denied

more than the necessary quantity thereof remains. For as long as a man retains a single dirham to which his heart inclines he will be tied to it and veiled from God. The veil of status is only lifted by distancing oneself from such circumstances as reinforce it, and through modesty, a preference for obscurity, fleeing from things which might cause one's name to be mentioned, and doing things which repel the hearts of others. As for the veil of imitation, this can only be removed by renouncing one's fanaticism for the school of thought [*madhhab*] to which one subscribes, whichever this may be, and by believing that 'there is no deity but God,' and that 'Muḥammad is the Emissary of God' with true faith, and by striving to render one's sincerity genuine by dismissing all objects of worship apart from God (Exalted is He!), the most powerful such object being one's desire.[A] When a man has done this the true nature of the doctrine which he had received through imitation will be disclosed, and this disclosure should be sought by means of spiritual strife, not through disputation.[B] Should a fanatical devotion to some doctrinal position so dominate him that he has no space in his heart for any other thing, then this likewise will become a tie and a veil, since it is not a requirement of aspi-

---

spiritual unveiling 'by reason of a dogma he had held since the time he acquired it by imitation in childhood through holding a good opinion [of his teachers]; this will form a barrier between him and the reality of God, and prevent the unveiling in his heart of anything which conflicts with what he had accepted through imitation. This is a great veil, which has veiled most theologians (*mutakallimīn*) and people who are fanatics for schools of thought; nay, even the majority of the righteous who contemplate the *kingdom of the heaven and the earth*.' (*Iḥyā'*, III. 12 [*K. ʿAjā'ib al-qalb*, Bayān mathal al-qalb]; cf. above. p.LXVI.) For Ghazālī's use of the term see Poggi, *Un Classico della Spiritualitá Musulmana*, 138–152; Watt, *Muslim Intellectual*, 164–5.

[A] Cf. Q.XLV:23: *Have you seen him that takes his desire to be his god?*

[B] In the *Munqidh* (pp.35–44), Ghazālī has already explained at length how ratiocination alone cannot lead man to metaphysical truth. Cf. also *Iḥyā'*, I. 21 (*K. al-ʿIlm*, bāb 2, Bayān ʿilm ... farḍ kifāya); IV. 212 (*K. al-Tawḥīd*, Bayān ḥaqīqat al-tawḥīd).

rancy that one adhere to any particular school of thought.[A] As regards the matter of sin, this constitutes a veil which can only be removed through repentance, the renunciation of wrongdoing, a resolute intention never to repeat any transgression one might have committed, genuine sorrow over past sins, and making reparations and giving satisfaction to those with whom one had disputed.[B] For the man who does not soundly repent and renounce the visible sins, and yet wishes to have discovered to him the secrets of religion through unveiling, is like the one who has not learnt Arabic but who nonetheless wishes to discover the secrets and the true interpretation of the Qur'ān. For in order to interpret the obscure passages[6] of the Book it is incumbent first to learn its tongue, whereupon one may proceed to its secret mysteries; likewise is it necessary to adhere in a proper fashion both at the commencement and the conclusion [of the Path] to the external forms of the Law, whereby one may be enabled to progress to its secrets and its depths.[C]

When these four requirements [of repentance] are satisfied, and when a man has stripped himself of his wealth and reputation, he will be as one who has purified himself and made the ritual ablutions so as to remove the state of ritual defilement and

[A] This advice is drawn almost verbatim from the *Risāla* of al-Qus̲h̲ayrī, who explains that 'it is an ugly thing for an aspirant to adhere to one of the schools of thought (*mad̲h̲āhib*) which are not attached to Sufism', a reference to some of the competing theological alignments of the day. Qus̲h̲ayrī goes on to explain that since the Sufi *ʿulamā'* are the most accomplished exponents of all the Islamic sciences, the novice has no need of sitting with anyone else. (*Risāla*, 731, 734.) See Introduction, p.LXVI.

[B] These are the conditions of repentance set out in the book devoted to the subject in the *Iḥyā'*; see IV. 30–8 (rukn 3, fī tamām al-tawba wa-s̲h̲urūṭihā ..., tr. Gramlich, *Lehre*, 85–102).

[C] A reminder of the eternal validity of the Sacred Law. The overwhelming majority of classical Sufi writers assume loyalty to the exoteric norms of Islam as a matter of course; not out of dissimulation (as an older school of European writers has tended to assume), but as a sincere expression of their faith that Sufism was the culmination of Islam. (Cf. Molé, 22–6.) As G̲h̲azālī

become fit for the Prayer, whereupon he needs an *imām* to lead him; in like wise the aspirant needs a Shaykh whom he will follow under every circumstance to guide him to the Straight Path. For the road of religion is obscure, and the ways of the devil many and manifest, so that whosoever has no Shaykh to guide him[7] must needs be led by the devil to his own paths. A man who sets out alone and with no guide along the dangerous roads which lie across a desert has exposed himself to grave peril, and will be lured to destruction. Similarly, someone who treats his soul by himself is like a tree which grows without husbandry, which must soon dry up; even should it survive for a while and put out leaves, yet will it not bear fruit.[8] The aspirant's safe refuge, these four requirements having been fulfilled, is his Shaykh; let him therefore hold fast to him in the way that a blind man might clutch his guide on a riverbank, putting himself entirely in his hands and never contravening his instructions whether in the matter of his regular religious duties or of anything else. He should leave nothing outside the compass of his aspirancy, since he must know that he would benefit more even from a mistake of his Shaykh (were he to make one)[A] than from any correct opinion or act which might proceed from his own soul.

When a man has found such a refuge it is incumbent upon the person he has found to protect him and keep him safe in an impregnable fortress from which the highwaymen will be repulsed. This fortress is built of four things: solitude, silence, hunger and sleeplessness. For it is the aspirant's purpose to mend his heart that he might behold therewith his Lord and be fit for

---

states very firmly: 'Whoever claims that the Reality (*ḥaqīqa*) contradicts the law (*Sharīʿa*), or that the inward (*bāṭin*) invalidates the outward (*ẓāhir*), is closer to unbelief than faith.' (*Iḥyā'*, I.89 [*K.Qawāʿid al-ʿaqā'id*, faṣl 2; tr. Faris, *Foundations*, 38].)

[A] Unlike the Prophets, the Sufi masters are not inerrant (*maʿṣūm*). But they may be *maḥfūẓ*; that is, protected from persistence in sin, although small faults may sometimes proceed from them. (Qushayrī, *Risāla*, 665, 743; Ghazālī, *Ayyuhā*, 130; and p. 173A below.)

His proximity. Hunger reduces the quantity of blood in the heart, and lightens its coloration, whereby will it be illuminated and the fat which is around it melted away, thus rendering it tender, which thing is the key to unveiling just as its hardness is the source of the veil. When the volume of blood in the heart is reduced, the paths available to the enemy will be straitened, for his courses lie in the veins, which are full of desires.[A][9] Jesus (upon whom be peace) once said, 'O assembly of disciples! Make your bellies hungry, that haply your hearts may behold your Lord!'[10] And Sahl ibn ʿAbd Allāh al-Tustarī said, 'The *Abdāl*[B] only attained their degree through four attributes: hungering the belly, sleeplessness, silence, and isolation from men'.[11] The benefit yielded by hunger to the illumination of the heart is an obvious thing to which experience attests; the method of progress therein shall be expounded in the *Book of Breaking the Two Desires*.

Sleeplessness also clears, purifies and illuminates the heart. When this is added to the clarity brought about by hunger the heart will be as *a shining star*,[12] and a polished mirror in which the beauty of the Truth blazes, so that a man comes to behold the exalted degrees of the Afterlife and the vileness and vices of the world, at which his turning away from this world in favour of the next will be complete. Sleeplessness is also a consequence of hunger, for it is impossible to stay

[A] As suggested in the well-known *ḥadīth*: 'The devil courses in man with the blood' (*Ma'thūr*, II. 374; ʿAjlūnī, 221; *Rasā'il Ikhwān al-ṣafā*, I. 364); expounded in Muḥāsibī, *Masā'il fi'l-zuhd*, 83ff, Abū Nuʿaym, *Ḥilya*, X. 272 (al-Junayd), Ibn al-Jawzī, *Talbīs*, 33–5, and Ibn ʿArabī, *Futūḥāt*, II. 248. Cited again below, p.111.

[B] The forty 'apotropean' saints who, although hidden, direct the world's spiritual activity. When one dies, his (or her) place is taken by another. Ranked above them, it is often held, there are seven *abrār*, four *awtād*, three *nuqabā'* and one *quṭb*. All are in continual communication and agreement. (Cf. Makkī, *Qūt*, I. 109; Hujwīrī, 214; Massignon, *Essai*, 132–4; *Passion*, I. 26–8; Jabre, *Lexique*, 23.)

awake at night on a full stomach. Sleep hardens and deadens the heart, unless, that is, it be done only in that amount which is needful, when it will conduce to the unveiling of the secrets of the Unseen. It has been said, describing the *Abdāl*, that they eat only what they need, sleep only when overcome, and speak only when necessary.[13] Said Ibrāhīm al-Khawwāṣ (may God have mercy upon him), 'Seventy Truthful Saints have agreed that abundant sleep is the result of drinking water in abundance.'

As for silence, this is facilitated by isolation.[14] However, the man who isolates himself by entering a retreat [*khalwa*] cannot help seeing the person who brings him his food and drink and who arranges his other affairs. He should therefore speak to him no more than is necessary, for speech distracts the heart, which is possessed of a tremendous greed for it since it is made relaxed thereby, and finds it a burdensome thing to apply itself exclusively to contemplation and the remembrance of God. Silence brings about a fecundity of the intellect, conduces to scrupulousness [*wara*ᶜ], and instructs one in piety.[A]

The advantage of entering a retreat[B] is that it dispels distractions and enables one to control one's hearing and vision, which are the entrance-halls of the heart, in the manner of a lake into which foul and turbid[15] water pours from the rivers of the senses: the purpose of spiritual discipline is to empty this lake of the water and the mud which it carried in with it, so that from the bottom of the lake clean and pure water might well up. How could such water be removed from the lake when these rivers continue to open into it, so that the water is constantly renewed even more rapidly than it can be drained away?

[A] The advantages of holding one's tongue are explored in detail elsewhere in the *Iḥyā'* (III. 92–142: *K. Āfāt al-lisān*).

[B] Another 'book' (II. 197–217: *K. Ādāb al-ᶜuzla*) of the *Iḥyā'* is consecrated to the advantages and disadvantages attaching to the practice of withdrawal from the world. Cf. also Introduction, p.XXIX above.

Whence is there no alternative to controlling the senses and preserving them from all save that which cannot be avoided. This can only be effected by going into a retreat in a darkened room,[16] or, if no such place is available, then by pulling up one's shirt so as to wrap the head in it, or by covering oneself with some other garment. At such times one may hear the call of the True God and behold the glory of the Lordly Presence.[A] Do you not see that the Summons to God's Emissary (may God bless him and grant him peace) reached him while he was in this state, so that it was said, *O thou wrapped one in thy raiment!*[17] and *O thou wrapped one in thy cloak!*?[B] [44]

These four things constitute a shield and fortress with the aid of which one may deflect the passing things [*ʿawāriḍ*] which block the path. Having done this, a man may then devote himself to treading it. This can only be achieved by travelling over the hills through which it passes, the highest of which are those attributes of the heart which are occasioned by one's inclination towards the world. Some of these are higher than others, and are to be overcome in a particular order, namely, that one should address oneself to the easier ones first, which will then help one to overcome the rest.[45] By these 'attributes' I refer to the inward realities of the attachments which one [ostensibly] severed at the outset of one's aspirancy, and also their effects (by which I mean wealth, reputation, love of the world, turning towards created things, and the yearning for sin): for one must empty one's inward aspect of these effects just as one divested one's outward of their visible causes. Although a protracted effort is required for this, it does differ in accordance with circumstance: some people have been preserved from some of

[A] Ar. *al-ḥaḍrat al-rubūbīya*: God as perceived by the gnostics through *kashf*. Cf. *Iḥyā'*, III. 13 (*K. ʿAjā'ib al-qalb*, Bayān mathal al-qalb); Jabre, *Lexique*, 67.

[B] In a celebrated incident of his biography, he had received one of the earliest revelations while in this condition. (See e.g. Bayḍāwī, 766 and 769; and, for an English account, Lings, *Muhammad*, 48.)

UNIVERSITY OF WINCHESTER
LIBRARY

these attributes, and must therefore labour for a shorter time.

We have already mentioned that the path of struggle comprises the opposing of one's desire and the disobedience of all the whims which may arise with regard to each dominant attribute of the aspirant's soul. When these things have been destroyed, or weakened by virtue of struggle, whereby not a single attachment remains, he must unceasingly occupy his heart with some form of remembrance and prevent it from engaging in any great variety of outward spiritual activities, restricting himself instead to the obligatory and regular supererogatory prayers. He should be performing only one spiritual activity, which is the kernel and fruit of all such acts: holding his heart to the remembrance of God (Exalted is He!), having emptied it of the remembrance of all else. Yet he may not busy himself with this for as long as his heart remains turned to its worldly ties.

Al-Shiblī once said to al-Ḥuṣarī, 'If, from one Friday when you pay me a visit to the next, there should occur to your heart anything but the remembrance of God, then you are forbidden to visit me.'[20] Such dedication can come about only when a man's aspirancy is true and his heart so overmastered by the love of God that he becomes like a passionate lover who has one concern alone.[A] When he arrives at this state the Shaykh will require him not to leave the lodge [*zāwiya*],[B] where he will stay on his

[A] Zabīdī (VII. 374) quotes here al-Rūdhbārī's definition of *irāda*: 'a pain in the heart, a passion in the mind, and a commotion in the soul'. The emotional intensity experienced by the beginner on the Way, generated both by his renunciation of old habits and by the appearance of the first gleams of the spiritual realities, is a favourite theme of Sufi literature, and of poetry in particular.

[B] By Ghazālī's time, Sufi groups had begun to gather in their own meeting houses, where certain novices would reside, and which would also be places for regular assemblies of 'lay' members, who would attend sessions of the invocation of God in the presence of the Shaykh. (See Schimmel, *Dimensions,* 231-4; E. Lévi-Provençal, art. 'Zāwiya', in *EI*, IV. 1220; Babs Mala, 'The Sufi Convent'.)

own, and be served by someone deputed to provide him with small quantities of licit food (for the religious path is founded on licit food).[A] The Shaykh will teach him a certain *dhikr*[B] with which he should occupy his tongue and his heart. He should sit and say, for example, '*Allāh, Allāh, Allāh,*' or '*Subḥān Allāh, Subḥān Allāh,*'[C] or such other phrases as his Shaykh may deem appropriate,[D] and persist in them until his tongue ceases to move and the phrase remains as though pronounced by it, but without the tongue moving at all.[21] Then he should continue until even the effect of the phrase disappears from the tongue and its form alone abides in the heart. He should next persevere until the form and letters of the phrase are erased from his heart while the reality of its meaning remains therein, is present with it, and prevails in it entirely.[E] The heart will then be empty of all else, since whenever it is preoccupied with some matter it will be void of all others, whatever these might be; therefore when it is occupied with the remembrance of God, which is its true function, will it needs fall empty of all other things.

[A] The importance of nourishing the body, which is connected in a subtle fashion with the spirit which pervades it, on *ḥalāl* sustenance, that is, food and drink whose origin is demonstrably lawful, is routinely stressed in the Sufi literature. For instance, Abū Yazīd, cited in Sahlajī's *K. al-Nūr* (published in Badawī, *Shaṭaḥāt*, 168): 'The concern of the ascetic [*zāhid*] is not to eat, while the concern of the gnostic [*ʿārif*] is what to eat'. It is addressed by Ghazālī in the *K. al-Ḥalāl wa'l-ḥarām* of the *Iḥyā'* (II. 79–138). See also note A on p. 133 below; cf. also Bayhaqī, *Seventy-Seven Branches of Faith*, tr. Murad, 30–5.

[B] Here, any set formula by which God is recalled and invoked.

[C] Meaning, 'Glorious/Transcendant is God!' For the use of this formula in Ghazālī's Sufism see *Iḥyā'*, I. 269-71 (*K. al-Adhkār*, Faḍīlat al-tasbīḥ), tr. Nakamura [2nd ed.], 15-20); for its interpretation see Nakamura, 115, and references there given.

[D] Other such phrases are listed by Ghazālī in the *K. al-Adhkār*, passim; cf. also *Iḥyā'*, IV. 71 (*K. al-Ṣabr*, rukn 1, Bayān ḥadd al-shukr; tr. Gramlich, *Lehre*, 182).

[E] Ghazālī has here given a brief summary of the doctrine of the three degrees of *dhikr*, for which see Nakamura, XXVI.

At this time he should guard his heart against whisperings and notions[A] connected with the world, and against the recollections it holds of his former circumstances and those of other men. For whenever it concerns itself with such things, even for a moment, it is guilty of remissness: this is something he should therefore strive diligently to avoid. When he repels all such whisperings and returns his soul to the phrase, certain other whisperings may emerge from the phrase itself: about its nature, about what we mean by the word 'Allāh,' and for what reason He is a god and is to be worshipped, so that notions come to him which open a gateway into thought.[B] The devil may whisper to him things which constitute disbelief, or heresy [*bid*ᶜ*a*]; however, insofar as he is repelled by these and strives to extirpate them from his heart, will they do him no harm.

Passing notions may be divided into two categories. There are those concerning which one knows for certain that God is far exalted above what they purport, but which are cast by the devil into the heart and made to run in the consciousness: to these one must pay no heed, but should rather rush fearfully back to the remembrance of God, and pray humbly that He should drive them away. As God has said: *And if a whisper from the devil come to you, then seek refuge in God. Truly, He is Hearing, Knowing. And those who are Godfearing, should a suspicion from the devil trouble them, remember God,*[C] *and behold, they see!*[22] [Secondly,] there are those

[A] For these *wasāwis* and *khawāṭir*, see Introduction, LXVII.

[B] Thought (*fikr*) is hardly discouraged by Ghazālī, as we will shortly discover; this passage is simply a warning against the Satanic insinuations and poor concentration common at a certain stage of the Path.

[C] Ar: *tadhakkarū*, which Bell renders as 'recollect themselves'. (*The Qur'ān Translated*, I. 157.) Asad (*The Message of the Qur'an*, 235) has 'bethink themselves [of Him]', while Suyūṭī and Maḥallī (*Jalālayn*, on this verse), suggest 'remember [His punishment and reward]'.

For a Sufi interpretation of the entire verse see Muḥāsibī, *Masā'il fi'l-zuhd*, 67–8; also *Iḥyā'*, x. III (*K. ᶜAjā'ib al-qalb*, Bayān majāmiᶜ awṣāf al-qalb), where Ghazālī uses it as a proof-text to establish that *dhikr* purifies the heart.

which give rise to doubts. These the aspirant should put before his Shaykh (just as he should put before him every state which he discovers in his heart, whether this be lassitude, zeal, inclination to some attachment, or sincerity in his aspirancy, and hide these things from others so that no other man comes to know of them). His Shaykh will then look into his state and study his intelligence and perceptiveness. If he discovers that were he to leave the aspirant and enjoin him to think he would spontaneously come to understand the truth, then he should induce him to think, and instruct him to use his mind constantly until such light is cast into his heart as will unveil this to him. However, should he know that the aspirant is not sufficiently strong for such a practice he will simply restore to him his certainty in his doctrine by means of such admonitions and proofs acceptable to his understanding as his mind may bear.[23]

The Shaykh should be kind and gentle with him, for it is these things which constitute the deadly traps and hazardous places which lie along the Path. Many an aspirant has busied himself with self-discipline only to be overcome with some unsound imagining which he proved unable to renounce, so that the Path became blocked for him and he occupied himself with a vain and distracting idleness, and followed the way of antinomianism [*ibāḥa*], which leads to complete destruction.[A] A man who devotes himself

[A] *Ibāḥa* is the term for an attitude of indifference to the revealed law, a position, as stated above, p.87C, which was evidently repugnant to mainstream Sufism.

In the *Iḥyā'*, Ghazālī speaks of three main types of *ibāḥa* known to him. Firstly, there is the man who claims that since God can have no need of his works, these may therefore be dispensed with. Secondly, there is he who asserts that acts of worship and self-purification have no effect on the soul, and hence may as well be abandoned. Thirdly, and most dangerously, there is he who claims that when the love of God supplants every other love in the heart, the legal obligations and interdictions can no longer be of value. All of these people, Ghazālī writes, have been led astray by the devil, because they have undertaken acts of spiritual discipline without the benefit of sufficient knowledge, or the guidance of an authentic and knowledgeable Shaykh. (*Iḥyā'*, III.

to remembrance[24] and to fending off distracting attachments from his heart will necessarily be exposed to such thoughts as these. It is as though he had boarded a ship for a dangerous voyage; if he arrives safely he will be one of the kings of the Faith, while should he make a mistake he will most certainly go to perdition. It was for this reason that the Emissary of God (may God bless him and grant him peace) said, 'Follow the religion of old women!'[A 25] By this he meant taking the fundamentals of faith and the exoteric doctrine by imitation [*taqlīd*], and busying oneself with good works; for to diverge from this is a thing perilous indeed. Therefore has it been said that it is vital that the Shaykh look inside [*yatafarras*] his aspirant,[B] and, if he find him to be neither intelligent nor perceptive, yet solidly rooted in the exoteric doctrine, should not occupy him with remembrance and meditation, but should rather cause him

348-9 [*K. Dhamm al-Ghurūr*, ṣinf 3].) For more on *ibāḥa*, see Hujwīrī, 312; Qushayrī, *Risāla*, 117; Ghazālī, *Mustaẓhirī*, 111; Muḥāsibī, *Masā'il fi'l-zuhd*, 70; Ibn al-Jawzī, *Talbīs*, 463-9; Çubukçu, *Şüphecilik*, 51; Massignon, *Passion*, III. 207.

There exists a work known as the *Refutation of the Ibāḥīya*, (*al-Radd ʿalā al-ibāḥīya*), which is often ascribed to Ghazālī, and has been edited and translated into German by Otto Pretzl as an authentic Ghazālian composition. Its provenance has been seriously questioned, however, by Badawī (*Mu'allafāt*, 467-8).

[A] A well-known proverb intended to encourage simplicity and sincerity in faith. (Suyūṭī, *Durar*, 136.)

[B] *Tafarrus*, the practice of *firāsa*, refers to 'knowing the noble aspects of the soul by [noticing] the dispositions of the body ['body language'], so that they said: "The face and the eye are the mirrors of the heart".' (*Iḥyā'*, IV. 91 [*K. al-Ṣabr*, rukn 2, Bayān ḥaqīqat al-niʿma; tr. Gramlich, *Lehre*, 226].) Elsewhere, Ghazālī explains the more supernatural and telepathic aspects of this art (*Iḥyā'*, III. 20-2 [*K. ʿAjā'ib al-qalb*, Bayān shawāhid al-sharʿ ...]), which enable the Shaykh to look within the soul of his disciple by virtue of a light granted his own heart by God. Cf. further Kalābādhī, tr. Arberry, 8, 132; Anṣārī Harawī, *Manāzil*, 136-8; Qushayrī, *Risāla*, 480-93; ʿAbbādī, *Manāqib*, 127-31; Corbin, *Avicenna*, 296n. The definitions of Jabre (*Lexique*, 221) are insufficient, reducing *firāsa* to a mere art of physiognomic divination without the deployment of any higher spiritual perception.

to persevere in exoteric works and the well-known duties of religion, and make him serve those who have divested themselves of all things but meditation, so that he gains from the blessing of their company. For a man who is unable to participate in the front lines of battle in the *Jihād* should provide water for the warriors and look after their mounts, that he might be resurrected on the Day of Arising in their company and be included in their blessedness even had he not attained to their degree.

An aspirant who has devoted himself to remembrance and meditation [*fikr*] may be divided from the Path by many things, such as self-satisfaction, ostentation, or joy at the states which are unveiled to him, and at the initial charismata [*awā'il al-karāmāt*].[A] To the extent that he pays attention to such things, so that his soul is occupied[26] with them, he will be caused to slacken or[27] stop altogether in his wayfaring on the Path. He should instead keep to his [directed] condition all his life in the manner of a thirsty man whose craving for water would not be slaked by whole oceans

[A] A frequent and grave hazard. So powerful is the impact of a supernatural event on the consciousness that God may distinguish thereby the true from the false saints. The former are made 'all the more humble, submissive, fearful and lowly towards God, and the more contemptuous of themselves,' while the latter 'imagine that they are miracles which they have merited by their actions' (Kalābā<u>dh</u>ī, tr. Arberry, 59).

'A man once came to Sahl al-Tustarī, and said: Abū Muḥammad, sometimes when I perform the ablution for ritual prayer (*ṣalāt*), the water flows from my hands and forms into a rod of gold and a rod of silver. Sahl said to him: My friend, you know that boys when they weep are given a rattle to keep them busy. So watch out what you are doing'. (Tustarī, *Tafsīr*, 46, cited in Böwering, 84.)

Cf. Abū Yazīd: 'It is not remarkable for someone to walk on water. There are many people who walk on water who are not of the least value in God's sight.' (Cited by Sahlajī [Badawī, *<u>Sh</u>aṭaḥāt*, 172].)

For the question of *karāmāt* generally, a phenomenon acknowledged by both the *falsafa* and Sunnī orthodoxy but distinguished carefully from that of the *muʿjizāt* (miracles worked by prophets), see, for instance, Hujwīrī, 218-35; Antes, *Prophetenwunder*, 32-4; Gardet, *Pensée*, 183-4; idem, *La Connaissance Mystique*, 49-52; Andrae, 88-9; Massignon, *Passion*, I. 291-5.

were they to be poured over him. Thus should he continue, making use of his capital, which is isolation from creation in order to be with the True God,[28] and living in a state of retreat.

An itinerant dervish once said, 'I asked one of those *Abdāl*[A] who have isolated themselves from mankind how one attains to realisation. And he replied, "Be in this world as though a wayfarer."'[B] On another occasion he said, 'I asked him to tell me of an action through which I would find my heart to be in God's presence at all times, and he told me, "Do not look at mankind, for to look at mankind brings darkness [to the heart]." "I cannot avoid doing so," I told him. "Then do not listen to what they say," he said, "for their words induce a hardness [in the heart]." "I cannot avoid doing so," I said. And then he told me, "Do not have any dealings with them, for to do so brings disharmony." "I live amongst them," I said, "and cannot renounce my dealings with them." "Then do not feel calm in their presence," he said, "for this leads to destruction." "That is the basis [of my happiness]," I remarked. And he said, "An astonishing thing it is that you would have! You look at the heedless, listen to the ignorant, deal with the idle, and still hope that you will find your heart to be in God's presence at all times! Such a thing can never be".'[29]

The final purpose of self-discipline, then, is to find one's heart constantly in the presence of God. This it will only be able to attain when by virtue of long inward strife[30] it has been emptied of all else. When the heart comes into God's presence, the glory of the Lordly Presence will stand unveiled before it, and the True God will become manifest to it, and from the subtle effusions of His mercy will appear a thing which it is forbidden to describe, or which rather cannot be compassed by any description at all.[C]

When some part of this has been unveiled to the aspirant the

[A] For the *abdāl* see note B on p.89 above.

[B] 'Be in this world as though a wayfarer' is a well-known saying of the Prophet (Bukhārī, Riqāq, 3).

[C] See Introduction, p.LXVIII.

greatest barrier for him is to speak about it, whether as advice or as part of a sermon. For the soul will find intense pleasure in this, which will induce him to think about how to express what he has seen in an attractive way, and how to set it in the correct order, and how to adorn it with stories and supporting texts from the Qur'ān and the Traditions, and how to make his discourse eloquent so that the hearts of others may incline to it. The devil may well deceive him into thinking that he is thereby bringing life to the hearts of the dead, who are heedless of God (Great and Glorious is He!), and tell him that 'You are a mediator between God and man, whom you call to Him. You yourself have no interest in the matter, neither does your soul find any delight therein.' The devil's ruse is exposed when there appear among such a man's associates people whose discourse is finer and more lucid than his own, and who are more able to attract the hearts of the commonalty, so that if his motive had been the desire for a responsive audience the scorpion of envy will stir within him, while had it truly been a desire to call the bondsmen of God to His *Straight Path*, then will he be possessed by exceeding joy, and declare, 'Praised be God, Who has supported and aided me with someone who shares my burden in the reform of His bondsmen!' This is like the case of someone who—for example—is obliged by the Law to carry a man who had died in poverty to his place of burial, and who is joined by someone who helps him: he will rejoice at this, and will not feel any envy of his assistant. The people of heedlessness are themselves dead, while those who deliver religious discourses wake them up and give them life. Therefore, when they are numerous there obtains ease and mutual support, which is something which ought to inspire rejoicing. (Such a thing, however, is exceedingly rare.) Therefore the aspirant should be on his guard against such notions, for they are the greatest artifices the Devil possesses in blocking the Path for those to whom its initial stages have been discovered.[A]

[A] The dangers of speaking in public are examined in Muḥāsibī, *Masā'il fī*

A preference for the life of this world is man's dominant trait: God (Exalted is He!) has said, *Yet do you prefer the life of this world, while the Afterlife is finer and more lasting.*[31] Then He states that evil is an ancient part of human nature, and that this was mentioned in the earlier scriptures: *This was in the former scrolls; even the scrolls of Abraham and Moses.*[32]

In this wise, then, is the method by which the aspirant should be progressively disciplined and trained until he comes to the encounter with God (Exalted is He!). The details of self-discipline as these are to be applied to each trait of character shall be set forth in due course. The most powerful of these are the desires associated with eating, sexuality and speech, and also anger, which is like an army set up for the protection of the desires. To the extent that a man loves and takes pleasure in his greed and his lust he will love the things of this world. And these, in turn, he can only acquire properly when he has money and a reputation, which lead him on to pride, self-satisfaction and authority. When he reaches this state his soul will not permit him any renunciation of the world, and he will hold fast to those aspects of religion which involve leadership, and will be overcome by self-delusion.

Having presented these two books,[A] we must, God willing, now complete the 'Quarter of the Destructive Vices' with eight further Books. These shall be as follows: a Book on Breaking the Two Desires (of Gluttony and of Sexual Desire); a Book on the Faults of the Tongue;[33] a Book on the Subjugation of Anger, Rancour and Envy;[34] a Book on the Condemnation of the World, which will detail the deceptions which it contains; a Book

aʿmāl al-qulūb, 133-9. Perhaps the most famous instance of a Sufi declining to speak publicly is that of Junayd, who only changed his mind when the Prophet himself appeared to him in a dream, and instructed him to do so (Hujwīrī, 129).

[A] The present work, and the *Book of Expounding the Wonders of the Heart* which immediately precedes it, which is summarised below, 233-243.

on Subjugating the Love of Money, and the Condemnation of Avarice; a Book on the Condemnation of Ostentation and the Love of Status; a Book on the Condemnation of Pride and Self-Satisfaction; and a Book on the Sources of Self-Delusion.[A] When we have discussed these destructive vices and expounded the ways in which they may be cured, our purpose in writing this Quarter shall, God willing, have been satisfied. For our discourse in the first Book[B] constituted an explanation of the attributes of the heart, which is the place of origin of the destructive vices and the saving virtues, while this second Book is an overall indication of the way by which the traits of character may be refined and the diseases of the heart cured. God willing, these traits shall be treated in a more detailed fashion in the forthcoming Books.

Here concludes, with praises to God, and by His aid and good providence, the *Book of Disciplining the Soul and Refining the Character.* God willing, it shall be followed by the *Book of Breaking the Two Desires.* Praised be God Alone. May He bless our Master Muḥammad, his Family and Companions, and His every chosen bondsman on earth and in heaven. *My success is from God alone; upon Him do I rely, and unto Him do I repent.*[35]

[A] Ar. *ghurūr*, a difficult word to translate. Asín (*Espiritualidad*, I. 458) suggests 'ilusión espiritual', which conveys the intention quite well. *Ghurūr* denotes an attitude of beguilement, illusion, vainglory, temptation, self-satisfaction, distraction: a vice which turns man aside from the quest for God.

[B] On the Wonders of the Heart.

THE BOOK OF BREAKING THE TWO DESIRES

Kitāb kasr al-shahwatayn

BOOK XXIII OF THE REVIVAL OF THE RELIGIOUS SCIENCES

Ihya' ʿUlūm-al-Dīn

THE BOOK OF BREAKING THE TWO DESIRES

Being the Third Book of the Quarter of Mortal Vices

[PROLOGUE]

In the Name of God, Most Compassionate and Merciful

PRAISED BE GOD, in His glory and height the sole possessor of majesty, Who is worthy to be praised, hallowed, extolled and exalted above all comparison; Who is ever Just in His judgements and decrees; Gracious without cause in His blessings and gifts; Who has taken it upon Himself to protect His bondsman in his every provenance and course; and Who does grant to him more than is his need, and even that which fulfills his hopes. For He it is that guides and leads him, slays and quickens him, heals him when he ails, strengthens him when he weakens, guides him to His obedience until He is well-pleased with him, feeds and waters him,[1] protects him from perishing and preserves him, and by means of food and drink safeguards him from his death and destruction. With little nourishment strengthens He him[2] and makes him content, so that the courses of Satan's assails are straitened, and he subjugates thereby the desires[3] of his soul which makes war on him. Wherefore, having warded off its evil, does he worship his Lord, and hold Him in fear and piety.

Then has He bestowed upon him such things as give him delectation and delight, and has abundantly aroused inducements in him and reinforced his temptations,[4] in order that He might prove and try him, and behold how he might prefer Him over his desires and ambitions, and in what manner he shall respect His ordinances and prohibitions, persevere in His obedience, and restrain himself from sinning against Him.

AND MAY BLESSINGS BE INVOKED upon our master Muḥammad, His noble bondsman and excellent Emissary, whereby his rank and degree may be exalted and his closeness to his Lord increased, and upon the righteous of his Family and House, and the best of his Companions and Followers.

To proceed. The greatest of the mortal vices which a man may harbour is the desire of the stomach. Because of it were Adam and Eve (upon whom be peace) expelled from the Abode of Permanence into the abode of humiliation and poverty; for although they had been forbidden the Tree their desire overcame them so that they ate from it, and *their private parts did become apparent unto them.*[5] After the belly, which is the very wellspring of desires and the source of diseases and disorders,[A] comes the desire of the sex and voracious appetite for women, and then yearning after fame and wealth, which are no more than means which enable one to indulge one's greed and desire in still greater measure. And after the acquisition of fame and wealth come the several kinds of frivolities, competitions and jealousies. They also give rise to the vices of ostentation, boasting, competition for

[A] Cf. the alleged statement of the Prophet, 'the stomach is the house of sickness', a belief deeply entrenched in medieval Muslim culture. This *ḥadīth* is recorded in Sakhāwī, 611; Ibn Ḥajar, *Lisān al-mīzān*, I. 43; Zamakhsharī, *Fā'iq*, I. 102. Cf. also *Qūt*, II. 179; Maghribī, *Siyāsa*, 58. In the *Mukhtār al-ḥikam*, the anthology of popular Greek wisdom compiled by Mubashshir ibn Fātik, the Arabs were reminded of Hippocrates' teaching that health can be preserved by not eating to satiety (p.49).

wealth, and arrogance, which in turn lead to rancour, envy, enmity and hate, which go to cause iniquity, injustice and corruption. All of these things are the consequence of paying insufficient heed to the stomach, and of the arrogant exulting which is begotten of satiety and eating one's fill. Were the bondsman only to humble his soul through hunger, and thereby narrow the courses which the devil pursues within him, it would give itself up to the obedience of God (Great and Glorious is He!) and would renounce the way of exultation and excess, so that he would be preserved from being dragged by these things into a preoccupation with the world and into preferring this present abode to that which is to come, and would never be so avid for worldly things.

Since the defect of the stomach waxes so powerful, it is incumbent to provide an exposition of its dangers and evils so that this may act as a warning in its regard, and likewise to explain the way in which it is to be resisted, and to draw attention to the merit which lies in this, by way of encouragement; likewise in the case of sexual desire, which is its subordinate. With God's help, we shall expound this in a number of Sections. These are: an Exposition of the Merit of Hunger, followed by a Mention of its Benefits, then the Method by which Discipline is Used to Subjugate the Greed of the Stomach by Delaying and Reducing the Food of which one Partakes, an Exposition of the Variance of the Rule and Merit of Hunger in Accordance with the Circumstances of Men, an Exposition of the Ostentation[6] which may follow from the Renunciation of Desire,[7] a Discourse on Sexual Desire, an Exposition of the Disciple's Obligations regarding the Renunciation or Undertaking of Marriage, and an Exposition of the Merit of him who Counters Greed and the Desire of the Sex and of the Eye.

[23.1]

An Exposition of the Merit of Hunger and a Condemnation of Satiety

THE EMISSARY of God (may God bless him and grant him peace) said, 'Make war on your souls with hunger and with thirst, for the reward which this brings is as that of participation in the *Jihād*. There is no action more beloved in the sight of God than to hunger and to thirst.'[8]

And Ibn ᶜAbbās said, 'The Emissary of God (may God bless him and grant him peace) said, 'Whoso fills up his belly shall not enter into the Kingdom of Heaven.'[9]

He was once asked, 'O Emissary of God! Who is the best of men?' And he replied, 'He who eats and laughs but little, and is content with such [clothes] as suffice to cover his private parts.'[10]

And the Prophet said (may God bless him and grant him peace), 'Hunger is the lord of all actions, while the wearing of wool brings about humility of soul.'[11]

Said Abū Saᶜīd al-Khudrī, 'The Emissary of God (may God bless him and grant him peace) once said, "Wear your clothes, and eat and drink up to the middle of your stomachs, for to do this is part of Prophethood".'[12]

Said al-Ḥasan, 'The Prophet (may God bless him and grant him peace) once remarked, "Meditation is half of worship, while eating frugally is all of it".'[13]

And al-Ḥasan said also,[14] 'The Prophet (may God bless him and grant him peace), once said, "The most exalted amongst you in God's sight on the Day of Judgement shall be those who hungered and meditated the longest for His sake (Glorified is He!), while the most loathsome amongst you in His sight on that Day will be those who slept, ate and drank abundantly".'[15]

It is related in Tradition that the Prophet (may God bless him and grant him peace) used to hunger without any exigency, that is, by choice.[16]

And he said (may God bless him and grant him peace), 'Truly, God (Exalted is He!) glories before His angels regarding the man who eats and drinks but little in the world,[17] saying, "Behold My bondsman! I did try him with food and drink in the world, yet was he steadfast and renounced them. Bear witness, O My angels, that he renounced not a single morsel but that I vouchsafed him thereby a higher degree in Heaven".'[18]

And he said (may God bless him and grant him peace), 'Slay not your hearts with much food and drink, for the heart is like a farmland which dies if watered excessively'.[19]

And he said (may God bless him and grant him peace), 'A descendant of Adam can fill no container worse than his own belly. A few small mouthfuls should suffice to keep his back straight; if he cannot keep to this, then let him fill one third with his food, one third with his drink, and keep the other for his breath.'[20]

The meritorious nature of hunger is mentioned in the long Tradition told by Usāma ibn Zayd and Abū Hurayra, in which the Prophet (may God bless him and grant him peace) said, 'The nearest of all men to God (Great and Glorious is He!) on the Day of Arising[21] shall be those who were often hungry, thirsty and sad in this world, and who were affectionate and Godfearing; who, when seen, went unrecognised, and who, when absent, were never missed by men, but yet were known to the provinces of the earth and were compassed by the angels of heaven. Others rejoiced in the world, but they rejoiced in their obedience to God (Great and Glorious is He!). Others made soft beds for themselves, while they rested only on their foreheads and their knees. Others caused the works and morals of the Prophets to be lost, while they observed them. The earth itself weeps when it loses them, and the Almighty's wrath descends upon every land in which they are not found. They did not rush into the world as dogs descend upon a carcass; rather did they eat such food as was sufficient to retain life, wear patched raiment, and were dishevelled and dusty-headed. When people saw them they thought them to be sick, yet they were not sick. It was said, "They are deranged; they have lost their minds"; yet they were of sound mind, it was only that the people's hearts beheld the decree of God, which had divested them of the world, so that for the world's people they walked without minds. Yet when the minds of the people had departed from them, it was they who understood. Theirs is the honour of the Afterlife. O Usāma![22] When you see them in a land, know that they are a source of protection for its people, for God shall never loose His chastisement upon a nation amongst whom they live. The very earth rejoices at them, and with them the Almighty is well-pleased. Therefore hold them for your brethren, that perhaps they will be the cause of your salvation. And if you can live so that when death comes to you your stomach hungers and your liver thirsts, then you shall attain to the most exalted ranks, and shall abide with the Prophets; the angels themselves shall rejoice at the advent of your spirit, and the Almighty shall grant you His blessing.'[23]

Al-Ḥasan (may God be pleased with him) relates on the authority of Abū Hurayra that the Prophet (may God bless him and grant him peace) said, 'Wear garments of wool, and roll up your sleeves, and eat with only half your bellies; for thereby shall you enter into the Kingdom of Heaven'.[24]

Jesus (upon whom be peace) once said, 'O company of disciples! Cause your livers to hunger and your bodies to go naked, that perhaps your hearts may behold God (Great and Glorious is He!)'.[25] This [saying] has also been handed down from our own Prophet (may God bless him and grant him peace) on the authority of Ṭāwūs.[26]

It is said that it is written in the Torah that God loathes a corpulent divine.[27] This is because corpulence is a sign of heedlessness and an abundant indulgence in food, something which is especially ugly in the case of a divine. It was for this reason that Ibn Masʿūd (may God be pleased with him) said, 'God abhors a reader [of the Qur'ān] who has become corpulent through frequent satiety'.[28]

In a *mursal*[A] Tradition it is said that 'The devil courses with the blood in the descendants of Adam; straiten, therefore, his courses with hunger and thirst'.[B 29]

It is related in Tradition that to eat when already sated is conducive to leprosy.[30]

And he said (may God bless him and grant him peace), 'The believer eats with one gut, while the hypocrite[31] eats with seven'[32]. Or, 'his appetite is seven times as great as that of the believer', using the word 'gut' as a metaphor for 'appetite', for this latter accepts food just as does the gut: the meaning is not that the hypocrite actually has more numerous guts than the believer.

Al-Ḥasan relates that ʿĀ'isha (may God be pleased with her) said, 'I once heard the Emissary of God (may God bless him and grant him peace) say, "Knock persistently on Heaven's door, and it shall be opened unto you". "How should we do that?" I asked, and he replied, "With hunger and thirst".'[33]

It is related that Abū Juḥayfa once belched while sitting with the Emissary of God (may God bless him and grant him peace), who said, 'You should belch less; for those who were most sated in this world shall hunger the longest on the Day of Arising'[34].

ʿĀ'isha (may God be pleased with her) used to say, 'The Emissary of God (may God bless him and grant him peace)

[A] Variously defined, a *ḥadīth mursal* is a Tradition impaired by the omission of an early transmitter from its chain of authorities. Cf. Jurjānī, *Taʿrīfāt*, 15; Kamali, *Principles*, 79.

[B] For this statement see above, p.89A.

never ate to satiety: sometimes, seeing his hunger, I would weep out of pity for him, and rub his belly with my hand, saying, "May I be your ransom![A] Why do you not partake in the things of this world inasmuch as would strengthen you and preserve you from hunger?" But he would only say, "O ʿĀ'isha! My brethren, the resolute among the Emissaries, were steadfast in the face of circumstances still harsher,[B] but persevered, so that when they came to their Lord He vouchsafed them a generous place of return and a munificent reward. Thus it is that I find myself ashamed to enjoy any comforts in this life, lest on the morrow I might not attain to their degree. Steadfastness for a few days is preferable to me than to see my lot reduced tomorrow in the Afterlife; for of all things, that which I desire most is that I should catch up with my companions and my brethren".' She remarked, 'And, by God, it was no more than a week thereafter when God took him unto Himself.'[35]

Said Anas, 'Fāṭima (may God be pleased with her) once brought a piece of bread to the Emissary of God (may God bless him and grant him peace). "What is this?" he enquired, and she said, "I have just baked a loaf, and my soul would not be still until I had brought this piece to you." "It is the first food to have passed the lips of your father for three days", he remarked.'[36]

Said Abū Hurayra, 'Never did the Prophet (may God bless him and grant him peace) eat his fill of wheat-bread for three consecutive days until he left this world'[37].

And he said (may God bless him and grant him peace), 'Those who hunger in this world shall be fed handsomely in the next. Truly, the most hateful of men in God's sight is he who is replete and suffers from indigestion. No bondsman renounces a morsel which he had desired without it raising his degree in Heaven.'[38]

[A] A stock expression indicating devotion.

[B] A reference to Q.XLVI:35: *And be steadfast, even as were the resolute among the emissaries* [*of old*]. These are commonly identified as Noah, Abraham, Moses, and Jesus. (Bayḍāwī, 670.)

The Narratives

ʿUmar (may God be pleased with him) has said, 'Beware of satiety, for it is a burden in life and a source of corruption after death.'

Said Shaqīq al-Balkhī, 'Worship is a trade, the shop of which is one's retreat, and whose tool is hunger'.

Luqmān once said to his son, 'O my son! When the belly is full, then the intellect sleeps, wisdom is silenced, and the members of the body are too slothful to perform any act of worship.'

Al-Fuḍayl ibn ʿIyāḍ used to say [to his soul], 'What is it that you fear? Are you afraid of hunger? Be not so, for you are of too little account in God's sight for that. Only Muḥammad (may God bless him and grant him peace) and his Companions were [truly] hungry'.

Kahmas used to say, 'God of mine! Thou hast rendered me hungry and naked, and hast caused me to sit in the darkness of the night without any lamp. For what cause hast Thou given me to attain this thing?'

Whenever Fatḥ al-Mawṣilī was hungry and grievously ill he would say, 'God of mine! Thou hast tried me with hunger and disease, as is Thy wont with Thy Saints; by what act, therefore, may I show my gratitude for that with which Thou hast blessed me?'[39]

Said Mālik ibn Dīnār, 'I once said to Muḥammad ibn Wāsiʿ, "O Abū ʿAbd Allāh! Blessed is he who has a source of income which strengthens him and makes him independant of other men." But he said, "O Abū Yaḥyā! Blessed is he who hungers morning and night, and yet is well-pleased with his Lord".'

Al-Fuḍayl ibn ʿIyāḍ used to say, 'O my God! Thou hast made me and my family to hunger, and hast left me without a lamp in the darkness of the night. In this wise dost Thou act with Thy Saints; by what rank, then, have I won from Thee this thing?'

Said Yaḥyā ibn Muʿādh, 'The hunger of the yearners wakes them, the hunger of the penitent[40] tests them, the hunger of the strivers ennobles them, the hunger of the steadfast gives them power, and the hunger of the ascetics invests them with wisdom.'[41]

In the Torah it is written: 'Fear God; and when you are sated, recall the hungry'.

Said Abū Sulaymān, 'To forsake one morsel of my supper is preferable to me than to spend the whole night in prayer'.[42]

And he said also, 'Hunger reposes in the storehouses of God, Who gives it only to those He loves'.[43]

Sahl al-Tustarī used to go for twenty-odd days together without eating.[44] One dirham would suffice him for the whole year.[45] He used to stress the importance of hunger, and go to extreme lengths in it, to the extent that he said, 'On the Day of Arising, no good work shall be finer than the renunciation of unnecessary food done in imitation of the Prophet (may God bless him and grant him peace).' And he said also, 'Men of intelligence have never seen anything more beneficial to one's religious and mundane life than hunger.' And he said, 'I know of nothing which is more damaging to those who seek the Afterlife than food.' And he said, 'Wisdom and knowledge have been set in hunger, and ignorance and sin in satiety.'[46] And he said, 'There is no finer means of worshipping God than to disobey one's whims by renouncing something lawful'.

Regarding the Tradition of 'one-third for one's food'[A] he [Sahl] said, 'Whoever exceeds this is merely eating up his own good works'. He was asked how one could do more, and replied, 'He shall not do more until refraining is more desirable to him than eating, and until, when he hungers for one night he prays God to make him hunger for two; when this occurs he will be doing more'.

And he said, 'The *Abdāl* attained their rank only by making their bellies slender, and through sleeplessness, silence and solitude'.[47]

[A] See above p. 109.

And he said, 'The beginning of every virtue sent down from heaven to earth is hunger, and the beginning of every vice which exists between the twain is satiety'.

And he said, 'Whosoever makes himself hungry is severed from the whisperings [of the devil]'.[A]

And he said, 'God draws nearer to His bondsman through his hunger, illness and tribulation—save those whom He will.'[48]

And he said, 'Know that this is an age in which no man shall attain to salvation save by slaughtering his soul, which is to be done by means of hunger, sleeplessness and [inner] strife'.[B 49]

And he said, 'Not a single man who has walked the face of the earth has drunk his fill of water and remained safe from sin, even if he rendered thanks to God (Exalted is He!); what therefore must the case be when one is sated on food?'

A sage was once asked, 'By what rope may I tie my soul?' and he replied, 'You should tie it with the rope of hunger and thirst, and bring it low by extinguishing your pride and forsaking being mentioned,[50] and should reduce it by setting it under the feet of the sons of the Afterlife,[C] and break it by renouncing the appearance of the rich.[51] Save yourself from its defects by always harbouring a poor opinion of it, and make it tractable by disobeying its whims'.

ʿAbd al-Wāḥid ibn Zayd used to swear by God that God has never purified anyone save through hunger, and that no-one has walked on air and[52] water or has had the distances of the earth folded up for him, or has been made one of His saints, save by virtue thereof.[53]

Said Abū Ṭālib al-Makkī, 'The stomach is like a *muzhir*,[D]

[A] 'Because hunger restricts the courses by which the devil reaches the heart' (Zabīdī, VII. 393). See also above p. LXVII.

[B] Tustarī continues: 'because of the corruption of the people of our age' (*Muʿāraḍa*, 23).

[C] That is, the people who strive for salvation.

[D] Although this word was applied to various musical instruments, including drums, what is intended here is probably a kind of lute. (Cf. Maḥfūẓ, *Muʿjam al-mūsīqā al-ʿarabīya*, 49.)

which is a hollow stick with strings, for the beauty of its sound proceeds only from its lightness and delicacy, and because it is hollow and not filled. The stomach is similar to it, for when it is empty of food and drink[54] it renders one's [Qur'ānic] recitation sweeter, one's standing [in night prayer] more constant, and one's sleep briefer.'

Said Bakr ibn ᶜAbd Allāh al-Mazanī, 'Three men are beloved of God (Exalted is He!): he who sleeps little, he who eats little, and he who rests little'.

It is related that Jesus (upon whom be peace) once communed with his Lord for sixty days, during which time he did not eat. While he was doing this, the thought of bread entered his mind, and his communing was broken off; and behold! a loaf had been set before him. He sat down and wept over having lost his communing, and lo! there before him stood an old man, looking over him. 'O Saint of God!' Jesus said, 'May God bless you![55] Pray God for me, for I was in a state which was interrupted when the [mere] thought of bread occurred to me!' And the old man [prayed, and] said, 'O Lord God! Shouldst Thou know that I have thought of bread since the time I attained knowledge of Thee, then never forgive me. Rather, whenever something came before me I ate it without any thought or distraction'.[56]

It is told that when Moses (upon whom be peace) was brought nigh in communing[A] he had forsaken food for forty days: first thirty, and then ten more, as is stated in the Qur'ān;[B] for one night he had not fasted, and was given ten more days as a result.

[A] Cf. Q.XIX:52: *We called unto him from the right slope of the Mount, and brought him nigh in communing.*

[B] Q.VII:142: *And when We did appoint for Moses thirty nights, and added to them ten more, wherefore he completed the time appointed by his Lord of forty nights.*

[23.2]
An Exposition of the Benefits of Hunger and the Evils of Satiety

THE EMISSARY of God (may God bless him and grant him peace) said, 'Make war on your souls by means of hunger and thirst, for the reward which this brings ... '[A]

Now, you may ask: 'This great merit which attaches to hunger: from what thing does it proceed, and what reason is there for it? For hunger comprises no more than hurting the stomach and enduring torment, and if there be reward in such things then man should be rewarded generously for every hurt which he sustains, including blows which he directs against himself, cutting his own flesh, swallowing loathsome objects, and similar actions'. You should know, however, that such words resemble the statement of a man who takes and profits from medicine, and who, declaring that its benefit proceeds from its unpleasantness and its bitter taste, then takes to swallowing everything which tastes unpleasant. This is a mistaken attitude, for the benefit lies in a special property which is present in the medicine, not in its bitter taste. Just as the physicians alone are aware of this property, so too is the reason for the beneficial nature of hunger known only to the great scholars. Whoever makes himself hungry, having believed the revealed texts which praise hunger, must needs benefit, even if he does not know why it is beneficial, in the manner of the man who takes medicine, and benefits without being told how it profits him.

[A] For the remainder of this *ḥadīth* see above, p.108.

But despite this, we shall explain this matter for the benefit of those who wish to rise from the level of belief to that of knowledge, for God has said, *God shall exalt those that believe among you, and those who have knowledge, to high degrees.*[1]

Hunger has ten benefits. The first of these is the purification of the heart, the illumination of the natural disposition [*qarīḥa*] and the sharpening of one's insight.[A] For satiety engenders stupidity and a blindness in the heart, and increases the vapours of the brain to produce a form of inebriation, so that the sources of thought are repressed[2] and the heart finds it a burdensome thing to think and to perceive things with any rapidity. A child, when it eats too much, becomes unable to memorise things, and its mind is corrupted so that it becomes slow and dull-witted.

Said Abū Sulaymān al-Dārānī, 'Make yourselves hungry, for this abases the soul, softens the heart, and yields heavenly knowledge.'[3]

And [the Prophet] (may God bless him and grant him peace) said, 'Give life to your hearts by laughing rarely, and purify them with hunger, for they will thereby become clear and soft'.[4]

And it is said,[5] 'Hunger is like thunder, contentment with one's lot is like a cloud, and wisdom is like rain'.

And the Prophet said (may God bless him and grant him peace), 'When a man causes his belly to hunger he causes his mind to think powerfully and his heart to grow in sagacity'.[6]

Said Ibn ʿAbbās, 'The Prophet (may God bless him and grant him peace) once said, "The heart of whomsoever eats his fill and then sleeps will grow harder". Then he declared, "There is a tithe [*zakāt*] for everything, and the tithe of the stomach is hunger".'[7]

Said al-Shiblī, 'I have never hungered for a single day without beholding in my heart an open door of wisdom and an ability to be admonished which I had never seen before.'

It is obvious that that the purpose for which the acts of

[A] Ar: *baṣīra*, a term which for Ghazālī denotes the intuitive aspect of the intellect. Cf. Jabre, *Lexique*, 32-6.

worship are intended is an intellection [*fikr*] which leads one on to gnosis [*maʿrifa*] and an inner perception into the realities of God [*al-istibṣār bi-ḥaqā'iq al-Ḥaqq*]. Satiety precludes this, while hunger opens wide its gate. Gnosis is one of the gates of Heaven, and it is only right that constant hunger should constitute a knocking on one of these gates.[A] It was for this reason that Luqmān told his son, 'O my son! When the stomach is full, then the intellect sleeps, wisdom is silenced, and the members of the body are too slothful to perform any act of worship.'

Said Abū Yazīd al-Bisṭāmī, 'Hunger is a cloud; whenever a bondsman is hungry his heart rains down wisdom.'[8]

Said the Prophet (may God bless him and grant him peace), 'The light of wisdom comes from hunger, while remoteness from God (Great and Glorious is He!) comes from satiety, and proximity to Him comes from loving the poor and being close to them. Therefore never eat to repletion, for you would thereby extinguish the light of wisdom which is in your hearts. The man who spends his night praying,[9] having eaten only lightly, is surrounded all night by the Houris until the dawn comes.'[10]

The second benefit is a softness and purity of the heart, by which it is readied to attain the delight of intimate discourse with God and to be affected by His remembrance. How many acts of remembrance there are which are done with the tongue and with an attentive heart, while the heart nonetheless fails to find any delight therein and is not affected, to the extent that it were as though a veil existed composed of the heart's hardness! When, however, it is softened due to certain circumstances, it will be affected most powerfully by the remembrance and will take great delight in communing with Him. Usually an empty stomach is the reason for this.

Said Abū Sulaymān al-Dārānī, 'Worship is sweetest for me when my belly cleaves to my back'.

Said al-Junayd, 'Can anyone put a measure of food between him and his chest, and still hope to find the sweetness of inti-

[A] See above p. 111.

mate communion with God?'

Said Abū Sulaymān, 'When the heart is hungry and thirsty, it becomes clear and soft, whereas when it is sated it becomes blind and rough.'

In this way, the influence exercised upon the heart by the delight of intimate communing [*munājāt*] facilitates thought and the acquisition of gnosis, thereby providing a second benefit.

The third benefit lies in mortification and abasement, and the removal of exultation, rejoicing and exuberance, which comprise the beginning of rebellion and heedlessness of God (Exalted is He!). For the soul is mortified and abased by nothing more effective than hunger, which, when it prevails, causes it to have placid trust in its Lord and fear of Him, and to be aware of its helplessness and abasement when it weakens and becomes desperate for the morsel of bread which it misses, so that the whole world appears dark to a man because one drink of water did not come when he desired it. For as long as he fails to behold the baseness and helplessness of his own soul he will be unable to behold the glory and power of his Lord: his saving felicity, therefore, lies in his seeing himself at all times to be base and helpless, and his Lord to be Glorious, Mighty and Powerful. Let him therefore be hungry without cease, constrained to turn to his Lord in such a way that he witness his constraint through experience [*dhawq*]. For this reason, when the world and all its treasures were offered to the Prophet (may God bless him and grant him peace), he said, 'No! Instead I shall hunger on alternate days, so that when I hunger I have patient endurance, and that when I eat my fill I have gratitude' (or as he said).[11] [A] For the craving for food and women constitutes one of the gates of Hell, and originates in satiety. By contrast, abasement and humility are one of the gates of Heaven, and originate in hunger. Whoever closes one of the gates of Hell has of neces-

[A] The parenthetical phrase is an indication by Ghazālī that he was unsure of the original wording.

sity opened one of Heaven's gates thereby, since they oppose each other, like the east and the west: proximity to one is remoteness from the other.

The fourth benefit is that one comes never to forget God's trials and torments, or those who are afflicted by them. For the man sated is liable to forget those people who are hungry, and to forget hunger itself. The intelligent bondsman never beholds a tribulation without recalling the tribulations of the Afterlife: when he thirsts, he remembers the thirst from which people will suffer on the wide plains of the Day of Arising,[A] and when he hungers he recalls the hunger of the people of Hell, which is so extreme that they shall long to eat even thorn-fruit, and the fruit of the Zaqqūm tree, and drink *g͟hassāq* and molten lead.[B] Never should a bondsman forget the punishment, torments and calamities[12] of the Afterlife, for it is they which arouse fear: whoever is not in a state of humility, sickness, poverty and tribulation[13] will forget the Afterlife, which will therefore fail to be manifest in his soul or prevalent in his heart. It is for this reason that the bondsman should suffer a trial, or witness the trial of others—and the most appropriate thing with which he should be tried is hunger. For in addition to the simple reminding of the torment of the Afterlife, it contains a great number of other benefits; which is one reason why the Prophets and Saints were particularly afflicted with trials, the best among them being the most sorely afflicted of all.[C] Therefore, when Joseph (upon whom be peace) was asked, 'Why do you hunger, when you hold in your hands the storehouses of the land?' he replied, 'I fear that I may eat my fill, and forget the hungry'. To remember those who are hungry

[A] For this thirst see *Iḥyā'*, IV. 439 (K. *D͟hikr al-mawt*, s͟haṭr 2, ṣifat ṭūl...; tr. Winter, *Remembrance of death*, 182).

[B] These delicacies shall be the sustenance of the damned; see respectively Q. LXXXVIII:6, LVI:52, LXXVIII:25, XVIII:29.

[C] Cf. the Tradition in which the Prophet says, 'We, the Prophets, are of all people the most grievously tried, the best of us most sorely'. (Tirmid͟hī, Zuhd, 57; Ibn Māja, Fitan, 23; al-Ḥakīm al-Tirmid͟hī, *Bayān al-farq*, 90.)

and needy is therefore one of the benefits of hunger, since this condition will conduce to compassion, feeding the hungry, and charity towards God's creatures; the man who is sated, by contrast, is heedless of those who hunger.

The fifth and greatest benefit lies in the breaking of all one's desires for sin, and in achieving mastery over the soul which commands evil.[A] For all sins originate in one's desires and strengths, the stuff of which is food in every case: when one eats less, every one of one's desires and strengths will be enfeebled. The saving felicity [*saᶜāda*] of man consists entirely in the control he wields over his own soul, while damnation and misery ensue when his soul controls him. Just as you cannot master a stubborn riding beast without weakening it through hunger, for when it eats its fill it becomes strong, obstinate and defiant, so it is with the soul.

Someone was once asked, 'Why is it that despite your age you do not take care of your body, which has become decrepit?'[15] He replied, 'Because it is quick to become exuberant and exultant: I am afraid that it might bolt and throw me. I prefer to force it to perform difficult actions than to be forced by it into acts of corruption'.

Said Dhu'l-Nūn, 'Never have I eaten my fill without then committing, or wishing to commit, some sin'.

Said ᶜĀ'isha (may God be pleased with her), 'The first innovation [*bidᶜa*] to appear after God's Emissary died was that people would eat their fill, and when the people's bellies were sated, their souls bolted with them into the things of the world'.[16]

This does not constitute one single benefit; rather is it the storehouse of all benefits. For this reason has it been said that 'hunger is one of God's storehouses'. The least[17] thing that is deflected by hunger is sexual desire, and also the desire for speech; for in the case of a hungry man the desire for unnecessary talk is not aroused, and this enables him to save himself from the

[A] Ar: *al-nafs al-ammāra bi'l-sū'*. See Introduction, p. XXVIII.

faults of the tongue, such as slander, obscenity, lying, backbiting and so forth, from all of which he is restrained by hunger. When, by contrast, he is sated, he will need to be entertained, and will necessarily amuse himself by deprecating other people, and 'people are cast down on their noses into Hell only by the harvests reaped by their tongues'.[18]

As for sexual desire, the hazard is quite apparent. Hunger overcomes the evil which it contains, whereas when a man is sated he cannot govern his sexual desire: even if preserved by the fear of God, he will be unable to control his eye, and the eyes commit fornication even as do the genitals.[A] And should he be able to master his eyes by lowering his gaze, he will still be unable to govern his thoughts, which will become foul, so that his soul's discourse to him regarding the causes of sexual desire will distract him from his intimate communing [with God], perhaps even while he performs the Prayer [*ṣalāt*]. We mention the danger of the tongue and the genitals only as an example; however, all the sins of the seven extremities[B] ensue from the strength which proceeds from eating one's fill. A wise man once said, 'When a man patiently restrains himself, and perseveres in eating bread and nothing else for a year, and only half-fills his belly, God relieves him of his desire for women.'

The sixth benefit consists in the repulsion of sleep, and acquiring the ability to remain awake for long periods. A man who eats his fill will drink abundantly, and whoever drinks abundantly will sleep abundantly also. For this reason one of the S͟hayk͟hs used to say whenever food was served, 'Assembled aspirants! Do not eat much, lest you drink much, which will cause you to sleep much, and therefore to lose much.'[19] Seventy Truthful Saints have agreed that abundant sleep is the

[A] Cf. the *ḥadīt͟h*, 'the fornication of the eyes is their gaze' (Buk͟hārī, Isti'd͟hān, 12; Muslim, Qadar, 21). See below, pp.172–5.

[B] The eye, the ear, the tongue, the genitals, the feet, the hands and the stomach. (G͟hazālī, *Bidāya*, 74 [tr. Abul Quasem, 73].)

result of drinking water in abundance.[A] Sleeping abundantly is a waste of one's lifetime, and causes one to miss the *Tahajjud* prayer[B] and results in a dull disposition and a hardness of heart. A lifetime is the most precious of jewels, and constitutes a bondsman's capital with which he trades; sleep, on the other hand, is a [kind of] death,[C] for when indulged in to excess it shortens one's lease on life. In addition, the manifestly great merit which attaches to the *Tahajjud* prayer will pass one by if one sleeps abundantly, and to the extent that one is overcome by drowsiness one will not taste the sweetness of worship.

An unmarried man, when he sleeps sated, is likely to experience a wet dream, which also will prevent him from performing the late night prayer, since he will need to carry out the major ablution, either with cold water, which he will find unpleasant—or in the public baths [*ḥammām*], which he may not be able to visit at night, so that he misses the *witr*[D] (should he have delayed this until the time of the *Tahajjud* prayer). He will also need to pay for the *ḥammām*, where his glance may fall upon the private parts of the people who are there with him: for this place contains many hazards (which we have mentioned in the *Book of Purity*).[E] All of these

[A] See above, p.90.

[B] A voluntary, though highly meritorious prayer which should be offered at the beginning of the final third of the night. Cf. *Iḥyā'*, I. 176 (*K. Asrār al-ṣalāt*, bāb 7, qism 1); also *Iḥyā'*, I. 321–4 (*K. Tartīb al-awrād*, bāb 2).

[C] Cf. the *ḥadīth* 'Sleep is the brother of death' (*Iḥyā'*, IV. 431 [*K. Dhikr al-mawt*, bāb 8; tr. Winter, *Remembrance of death*, 153].) which Ghazālī interprets as proof that glimpses of the next world may be achieved during dreams.

[D] A prayer which may either be said before sleeping at night, or postponed until the end of the *tahajjud*. (*Iḥyā'*, I. 175 [*K. Asrār al-ṣalāt*, bāb 7, qism 1].)

[E] *Iḥyā'*, I. 123–5 (*K. Asrār al-ṭahāra*, qism 3, naw[c] 1). The other dangers include losing one's sense of modesty, being looked at by others, wasting water, and so forth. Allegedly, Ibn [c]Umar used to wear a blindfold in the *ḥammām*.

Islam is here continuing an old debate. St. Augustine's horror of the public baths of his day is well-known, while Plotinus avoided the public bath for moral reasons (cf. Wallis, *Neoplatonism*, 9). Needless to remark, the sexes were decently segregated in the baths of the Near East under the Islamic order.

things ensue from eating one's fill. Abū Sulaymān al-Dārānī once remarked that 'Nocturnal emission is a punishment',[20] because it obstructs one from performing many forms of worship by reason of the impossibility of performing the major ablution at once.[A]

Sleep, therefore, is the very well-spring of disadvantages, and satiety conduces to it, while hunger cuts it short.

The seventh benefit is that lengthy acts of worship are made easier. Food prevents a man from worshipping much, since he needs a time in which he busies himself with eating, and may require time for buying and cooking food as well. He needs time to wash his hands, and to pick his teeth, and will make many visits to the privy because of having drunk so much. Were he to spend the hours he used up in these activities in the remembrance of God, intimate communing with Him, and the other varieties of worship, he would profit greatly.

Said al-Sarī, 'I once saw ʿAlī al-Jurjānī eating barley porridge with his fingers. "What made you do this?" I asked him. "I have calculated," he replied, "that the difference between chewing [bread] and eating in this way is seventy 'Glory be to God's'. So I have not chewed bread for forty years." '[21]

See how concerned he was for his time: he would not even waste it in chewing! Every breath of a man's lifespan is a precious and priceless gem, and, since he must lay up a great treasure-house of these gems which will survive into the Afterlife, he must address himself to the remembrance and worship of God (Exalted is He!).

Among the things which are made impossible by excessive eating are retaining the condition of ritual purity and spending much time in the mosque, for someone who eats abundantly is obliged to leave the mosque in order to pass water. Among them

[A] The resultant state of defilement (*janāba*) renders it unlawful for a Muslim to perform the canonical prayer, to touch or recite the Qur'ān, or to enter a mosque until he or she has performed *ghusl*: a bathing of the entire body. (*Iḥyā'*, I. 121 [*K. al-Ṭahāra*, qism 2].)

likewise is fasting, which is easier for a man who is accustomed to hunger. Fasting, together with spending much time in the mosque, and remaining in the state of ritual purity, and turning one's mealtimes into times of worship, yield a great profit which can only be despised by those who are heedless and do not know the value of religion, and who instead are *content with the life of this world, and feel secure therein,*[22] *and who know only the appearance of the life of this world, and are heedless of the Afterlife.*[23] Abū Sulaymān al-Dārānī has pointed out six disadvantages of satiety by saying, 'Whosoever eats his fill is attended by six defects: he loses the sweetness of communing with God, he is unable to memorise Divine[24] wisdom, he is denied compassion for others (since when he is full he imagines that everyone else is full likewise), he finds worship to be burdensome, his desires become stronger, and, while other believers are at the mosques, those who have eaten their fill are at the rubbish heaps and the latrines, emptying their stomachs'.[25]

The eighth benefit is the bodily health which results from eating little. For diseases are caused by overeating, and by the presence of a residue of humours in the stomach and the arteries. Illness prevents one from worshipping; it distracts the heart[26] and stands in the way of remembrance and reflection; it spoils one's life, and obliges one to submit to bloodletting and cupping, and to drinking medicines and seeing physicians, all of which requires money, which in turn can only be obtained through things which require that one exhaust oneself in avoiding various kinds of sins and desires. Hunger makes all of this unnecessary.

It is told that [Hārūn] al-Rashīd once summoned four physicians: an Indian, a Greek, an Iraqi and a Sawādī,[A] and said, 'Let each one of you describe that medicine which itself results in no sickness'. The Indian spoke up, and said, 'In my opinion, the medicine which contains no sickness is black myrobalan.'[B] Then

[A] A native of the Sawād, the agricultural region of south-central Iraq.

[B] Ar. *al-halīlaj al-aswad.* An Indian herb used to treat various ailments,

the Iraqi[27] said, 'For me, it is nasturtium cress'.[A] The Greek[28] said, 'I think it is hot water'. And the Sawādī (who was the most learned of them) said, 'Myrobalan scours the stomach, and that constitutes a sickness. Nasturtium cress renders the stomach oily, and that is a sickness also. Hot water slackens the stomach, and that also constitutes a sickness.' And so al-Rashīd asked him, 'Then what is your answer?' And he replied, 'In my opinion, the medicine which contains no sickness consists in refraining from food until one has an appetite, and in ceasing to eat when one is yet unsated'. 'You have spoken truly,' he declared.

One of the People of the Book,[B] who was a philosopher and also a physician, once heard the statement of the Prophet (may God bless him and grant him peace), 'One third for food, one third for drink, and one third for the breath.'[C] Astonished, he declared, 'I have never heard wiser words than these concerning frugality in eating. These are wise words indeed!'[D] The Prophet (may God bless him and grant him peace) once said, 'Satiety is the beginning of sickness, and fever the beginning of physic. Let every body be accustomed to that to which it is used'.[29] It is my opinion that the surprise of the aforementioned physician was at this latter Tradition, not the former.

Said Ibn Sālim, 'Whoever eats wheat-bread and nothing else, and does so with due propriety, shall never fall sick, save with his mortal illness.' He was asked what the due propriety might

---

including leprosy (*judhām*). See Ibn Sīnā, *Qānūn*, 65-7; Ibn al-Ḥashshā', *Mufīd*, 129-30; Levey, *Medical Formulary of Al-Samarqandī*, 26.

[A] Ar. *ḥabb al-rashād al-abyaḍ*. Used for leprosy, ailments of the spleen, and women's diseases. See Graziani, 'Ibn Jazlah's Eleventh Century Tabulated Medical Compendium', 307; Levey, 239.

[B] A Christian or a Jew. Non-Muslims dominated the medical profession during the ʿAbbāsid period. (Dols, *Medieval Islamic Medicine*, 41, and references there cited.)

[C] Referring to the stomach. See above p. 109.

[D] Or, 'these are the words of a philosopher/sage/physician' [*kalām ḥakīm*].

be, and replied, 'To eat after the onset of hunger, and to stop before the onset of satiety'.

A certain doctor of upright conduct once condemned overeating by saying, 'The most beneficial thing that a man can admit to his belly is a pomegranate,[30] [A] while the most damaging thing for it is salt.[31] [B] I prefer that one reduce one's intake of salt rather than increase the number of pomegranates one eats.'

In a Tradition it is said, 'Fast, and you will be healthy'[32]. Fasting, hunger, and eating less conduce therefore to the health of the body, so that it becomes free of disorders, and of the heart, which becomes free from the diseases of rebellion and exultation, as well as a number of other complaints.

The ninth benefit lies in reduced expenditure. Whoever becomes used to eating little will find a modest income sufficient, whereas a man who is habituated to eating his fill will find that his belly becomes a creditor impossible to shake off, who seizes him by the throat every day, saying, 'What will you eat today?' Therefore will he be compelled to enter into all sorts of activities, and either earn from unlawful pursuits, so that he sins, or from lawful ones, which will involve him in humiliation and exhaustion. He may even need to direct his wishful gaze towards other people,[C] which is the utmost form of abasement and degradation. A believer's needs are few: a sage once remarked that 'I satisfy most of my needs by renouncing them, which is, moreover, more restful for my heart'. Someone else said, 'Whenever I feel a wish to borrow money from someone for the sake of satisfying a desire or making an investment, I borrow from myself, whereupon I renounce the desire. Thus am I my own best creditor'.

[A] The commentator remarks here: 'Because [...] it does not fatten.' (Zabīdī, VII. 400), which is also the verdict of Ibn Sīnā (*Qānūn*, 278).

[B] Zabīdī tells us that salt 'inflames the blood, weakens the eyesight and harms the brain and the lungs' (Zabīdī, loc. cit.). See further Ibn Sīnā, *Qānūn*, 195–7.

[C] That is, he may be reduced to mendicancy.

Ibrāhīm ibn Adham (may God show him His mercy), used to ask his companions about the price of food. When told that it was high, he would say, 'Lower it with renunciation!'[33]

Said Sahl (may God show him His mercy), 'The glutton is base in three circumstances: if he spends his time in worship, he will grow lazy; if he has a trade, he will not be safe from the evils of his trade; and if he has a private income he will not give God His due'.

In sum, then, the reason why people are destroyed lies in their greed for the things of the world. This greed is in turn produced by desire for food, and sexual desire, the latter being the upshot of the former. All these gates may be closed by a frugal diet; they are gates to Hell, which, when shut, open gates into Heaven: as the Prophet (may God bless him and grant him peace) said, 'Make use of hunger to knock persistently on the gates of Heaven'. Therefore, whoever is satisfied with a single loaf each day will be satisfied in respect of his other desires also, and will be liberated, since he will have no need of others, and will find rest from worldly pursuits so that he may devote himself to the worship of God (Great and Glorious is He!) and to trading for the Afterlife, thereby joining those described by God as *Men whom neither commerce nor sale distract from the remembrance of God.*[34] Such people are freed from this beguilement merely because, by virtue of contentment with their lot, they can dispense with it. He who needs more, however, must needs be beguiled.

The tenth benefit is that the aspirant is enabled to put others before himself, and to give in charity to the orphans and the poor that which is surplus to his wants. On the Day of Arising he will be shaded by his charity, as is stated in Tradition.[35] That which he eats is stored in the privy, while that which he gives in charity goes to the storehouse which is God's grace: therefore man benefits from his wealth only insofar as he gives it away, when he will have rendered it permanent, just as when he eats it he destroys it and when he wears it he wears it out.[A] To give away what food one does not need is far better, therefore, than indigestion and satiety.[36]

Al-Ḥasan (may God show him His mercy) used whenever he recited God's word (Exalted is He!), *We offered the Trust unto the heavens and the earth and the mountains, but they shrank from bearing it, and were fearful of it; and it was assumed by man. Assuredly he has been a tyrant and a fool,*[37] [B] to say [by way of commentary]: 'He offered it to the seven tiered heavens, which are the *paths* [C] which He did ornament with stars, and the bearers of the *Great Throne*. He said to them (Glorious and Exalted is He!), "Will you bear this trust, and all that ensues from it?" "And what ensues from it?" they asked. He replied, "That if you do good, you will be rewarded, and if you do evil, you shall be punished." "No!" they answered. Then He offered it to the earth in the same wise, and it refused also. And He offered it to the firm, sheer and lofty mountains: "Will you bear this trust, and all that ensues from it?" "What ensues from it?" they asked. He mentioned the reward and the punishment[38] once again, and they refused. Then He offered it to man, who assumed it. *Assuredly he has been a tyrant* against himself, *and a fool* concerning the ordinances of his Lord. By God, I have seen people selling the Trust for the sake of their wealth, acquiring many thousands thereby. Yet to what use did they put them? They extended their houses, and narrowed their graves.[D] They fattened their horses, and starved their religion.

[A] An echo of a *ḥadīth*: 'Man asks, "Where is my wealth?" But O man! Is any wealth yours, save that which you eat and destroy, or wear and wear out, or give and thereby render permanent?' (Muslim, Zuhd, 3.)

[B] For the Trust [*amāna*] see Schimmel (*Mystical Dimensions*, 188), who observes that it 'has been differently interpreted: as responsibility, free will, love, or the power of individuation'. According to Qushayrī, whose opinions are regularly adopted by Ghazālī, it is to be identified with knowledge of the Divine Unity, and obedience to the revealed Law. (*Laṭā'if*, III. 173.) See further Ṭabarī, *Tafsīr*, XXII. 38-41; Massignon, *Passion*, III. 13.

[C] And We have created above you seven paths [*tarā'iq*] (Q. XXIII:17). Cf. Asad, 520: 'seven [celestial] orbits'.

[D] An allusion to the 'straitening of the grave', a punishment to which

They followed [the whims of] their souls by appearing morning and eve before the gates of the ruler, exposing themselves thereby to sore temptations, although God had granted them comfort enough. One of them says, "Seek such-and-such a thing for me, and bring me such-and-such a thing,"[40] reclining on his left side while he consumes the money of other men. His speech is mockery and derision,[41] his money was gained unlawfully, until, when his belly swells up, and indigestion afflicts him, he says, "Lad! Get me something which will help me digest my food!"[42] You scoundrel! Is it your food that you wish to digest? You are digesting your religion instead! Where is the pauper? Where the widow? Where the destitute? Where the orphan? It is they whom God has commanded you to assist!'

This constitutes a reference to the [tenth] benefit, which entails the donation of one's superfluous food to the poor so that one may store up something better than one would gain by eating it, and thereby avoid being burdened with another sin.

The Emissary of God (may God bless him and grant him peace) once saw a pot-bellied man, and indicated his belly with his finger. 'If that were elsewhere,' he remarked, 'it would be better for you', by which he meant, 'If you had sent it before you for your Afterlife instead, and used it to put others before yourself'.[43]

It is told that al-Ḥasan once said, 'By God, when I was young I knew people who, in the evening,[44] would have enough food for themselves, but who would say, when they began to eat, "By God, I shall not give this all to my belly, until I have given some of it to God"'.[A]

Such, then, are the ten benefits of hunger. Under each one are subsumed countless subdivisions of incalculable advantage. For hunger is a great storehouse of the benefits which help one in the Afterlife: as one of the Predecessors declared, 'Hunger is

some sinners will be subjected between the time of their interment and the Resurrection. See *Iḥyā'*, IV. 429–30 (K. *Dhikr al-mawt*, bāb 7, bayān su'āl...; tr. Winter, *Remembrance of death*, 144–8).

[A] Through almsgiving.

the key to the Afterlife, and the gateway to renunciation, while satiety is the key to the world and the gateway to greed.' This is very evident from the Traditions which we have cited, which you may understand with insight by studying the details of each benefit, so that you rise above the level of mere faith.[45] However, if you do not come to learn these things, but simply believe in the merit of hunger, you shall be at the level of those who receive their faith through imitation [*taqlīd*].

And God knows best.

[23.3]
An Exposition of the Method by which Discipline is Used to Break the Greed of the Stomach

KNOW that four duties [*waẓā'if*] are incumbent upon the aspirant with regard to his belly and his diet. The first is that he should only eat food that is lawful [*ḥalāl*], for to worship on a diet of unlawful food is like building on the waves of the sea. We have already made mention of the degrees of scrupulousness which must be observed in this regard in the *Book of the Lawful and the Unlawful.*[A] But there are three other duties concerning food: to estimate the quantity of food one eats, whether

[A] *Kitāb al-Ḥalāl wa'l-ḥarām*: Book 14 of the *Iḥyā'*. There is a French translation by Régis Morelon: *Le Livre du licite et de l'illicite*. The passage referred to here appears at *Iḥyā'*, II. 85 (=Morelon, pp.24–5). There are four degrees of scrupulousness (*wara*ᶜ), Ghazālī tells us, with regard to what is lawful. Firstly, there is that of ordinary Muslims, who simply avoid what is known to be forbidden by religion. Secondly, there is that of the 'righteous' (*ṣāliḥūn*), who avoid that which seems lawful, but concerning which there might be some doubt. Thirdly, the 'Godfearing' (*muttaqūn*) avoid that which is incontrovertibly lawful, but which might lead to something reprehensible. Finally, there is the scrupulousness of the 'Truthful Saints' (*ṣiddīqūn*), who avoid that which is lawful, and cannot lead to what is unlawful, but which they renounce because it will not help them in the service of God. Ghazālī's understanding of *wara*ᶜ is based on that of al-Muḥāsibī, who had defined it as 'a pause of the heart to distinguish lawful from unlawful before engaging in an act' (*Qaṣd*, 46). Elsewhere, Muḥāsibī had explained how the principle of disciplining the self was implicit in *wara*ᶜ (*Makāsib*, 200–8, 216).

great or small, to estimate the speed with which one eats it, and to know which varieties of food are most conducive to the satisfying or the renunciation of one's desire.

As for the first of these [three] duties, which concerns the reduction of one's intake of food, the method by which one may discipline oneself therein consists in gradualness. This is because the constitution of a man who is accustomed to eating much, and who then changes all at once to eating only a little, will not be able to sustain this, and will be weakened, resulting in considerable hardship and distress.[1] He should therefore proceed a little at a time by eating progressively less and less of his accustomed nourishment: should, for example, he customarily eat two loaves, and wish to restrict himself to no more than one, he should reduce his consumption each day by a quarter of one-seventh of a loaf (so that he eats one twenty-eighth or one thirtieth of a loaf less) which will enable him to eat only one loaf a day by the end of the month without hardship or any noticeable effect. If he so desires, he may do this with the aid of scales, or simply through his own judgement, by eating every day one morsel less than the day before.

This, in turn, has four degrees. The highest is where one forces oneself to partake only of that which is necessary for life. This was the custom of the Truthful Saints, and[2] was the preferred practice of Sahl al-Tustarī, who said, 'God has rendered mankind His bondsmen through three things: life, intelligence and strength. Should someone fear for two of these, that is, life and intelligence, he will eat, and, should he be fasting, will break his fast, and, should he be poor, will strive for his livelihood. Should he not fear for them, but fear only for his strength, he should pay no heed, even if he should weaken, until such time as he is obliged to pray in a sitting position, and is of the opinion that to pray thus and be hungry is better than to pray standing and to eat abundantly.'

Sahl was once asked about the beginning [of his spiritual career], and what he used to eat. He replied: 'Every year my food was purchased for three dirhams, one of which I would spend on black treacle, one on rice flour, and one on clarified butter. I would mix them all together, and make three hundred and sixty round cakes, one of which I would take each evening in order to break my fast.' He was then asked, 'How do you eat now?' and he replied, 'Without any particular limit, or any fixed time'.[3]

It is related that certain[4] monks used to compel themselves to make do with only a single dirham's worth of food [in a year].

As for the second degree, this is attained when one has disciplined oneself to a daily diet of no more than half a *mudd*,[A] which is a little more than one loaf (four of which would make up one *mann*).[B] For most people this is approximately one third of the stomach, as the Prophet (may God bless him and grant him peace) stated, and is more than 'a few small morsels,'[C] since this form of the plural is used to indicate paucity, that is, a number less than ten. Such was the custom of ᶜUmar (may God be pleased with him), who used to eat seven or nine morsels.

The third degree is attained when one reduces oneself to the quantity of one *mudd*, which is two and a half loaves. For most people this is in excess of a third of the belly, and is almost two thirds, so that one third remains for drink and nothing at all for the remembrance of God. In some variants [of the Tradition] the phrase 'for one's remembrance' instead of 'for one's breath' is given.

The fourth degree is to exceed one *mudd* to the quantity of a *mann*,[5] beyond which lies a prodigality which violates His

[A] A measure of corn (Lane, 2697).

[B] For these measures see Lane, s.v. *riṭl*.

[C] This is a reference to the Tradition in which the Prophet says, 'Sufficient for the descendant of Adam are a few small morsels [*luqaymāt*] which will keep his back straight. But if there be no alternative, then one third of the belly should be for food, one third for drink, and one third for one's breath'. (Ibn Māja, Aṭᶜima, 50.) Cf. above p. 127.

commandment (Exalted is He!): *And be not prodigal.*[6] This applies in the case of most people, for people need food in varying degrees, according to their age, build and profession.

There exists also a fifth way, which is of no account, but nevertheless constitutes an error. This consists in eating when truly hungry, and restraining one's hand when one feels genuine greed. It is usually the case, however, that someone who has not set himself a limit of one or two loaves is unable to discern the point at which hunger becomes genuine, and will mistake a deceptive appetite for this. True hunger has signs which people have mentioned: one is that the soul does not demand that one eat something along with bread, but rather eats bread alone, whatever its form, with an appetite: whenever the soul requires that one eat a particular kind of bread, or that it be accompanied by something else, it is not acting in response to true hunger. It has been said that one of its signs is that if one spits, no flies gather on the spittle, because it contains no residual oils or fatty substances; this being an indication that the stomach is empty. To ascertain this thing is difficult, and the aspirant should therefore determine a quantity which, in the case of his own soul, will not enfeeble his capacity for the worship which lies before him, but at which limit he stops, even if his appetite remains unsatisfied.

In fine, it is impossible to specify the [correct amount of] food, since it varies with the circumstance and the individual. Certainly, the sustenance of a number of the Companions[7] was no more than one *sāʿ*[A] of wheat in every week. When they ate dates they sufficed themselves with one *sāʿ* and a half. One *sāʿ* of wheat is four *mudds*, so that each day they ate about half a *mudd*, which corresponds to what we mentioned as being equivalent to a third of the stomach. A greater quantity was required in the case of dates because these contain pits which must be discarded.

[A] A measure said to have been equivalent to four times a *mudd* in the time of the Companions of the Prophet.

Abū Dharr (may God be pleased with him) used to say, 'Every week my food amounts to one *ṣāʿ* of barley, in accordance with the usage of God's Emissary (may God bless him and grant him peace). And, by God, I shall not eat more until I meet him again! For I once heard him say, "The closest and most beloved person to me on the Day of Judgement shall be he who dies in the state in which he is today".'[8] And he used to say, criticising thereby some of the other Companions, 'You have differed:[A] you sift your barley-flour, and he did not; you bake fine bread, and eat it with two kinds of food at once, and partake of a variety of dishes; likewise do you wear one garment in the morning, and another in the evening. In the day of God's Emissary (may God bless him and grant him peace) you did not do these things.'

The daily food of the People of the Veranda[B] was one *mudd* of dates shared between two of them[9] (a *mudd* being one *riṭl* and a third), from which the pits had to be discarded. Al-Ḥasan (may God have mercy upon him) used to say, 'A believer is like a goat,[10] which is sufficed by a handful of dry, rotten dates,[11] a fistful of parched barley,[12] and a single gulp of water. A hypocrite, however, is like a predatory beast, which gulps and swallows again and again; he does not straiten his own belly in hunger for his neighbour's sake, and does not prefer his brother over himself in his surfeit.'

Said Sahl, 'If the world was of pure blood, the believer's food therein would still be lawful'.[13][C] This he said because the believer eats when necessary, and only inasmuch as will keep him alive.

[A] i.e. from the precedent set by the Prophet.

[B] Ahl al-Ṣuffa: a group of impoverished Companions of the Prophet who lived in a veranda at the Mosque in Medina. Their reputation for asceticism and sanctity, and in particular the emphasis they laid on fasting and hunger, made them a revered model for the Sufis, whose name is sometimes said to be derived from them. (Ḥākim, *Mustadrak*, III. 15-7; Muḥāsibī, *Makāsib*, 226; Kalābādhī, *Taʿarruf*, 6-8 [tr. Arberry, 5-9]; Suhrawardī, *ʿAwārif*, 78-81 [tr. Gramlich, *Gaben*, 110-3]; Massignon, *Essai*, 156.)

[C] Blood upon emerging from the body, is an impure substance according to Islamic Law (Ghazālī, *Wajīz*, I.7). Cf. above, p. 42

The second duty[A] concerns the time of eating, and the extent to which this should be delayed. This also consists of four degrees. The highest is that one should go without food for three days, or more: seven, ten or fifteen.[14] Some aspirants make continual fasting, rather than restricting the amount of food they eat, the basis of their self-discipline, to the extent that they fast without interruption for thirty or forty days. This was the practice of a considerable number of scholars, including Muḥammad ibn ʿUmar[15] and al-Qaranī[16] and ʿAbd al-Raḥmān ibn Ibrāhīm[17] Duḥaym, Ibrāhīm al-Taymī, Ḥajjāj ibn Furāfiṣa, Ḥafṣ al-ʿĀbid al-Maṣīṣī, al-Muslim ibn Saʿīd,[18] Zuhayr, Sulaymān al-Khawwāṣ, Sahl ibn ʿAbd Allāh al-Tustarī, and Ibrāhīm ibn Aḥmad al-Khawwāṣ. Abū Bakr al-Ṣiddīq (may God be pleased with him) used to eat nothing for six days on end, while ʿAbd Allāh ibn al-Zubayr ate nothing for seven, which was also the practice of Abu'l-Jawzā', the companion of Ibn ʿAbbās. It has been related that al-Thawrī and Ibrāhīm ibn Adham regularly went without food for three days at a stretch.

All of this they did in order that hunger might assist them along the way of the Afterlife. One of the scholars[B] said, 'To whomsoever goes without food for forty days for the sake of God shall appear a potency from the Kingdom [*malakūt*] that is, certain of the Divine Secrets shall be unveiled to him'. It is told that one of the people of this community[C] once passed by a monk who reminded him of his own state. Desiring that he should accept Islam and renounce the delusion in which he was engaged, he spoke to him for some time. At length, the monk said to him that the Messiah had spent forty days without eating or drinking, and that this was a miracle which could proceed only from a Prophet or a Truthful Saint. The Sufi replied to him:

[A] Of the three mentioned above, p. 133-4.

[B] Sahl al-Tustarī, according to Suhrawardī, *ʿAwārif*, 162 (tr. Gramlich, *Gaben*, 209).

[C] Sc. the Sufis.

'If I were to go without food or drink for fifty days, would you abandon your creed and enter into the religion of Islam, knowing it to be the truth, and that you had been engaged in falsehood?' 'Certainly,' the monk replied. So he sat down, and then did not go out of his sight until he had passed fifty days without eating or drinking. Then he said, 'I shall do more for you', and continued until he had reached sixty. The monk was astonished at this, and declared, 'I had never thought that anyone could do more than the Messiah'. And this became the cause of his Islam.

This constitutes a very exalted degree, which is seldom attained by any save men of unveiling [*mukāshafa*] and great good fortune, who have been occupied with the vision of that which severed them from their nature and custom so that they gained a pleasure so complete that they forgot their hunger and their need.

The second degree [of the second duty] is achieved when one goes without food for two or three days together. This is not a miraculous thing; rather it is quite attainable, although it may only be reached though effort and struggle.[19]

The third degree, which is the lowest, is that one restrict oneself in every day and night to one meal. This is the least one should do; everything beyond it constitutes extravagance, and persistence in satiety, so that the condition of hunger never occurs at all, which is the state—far removed from the *Sunna*—of those who live in luxury. It is related by Abū Saʿīd al-Khudrī that when the Prophet (may God bless him and grant him peace) ate in the middle of the day, he would not eat in the evening, and *vice versa*.[20] The Predecessors[A] used to eat only once a day. And the Prophet (may God bless him and grant him peace) once said to ʿĀ'isha, 'You should beware of extravagance, and it is extravagant to eat twice in a single day'.[21] One meal every two days is poverty, while a meal every day is a firm

[A] Ar: *al-Salaf*: the early Muslims.

station between the two; which is praised in the Book of God (Exalted is He!).[A]

It is preferable that the man who restricts himself to one meal a day should take it during the period before daybreak, so that he eats after his *tahajjud* prayers and before the Dawn Prayer. This will render him hungry during the day while he fasts, and during the night while he prays. His heart will be emptied because of the emptiness of his belly, his thoughts will become more precise, his intention more collected, and his soul, being reconciled to a known [mealtime] will not struggle against him before the appropriate time. In a Tradition related by ʿĀṣim ibn Kulayb from his father, Abū Hurayra said, 'The Emissary of God (may God bless him and grant him peace) never prayed at night in the way you do: he used to stand in prayer until his feet became swollen;[22] neither did he fast from one day to the next as you do, rather he used to delay breaking his fast until the last part of the night'.[23] ʿĀ'isha once said (may God be pleased with her), 'The Prophet (may God bless him and grant him peace) used to prolong his fasts until the end of the night'.[24]

Should sunset come, and the heart of a man who is fasting incline towards food to the extent that he is too distracted to be attentive during his night prayers, he should divide his food in two: if, for instance, this takes the form of two loaves he should eat one loaf at sunset and one just before dawn, so that although his soul is silenced his body remains light for the late night prayer, and so that he does not suffer greatly from hunger during the daytime because of having eaten before first light. Thus the first loaf will help him in his night devotions, and the second in his fast. Someone whose custom it is to fast on alternate days may without harm eat at midday on the day in which he does not fast, and before dawn when he does.

[A] Cf. Q. xxv:68: *And those who, when they spend, are neither extravagant nor grudging, and there is ever a middle point between the two.* Cited above, p. 28-9.

Thus is the way to time one's eating, and to determine the periods in which one abstains.

The third duty concerns the varieties of food one eats, and which of these one should renounce. The best form of bread is made from finely-ground flour, which constitutes an extreme form of luxury. Beneath it comes bread from sifted barley flour, while the most inferior kind is barley flour that has not been sifted. Of things which may be eaten with bread, the finest are meat and sweetmeats,[25] the lowest are vinegar and salt, while in between lie dishes of vegetables served with oil but with no meat. The custom of the wayfarers on the Path of the Afterlife is to abstain always from eating anything other than bread, and from indulging every other appetite, for each delicious thing which a man desires and eats leaves behind it an exuberance in his soul and a hardness and forgetfulness in his heart engendered by the delights of the world, so that he comes to be familiar with these, and conceives a dislike for death and the meeting with God (Exalted is He!). The world becomes like Heaven for him, while death turns into a gaol.[A] However, when he forbids his soul its passions and delights, and restricts it, the world becomes a gaol and a constraint for him,[26] so that his soul desires to escape from it immediately, and death becomes a liberation. This is indicated in the following saying of Yaḥyā ibn Muʿādh: 'O company of Truthful Saints! Hunger your souls for the sake of the banquet of Paradise, for the desire for food is in proportion to one's causing oneself to hunger'.[B]

Since all the things that we have mentioned concerning the evils of satiety apply to every one of man's desires and delights,

[A] An echo of a *ḥadīth*: 'The world is the believer's prison and the unbeliever's heaven.' (Muslim, Zuhd, I. Cf. *Iḥyā'*, IV. 383; tr. Winter, *Remembrance of Death*, 9.)

[B] In other words, the more a man wages war on his cravings, the more powerful they will become, and this will bring a yet greater reward in Heaven (cf. Zabīdī, VII. 412).

we shall not commit prolixity by repeating the matter.

In this way is a substantial reward granted for renouncing those lawful things which one desires, while great danger lies in partaking of them, so much so that the Prophet (may God bless him and grant him peace) said, 'The worst of my nation are those that eat wheat flour'.[27] This does not constitute a prohibition, for wheat flour is lawful in the sense that a man who eats it once or twice commits no sin; neither does a man who partakes of it regularly. Nevertheless, the soul of the latter is thereby habituated to pleasure, so that it finds solace in the world and becomes accustomed to its delights and strives to acquire them, which thing leads to acts of sin: such people are thus the worst of the nation, since wheat flour leads them into transgression. Also, the Prophet (may God bless him and grant him peace) said,'The worst of my nation are those who are nourished on pleasure, so that their bodies are built of it. Their sole concern is for the various kinds of food and dress, and they affect eloquence in their speech.'[28] And God (Exalted is He!) revealed to Moses (upon whom be peace): 'Remember that you shall dwell in the grave, for this [thought] will prevent you from indulging in many desires.'

The Predecessors lived in great fear of eating delicious things and allowing their souls to be accustomed to this, and were of the opinion that such a thing was a token of damnation, and that to be kept from it by God was the very height of felicity. It is even related by Wahb ibn Munabbih that 'Two angels once met in the Fourth Heaven [*samā'*]. One said to the other, "Whence have you come?" and he replied, "I have just instructed a fish to be brought from the sea to such-and-such a Jew, may God curse him". And the other said, "I have just ordered that some oil which such-and-such a worshipper desired be spilt".' This constitutes an indication that it is not a good sign that one's desires be made easy of access. ʿUmar (may God be pleased with him) for this reason refrained from drinking cold water, saying, 'Keep me from being called to account for it!'

Therefore is there no form of worship greater than contradicting the soul and renouncing delightful things (as we have stated in the *Book of Disciplining the Soul*).[A]

Nāfiᶜ related that when Ibn ᶜUmar (may God be pleased with him) was ill once, he desired a fresh fish. One was sought in Medina, but there were none to be had. After a certain number of days, one was found, which was purchased for a dirham and a half: it was roasted and taken to him on a loaf of bread. A beggar came to the door, and Ibn ᶜUmar said to the boy [Nāfiᶜ]: 'Wrap it in the bread, and give it to him'. 'May God set you aright!' the boy said. 'You desired it for such-and-such a period, and I could not find it; and when I did I bought it for one and a half dirhams. Let us give him its price instead!' But he only said, 'Wrap it up, and give it to him'. The boy said to the beggar, 'Will you accept one dirham and not take it?' and he said that he would, so he gave him the dirham and took the fish, and came back to him with it, setting it before him with the words, 'I gave him a dirham and took it from him'. 'Wrap it up,' he told him again, 'and give it to him, and do not take back the dirham, for I once heard the Emissary of God (may God bless him and grant him peace) say, "God shall forgive the sins of any man who desires something, and then overcomes his desire, preferring that someone else should have the enjoyment instead".'[29]

And he said (may God bless him and grant him peace), 'When one's rabid hunger may be satified with a loaf and a mugful of pure water, then destruction upon this world and its people!'[30] By this he was saying that the purpose [of eating] is to stop the rabidity and harm of hunger, and not to take pleasure in worldly delights.

ᶜUmar (may God be pleased with him) once heard that Yazīd ibn Abī Sufyān used to eat several kinds of food. ᶜUmar therefore said to one of his clients [*mawālī*], 'When you know that

[A] See above, p. 55-66.

his supper is served, tell me'. This he did, and ᶜUmar went in, and was offered some food, which was a bread broth and some meat,[31] and he ate with him. Then some roast meat was served, to which Yazīd stretched out his hand, while ᶜUmar refrained, saying, '*Allāh! Allāh!* O Yazīd ibn Abī Sufyān! One dish after another? By Him in Whose hand lies ᶜUmar's soul, if you differ from their usages,[A] then you shall certainly be caused to diverge from their way'.

Yasār ibn ᶜUmayr said, 'Whenever I sifted wheat for ᶜUmar I was disobeying him'.[32]

It is told that ᶜUtba al-Ghulām used to make his own dough, dry it in the sun, and then eat it, saying, 'A crust and some salt, until roast meat and good food are prepared for me in the Afterlife!' It was his custom to pick up his mug and dip it into a jar which was standing in the midday sun, when a servant woman of his would say, 'O ᶜUtba! Why do you not give me your flour, and allow me to bake for you, and cool some water for you?' But he would only reply, 'O mother of So-and-so! I have driven from myself the rabidity of hunger'.[33]

Said Shaqīq ibn Ibrāhīm, 'I once met Ibrāhīm ibn Adham at Mecca in the Sūq al-Layl[B] on the Prophet's birthday (may God bless him and grant him peace). He was seated, weeping, on one side of the road. I went over to him, and sat down beside him. "What are these tears, Abū Isḥāq?" I asked him, and he replied, "They come from good news". I asked him again, and then a third time, until he said, "O Shaqīq! Conceal my words!" "My brother," I told him, "say what you wish". And he said, "For thirty years my soul desired *sikbāj*,[C] and I used my best efforts to prevent it from having its desire. But yesterday I was sitting down when I was overcome by drowsiness, and there before me

[A] The austere conduct of the righteous Companions of the Prophet.

[B] A district by this name still exists in the Holy City (Bilādī, *Maᶜālim Makka*, 38).

[C] A dish usually prepared of meat and vinegar (Lane, 1389).

stood a young man bearing a green vessel from which steam and the aroma of *sikbāj* were rising. I was fully determined to refuse, and when he said to me, "Eat, Ibrāhīm!", I answered, "I will not! I have forsaken it for the sake of God (Great and Glorious is He!)". But he replied, "God has given you food, so eat!" And my only answer was to weep. "Eat, may God show you His mercy!" he said again. "He has commanded us," I said, "not to cast anything that we do not know about into our bellies." "Eat, may God give you health!" he said, "I have only been given this, with the words, 'O Khiḍr![34] [A] Take this, and feed the soul of Ibrāhīm ibn Adham, for God has had mercy upon it on account of its long perseverence under the prohibitions with which it has been burdened'. Know, Ibrāhīm, that I heard the angels saying,'Whosoever does not take what he is given, will not be given that for which he asks'." And so I said, "If that be so, then here I am before you for the sake of the covenant of God (Great and Glorious is He!)". Then I turned around, and there before me was another youth, who was also bearing something. "O Khiḍr!" he said. "Put a morsel into his mouth!" And he fed me. At last, I was overcome with sleep, and when I awoke, I could taste the sweetness in my mouth."' Said Shaqīq, 'I asked him to show me the palm of his hand, and I took hold of it, and kissed it. Then I said, "O Thou Who feedest the hungry, when they forbid themselves aright! O Thou Who castest certitude into the mind! O Thou Who curest their hearts of the love of all else! Dost Thou behold in Thy bondsman Shaqīq any [spiritual] state?" Then I raised the hand of Ibrāhīm up to the heavens, and said, "By the esteem in which Thou holdest this hand, and by the worth of him who owns it, and by the generosity which he found in Thee! Be generous to Thy bondsman, who is needful of Thy grace, beneficence and mercy, though he deserve them

[A] The immortal spiritual guide usually believed to have been the companion of Moses mentioned in the Qur'ān. See A.J. Wensinck, art. 'al-Khaḍir (al-Khiḍr)' in *EI*[2], IV. 902-5; Schimmel, *Mystical Dimensions*, index, s.v. 'Khiḍr'.

not". Then Ibrāhīm got to his feet, and walked home with me.'[35]

It is related of Mālik ibn Dīnār that he desired yogurt for forty years, but never once ate it.[36] One day, he was given some fresh dates as a present. 'Eat,' he said to his companions, 'for I have not eaten fresh dates for forty years'.

Aḥmad ibn Abi'l-Ḥawārī said, 'Abū Sulaymān al-Dārānī once desired a hot loaf of bread with some salt. I brought one to him, and he bit into it, and then cast it aside and burst into tears. "After long struggling and suffering", he said, "I made haste to gratify my desire. I am determined to repent!"' And Aḥmad said, 'I never saw him eat salt thereafter until he went to meet God (Exalted is He!).'

Said Mālik ibn Ḍaygham, 'I once passed through the souk at Basra, where I espied some green vegetables. My soul said to me, "If you would only give me some of those to eat tonight!" And I swore by God that I would not give it green vegetables to eat for forty nights'.[37]

Mālik ibn Dīnār spent fifty years at Basra, but never ate a single one of its dates, whether ripe or not. 'O people of Basra!' he said. 'For fifty years have I lived among you, and have not eaten a single one of your ripe or unripe dates, which thing has neither harmed me, nor benefited you.'[38]

He also said, 'Fifty years ago I divorced the world, and my soul has been desiring fine flour[39] for forty years, but, by God, I shall not feed it with any until I go to join God (Exalted is He!).'

Said Ḥammād ibn Abī Ḥanīfa, 'I once went to visit Dāūd al-Ṭā'ī, and found his door to be closed. I could hear him saying within, "You desired carrots, so I fed you with some; then you desired dates, and I swore that you would never eat them". I pronounced a greeting, and entered, and found him to be alone'.[40]

One day, Abū Ḥāzim[41] was passing through the souk. Seeing some fruit, he conceived a desire for it, and told his son, 'Buy for us some of that fruit which is out of *reach and forbidden*, that perhaps we may go on to the fruit which is *neither out of reach, nor yet forbidden.*'[42] When his son made the purchase and brought it to him, he said to his soul, 'You tricked me into looking and desiring, and you defeated me so that I bought. By God! You will not taste it!' And he sent it off to some poor orphans.

It is told that Mūsā ibn[43] al-As͟hajj once said, 'My soul has desired coarse salt for twenty years.'

It is related that Aḥmad ibn K͟halīfa said, 'My soul has harboured desire for twenty years, asking me only for enough water to quench its thirst, yet I have not given it even that'.

It is told that ʿUtba al-G͟hulām desired meat for seven years. Afterwards he said, 'I was ashamed before my soul to resist it for seven consecutive years, so I bought a piece of meat on some bread, and roasted it. Then I left it on its bread. I then met a boy, and asked him, "Are you not the son of So-and-so?" (his father having died). "Yes", he replied. So I gave it to him'. Then he began to weep, reciting *And for their love of Him*[A] *they feed the needy wretch, the orphan and the prisoner,*[44] and never tasted meat thereafter.[45]

He also spent years with a desire for dates. One day he bought a *qīrāṭ's*[B] worth of them, and put them away until nightfall when he would break his fast on them. Then a strong wind struck up, and the sky grew so dark that the people were afraid, and ʿUtba addressed his soul, saying, 'This is the result of my foolhardiness with you in buying a *qīrāṭ*'s worth of dates!' Then he said to his soul, 'I think that the people are to be punished by reason of your sin alone. I must not allow you to taste them!'[46]

Dāūd al-Ṭā'ī once spent half a *fals*[B] on green vegetables,[47] and half a *fals* on vinegar, and then spent the following night saying to his soul, 'Woe betide you, Dāūd! How lengthy your judgement

[A] Alternative senses: 'And despite their love of food' (Qus͟hayrī, *Laṭā'if*, III. 663); 'And for their love of giving food' (Bayḍāwī, 774). Cf. Asad, 916n; Lyall, 'The meaning of the words *'Ala hubbihi* in Qur. II, 172'.

[B] A coin of small denomination.

will be on the Day of Arising!' After that he ate nothing save dry bread.

ʿUtba al-Ghulām said one day to ʿAbd al-Wāḥid ibn Zayd, 'So-and-so describes his soul as being at a degree which I do not recognise my own soul to have attained'. He replied, 'That is because you eat dates as well as bread, while he eats only bread'. 'If I ceased to eat dates,' he asked, 'would I too attain to that degree?' 'Yes indeed,' he replied, 'and to others also'. At this, ʿUtba wept, and was told by one of his companions, 'May God dry your eyes! Are you weeping because of dates?' But ʿAbd al-Wāḥid said, 'Let him be, for his soul has learnt that he sincerely resolves to renounce them, and when he has renounced something he nevermore returns to it'.

Said Jaʿfar ibn Nuṣayr, 'Al-Junayd once instructed me to buy some *wazīrī*[48] figs. When I had done so, and when the time came for him to break his fast, he took one and set it in his mouth. Then he took it out, and began to weep. "Take them away!" he ordered. I asked him about this, and he replied, "A Voice[A] sounded in my heart,[49] saying, 'Are you not ashamed, that you once renounced them for My sake and then returned to them?'"'[50]

Said Ṣāliḥ al-Murrī, 'I once said to ʿAṭā' al-Sulamī, "There is a favour which I would render to you, so do not offend me by refusing." "Do what you will," he replied. So I sent my son to him with a bowl of barley-meal moistened with honey and clarified butter, having told him, "Do not leave him until he has eaten it". The next day I sent him another, but he returned it uneaten. I reproached him for this, saying, "Glory be to God! You have offended me!" When he saw my strong feelings about the matter he said, "Do not be hurt. The first time I ate, while the second time I tried to coax my soul into eating, but it would not: whenever I wished to do so, I remembered the word of God (Exalted is He!): *he gulps it down, scarcely able to swallow it, and death cometh unto*

[A] Ar. *hātif*, a disembodied voice sometimes heard by Sufis, which reproaches or guides them. Cf. T. Fahd, art. '*Hātif*' in *EI*², III. 273.

him from every side while yet he cannot die, and before him is a harsh punishment[51]".'[A] And Ṣāliḥ said, 'Then I wept, and said to myself, "I am in one valley, and he in quite another".'[52 B]

Said al-Sarī al-Saqaṭī, 'For thirty years my soul has been demanding that I dip a carrot into some black treacle, but I have not done so'.[53]

Said Abū Bakr ibn al-Jallā', 'I know a man whose soul told him, "I shall persevere for ten days without any food if you afterwards give me something to eat which I desire". But he replied, "I do not wish to go without food for ten days. Renounce the desire instead!"'

It is told that one of those men who are much given to worship once invited one of his brethren round, and served him with loaves of bread. His brother turned the loaves over in order to choose the best. 'What are you doing?' the worshipper asked him. 'Do you not know that the loaf you rejected contains many wisdoms, and that a great many forces were at work to make it, until it finally became rounded: the clouds which bore the water, which in turn watered the earth, the winds, the soil, the beasts and the descendants of Adam, until it came to you. And then you turn it over, and are not satisfied with it?'

It is related in a Tradition[54] that no loaf is rounded and set before you until three hundred and sixty forces have been at work on it, the first being Michael[C] (upon whom be peace), who measures out water from the storehouses of Mercy, and then the angels which drive along the clouds, the sun, moon, and planets, and the angels of the air, and the beasts of the earth, the last of whom is the baker. *And if you would count the blessings of God, you shall never count them.*[55]

One [of the Sufis] said, 'I once visited Qāsim al-Jūʿī, and asked

[A] The reference is to the putrid food which will sustain the damned.

[B] The final phrase is a common idiom implying a great distance.

[C] The angel responsible for distributing God's blessings, both physical and intellectual. See S. Murata, 'The Angels', 327–8.

him to define asceticism. "What have you heard about it?" he asked me, and I quoted several statements. He remained silent, so I said, "What do you say it is?" He replied, "Know that the belly is the world [*dunyā*] of God's bondsman, and that to the extent that he masters it, he has mastered asceticism, while to the extent that his belly masters him, he is mastered by the world".'[56]

Bis̲h̲r ibn al-Ḥārit̲h̲ once fell ill. He repaired to ʿAbd al-Raḥmān al-Ṭabīb[57] to ask him which foods would be suitable for him. He replied, 'You may ask, but when I have prescribed them for you, you will not accept what I say'. 'Tell me what they are,' he said, 'so that I may know'. And he told him, 'You should drink oxymel,[A] and suck on a quince,[B] and then eat blanquette.'[C] 'Do you know of anything inferior to oxymel which could supply its place?' asked Bis̲h̲r, and he replied that he did not. 'But I know of something,' Bis̲h̲r said. 'What?' [the physician] enquired. 'Endives[D] with vinegar', he said. Then [Bis̲h̲r] said, 'Do you know of anything inferior to quinces which could supply their place?' and he replied that he did not. 'But I know of something,' Bis̲h̲r said. 'What?' [the physician] demanded. 'Syrian carob,'[E] he said. 'And do you know of anything inferior to blanquette which could supply its place?' 'No,' he told him. 'But I know,' he said. 'What?' [the physician] asked, and he said, 'The juice of chickpeas in beef tallow'. And ʿAbd al-Raḥmān

[A] Ar. *sakanjubīn*, from Persian, *sirka-anjubīn*: a mixture of vinegar and honey, regarded as a remedy for arthritis and gout, amongst other ailments. (Dols, 126n; Graziani, 322.)

[B] A cure for coughs. (Ibn Sīnā, *Qānūn*, 237.)

[C] Ar. *isfid̲h̲bājā*. A specific for colds in the kidneys. (ʿAlī al-Ṭabarī, *Firdaws al-ḥikma*, 28; cf. Dozy, I. 22; Siggel, *Gifte*, 216.)

[D] Ar. *hindibā*. See Freytag, IV. 375 for the various forms of this word. A leguminous plant useful for the stomach, liver and spleen when eaten. (Graziani, 309; Lane, 2884; Ibn Sīnā, *Risāla fī amr al-hindibā*; cf. Tabarsī, 202; *Ma't̲h̲ūr*, III. 246; Massignon, *Passion*, I. 234.)

[E] Ar. *al-k̲h̲arnūb al-s̲h̲āmī*: probably *Ceratonia ciliqua*, which is possessed of some medicinal value, and is disagreeable in taste. (Ibn Sīnā, *Qānūn*, 319-20; Lane, 716-7; Graziani, 313.)

told him, 'You know medicine better than I; why, therefore, are you asking me questions?'

You have thus learnt that these men refrained from eating the things they desired, and from sating themselves on food, and that they refrained for the sake of the benefits which we have mentioned above. This they did with regard to certain foods,[58] which although lawful were not entirely pure in their eyes, so that they did not permit themselves to partake of them save in that quantity which was quite indispensable. The things which one desires are not indispensable: Abū Sulaymān al-Dārānī once said that 'salt is a desire, since it is an addition to bread, and everything more than bread is a desire'. This constitutes the utmost limit; but whoever is unable to attain it should not be heedless of his soul or become engrossed in his desires: it is sufficient extravagance for a man that he eat all that he desires,[A] and act in accordance with all his whims. Therefore one should not be in the habit of eating meat: it was said by ʿAlī (may God ennoble his face) that 'When a man renounces meat for forty days his character deteriorates, and when he eats it regularly for forty days his heart is hardened.' It has been said that[59] to eat meat regularly results in an addiction similar to the addiction to wine.

When a man is hungry, and his soul desires sexual intercourse, he should not eat and then go in to a woman, for he would thereby be permitting his soul two desires, which would strengthen it against him.[60] The soul often demands food in order to gain greater energy for sexual union. Similarly, it is preferable that one avoid sleeping on a full stomach, for this would be to conjoin two forms of heedlessness, which would habituate oneself to sloth and would harden the heart. Instead one should pray, or engage in the remembrance of God

[A] An echo of a Tradition: 'It is part of extravagance to eat all that one desires'. (Ibn Māja, Aṭʿima, 51.)

(Exalted is He!), for this is a better way to give thanks. It is said in Tradition, 'Melt away your food with prayer and the remembrance of God, and do not sleep after eating, lest your hearts become hard'.[61] The lowest form of this is to pray four *rakʿas*,[A] or to say 'Glory be to God!' [*subḥān Allāh*] a hundred times, or to recite one thirtieth-part of the Qur'ān; these things to be done after finishing a meal. Sufyān al-Thawrī, whenever he ate his fill in the evening, would spend his night in prayer, and when he ate his fill during the daytime would pray and remember God afterwards. He used to say, 'The slave is sated, and must work,' or 'the donkey is sated, and must work'.

Whenever a man desires some form of food or delicious fruit, he should forsake bread, and eat that food instead, so that his meal may provide sustenance and not exuberance, and so that his soul does not enjoy both a habit and a desire at once.

Sahl once looked at Ibn Sālim, who had some bread and dates in his hand. 'Begin with the dates,' he told him; 'if you find them sufficient, then stop; if not, then take such bread as you need.' Whenever a man has before him both light and heavy foods, then he should commence with the former, so that he will not then have a desire for the latter.[62] If he eats the heavy dish first, he will eat the light one as well because of its pleasantness. One [of the Sufis] used to say to his companions, 'Do not eat the things which you desire; and if you do, then do not seek them out, and if you seek them out, then do not love them'. Even to seek out some kinds of bread constitutes a desire. ʿAbd Allāh ibn ʿUmar said, 'There is no fruit which comes to us from Iraq that is more beloved to us than bread.' In this way he considered bread itself to be a kind of fruit.

In sum, then, one must not in any way neglect the soul so that it indulges in the lawful things which it desires, or follow its whims. To the extent that a bondsman satisfies his desire, it may be feared that he will be told on the Day of Arising, *You squan-*

[A] *Rakʿa*: unit of the Muslim ritual prayer.

dered your good things in the life of the world, and took pleasure therein[63]; whereas to the extent that he struggles with his soul and renounces its desires, he will enjoy the consummation of his desires in the Abode of the Afterlife.

An inhabitant of Basra once said, 'My soul fought with me for rice-bread[64] and fish, but I refused it. Its demands grew stronger, and I fought more bitterly, until twenty years had passed'. 'When he died,' someone else said, 'I saw him in a dream,[65] and asked him, "How has God dealt with you?" "I am unable to describe," he responded, "the blessings and honours which my Lord has granted me. First of all, he gave me rice-bread and fish, saying, 'Eat this day what you desire, contentedly and without fear of reckoning'."' God (Exalted is He!) has said, *Eat and drink at ease for what you sent before you in days gone by*:[66] they had sent before them the renunciation of their desires. It was for this reason that Abū Sulaymān al-Dārānī said, 'To renounce one desire is more profitable to the heart than to fast and pray for a whole year.'

God grant us success in pleasing Him![67]

[23.4]
An Exposition of the Variance in the Rule and Merit of Hunger in Accordance with the Circumstances of Men

KNOW that the most exalted desideratum in all matters and morals is moderation. For 'the best of affairs is the middle course',[A] and both extremes in any matter are blameworthy. Our discourse concerning the merits which attach to hunger may have suggested that extremeness is required in this regard, but this is certainly not the case. For it is one of the secret wisdoms of the Law [*Sharīʿa*] that whenever man's nature demands that he go to an unsound extreme, the Law also goes to extremes in forbidding this, in a fashion which to an uninformed man might suggest that it requires the complete opposite of what human nature [*ṭabʿ*] demands. The man of knowledge, however, realises that it is the mean that is required. This is because human nature, demanding as it does the maximum of satiety, must be countered by the Law with praises of extreme hunger, so that the instincts of man's nature and the prohibitions of the Law stand opposite one another, thereby bringing about an equilibrium. For it is an unlikely thing that a man might suppress his nature entirely; rather will he realise that he shall never reach this goal. Even were he to go to the greatest extremes in countering his nature, the Law would indicate that he had erred. The Law praises to the utmost those

[A] For this *ḥadīth* see above, p. 29.

who pray all night and fast by day; yet when the Prophet (may God bless him and grant him peace) learnt that someone[A] was fasting every day, and praying all night, he forbade him to continue.

Having learnt this, you should also know that the best course for a man of moderate nature is to eat so that his stomach is not heavy, but without feeling the pangs of hunger. One should forget one's belly, and not harbour any preference for hunger. For the purpose of eating[I] is the preservation of life and the gaining of strength for worship: a heavy stomach is an obstruction to worship, and so are the pangs of hunger, for they distract the heart. What is required is that one eat so as to prevent one's food from having an effect, at which one will be emulating the angels, who are too holy either for the heaviness of food or the pangs of hunger, and it is man's utmost purpose to emulate them. If a man remain unredeemed from satiety and hunger, then the furthest he can go from both extremes is the mean, which is the place of equilibrium. A human being, in his striving to distance himself from these opposite extremes by returning to the middle, can be compared to an ant thrown into the centre of a ring heated in fire and set on the earth: it will flee from the ring's heat which surrounds it, but, being unable to escape, will continue to run about until it comes to rest in the centre (should it die, it will die there); because the centre is the furthest point from the heat of the encompassing ring. Man's desires surround him like the ring which contains the ant, while the angels are outside the ring, whither man cannot hope to escape. Still, he desires to imitate them in their liberty, and finds that he resembles them most when he is far from his desires, and he is never further from those desires than when he is at the centre.[B] Thus is the mean required

[A] ʿAbd Allāh ibn ʿAmr ibn al-ʿĀṣ, according to the story in Bukhārī (Nikāḥ, 1; tr. Robson, *Mishkāt al-maṣābīḥ*, I. 435–6).

[B] The image of the mean as the centre of a circle is found in Miskawayh, *Hawāmil*, 238–9; cf. Arkoun, *Contribution*, 249, 300.

UNIVERSITY OF WINCHESTER LIBRARY

in all traits of character which have opposites.[2] This was expressed by the Prophet (may God bless him and grant him peace) when he said, 'The best of affairs is the middle course', and is indicated in the statement of God (Exalted is He!): *Eat and drink, but do not be extravagant.*[3] To the extent that a man feels neither hunger nor satiety, he will find worship and contemplation easy, and, being light, will have the strength to act.

This, however, comes about after one's nature has been set in equilibrium. At the outset, should the soul have a tendency to bolt, crave the satisfaction of its desires, and incline to excess, the mean will yield it no advantage; instead one must go to extreme lengths to hurt it with hunger, in the way that one must employ hunger, blows and other things to hurt a riding beast that is not broken in until it becomes moderate in its temperament. When it is broken in, becomes balanced, and reverts to the equilibrium, one may cease training and hurting it. It is for this secret reason that a Shaykh may command his aspirants to perform things which he himself does not do: he instructs them to be hungry, while he himself is not, or he may forbid them to eat fruits and other desirable things which he himself does not refrain from, having concluded the discipline of his own soul so that he no longer stands in need of such training.

Since the dominant condition of the soul is one of greed, desire, rebellion, and refusal to worship, the most profitable thing for it is hunger, the pain of which it feels under most circumstances, and which leads to its subjugation. The intention is that the soul should be broken in this way until it becomes balanced, which condition will abide even after it returns to its food. Among wayfarers on the Path of the Afterlife, the only people who refrain from hunger are Truthful Saints and self-deluded imbeciles: the former because their souls are following the *Straight Path* with perfect rectitude, and because they have no need of being driven with the whip of hunger to the True God, and the latter because they think themselves to be like the saints, and have a high opinion of their own souls. This is a serious form of illusion, and has become prevalent, since the soul is seldom disciplined completely, and frequently falls into illusion, so that it looks at the manner in which the Truthful Saints permit their souls certain things, and is permissive itself. In this way it resembles a sick man who watches someone who has been cured, and follows the same diet, thinking that he himself is being cured also, which thing will lead to his destruction.

There is a proof text which shows that to fix the quantity and variety of food one eats, and the time when one eats it, is not required in itself, but only insofar as it is a valuable form of struggle against a soul which is remote from the True God and has not attained the rank of perfection. This consists in the fact that the Emissary of God (may God bless him and grant him peace) did not fix a specific quantity or time for his meals. ʿĀ'isha (may God be pleased with her) said, 'The Emissary of God (may God bless him and grant him peace) used to fast until we would say that he would never break his fast, and then not fast until we would say that he would never fast again'.[4] He used to go in to his family, and ask, "Do you have anything?" If they said yes, he would eat, and if they said no, he would say, "Then I am fasting".'[5] If he was served with anything, he would declare, 'I had wanted to fast,' and then eat.[6] One day, he went out (may God bless him and grant him peace), saying, 'I am fasting', and ʿĀ'isha (may God be pleased with her), told him, 'We have been given some *ḥays*.'[A] 'I had wanted to fast,' he said, 'but serve it instead.'[7] For this reason it has been related that when someone asked Sahl how he had begun [his devotional life], he answered that he had performed many kinds of spiritual exercises, such as living for a time on the leaves of the lote-tree,[B] and then, for three years, on chaff, and that he had lived for three more years on only three dirhams. Then he was asked, 'What do you do now?' and he replied, 'I eat

[A] Usually a mixture of dates, clarified butter and a kind of cheese (Rodinson, 'Récherches sur les documents arabes rélatifs à la cuisine', 148; Lane, 686).

[B] Ar. *nabaq*, of which there are several varieties. (Cf. Dozy, II. 644.)

without observing any particular limit, or any fixed time'.[8] By saying 'without any particular limit, or any fixed time' he did not mean that he ate abundantly, but rather that he did not fix a single quantity of food in advance.

Maᶜrūf al-Karkhī was once given some delicious food, which he ate. Someone told him, 'Your brother Bishr does not eat such things', and he replied, 'My brother Bishr is in a state of Constriction[A] begotten of scrupulousness [*waraᶜ*], while I am in a state of Expansion[B] resulting from gnosis [*maᶜrifa*].' Then he said, 'I am no more than a guest in my Lord's house. When He gives me food, I eat; when He gives me hunger, I endure patiently. What have I to do with repudiation, and making distinctions?'

Ibrāhīm ibn Adham once gave some dirhams to one of his companions with the words, 'Buy some butter, honey and white bread for us'. 'O Abū Isḥāq!' someone said. 'All that?' And he replied, 'Shame on you! When we have money, we eat like men, and when we have none, we endure like men'. One day he prepared a large meal, and invited a small company, which included al-Awzāᶜī and al-Thawrī, to partake of it. This latter asked him, 'O Abū Isḥāq! Are you not afraid that this might constitute prodigality?' 'There is no prodigality in food,' came his reply; 'prodigality obtains only in respect of clothes and furnishing'.[9]

Someone who acquires his knowledge imitatively [*taqlīd*[an]], from lectures and transmitted authority, would see Ibrāhīm ibn Adham doing this, and at the same time hear Mālik ibn Dīnār say-

[A] Ar. *qabḍ*: 'the oppressive desert of loneliness in which the mystic spends days and sometimes months of his life' (Schimmel, *Mystical Dimensions*, 129). For the Central Asian school of Sufism in Ghazālī's day, *qabḍ*, a term thought to derive from Qur'ān, II:246: *God constricts and expands*, was the semi-permanent 'station' (*maqām*) experienced in response to the fear of God's wrath and chastisement.

[B] Ar. *basṭ*: the complementary 'station' of hope and confidence in God's forgiveness and proximity, which may be a prelude to ecstatic states. For *qabḍ* and *basṭ* see e.g. Hujwīrī, 374-6; Anawati and Gardet, *Mystique musulmane*, 89-90; Nicholson, *Studies*, 24.

ing, 'No salt has entered my house for twenty years',[10] and al-Sarī al-Saqaṭī declaring that for forty years he had desired to dip a carrot into some treacle, but had not done so,[11] and think that there was a contradiction here, and be puzzled, and declare that one of them must surely have been in error. The man who has insight, however, into the hidden sciences, will be aware that all of these [attitudes] are correct, but in relation to differing circumstances. When these situations are spoken of to an intelligent, prudent man, and to someone else who is foolish and self-satisfied, the former will say, 'I am no gnostic, that I might be gentle with my soul; for it is no more obedient than the soul of Sarī al-Saqaṭī and Mālik ibn Dīnār, who were among those who refrained from their desires; therefore shall I follow in their footsteps'. The man who is self-satisfied, however, will declare, 'My soul is no more disobedient to me than the soul of Maʿrūf al-Karkhī and Ibrāhīm ibn Adham, so it is they that I shall follow. I will permit myself any amount of food, for I too am a guest in my Lord's house: what have I to do with repudiation?' This provides the devil with much scope against the foolish; not to observe any limits in the matter of food, [supererogatory] fasting, or eating what one desires, is safe only for those who look into[12] the niche [*mishkāt*] of Sainthood and Prophethood, and who receive signs from God to the effect that they must eat or refrain. This can only take place when the soul has fully emerged from obedience[13] to its whims and to habit, so that when it eats, or refrains from eating, it does so with the appropriate intention, and works for God in both cases. One should learn determination from ʿUmar (may God be pleased with him), who saw that the Emissary of God (may God bless him and grant him peace) used to like and eat honey,[14] but did not draw an analogy from this for his own situation, and instead, when offered a cold drink which contained honey, turned the container around and around in his hand, saying, 'Shall I drink it, only for its sweetness to depart and its consequences to remain? Preserve me from being called to account for it!' And he left it alone.[15]

These secrets should not be unveiled by a Shaykh of the Path to his aspirants. Instead he should confine himself to praising hunger, and not summon them to moderation, for if he did so they would certainly fall short of it: he should rather summon them towards the very extremes of hunger, in order that such moderation might become easy for them. He should not tell them that the perfect gnostic may dispense with self-discipline, for this would furnish the devil with a pathway to their hearts, so that he would constantly be whispering to each of them, 'You are a perfect gnostic; what more gnosis and perfection could you need?' By contrast, the custom of Ibrāhīm al-Khawwāṣ was to engage in every form of self-discipline which he instructed his aspirants to perform, so that they would not think that the Shaykh was telling them to do things which he did not do himself, which would cause them to shy away from such forms of discipline. The strong man, when he devotes himself to self-discipline and the reform of others, must descend to the level of the weak in order that he might resemble them and be gentle when driving them towards their saving felicity. For the Prophets and Saints, this is a great trial.

Since the point of equilibrium for each person is hard to discern, determination and caution should under no circumstances be abandoned. It was for this reason that ʿUmar (may God be pleased with him) disciplined his son ʿAbd Allāh, when he once went in to find him eating some meat cooked in clarified butter. ʿUmar struck him with his stick, saying, 'Wretch! Eat bread and meat one day, and on the next bread and curd, on the next bread and clarified butter, on the next bread and oil, on the next bread and salt, and on the next bread alone!' This is the position of equilibrium. Constantly to eat meat and other desirable things is a form of prodigality and extravagance; to renounce meat altogether is to be grudging, while this is *a middle point between the two.* [16] [A]

[A] For this verse see above, p.29.

[23.5]

An Exposition of the Ostentation which may follow from the Renunciation of Desirable Foods and from Eating Frugally

KNOW that those who renounce desirable foods may be afflicted by two great evils which are even more pernicious than indulging in them.

The first obtains when the soul, being unable to forsake some of the things it finds desirable, and not wishing the fact to be known, conceals its desire, and eats things in secret which it does not eat when others are present. This constitutes a form of hidden polytheism.[A]

A scholar was once asked about a certain ascetic, and refused to speak of him. 'Has he any faults that you know of?' he was asked, and he answered, 'He eats things in private which

[A] This idea of *shirk khafī*, or *shirk aṣghar*, is alluded to by a *ḥadīth*: 'Polytheism is more hidden than the creeping of black ants.' (Ibn Ḥanbal, *Musnad*, IV. 403.) The Sufis took readily to this concept: 'Just as polytheism [*shirk*] invalidates monotheism, so also does ostentation invalidate works'. (Tustarī, in *Muʿāraḍa*, 41.) According to Ghazālī, 'Polytheism is of two kinds: hidden, which does not lead to eternal damnation, and which is escaped only by a few, being more hidden than the crawling of a black ant, and clear polytheism, which leads to eternal residence in Hell.' (*Iḥyā'*, II. 203-4 [*K. Dhamm al-bukhl*, Bayān madḥ al-māl].) Cf. also *Iḥyā'*, IV. 327-8 (*K. al-Nīya*, bāb 2, Bayān darajāt al-shawā'ib, daraja 4); *Iḥyā'*, III. 263-8 (*K. Dhamm al-jāh*, shaṭr 2, Bayān al-riyā' al-khafī ..., and Bayān mā yuḥbiṭ al-ʿamal ...); Muḥāsibī, *Masā'il fi'l-zuhd*, 64-5; Obermann, 150.

he does not eat with others'. Now this is a serious fault. If a bondsman of God be tried with desires which he loves to gratify, he ought to make them public, for his state will thus be one of honesty, compensating for the absence of acts of spiritual struggle. To conceal one's shortcomings and to make a show of their excellent opposites are themselves two compounded shortcomings, and to lie, and to hide one's lying, are themselves a twofold lie, so that a man guilty of this deserves two chastisements, and will not be acceptable again in his works until he has repented twice. It is for these reasons that God has laid such emphasis upon the issue of the hypocrites, saying, *Hypocrites shall be in the lowest chasm of Hell:*[1] the unbeliever makes public his unbelief, and is sincere in it,[2] while the hypocrite keeps his unbelief hidden, so that this concealment becomes another form of unbelief, since he makes light of God's gazing into his heart, and makes much of the gaze of His creatures by effacing unbelief from his outward aspect. The gnostics too are tried with desires, and even with sins, but are never tried with ostentation, deceit or concealment: the perfect gnostic renounces his desires for the sake of God (Exalted is He!) and affects their presence in himself in order to diminish the respect in which other men hold him. One of them used to go out and buy delicious things, and display them in his house, although he never partook of them. This he did merely to deceive people regarding his state and to repel the hearts of the heedless, so that he would not be distracted from his state.[A] The highest form of

[A] A reference to the method of *malāma*, 'blame', adopted by some early Sufis such as D͟hu'l-Nūn al-Miṣrī, by which the adept would conceal his piety by pretending to a casual attitude towards the *S͟harīʿa*. It was debated whether the objective of *ik͟hlāṣ*, 'pure sincerity' was always attainable by this technique. According to G͟hazālī, *malāma* is a technique to be used only by those with no following of students or disciples, and should be confined to the performance of actions which, although looked down upon by the public, are entirely permissible (*Iḥyā'*, III. 249 [*K. D͟hamm al-jāh*, s͟haṭr I, Bayān wajh al-ʿilāj...]). See Molé, 72-8; Sulamī, *Risālat al-malāmatīya*; Schimmel, *Mystical Dimensions*, 86-7 and the references there given.

renunciation is to renounce renunciation itself by outwardly appearing to do its opposite: this is the practice of the Truthful Saints, since it combines two veracities, just as the former combines two lies. It weighs down the soul with two burdens, and forces it to quaff the cup of endurance twice: once by actually drinking it, and once again by suffering insults. *Assuredly, such will be given their reward twice on account of their endurance.*[3] This is comparable to the way of those who are given and accept money publicly, but who secretly return it, in order to subjugate their souls through public humiliation and private poverty.

All those who cannot accomplish this should at least make their desires and weaknesses public, for the sake of honesty, and should not be beguiled by the devil's saying to them, 'If you make these things known, other men will follow you into doing them. So hide them away, and you will reform such people!' For the man who wishes to reform others should first reform himself. Such a person can only intend sheer ostentation, and the devil encourages him in this by suggesting that he will reform others; for this reason he would find the noising abroad of his desires unpleasant, even if he knew that those who came to know of them would not imitate his actions or renounce something in the belief that he himself had renounced his desires.

The second evil arises when a man genuinely engages[4] in the renunciation of his desires, but rejoices that he is known to do so, and that he is famous for his continence in the face of his cravings. By doing this he has merely disobeyed a weak desire, namely that of food, and surrendered to a desire which is far worse: that of the love of status. This is a 'hidden desire'.[A] When one detects such a desire in the soul, it is more important to defeat it than to defeat the desire for food itself: in fact, it is more appropriate that such a person should eat.

[A] This may be a reference to the Tradition: 'I fear that my community [may be tempted by] ostentation and hidden desire.' (Ibn Ḥanbal, *Musnad*, IV. 124.) According to Zabīdī (VII. 427) this should be interpreted to mean 'a desire to be known and spoken of as one who abstains from his desires'.

Abū Sulaymān said, 'If something is put before you in the nature of a desire which you have renounced, then partake of it just a little, but do not give your soul all it hopes for. In this way you will banish a desire without making it pleasurable for your soul.'

Said Jaʿfar ibn Muḥammad al-Ṣādiq, 'Whenever I am confronted with a desire, I look to my soul. If it displays desire, I give it something of it, which is better than to deprive it, whereas if it hides its desire, and displays indifference to it, I punish it by abstaining, and do not give it anything at all.' Such is the way to punish the soul for this hidden desire.

In sum, the man who renounces his desire for food only to fall prey to the desire which is ostentation, resembles a man who flees from a scorpion and takes refuge with a viper, for ostentation is more harmful than the desire for food.

[23.6]
A Discourse on Sexual Desire

KNOW that man has been made subject to sexual desire for two beneficial reasons. The first of these is that by knowing its delight he is able to draw an analogy which suggests to him what the delight of the Afterlife must be like. For the delight of the sexual act, were it to last, would be the greatest pleasure of the body, just as the pain of a burn is the body's greatest agony. Encouragement and deterrance [*al-targhīb wa'l-tarhīb*], which drive people towards their saving happiness, can only be brought about by means of palpable pain and pleasure, since what cannot be perceived through experience will never be greatly desired. The second reason is that it allows the human race to continue and the world [*ʿālam*] to abide. Such are its benefits.[A]

However, sexual desire also contains evils which may destroy both religion and the world if it is not controlled and subjugated, and restored to a state of equilibrium. It has been said that His word (Exalted is He!), *O our Lord! Burden us not with more than we can bear!*[1] refers, when correctly interpreted, to powerful lust.[2] And Ibn ʿAbbās understood His word

[A] Cf. also the five 'benefits of marriage' expounded by Ghazālī in *Iḥyā'*, II. 22-30 (*K. Ādāb al-nikāḥ*, bāb 1, Āfāt al-nikāḥ wa-fawā'iduh), namely: (1) obtaining children who will serve their parents and pray for them; (2) gaining a lawful outlet for sexual desire, thereby thwarting the devil; (3) relaxation of the heart through intimacy with a woman; (4) relief from domestic chores; (5) an opportunity to struggle against the *nafs* when making an honourable living for one's family, and tolerating the difficulties of married life.

(Exalted is He!), *wa-min sharri ghāsiq^in idhā waqab*[3] [A] to refer to 'the erection of the male member'.[4] A certain Traditionist has traced back to the Emissary of God (may God bless him and grant him peace) the saying [interpreting the same verse], 'The male member when it enters'.[5] It has been said that 'an erection results in the loss of two-thirds of the intelligence'.[6] And the Prophet (may God bless him and grant him peace) used to say in his prayers, 'I seek refuge in Thee from the evil which may be in my ear, my eye, my heart[7] and my semen'.[8] And he said (upon him be peace), 'Women are the snares of the devil' [9B]—and indeed, were it not for this desire women would have no power over men.

It is told that Moses (upon whom be peace) was once sitting in company[10] when Satan came up to him wearing a cloak in which he assumed many colours [*yatalawwanu fīhi alwān^an*]. When he drew near to him he took this off and set it aside. Then he said, 'Peace be upon you, Moses!' Moses asked him who he was, and he replied, 'I am Satan'. 'God slay you!' Moses said. 'What brings you here?' And he answered, 'I have come to greet you in view of your great rank in the sight of God'. 'What was it that I saw you wearing?' he asked, and he replied, 'A cloak with which I snatch away the hearts of the descendants of Adam'. 'What is it then,' Moses asked, 'that a man does which enables you to prevail over him?' And he replied, 'He becomes pleased with himself, and considers that he has many good deeds to his credit, and forgets his sins. Now, I would warn you against three things! Never be alone with a woman who is not

[A] As Ibn ʿAbbās' gloss suggests, this verse caused confusion among the exegetes. *From the evil of dusk when it dimmeth into night* (Lings, *Muhammad*, 261) recalls a more mainstream interpretation. Ṭabarī (*Tafsīr*, xxx. 226-7) speculates that *waqab* may refer to nightfall, the Pleïades, or the moon. Cf. further Bayḍāwī, 814; Asad, 986n2.

[B] There are a number of misogynous apophthegmata of this type, which may be of Christian origin. See Sakhāwī, 400-1 (under *shāwirūhunna wa-khālifūhunna*), where they are all dismissed as spurious.

lawful for you, for never does a man do so without having me, not my companions, as his companion, so that I tempt them both with one another. Never make a vow to God without fulfilling it. And never prepare something to give as charity and then fail to give it, for never does a man do so without having me, not my companions, as his companion, so that I prevent him from giving it [at a later time]'. Then he went away, crying, 'Woe is me! Moses has learnt something against which to warn the descendants of Adam!'

Saʿīd ibn al-Musayyib once said, 'Satan never despaired of destroying any previous prophet by means of women.[A] In my opinion they are to be feared more than anything else. I do not enter a single house in Medina—apart from my own and that of my daughter, which I take a bath in on Fridays and then leave'.[11]

Someone once said, 'The devil says to woman: "You are half my army! You are my arrow with which I do not miss! You are my confidante! You are my messenger with whom I achieve my wants!" Thus half his army is desire, the other half being anger.'

The desire for women, which is the greatest of all desires, is susceptible to excess, defect, and equilibrium. Excess obtains when the intellect is overcome, so that a man's concern is so distracted towards the enjoyment of women and slavegirls that he is unable to tread the path of the Afterlife; or it may overcome a man's religion, so that he is drawn into obscene activities. This may become so extreme in some cases that two foul habits are acquired. Firstly, he may partake of something which makes him desire to have intercourse more often, just as some people take certain drugs which strengthen the stomach and allow them to eat more of the things which they desire.

[A] 'With the exception, that is,' comments Zabīdī (VII. 430), 'of our own Prophet (may God bless him and grant him peace), whom God had helped against him'.

This resembles nothing so much as a man tormented by savage beasts and snakes[12] which sleep from time to time, but which he finds methods of awakening and arousing, and then has to make his peace with. For the desires for food and intercourse are in reality pains, which a man would rather be free of so as to gain another form of delight.[A] Should you object that it has been narrated in a *gharīb*[B] Tradition that the Emissary of God (may God bless him and grant him peace) said, 'I complained to Gabriel that I would like more strength when having intercourse with my wives, and he instructed me to eat *harīsa,*[C]'[13] then you should know that he had (may God bless him and grant him peace) nine wives, and that he was obliged to satisfy them all, and that no-one was permitted to marry them after his death, or even if he divorced them: his request for strength was therefore for this, and not for enjoyment.[14 D]

The second thing is that in the case of some misguided people this desire may end in amorous passion [*ʿishq*], which constitutes utter ignorance of the intended purpose of sexual congress, and a descent to a level lower than that of the animals. For such people are not content merely to gratify their lust, which is the unsightliest of all desires and the one of which

[A] This understanding has found its way into the thought of al-Fakhr al-Rāzī, according to Maʿṣūmī, *Imām Rāzī's 'Ilm al-Akhlāq*, 178, 191.

[B] A *ḥadīth* which contains unusual lexis, or which is related by only one chain of authorities. (Jurjānī, *Taʿrīfāt*, 167.)

[C] *Harīsa*, of which there are several varieties, is a highly nourishing dish made from wheatflour (cf. Ibn Sīnā, *Qānūn*, 72; Rodinson, 'Récherches', 241-2).

[D] This somewhat austere view of the Prophet's sexuality does not fully coincide with the traditional picture presented in his biography, where his prowess is celebrated as a further aspect of his human perfection. According to one account, 'the Prophet, may God bless him and grant him peace, used to visit all of his wives in a single day and night—and there were eleven of them.' (Qāḍī ʿIyāḍ, *Shifā'*, I. 195.) And in this connection, 'he had been given the strength of thirty men' (Bukhārī, Ghusl, 12). The Imām may be introducing this attitude for 'strategic' reasons; see Introduction, p. LXVIII above.

a man should most be embarrassed, but instead believe that their lust can only be satisfied by one person. An animal finds it enough to satisfy its lust anywhere it can, whereas these people will only be satisfied with one person in particular, which thing heaps abasement upon abasement, and enslavement upon enslavement, until their intellects are subordinated to the service of their cravings, even though the intellect has been created to be obeyed, not to obey desires and devise means of gratifying them. Amorous passion is nothing but a wellspring[15] of excessive sexual desire, and is the disease of an empty and unconcerned heart. One should be on one's guard against its preliminaries by abstaining from repeated glances and thoughts. Otherwise, it will take firm hold of one and be difficult to shake off. In this it resembles the passion which certain people harbour for wealth, status, land and children, or even for playing with birds[16], lutes[17], backgammon, or chess, all of which may possess them to such a degree that their religious and worldly lives are adulterated and they are unable ever to abstain from them. To break the power of amorous passion in its early stages is like pulling at the reins of a riding-beast when it heads for a gate it would like to enter: to rein it back is a very easy thing, whereas to treat such a passion after it has taken hold of one is like letting the beast go in, and then catching it by its tail and pulling it from behind: a much more difficult task. One should therefore take precautions at the onset of these things, for later they can only be treated with an effort so intense as almost to lead to death.

Excess in the matter of sexual desire, then, causes the intellect to be overcome to this degree, which is very much to be condemned. Insufficient sexual desire, however, leads to an indifference to women, or to giving them insufficient pleasure, which is also to be condemned. Sexual desire is a praiseworthy thing when it stands in a state of equilibrium, obedient to the intellect and the Law in all its movements. Whenever it becomes excessive, it should be broken with hunger and marriage. The Prophet (may God bless him and grant him peace) said: 'O young men! You should marry, and whosoever cannot should fast, for fasting is a form of castration.'[18]

[23.7]
An Exposition of the Aspirant's Obligations Regarding the Renunciation or Undertaking of Marriage

KNOW that at the outset the aspirant should not occupy his heart and his soul with marriage, for this would distract him very seriously from treading the Path, and would cause him to find solace in his wife; and all who find solace in other than God must necessarily be distracted from Him. You should not be deceived by the fact that the Emissary of God (may God bless him and grant him peace) married frequently, for the entire world could not have distracted his heart from God: one cannot compare angels to prison warders.[A] In this way, Abū Sulaymān al-Dārānī said, 'Whoever marries has inclined toward the world'. He also remarked, 'I have never known an aspirant to marry and retain his former state.' And when he was once told, 'How greatly you need a woman in whom you can take solace!' he replied, 'May God not grant me solace in her!'—for that would bar him from finding solace in God (Exalted is He!). He likewise said, 'Everything which distracts you from God, whether it be family, property or children, is an ill omen for you.' How, then, could one draw such an analogy in the case of the Emissary of God (may God bless him and grant him peace),

[A] Or: 'blacksmiths'. The translation given follows the interpretation of Maydānī (*Majmaʿ al-amthāl*, I. 136). The trope is a favourite with Ghazālī; cf. Lazarus-Yafeh, 127-9.

whose burning love of God sometimes so engulfed him that he feared that it might overflow upon his physical body and destroy it? For this reason (because of his frame's insufficient capacity) he would at times slap the thigh of ʿĀ'isha, and say, 'Talk to me, ʿĀ'isha!'[1] so as to be distracted by her words from the overwhelming nature of his state. Intimacy with God (Great and Glorious is He!) was part of his nature, while his intimacy with His creatures was temporary, and a form of clemency to his body. He found his perseverence in sitting with God's creatures hard to bear, and would say, 'Relieve us with it, Bilāl!' in order to return to that which was his true delight.[2A] A weak person, observing how his circumstances were in such matters, will be deceived, since no mind can comprehend the secret wisdom behind his acts (may God bless him and grant him peace).

Accordingly, it is a condition that the aspirant remain celibate at the outset, until such time as his gnosis becomes well-established. This, however, is the case only if he is not overcome by desire. If he is so overcome he should break it with constant hunger and fasting. Should his desire still not be subjugated, and he find himself unable to restrain his eyes, for instance, even if able to preserve his chastity, then for him marriage is the better state, for it will quieten his desire.[B] Otherwise, to the extent that he cannot restrain his eyes he will be unable to restrain his thoughts, and his concentration will be destroyed; he may even be tried with something beyond his capacity. The 'fornication of the eye' is one of the major venial faults, and soon leads on to a mortal and obscene sin, which is the fornication of the flesh. The man who is

[A] With these words he was asking Bilāl, his muezzin at Medina, to give the Call to Prayer, in which, according to another *ḥadīth* (Nasā'ī, Nisā', 1), he would find his 'true delight' (literally the 'coolness of his eye').

[B] As Bercher observes: 'Point de vue absolument contraire à celui de la religion catholique romaine' (Bercher, 'Extrait', 319).

unable to turn away his eyes will not be able to safeguard himself against unchastity.[3]

Jesus (upon whom be peace) said, 'Beware of glances, for they sow desire in the heart, which is temptation enough.'[4]

Saʿīd ibn Jubayr said, 'Temptation came to David (upon whom be peace) merely through a glance.[A] Therefore he told his son [Solomon] (upon whom be peace), "O my son! Walk behind a lion or a black cobra, but never walk behind a woman".

John [the Baptist] (upon whom be peace) was once asked, 'How does fornication begin?' and he replied, 'With looking and wishing'.[5]

Al-Fuḍayl said, 'Satan says: "It is my ancient bow, and my arrow with which I do not miss", referring to looking.'

And the Emissary of God (may God bless him and grant him peace) said, 'A gaze is a poisoned arrow from Satan. Whoever abstains from it in fear of God shall receive from Him an increase in faith, the sweetness of which he will feel in his heart'.[6]

He also said (may God bless him and grant him peace), 'I leave behind me no temptation more damaging to men then that of women'.[7]

And he said (may God bless him and grant him peace), 'Beware of the temptation of this world and the temptation of women, for truly, the first temptation of the sons of Israel was through women'.[8]

[A] 'And it came to pass in an eveningtide, that David arose from off his bed, and walked upon the roof of the king's house; and from the roof he saw a woman washing herself; and the woman was very beautiful to look upon. And David sent and enquired after the woman. And one said, Is not this Bath-sheba, the daughter of Eliam, the wife of Uriah the Hittite? And David sent messengers, and took her, and she came in unto him, and he lay with her.' (2 Samuel 11, 2-4.) Needless to say, this was offensive to Muslims, who held the prophets to be divinely secured from sin. See Johns, 'David and Bathsheba. A Case Study in the Exegesis of Qur'anic Storytelling.'

God (Exalted is He!) says: *Tell the believing men to lower their gaze*[9] to the end of the verse.[A10]

And [the Prophet] said (upon him be peace), 'Every son of Adam has his share of fornication. The eyes fornicate, and do so by looking. The hands fornicate, and do so by touching. The feet fornicate, and do so by walking.[B] The mouth fornicates, and does so by kissing. And the heart forms thoughts and wishes, which the genitals confirm or deny.'[11]

Said Umm Salama, 'Ibn Umm Maktūm, the blind man, once asked leave of the Emissary of God (may God bless him and grant him peace) to enter while I was sitting with Maymūna. [The Prophet] asked us to go behind a screen, and we asked, "Is he not blind, and unable to see us?" And he replied, "Do you not see him?"'[12] This shows that it is not lawful for women to sit with blind men, as has become the custom today at banquets and funeral assemblies. A blind man is forbidden to be alone with women, and no woman may sit with a blind man or gaze at him without reason. It is only lawful for women to speak to men and to look at them for purposes of general necessity.[13]

Now, it may also be the case that a man is able to keep his eyes from women,[14] but not from adolescent boys, and for him too it is better that he marry. For the case of boys is even more damaging, since if a man's heart inclines to a woman he may at least render her lawful to him by marrying her. To look with desire at the face of a boy is forbidden; in fact, everyone whose heart is affected by the form of beautiful boys to the extent that he senses that they are different from bearded adults, is forbidden to look at

[A] The rest of the verse runs: *and to preserve their chastity. That is purer for them. Assuredly, God is Aware of what they do.* This virtue is required also of women: the following verse begins: *And tell the believing women to lower their gaze and preserve their chastity.*

[B] To an immoral act or place. (Cf. Muḥāsibī, *Masā'il fī aʿmāl al-qulūb*, 159-60; Nawawī, *Sharḥ*, XVI. 205-6.)

them.[A] Should you say, 'Everyone who has any perception necessarily knows the difference between someone who is beautiful and someone who is ugly, and yet the faces of young boys remain unveiled,' I would reply that I do not mean the mere distinction made by the eye, which resembles the distinction which one might make between a green tree and a desiccated one, between pure and polluted water, or a bush bearing blossoms and another denuded of leaves: one inclines towards the former in each case both with one's eye and one's nature, but in a fashion that is quite devoid of sexual desire, for one does not desire to touch and kiss flowers, or sources of light, or pure water. Likewise is the case with handsome old men, to whom one's eye may incline, and know the difference between them and old men who are ugly, but without any intrusion of desire. This may be recognised in one's inclination towards proximity and touching: to the extent that a man detects this inclination in his heart, and perceives the distinction between a handsome face and pleasant plants, embroidered garments, and gilded ceilings, his regard is concupiscent, and therefore forbidden.

This is a matter in which people are careless, and which drags them into destruction without their noticing. One of the

[A] The implications of this weakness, celebrated by a number of important Arab poets, are discussed in Bellamy, 'Sex and Society in Islamic Popular Literature,' 37-8; Schimmel, 'Eros in Sufi Literature and Life,' 131-3; for the more general Islamic understanding of inversion, see, e.g. *EI*², v. 776-9, art. 'Liwāṭ'; Yakan, *al-Islām wa'l-jins*, 47-50. The phenomenon may have been reinforced by the increasing segregation of higher-class women from the second century onwards, although this cannot be proved securely; indeed, it has been shown that among the ancient Greeks, homosexuality was often more common in regions which did not practise female seclusion than in areas which did. (Wilkinson, *Classical Attitudes to Modern Issues*, 115-6.) G͟hazālī is here echoing the concerns of other sober mystics of his tradition, such as Qus͟hayrī (*Risāla*, 744-5), who were alarmed by what seems to have been a widespread and unnatural interest in *aḥdāt͟h*, male teenagers present at Sufi gatherings. The *s͟hāhid*, the youth whose beauty bears witness to the beauty of the Divine, is nonetheless one of the commonest and most ambivalent figures of Persian mystical literature.

Followers said, 'A wild lion is less to be feared in the case of a youth given to worship than his sitting with an adolescent boy.'[15] Sufyān remarked, 'If a man so much as plays with two toes of a boy for the sake of lust, he is a sodomite'.[16] One of the Predecessors[A] said, 'There shall be three kinds of sodomites in this nation:[B] those who look, those who hold hands, and those who act.'

To gaze at adolescents is therefore a very serious matter. To the extent that an aspirant is unable to lower his eyes and control his thoughts, the appropriate thing is that he should break his desire by marrying, for there are many souls whose cravings cannot be subdued through hunger.

Someone once said, 'At the outset of my aspirancy I was unbearably oppressed by sexual desire. For a long time I beseeched God (Exalted is He!), until I saw someone in a dream. He asked me what was the nature of my complaint, and I informed him. "Come here," he told me, and I did so. He then placed his hand on my chest, and I felt its coolness in my heart and in all my body. When I awoke, my condition was at an end, and I remained free from it for a year. When it returned, I sought help once more from God, until someone again came to me in a dream, saying, "Would you like your state to be removed on condition that I chop off your head?" "Yes," I told him. "Then lean forward," he said, and when I did so he drew a sword of light, and cut off my head. When I awoke, the condition had ended, and again I was free from it from a year. Finally, it returned to me even more powerfully, and again I saw someone standing directly before me. He said, "Wretch! How many times[17] have you asked God to remove that which He does not like to remove?" And so I married, and that state departed from me at last, and I was given children.'

However much an aspirant may need to marry, he should not forsake the stipulations of aspirancy, either when he is first

[A] Ar. *salaf*: the early Muslims.

[B] Ar. *umma*: the community of Islam.

married or later on. When he is newly wed, he should respect them by having a correct intention, while during the course of his married life he should do so by means of goodness of character and behaviour, and respecting the rights which God (Exalted is He!) has granted to women[18] and which, since we have detailed them in the *Book of Marriage*,[A] we will not commit prolixity by reiterating. It is a sign of sincerity in aspirancy that one marry a woman who is poor but religious, rather than seeking after a wealthy one. Someone once said that 'The man who marries a rich woman will find five things in her: an expensive dower, a delayed wedding, a lack of service, constant expense, and an inability to divorce her should he wish to do so, because of his fear of losing her money.[B] The case of a poor woman, however, is quite the opposite.' And someone else remarked: 'A wife should be beneath her husband in four things or else she will despise him: age, height, wealth and lineage. She should be better than him in four others: beauty, manners, character, and scrupulousness in matters of religion.'

The mark of sincere aspirancy in married life is good character. A certain aspirant once married a woman whom he served so constantly that she was embarrassed, and complained to her father. 'I am quite bewildered,' she said, 'by this man. I have

[A] This book (*Iḥyā', K. al-Nikāḥ*) contains a chapter on 'A Wife's Rights over her Husband' (II. 52-5 [bāb 3, qism 2]). The English version by Farah (*Marriage and Sexuality in Islam*, 93-120) is unsatisfactory; but good German and French translations exist (see Appendix II), and also a Spanish synopsis by Asín (*Espiritualidad*, I. 160-2). Ghazālī lists twelve such rights, including the toleration of faults, provision of financial maintenance, and the equal treatment of co-wives.

[B] The property of Muslim women is secured to them by the *Sharīʿa*: marriage does not grant a husband any right to his spouse's money and possessions. The quotation reminds us of the reasonable degree of financial independence enjoyed by women in classical Islam. While there is insufficient space here to discuss the matter at length, it is interesting to recall in parenthesis the present situation in Saudi Arabia, where it is said that most property is owned by women. (Smith, *The Islamic Impact*, 96-7; also above, LXXX.)

been in his house for years, and not once have I gone to the privy without his arriving there before me with the water'. Another aspirant married a woman of great beauty, who shortly before the wedding was afflicted with the smallpox. Her family were beside themselves with grief, and feared that he would no longer find her beautiful. Instead, however, he pretended to them that he himself had been afflicted with ophthalmia, and then that he had gone quite blind, so that when she was given to him in marriage her family were no longer distressed. He continued in this way for twenty years until at last, when she died, he opened his eyes. When questioned about what he had done, he said, 'I did it deliberately so that her family would not be grieved.' 'You have outrun all your brethren,' he was told, 'through your goodness of character.'[19]

Another Sufi once married a bad-tempered woman, and endured her company patiently. When asked why he did not divorce her, he replied, 'I am afraid that someone might marry her who is unable to tolerate her, and will suffer accordingly'.

This is how an aspirant should be when he marries. But should he be able to forsake marriage, then this would be more appropriate, on condition that he be incapable of combining the merit which lies in marriage with his wayfaring on the Path, and that he be aware that marriage would distract him. In this wise, it is told that Muḥammad ibn Sulaymān al-Hāshimī, whose daily revenues on his worldly investments amounted to eighty thousand dirhams, once sent a letter to the people and scholars of Basra, asking whether they knew of a woman whom he could marry. They all concurred that Rābiʿa al-ʿAdawīya (may God show her His mercy) should be the one.[A] And so he wrote to her in this wise: 'In the name of God, most Compassionate and Merciful! To proceed. God (Exalted is He!) has given me an income of eighty thousand dirhams every

[A] According to Zabīdī (VII. 437), Rābiʿa was as beautiful as she was devout.

day out of the things of this world, and it will not be long before this becomes a full hundred thousand, of which I shall give you riches in proportion, so accept my offer!' And she wrote back as follows: 'In the name of God, most Compassionate and Merciful! To proceed. The renunciation of this world brings tranquillity to heart and body alike, whereas to desire it brings worry and grief. When you receive this letter of mine, then prepare your provisions, and address yourself to your fate. Be the counsellor of your own soul, and let not other men be your counsellors, lest they divide up your wealth.[20] Fast without cease, and break your fast with death. As for myself, were God (Exalted is He!) to give me many times what He has given to you, I would not be happy to be distracted from Him for the blinking of an eye'.[A]

This is an indication that everything that distracts one from God is a shortcoming: let, therefore, the aspirant scrutinise his condition and his heart: should he find that these are at peace in bachelorhood, then thus should he remain, whereas if they are not, and he cannot render them so, then it is better that he marry. The cure for this weakness is threefold: hunger, lowering the gaze, and busying oneself with some activity that will come to prevail in the heart. Should these three things be of no avail, then only marriage will cure the matter at its root.

It was for this reason that the Predecessors made haste to marry, and to marry off their daughters. Saʿīd ibn al-Musayyib said: 'Satan never despairs of anyone until he has endeavoured to tempt him through women'.[21] And [Ibn al-Musayyib] said, at the age of eighty-four, when he had lost the use of one eye, and was almost blind in the other, 'In my opinion, women are to be feared more than anything else'.[22]

[A] For this anecdote see Smith, *Rābiʿa*, 10–11. It is a generally recognised principle of Islamic law that women have the right to refuse a suitor: cf. Abū Zahra, *Muḥāḍarāt fī ʿaqd al-zawāj*, 90, 165; Nasir, *The Islamic Law of Personal Status*, 46.

ʿAbd Allāh ibn Abī Wadāʿa related: 'I used to attend the assemblies of Saʿīd ibn al-Musayyib, who once noticed my absence for a few days. When I returned, he enquired where I had been, and I replied that my wife had died and that I had been occupied on that account. "Would that you had told me," he said, "so that I could have attended her funeral". I then made to rise, but he asked, "Have you married again?" "God have mercy on you!" I said. "Who would allow me to marry his daughter, since I possess no more than two or three dirhams?" "I would," said he. "Would you do that?" I asked, and he replied, "Certainly." And he praised God (Exalted is He!), and called down blessings upon the Prophet (may God bless him and grant him peace), and married me to her for a dowry of two dirhams.' (Three, according to another version). 'Beside myself with joy, I got to my feet and went to my house, where I started to think whom I could ask for things, and from whom I could borrow. After attending the Sunset Prayer, I went home again, and lit a lantern. I had been fasting, and my supper, consisting of bread and oil, was brought for me to break my fast on. Suddenly, I heard a knock on the door. "Who is that?" I asked, and a voice answered, "Saʿīd". I thought of all the people I knew called Saʿīd, except Saʿīd ibn al-Musayyib, since for forty years he had been seen nowhere save in his house and at the mosque. I went out, and there was Saʿīd ibn al-Musayyib. I imagined that some idea had occurred to him, and I said, "O Abū Muḥammad! Had you only sent for me I would have come to you instead!" "No," he said, "It is more correct that I visit you." "What can I do for you?" I asked, and he replied, "You were a single man to whom I gave my daughter in marriage, and I was reluctant to make you spend this night alone. Here is your wife." And there she was, standing close behind him. He took her hand, guided her through the door, and then closed it, following which the woman fell to the ground out of shyness. I made sure the door was closed, and then went to the bowl of bread and oil and put it where the lamp's rays did not penetrate, lest she see it.[A] Then I went up onto the roof, and threw some pebbles to [attract the attention of] my neighbours. When they came, and asked what was the matter, I said, "Saʿīd ibn al-Musayyib today gave me the hand of his daughter, and came unexpectedly this evening!" "Saʿīd married her to you?" they asked, and I said, "Yes!" "And she is in the house?" they enquired, and I replied that she was, at which they went down to her. My mother was informed, and she arrived and said, "May I never see your face again if you touch her before I have spent three days reconciling her to me!" And so I waited three days before consummating the union, and found her to be surpassingly beautiful, and more erudite[B] than anyone in the Book of God and the Precedent [*Sunna*] of His Emissary (may God bless him and grant him peace), and well aware of the rights of her husband. After spending a month without either visiting Saʿīd or being visited by him, I went to see him. He was sitting in his circle, and, once I had greeted him, and he returned my greeting, he spoke to me no more until the people had dispersed. "How is that person?"[C] he enquired. "Very well, Abū Muḥammad," I told him, "as a friend would love, and an enemy hate". "Should you find anything doubtful in that person," he said, "then the disobedient one is yours [to deal with]!" And, after I had returned home, he sent me a gift of twenty thousand dirhams.[23]

ʿAbd Allāh ibn Sulaymān remarked: 'She had already received a proposal from [the Caliph] ʿAbd al-Malik ibn Marwān on behalf of his son al-Walīd when he made him his heir apparent, but Saʿīd had refused.[D] As a result, ʿAbd al-Malik

[A] He was ashamed of his poverty.

[B] For the question of women's education in early Islamic history see above, LXXXII.

[C] Ibn al-Musayyib here speaks with a proper neutrality, lest others be listening to his words.

[D] Not wishing to entrust his daughter to a man of the Umayyad dynasty, which was abhorred in many pious circles for its worldliness and oppression.

had taken endless measures against him, until he had him flogged with a hundred stripes on a cold day, and then had a jug of water poured over him and forced him to wear a woollen shirt.'[24]

Saʿīd's haste on that night to complete the marriage should inform you of the hazardous nature of sexual desire, and of the necessity in the eyes of religion of speedily extinguishing its flames through marriage. May God be pleased with him, and show him His mercy!

[23.8]
An Exposition of the Merit of him who Counters the Desire of his Sex and his Eye

KNOW that this desire wields more power than any other over man, and is the most disobedient to reason when it is aroused. Its consequences are unsightly and embarrassing, and one should be afraid to enact them. Most people refrain from acting upon their sexual desire either through incapacity, fear, embarrassment, or a wish to safeguard their reputations. None of these things, however, brings any reward [from God], for they constitute no more than a preference for one desire of the soul over another. Certainly, a man's inability to follow up his desire is a sign that he is protected, and all such obstacles are beneficial in that they ward off sin: a man who does not commit fornication will not incur the sin which attaches to it, whatever the reason that induced him to abstain may have been. But merit and great reward follow only when one refrains from such an act for fear of God (Exalted is He!), while able to perform it and in the absence of obstacles and the presence of suitable circumstances, and this is especially so when one's desire is genuine. This constitutes the degree of the Truthful Saints.

In this regard the Emissary of God (may God bless him and grant him peace) once said, 'Whoever feels amorous passion, but remains chaste, conceals his state, and then perishes, has died the death of a martyr.'[1][A]

[A] For this report, which still circulates as a proverb, see our Introduction, XLIV.

And he said (may God bless him and grant him peace), 'On the Day of Arising, seven people will be shaded by God under His Throne, when there is no shade but His.' And he enumerated among them 'a man invited by a woman of beauty and good family to lie with her, but who said, "I fear God, the Lord of the Worlds".'[2]

The tale of Joseph (upon whom be peace) and his refusal of Zulaykhā, despite his ability to accede to her demand, and in spite of her desire for him, is well-known: God (Exalted is He!) praised him for so doing in His mighty Book,[A] and he is the leader and examplar for all who have been granted success in struggling against the devil with regard to[3] this powerful desire.

It is told that Sulaymān ibn Yasār, who was one of the most handsome of all men, was once visited by a woman who asked him to lie with her. He refused, and fled the house, leaving her inside. Sulaymān said later, 'That same night I had a dream in which I saw Joseph (upon whom be peace). "You are Joseph!" I said, and he replied, "Yes, I am Joseph, who desired, and you are Sulaymān, who did not desire," referring thereby to His statement (Exalted is He!), *She desired him, and he desired her, had he not seen the argument of his Lord.*[4][B]

Another, even more astonishing thing is related of him. Accompanied by a companion, he once left Medina intending to perform the Pilgrimage. When they arrived at al-Abwā'[C] his companion got up to go to the souk to buy something, taking with him the mat of leather on which they used to eat. Sulaymān remained seated in the tent. Since his face was

[A] Qur'ān, XII:22-6.

[B] The 'argument', or 'evidence' (*burhān*) is explained in the following paraphrase by Asad: 'he desired her; [and he would have succumbed] had he not seen [in this temptation] an evidence of his Sustainer's truth.' (Asad, 340.)

[C] A place about three day's ride from Medina. A grave traditionally thought to be that of the Prophet's mother is located here, and continues to draw visitors. Cf. Yāqūt, I. 99-100; Wohaibi, *The Northern Hijaz*, 35-40.

unusually handsome, he had been noticed by a bedouin woman who was on a nearby hill, who now descended and went to him. When she saw the beauty of his face she drew closer until[5] she stood before him (he being of great beauty and scrupulousness in matters of religion)[6] wearing a veil and gloves.[7] She unveiled her face, and it was like a piece of the moon. 'Satisfy me!' she said. He thought that she was referring to food, so he picked up some leftovers and gave them to her. 'I don't want that,' she said. 'I want what a man gives to his wife.' 'Satan has sent you to me!' he exclaimed, and then, setting his head between his knees, began to sob and weep without interruption. Beholding this sight, she drew on her veil once more and went away to her family. His companion then came, and, upon seeing that his eyes were swollen from tears and that his voice was silent, asked what had made him weep. 'Something good,' he told him. 'I remembered my children'.[8] 'No, by God,' his companion said. 'You have some tale to tell. You were with your children three days ago or thereabouts'. And he persisted until he had heard about the bedouin woman. He thereupon put down the leather mat and started to weep bitterly, so that Sulaymān asked him, 'Why are you weeping too?' and he replied, 'It is more appropriate that I weep than you. I fear that had I been in your place I would not have refused her!' And then they wept together for a long time.

When Sulaymān reached Mecca, and performed the *saʿy* and the *ṭawāf*,[A] he went to the Black Stone,[B] where, after wrapping himself in his garment, he was overcome by sleep. And there he

[A] The *saʿy* ritual is a sevenfold procession between the hillocks of al-Ṣafā and al-Marwa observed in commemoration of Hagar's quest for water for the young Ishmael. The *Ṭawāf*, also one of the obligatory rites of both the Greater and Lesser Pilgrimages (*ḥajj* and *ʿumra*), involves circling the Kaʿba seven times. (Ghazālī, *Iḥyā'*, I. 224-6 [*K. Asrār al-ḥajj*, bāb 2, jumla 4, 5].)

[B] A stone set into one corner of the Kaʿba which, among other functions, indicates the spot from which the rite of *ṭawāf* commences.

beheld a handsome, tall man, fragrant and of pleasant aspect, to whom he said, 'God show you mercy! Who are you?' 'I am Joseph,' the man said. 'Joseph the Truthful?'[A] he asked, and he replied, 'Even he.' 'Your episode with Potiphar's wife was quite astonishing,' said Sulaymān; but Joseph replied, 'Your episode with the woman at al-Abwā' was more astonishing still'.[9]

It is related that ʿAbd Allāh ibn ʿUmar said, 'I once heard the Emissary of God (may God bless him and grant him peace) say, "Three men of yore once set out on a journey. When night fell, and they had entered a cave in order to sleep, a rock came down from the mountain and blocked the entrance. 'Nothing can save us from this rock,' they said, 'unless we pray that God (Exalted is He!) save us on account of our righteous works!' Accordingly, one of their number declared, 'O Lord God! Thou knowest that I have two elderly parents, and that I always drew milk for them before my other family and my slaves. One day the search for fodder caused me to go far afield, so that I did not return to them before they had slept. When I drew their milk, and found them to be asleep, I found it hateful that I should give others of my family or my slaves to drink before them, so I remained there with the vessel in my hand waiting for them to awake until daybreak, although the children were crying around my feet. Then they awoke, and drank their milk. O Lord God! If I acted thus for Thy sake, then deliver us from the misfortune of this rock!' At this, the rock moved slightly—but they were still unable to leave. Another man said, 'O Lord God! I had a niece whom I loved exceedingly, and I tried to seduce her,[10] but she refused. There then came a year of drought[11] in which she suffered greatly. She came to me, and I gave her a hundred and twenty dīnārs on condition that she put herself at my disposal. This she did. But when I was upon her,

[A] Ar. *al-ṣiddīq*. Joseph is given this epithet in the Qur'ān (XII:46).

she said, 'Fear God! Break not the seal, save in a lawful way!' So I refrained from going into her, and went away, even though she was dearer to me than all else, leaving her with the gold which I had given her. O Lord God! If I acted thus for Thy sake, then deliver us from our plight!' And the rock moved—but they were still unable to emerge. And then the third man spoke up, saying: 'O Lord God! I once hired some men, and paid them their wages, with the exception of one man who went away and omitted to take his due. So I invested[12] his wage until a large sum had accumulated. After a time, he returned to me, saying, 'Bondsman of God! Give me my wage!' 'Your wage,' I told him, 'is everything you can see, whether camels, cows, sheep or slaves.' 'Bondsman of God!' he said. "Are you mocking me?' 'I am not,' I said. 'Take it.'[13] And he rounded up [the animals and slaves] and took everything, leaving nothing behind. O Lord God! If I acted thus for Thy sake, then deliver us from our plight!' And the rock moved again—and they emerged and walked away.'"[14]

Such is the merit which attaches to remaining chaste when one is in a position to gratify one's desire.

Similar to this is the case of being able to gratify the sexual desire of the eye [and yet abstaining]. The eye is the beginning-place of fornication, and to guard it is therefore a matter of great importance. It is also difficult, in that it may be underestimated and not greatly feared, despite the fact that all evil derives from it. One will not be taken to task for the first glance, if it is unintentional, but one will certainly be taken to task for looking again. The Prophet (may God bless him and grant him peace) said, 'You may have the first, but the second is against you,'[15] by which he was referring to one's glance. Al-ʿAlā' ibn Ziyād has said, 'Do not follow the cloak of a woman with your eyes,[16] for a glance sows desire in the heart'.[17] It is rare indeed that a man in his comings and goings does not happen to glance at women and boys. To the extent that he senses their beauty his nature will demand that he look again, at which point he should make himself appreciate that looking again in this way is sheer ignorance.[18] For if he looks, and finds the object of his regard to be beautiful, his desire will be aroused, but since he will be unable to satisfy it, he will gain only regret; while if he looks and finds ugliness, he will gain no pleasure, and will in fact be pained, since he had desired pleasure and found ugliness instead. Both of these circumstances, therefore, entail sin and sorrow. However, to the extent that he guards his eye, a great number of disadvantages will be spared his heart. Should his eye stray [by looking], but he still restrain his sex when in circumstances which would permit him to gratify it, he has been granted the utmost strength and success.

Bakr ibn ʿAbd Allāh al-Mazanī related that a certain butcher once conceived a passion for the young girl of one of his neighbours. One day, her people sent her on an errand to a nearby village, and he followed her, and tried to seduce her. 'Don't do it!' she said, 'I love you even more than you love me, but I fear God!' 'You fear Him, and I do not?' he exclaimed, and he turned back in a state of great penitence. On the way, he was afflicted by a thirst so intense that he was on the point of death, when there before him stood the messenger [*rasūl*] of one of the Israelite Prophets. 'What is the matter?' the man asked, and he replied, 'I am thirsty!' 'Come,' he said, 'let us pray God to shade us with a cloud until we arrive at the village.' 'But I have no [righteous] works! You pray instead!' said the butcher. 'I shall pray, then,' said the messenger, 'and you say amen.' And so the messenger prayed, and the butcher said amen, and a cloud came and shaded them until they reached the village. When the butcher turned towards his place, the cloud moved with him, so that the messenger remarked, 'You claimed that you have no works: I was the one that prayed, while you said amen, but the cloud which shaded us then followed you! You must tell me about yourself.' And when he told him what had happened, the messenger remarked, 'A man who turns to God in repentance is higher in His sight than anyone else'.[19]

Aḥmad ibn Saʿīd al-ʿĀbid related that his father had told him the following: 'There was once with us at Kūfa a young man much given to devotional practices, who used to stay in the Friday mosque and hardly ever leave it. Since he had a fine face and bearing, and a pleasant manner, he was noticed by a beautiful and intelligent woman, who fell deeply in love with him. After having passed a long while in this condition, she stood in the road one day when he was going to the mosque. "Young man!" she said. "Hear a few words which I would say to you, and then do whatever you will." He walked on without speaking to her. Then she stood in the road when he was returning home, and said, 'Young man! Hear a few words which I would say to you!' He lowered his head for some time, and told her, "This is a situation which invites suspicion, and I do not like to be suspected." "By God," she told him, "I am not standing here because of ignorance of your disposition; God forbid that people should see me do this thing, yet I have been impelled to meet you myself; only a little of such things is considered by people to be too much, and you constant worshippers are like glass bottles which are damaged by the slightest thing. In sum, what I would say is that all my limbs are intent upon you: God, God help me with you!" The young man went home. He wanted to pray, but he could not concentrate, so he took out a piece of paper instead and wrote a message. He then went outdoors, where the woman was standing in the same place: he threw the message towards her, and went back in. The message ran: "In the name of God, Most Compassionate and Merciful. You should know, O woman, that when one of God's servants sins against Him, He deals with him leniently. Should he sin again, He conceals this for him. But should he don its garments,[A] then God conceives against him such wrath as the very heavens and the earth could not compass, *neither the mountains, the trees and the animals*:[20] what man could then withstand such

[A] That is, should he become a recidivist.

wrath? If what you said was spoken in deceit, then I would remind you of a *Day when the sky will become as molten copper, and the mountains as carded wool,*[21] when all nations shall crouch down before the onslaught of the Almighty. I am too weak to reform myself; how, then, may I reform others? However, if what you say was spoken truly, I would direct you to a physician of guidance, who cures festering wounds and burning pains; to wit, God, Who is *Lord of the Worlds*. So address youself to Him with sincere entreaties, for I am distracted[22] from you by His words (Exalted is He!): *And warn them of the Day of Destruction, when hearts shall choke throats, when there will be no friend for the evildoers, neither any intercessor who will be heard. He knows the traitor of the eyes and that which hearts conceal. God judges with verity!*[23] How may one escape from this verse?"

'A few days later, she came and stood in front of him again in the street. When he saw her from afar he wanted to return to his house so as not to see her. But she said, "Young man! Do not go back, for we shall never meet after today save in the presence of God (Exalted is He!)."[A] She broke into bitter tears, and said, "I ask God, in Whose hand lie the keys of your heart, to ease all your hardships." She then followed him, saying, "Grant me the kindness of an admonition, which I may take from you, and give me a counsel by which I may act." "I counsel you," he said, "to protect your soul from your soul,[B] and would remind you of His statement (Exalted is He!): *He it is who slays you at night, and knows what you commit by day.*[24C] At this, she lowered her head, and cried even more bitterly. When she recovered, she went home, and remained there, and occupied herself with continual worship until at last she died of grief. After her death, the young man would weep when he recalled her. "Why do

[A] On the Day of Judgement.

[B] 'The former "soul," Zabīdī explains (VII. 444), 'refers to the essence [*dhāt*], and the latter to the lower soul'.

[C] The 'slaying' here refers of course to sleep.

you weep?" he was asked, "when you kept her away from you?" And he would reply, "I killed her hope for me[25] at the outset, and through that rejection stored up a treasure with God (Exalted is He!). And then I was ashamed to take back a treasure of this kind."'[26A]

Thus, praised be God, and through His generosity, closes the *Book of Breaking the Two Desires*. It shall be followed, God willing, by the *Book of the Faults of the Tongue*. Praised be God, at the beginning and at the end, in what is apparent and in what is hidden. May His blessings and most abundant salutations rest upon our master Muḥammad, the best of His creation, and upon His every chosen bondsman among the dwellers of the earth and of the heavens.[27]

[A] The intended meaning is that he had felt an unlawful desire for her, and gained such grace in wrestling with it that when he too fell in love with her, he denied himself a legitimate marriage so as not to vitiate his original virtue.

NOTES

Notes to Prologue and Exposition 22.1

1 MA, A: *ʿaddala tarkīb al-khalq* (Z: *ʿaddala tartīb al-khalq*).

2 'and hardships' missing in Z.

3 A: *yustashraf* (Z: *t.stash.ff*; MA: *y.stansh.q*).

4 Z: *al-shayṭān al-laʿīn*. (MA, A: *al-shayāṭīn*: 'the devils'.)

5 Q.CIV:5,6.

6 MA, A: *fī maraḍihā fawt ḥayāt bāqiya*. (Z: *fīhā qurb ḥayāt bāqiya*.)

7 Q.XCI:9.

8 Q.XCI:10.

9 MA, A: *jumal min amrāḍ* (Z: *jumal amrāḍ*).

10 MA, A add here *al-ṭuruq allatī bihā yuʿraf tafṣīl*.

11 Z: *tajmaʿ maqāṣid al-kitāb* (MA, A: *yajmaʿ maqāṣidahā hādhā al-kitāb*).

12 Q.LXVIII:4.

13 Muslim, Ṣalāt al-musāfirīn, 139.

14 'And a man ... recited' missing in Z, MA.

15 Q.VII:199. Cf. Nasafī, IV. 210.

16 MA adds here: "to Gabriel (upon whom be peace), 'And how should this be done?' 'I do not know,' he replied, 'until I ask the All-Knowing.' And he ascended, and when he came down again he said, 'O Muḥammad! ...'" This addition is absent from Z and A, and also from the *Lajna Nashr al-Thaqāfa al-Islāmīya* (Cairo, 1356) edition, and that of Ḥalabī (Cairo, 1347 AH); as also the texts which we have identified as sources for this report.

17 Ibn Abi'l-Dunyā, *Makārim al-akhlāq*, 6; Qushayrī, *Laṭā'if*, III. 617; Kharā'iṭī, 14, 56; Hannād, II. 493.

18 *innamā* missing in Z.

19 *Muwaṭṭa'*, Ḥusn al-khuluq, 8; Ḥākim, II. 613; Kharā'iṭī, 1; al-Ḥārith ibn Abī Usāma, *al-Musnad* (*Maṭālib*, II. 391); *Lumaʿ*, 99; Miskawayh, *Jāvidān*, 106; Māwardī, 421.

20 *taqwā Allāh wa* missing in Z.

21 Ibn Ḥanbal, *Musnad*, VI. 442; Tirmidhī, Birr, 61.

22 Cf. Mundhirī, III. 405.

23 Abū Dāūd, Adab, 124; Ibn Ḥanbal, *Musnad*, III. 502; Qushayrī, *Risāla*, 500.

24 Tirmidhi, Birr, 55; Ibn Ḥanbal, *Musnad*, V. 158.

25 Unidentified (cf. Zabīdī, VII. 319).

26 Ṭabarānī, *al-Muᶜjam al-Awsaṭ* (Haythamī, *Majmaᶜ*, VIII. 21); al-Khaṭīb al-Baghdādī, III. 226.

27 Ibn Ḥanbal, *Musnad*, II. 440.

28 Unidentified (cf. Zabīdī, VII.320). Up to 'generosity' is to be found in Tirmidhī, Birr, 62.

29 Abū Nuᶜaym, *Ḥilya*, II. 160; Ṭabarānī, *al-Muᶜjam al-Awsaṭ* (Haythami, *Majmaᶜ*, VIII. 20).

30 Ṭabarānī, *al-Muᶜjam al-Awsaṭ* (Haythamī, *Majmaᶜ*, VII. 20); Abū Nuᶜaym, *Ḥilya*, II. 175; Daylamī, II. 140.

31 Kharā'iṭī, 3; Qushayrī, *Risāla*, 494. Cf. Abū Dāūd, Sunna, 14; Ibn Ḥanbal, *Musnad*, II. 250.

32 Abū Yaᶜlā, *al-Musnad* (Haythamī, *Majmaᶜ*, VIII. 22); Ḥākim, I. 124; Abū Nuᶜaym, *Ḥilya*, X. 25; Daylamī, I. 391-2; Ḥalīmī, III. 259; al-Bazzār, *al-Musnad* (Haythamī, *Kashf*, II. 408); Qushayrī, *Risāla*, 496; ᶜĀmirī, *Saᶜāda*, 150.

33 Ṭabarānī, *al-Muᶜjam al-Kabīr* (Haythamī, *Majmaᶜ*, VIII. 24); ᶜUqaylī, IV. 291; Ṭabarsī, 16; ᶜAbd ibn Ḥumayd (*Maṭālib*, II. 393). In Mubashshir ibn Fātik's *Mukhtār al-ḥikam*, p.131, the aphorism is attributed to Plato!

34 Kharā'iṭī, 2.

35 Kharā'iṭī, 2. Also in Muslim, Masājid, 267 (with variation).

36 A: 'Abū Saᶜīd al-Khudrī'.

37 Kharā'iṭī, 2; Ṭayālisī, 49; Ibn Ḥanbal, *Musnad* (Haythamī, *Majmaᶜ*, VI. 20).

38 Z: 'ibn ᶜAmr'.

39 Kharā'iṭī, 2.

40 Ibn Hanbal, *Musnad*, II. 365; *Muwaṭṭa'*, Jihād, 35.

41 Kharā'iṭī, 3; Ṭayālisī, 171; Ibn Ḥibbān (Haythamī, *Mawārid* 475); Ibn Māja (Zabīdī, VII. 322); Ibn Musarhad, *Musnad* (*Maṭālib*, II. 390); Hannād, II. 595.

42 Kharā'iṭī, 4; Ibn Ḥibbān (Haythamī, *Mawārid*, 473); Ibn Ḥanbal, *Musnad* (Haythamī, *Majmaᶜ*, VIII. 21); Wakīᶜ, III. 740; Bukhārī, *al-Adab al-Mufrad*, 60.

43 Kharā'iṭī, 5; Ibn Abi'l-Dunyā, *Ḥilm*, 50; Ṭabarānī, *al-Muᶜjam al-Awsaṭ* (Haythamī, *Majmaᶜ*, VIII. 24, 190).

44 Muslim, Musāfirīn, 201.

45 Kharā'iṭī, 7; Ṭabarānī, *al-Muᶜjam al-Awsaṭ* (Haythamī, *Majmaᶜ*, VIII. 24); Daylamī, VII.140.

46 Kharā'iṭī, 7; Quḍāᶜī, I. 199.

47 Kharā'iṭī, 7, 11; Quḍāᶜī, I. 66.

48 Kharā'iṭī, 8; Quḍāᶜī, II. 39; Ṭabarānī (Haythamī, *Majmaᶜ*, X. 283); Ibn Māja (Zabīdī, VII. 323).

49 Ṭabarānī, *al-Muᶜjam al-Kabīr* (Haythamī, *Majmaᶜ*, VII. 24), al-Ḥakīm al-Tirmidhī, 229; al-Bazzār, *al-Musnad* (Haythamī, *Kashf*, VII. 409).

50 Z: *ḍarībatihi* (MA, A: *martabatihi*). *Ḥadīth* in Ṭabarānī, *al-Muᶜjam al-Kabīr*, (Mundhirī, III. 404).

51 Tirmidhī, Birr, 62; Abū Dāūd, Adab, 7.

52 Kharā'iṭī, 10; al-Ḥakīm al-Tirmidhī, 229, 321.

53 Ṭabarānī, *al-Mu^c^jam al-Kabīr* (Haythamī, *Majma^c^*, VIII. 24–5; Zabīdī, VII. 324); Daylamī, III. 197; Ḥalīmī, I.259.

54 Bukhārī, Faḍā'il aṣḥāb al-Nabī, 6; Muslim, Faḍā'il al-ṣaḥāba, 22.

55 Z: *natūj* (A: *tafūḥ*; MA: *tanūḥ*).

56 Ṭabarānī, *Ṣaghīr*; Kharā'iṭī, *Masāwī al-akhlāq* (Zabīdī, VII. 324).

57 This is the completion of the foregoing *ḥadīth* (see note to Kāshānī, *Maḥajja*, V. 93).

58 Maydānī, II. 90; Miskawayh, *Jāvidān*, 177.

59 Qushayrī, *Risāla*, 499; *Luma^c^*, 177.

60 Z, MA: *bakaytuhu raḥmat[an] lahu* (A: *ataraḥḥamu ^c^alayhi*).

61 Qushayrī, *Risāla*, 495; Suhrawardī, 168; Hujwīrī, 39; cf. Anṣārī, *Manāzil*, 97.

62 *^c^azīz* missing in Z.

63 Q.XLIX:14.

64 Z: *al-īmān*: 'Faith'.

Notes to Exposition 22.2

1 'and Bad' omitted in Z.

2 Qushayrī, *Risāla*, 494.

3 ibid., 496.

4 ibid., 498.

5 ibid., 494.

6 'Abū Sa^c^īd' omitted in Z.

7 Qushayrī, *Risāla*, 495.

8 Q.XXXVIII:71; cf. Qushayrī, *Laṭā'if*, III. 262–3.

9 MA, A: *Rabb al-^c^ālamīn* (Z: *Allāh ta^c^ālā*).

10 Z: *ḥāla* (MA, A: *ḥāja*).

11 'and ... reputation' omitted in MA, A.

12 'of the act' omitted in MA, A.

13 'the mouth' omitted in Z.

14 Q. II:269.

15 Z: *yaqtaṣir ... ^c^alā* (MA, A: *yasīr ... fī*).

16 *al-shar^c^*. (Z: *al-dīn*: 'religion').

17 *manzilatuhu* (A: *mithāluhu*.)

18 *manzilatuhu* (A: *mithāluhu*.)

19 Z adds: 'and combines all the noble qualities; it is he that is praised by the verses and Traditions cited above.'

20 *a^c^ḍā'* (A: *ajzā'*).

21 *khūr* (MA: *jawr*: 'tyranny').

22 A adds *wa-muqābil*.

23 *khibb* (A: *khubth*).

24 *jurbuza* (MA: *jarīra*).

25 'It ... proceed' omitted in Z.

26 'excellence of discernment' omitted in Z.

27 *jurbuza* (MA: *jarīra*).

28 MA adds *wa'l-ḥiqd*: 'and spite'.

29 'heedlessness' omitted in MA, A.

30 *kibar al-nafs* (MA, A: *kasr al-nafs*).

31 *tawaddud* (Z: *tu'ada*).

32 *laṭāfa* (Z: *ṭalāqa*).

33 Q.XLIX:15.

34 Q.XLVIII:29.

Notes to Exposition 22.3

1 *man ghalabat ʿalayhi* (MA, A: *baʿḍ man ghalabat ʿalayhi*).

2 *bi-qamʿ* (MA: *yaqmaʿ*).

3 Ibn Lāl, *Makārim al-akhlāq* (Zabīdī, VII. 332).

4 *al-bāzī* (Z: *al-ṣayd*).

5 *wa'l-inqiyād* omitted in Z.

6 *wa'l-arḍ* omitted in A.

7 *takabbur* (Z: *tafakkur*).

8 *qalʿ* (A: *qadr*).

9 *min al-ʿanā' riyāḍat al-harim* omitted in Z.

10 Q.XLVIII:29.

11 *la'mtanaʿa jihād al-kuffār* (A: *la-baṭala al-jihād*).

12 Muslim, Birr, 95.

13 As stated in Bukhārī, Maghāzī, 53; Muslim, Faḍā'il, 129.

14 Q. III:134; *'and are forgiving toward people'* omitted in Z.

15 *maḥmūd* (Z: *maṭlūb*).

16 Q.XXV:67. Cf. *Laṭā'if*, II. 650.

17 Q.XVII:29.

18 Q.VII:31

19 Q.XLVIII:29.

20 Maydānī, I. 243; for other sources see Sakhāwī, 332; Suyūṭī, *Durar*, 107–8.

21 Q.XXVI:89.

22 *al-tabdhīr* (Z: *al-jūd*).

23 *salīm*[an] *baynahumā* (MA, A: *salīm*[an] *minhumā*, 'safe from both of them').

Notes to Exposition 22.4

1 *al-mutakhalliqīn bi-hādhihī al-akhlāq* (MA: *al-mutakhalliqīn bi-hādhihī al-asbāb*).

2 *khuluq* (Z: *fiʿl*).

3 *jamīʿ al-ʿādāt al-sayyi'a* (MA, A: *jamīʿ al-afʿāl al-sayyi'a*).

4 Nasā'ī, Nisā', 1; Ibn Ḥanbal, *Musnad*, III. 128.

5 Q.II:45.

6 Ṭabarānī, *Kabīr* (Zabīdī, VII. 328); *Qūt*, I. 263.

7 Quḍāʿī, I. 206; *Tārīkh Baghdād*, VI. 17.

8 *innā narā* (MA, A: *innā qad narā*).

9 'or the gibbet' omitted in MA, A.

10 *yuṣirru ʿalā al-inkār* (MA: *yuṣirru ʿalā al-ankāl*).

11 'and...ugliness' omitted in Z.

12 *ulzimat* (MA, A: *iltazamat*).

13 *yartafiʿ* (MA, A: *qad yartafiʿ*).

14 *qalb* (Z: *nafs*).

15 *akhlāq* (MA, A: *aʿmāl*).

16 *lā yuḥassu bi-atharihā* (A: *lā yaḥsunu ta'thīruhu*).

17 *yawm*[an] *yawm*[an] omitted in A.

18 Q.XXXVI:9.

19 *lumʿa* (MA, A: *nukta*: 'a speck').

20 *Qūt*, I. 113; Mufīd, *Ikhtiṣāṣ*, 237.

21 *yasriqu* (Z: *yastariqqu*).

22 Q.XCIX:8, 9.

23 Q.XVI:33.

Notes to Exposition 22.5

1 MA adds here *fī mizāj al-badan*.

2 *taʿtarī al-ʿilla al-mughayyira lahu* (MA, A: *taʿtarī al-māʿida al-muḍirra*).

3 Z: *tazkiya*.

4 *maraḍ* (Z: *ʿadhāb alīm*).

5 *bunyatihi* (MA: *nafsihi*).

6 'outwardly' omitted in Z.

7 *naẓīfa* (Z: *rafīʿa*).

8 *ʿājiz ʿan al-ṭawl* (Z: *ʿājiz ʿan al-nikāḥ*).

9 Q.LXXIX:41, 42.

Notes to Exposition 22.6

1 'remembering' omitted in Z.

2 Q.LI:56.

3 'Thus ... function' omitted in Z.

4 Q.IX:24.

5 *ʿalā ghayr al-mustaḥiqq* (Z: *li'l-mustaḥiqq*).

6 Q.IV:69.

7 Q.XIX:71,72.

8 Q.XI:112. The *ḥadīth* is given in Tirmidhī, Tafsīr Sūrat 56, 6; cited also in Bayḍāwī, 307.

9 This sentence omitted in Z.

Notes to Exposition 22.7

1 *man kamulat baṣīratuhu* (A: *man kānat baṣīratuhu nāfidha*).

2 *al-akyās* omitted in Z.

3 Ghazālī relates this same story in *Tibr* (tr. Bagley), 30.

4 *yukhshā an tadūm* (MA: *akhshā an tadūm* [the elative]).

5 *allatī athmarathā kathrat al-dhunūb* (Z: *allatī thamaratuhā kathrat al-dhunūb*).

6 A *ḥadīth* of the Prophet (Abū Dāūd, Adab, 49; Tirmidhī, Birr, 18).

7 Cited in Māwardī, 421; repeated in Ghazālī's *Bidāya*, 101 (tr. Abul Quasem, p.103). Asín (*Logia*, 361), finds no biblical source for this statement.

Notes to Exposition 22.8

1 Q. LVIII:11.

2 *aghwār* (MA, A: *aʿwān*).

3 Q. IV:95.

4 Q. LXXIX:41,42.

5 Q. XLIX:3.

6 Abū Bakr ibn Lāl, *Makārim al-akhlāq* (Zabīdī, VII. 351).

7 Qushayrī, *Risāla*, 398.

8 Cf. Asín, *Logia*, 361.

9 Mufīd, *Ikhtiṣāṣ*, 234.

10 Ibn Ḥanbal, *Musnad*, VI. 20; Ibn Abi'l-Dunyā, *Muḥāsaba*, 102; Hujwīrī, 200.

11 Unidentified.

12 Abū Nuʿaym, *Ḥilya*, VII. 5.

13 'the sword ... little sleep, and' present in all texts, including those of al-Ḥalabī and the *Lajna*,

except MA which reads: 'the swords of vengeance against them. For the stomach dries out when one eats little, and one sleeps less and one's eyes are opened so that one is able to perform the midnight prayer. This is because two arteries lead from the eyes to the stomach, so that when the stomach is filled the eyes become contented, so that one sleeps, in the manner of a table heavy laden. This takes place in consequence of little sleep. You should also ...'

14 *ḥattā tanqaṭiᶜ ᶜan al-ẓulm wa'l-intiqām fa-ta'man* (Z: *ḥattā tanqaṭiᶜ min al-dhull wa'l-intiqām mayāmin*).

15 *fī sā'ir al-ayyām* (A: *bayn sā'ir al-anām*).

16 Z: *rūḥānīya laṭīfa wa-nūrīya khafīfa* (A: *naẓīfa wa-nūrīya khafīfa rūḥānīya*; MA: *naẓīfa wa-nūrīya ḥaqīqa rūḥānīya*).

17 *tasīru fī* (MA: *tantashiru fī*).

18 *jubb* (Z: *ḥubb*).

19 'which-wish' omitted in Z.

20 A: Jaᶜfar ibn Ḥumayd.

21 MA: 'Abu'l-Ḥasan'.

22 Identified by Zabīdī as Wahb ibn Munabbih. A has 'Wuhayb ibn al-Ward'.

23 *shahwa* (MA: *hawā*).

24 Q.xii:55.

25 'and during... kingdom' omitted in Z.

26 A: *jaᶜala al-mulūk ᶜabīdan bi'l-maᶜṣiya* (MA: *jaᶜala al-mulūk ᶜabīd al-maᶜṣiya*).

27 'Glory-obey Him!' omitted in Z.

28 'which is the reward for the iniquitous' omitted in Z.

29 'as ... said' omitted in Z.

30 Q. xii:90.

31 Qushayrī, *Risāla*, 394-5.

32 Qushayrī, *Risāla*, 302.

33 *yankashifu bi-* (MA, A: *la yudrak illā bi-*).

34 'clothing' omitted in Z.

35 'and devotion to' omitted in Z.

36 'the strength ... alone' omitted in Z.

37 'O Lord ... of refuge' omitted in Z.

38 A well-known *ḥadīth* (Abū Nuᶜaym, *Ḥilya*, vi. 388, cf. Suyūṭī, *Durar*, 97; Sakhāwī, 296-7).

39 'and invalidates ... deed' omitted in Z.

40 Qushayrī, *Risāla*, 396; cf. ᶜAṭṭār, *Tadhkira*, ii. 83-4 (tr. Arberry, 275-6).

41 Qushayrī, *Risāla*, 397.

42 'the remembrance of God and' omitted in Z.

43 *thamila* (Z: *mumtali'a bihā*).

44 Z adds: 'of which Mālik ibn Dīnār said that the heart which is denuded of it is like a ruined house.'

45 Q. x:7. Omitted in Z.

46 Q. xiii:26: 'And they rejoice in the life of the world' omitted in A.

47 Q. lvii:20.

48 This sentence omitted in Z.

49 *baṭira* (A: *nafira*).

50 'punished ... ambiguous' omitted in Z.

51 *khallaṣū* (Z: *khalaʿū*).
52 *asr* (A: *athar*).
53 *insirāḥ* (A: *sarāḥ*; MA: *asrāj*).
54 *al-ashr wa'l-baṭr* (A: *al-naẓar wa'l-uns*).
55 Ṭabarānī, *Ṣaghīr*, I. 251; Hākim, IV. 325.
56 *yashqā lā maḥāla li-firāqih* (MA, A: *yasʿā lā maḥāla li-firāqih*).
57 'and the blindnesses ... said' omitted in Z.
58 Q. X:7.
59 Z adds: 'either evident or concealed'.

Notes to Exposition 22.9

1 *Bayān ʿalāmāt ḥusn al-khuluq* (MA: *Bayān tamyīz ʿalāmāt ḥusn al-khuluq*).
2 Q.XXIII:1-10.
3 Q.IX:112.
4 Q.VIII:2-4.
5 Q.XXV:63.
6 'all of' omitted in Z.
7 'their ... one' omitted in Z.
8 Bukhārī, Īmān, 7.
9 Bukhārī, Adab, 31; Muslim, Īmān, 73.
10 Bukhārī, Adab, 31; Muslim, Īmān, 73.
11 Bukhārī, Adab, 31; Muslim, Īmān, 73.
12 Kharā'iṭī, 3; Abū Yaʿlā, *al-Musnad* (*Maṭālib*, II. 388). See p. 9 above.
13 Ibn Māja, Zuhd, 1 (with variations).
14 Ibn Ḥanbal, *Musnad*, IV. 398.
15 Ibn al-Mubārak, *Zuhd* (Zabīdī, VII. 358).
16 Abū Dāūd, Adab, 85; Tirmidhī, Fitan, 3; Ibn Ḥanbal, *Musnad*, V. 362.
17 Ibn Lāl, *Makārim al-akhlāq*; Bayhaqī, *Shuʿab al-īmān* (Zabīdī, VII. 358).
18 'satisfied' omitted in Z.
19 'chaste' omitted in Z.
20 Unidentified (cf. Zabīdī, VII. 359).
21 *al-ṣabr* (A: *al-ʿibar*).
22 *li'l-siyāsa* (MA: *bi'l-siyāsa*).
23 Bukhārī, Adab, 68; Muslim, Zakāt, 128.
24 () omitted in Z.
25 Q.LXVIII:4. According to Zabīdī (VII. 359), the *ḥadīth* is narrated in Bayhaqī's *Dalā'il al-nubuwwa*.
26 Qushayrī, *Risāla*, 499; cf. ʿAṭṭār (Arberry), 77.
27 Z, A and MA have *laysa lī wajh*, which is problematic. Qushayrī (*Risāla*, 499) has *laysa al-ān waqt dukhūlika*.
28 *irjiʿ* (Z: *tarjiʿ ʿalā mā yūjib al-waqt*).
29 Qushayrī, *Risāla*, 499-500; cf. ʿAṭṭār (Arberry), 233-4.
30 'and made the prostration of gratitude' omitted in Z.
31 Qushayrī, *Risāla*, 500; cf. ʿAṭṭār (Arberry), 234.
32 'not finding him' omitted in Z.
33 Z and Qushayrī: *mudda*

UNIVERSITY OF WINCHESTER LIBRARY

(MA, A: *sana*).

34 Qus̲h̲ayrī, *Risāla*, 500.

35 *ḥilm* (Z: *ḥusn al-k̲h̲uluq*).

36 *ḥilm* (Z: *ḥusn al-k̲h̲uluq*).

37 Qus̲h̲ayrī, *Risāla*, 495–6.

38 Ibid., 496.

39 'yet he held his peace' omitted in MA, Z.

40 *fa-yu'd̲h̲ūka* (Z: *fa-yujībuka*).

The story comes from Qus̲h̲ayrī, *Risāla*, 496–7.

41 Ibid., 497. In the *Tibr* (tr. Bagley, 27), the story is told of ʿAlī Zayn al-ʿĀbidīn, not the ʿAlī who was the Prophet's son-in-law.

42 Qushayri, *Risāla*, 498.

43 Ibid., 498.

Notes to Exposition 22.10

1 This sentence omitted in Z.

2 'and all its teachers and preceptors' omitted in Z.

3 Q. LXVI:6.

4 ⌜⌝Miskawayh, 58, = Bryson, 186–7.

5 ⌜⌝Miskawayh, 57; cf. Bryson, 194.

6 *qalbihi* (A: *nafsihi*).

7 ⌜⌝Miskawayh, 57.

8 'of ... again' omitted in Z.

9 *hayba* (MA: *hay'a*).

10 ⌜⌝Miskawayh, 60; cf. Bryson, 189.

11 *lā y.sman badan.hu* (MA, Z: *lā yastak̲h̲iff badanuhu*). Miskawayh (*Tahd̲h̲īb*, 60) has *la yaṣlab badanuhu*.

12 ⌜⌝Miskawayh, 59–60.

13 ⌜⌝ Miskawayh, 60, = Bryson, 194.

14 ⌜⌝ Miskawayh, 60.

15 ⌜⌝ Miskawayh, 62, = Bryson, 200.

16 ⌜⌝Miskawayh, 61, = Bryson, 196.

17 ⌜⌝Miskawayh, 61, = Bryson, 196–8.

18 ⌜⌝Miskawayh, 61, = Bryson, 200.

19 ⌜⌝Cf. Miskawayh, 62; Bryson, 202.

20 ⌜⌝Miskawayh, 62, = Bryson, 202.

21 *al-g̲h̲is̲h̲s̲h̲* (A: *al-faḥs̲h̲*).

22 'in which we must abide ... pass' omitted in Z.

23 Buk̲h̲ārī, Janā'iz, 92.

24 MA, A: *sinīn*, as in Qus̲h̲ayrī, *Risāla*, 93. Z has *sanatayn*.

25 Qus̲h̲ayrī, *Risāla*, 92–4. Cf. Böwering, 32, 45, who also locates the story in ʿAṭṭār, *Tadhkira*, I. 252–3.

26 'for ... Lord' omitted in Z,

Notes to Exposition 22.11

1 *lā yatrukuhā* (Z, MA: *qad lā yatrukuhā*).

2 *hudāt* (Z: *hidāya*).

3 'and impermanence' omitted in Z.

4 Cf. *Qūt*, I. 94.

5 Q. xxxvi:9.

6 *g̲h̲arīb* (MA, A: ʿ*arabīya*).

7 *yahdīhi* (Z: *yuhadhdhibuhu*).

8 This image is drawn from Qushayrī, *Risāla*, 735.

9 The text here echoes *Qūt*, I. 94.

10 *Qūt*, I. 95. According to Asín (*Espiritualidad*, I. 195; *Logia*, 361), this apocryphal text is inspired by Matthew v.6–8.

11 *Qūt*, I. 95, 97.

12 Q. XXIV:35.

13 Qushayrī, *Risāla*, 266; *Qūt*, I. 95.

14 *tusahhiluhu al-ʿuzla* (Z: *yusahhilu al-ʿuzla*).

15 *kadira* (MA, A: *karīha*).

16 *bayt* (Z: *makān*).

17 Q. LXXIII:1.

18 Q. LXXIV:1.

19 'which... rest' omitted in A.

20 Qushayrī, *Risāla*, 736.

21 'and the phrase...at all' omitted in Z.

22 Q. VII:200–1.

23 This paragraph echoes closely the *Risāla* of al-Qushayrī, 738–9.

24 *dhikr* (Z: *fikr*).

25 For this *ḥadīth* see Suyūṭī, *Durar*, 136; Subkī, III. 260.

26 *shughilat* (MA: *qanaʿat*).

27 *aw* (A: *wa*).

28 'in order...God' omitted in Z.

29 *Qūt*, I. 100.

30 *bi-ṭūl al-mujāhada* (MA: *bi-ṭarīq al-mujāhada*).

31 Q. LXXXVII:16–17. 'although ... lasting' omitted in A.

32 Q. LXXXVII:18–19.

33 *āfāt al-lisān* (Z, MA: *kasr sharah al-kalām*).

34 Z has these two books in reverse order.

35 The contents of this paragraph are omitted in Z.

Notes to Prologue and Exposition 23.1

1 An echo of the famous sermon of Abraham (Q.XXVI:78–81).

2 *yuqwīh* (MA, A: *yaqrīh*).

3 *shahwa* (Z: *saṭwa*).

4 *wa-yu'akkidu dawāʿīh* (Z: *wa-j.lla dawāʿīh*).

5 Q.VII:22; XX:121.

6 *riyā'* (MA: *riyāḍa*).

7 'an Exposition of the Ostentation...Desire' omitted in A.

8 Unidentified (cf. Zabīdī, VII. 386). Cf. *Ma'thūr*, I. 104; Hujwīrī, 200.

9 Unidentified (cf. Zabīdī, VII. 386).

10 Unidentified (cf. Zabīdī, VII. 387).

11 *sayyid al-aʿmāl al-jūʿ wa-dhull al-nafs libās al-ṣūf* (A: *sayyid al-aʿmāl al-jūʿ wa-dhull al-nafs wa-libās al-ṣūf*). The *ḥadīth* is unidentified (cf. Zabīdī, VII. 387). But see Muḥāsibī, *Makāsib*, 227 for a similar sentiment.

12 Unidentified (cf. Zabīdī, VII. 387). Cf. *Ma'thūr*, I. 102; Ṭabarsī, 132 for a similar Tradition.

13 Unidentified (cf. Zabīdī, VII. 387).

14 'al-Ḥasan said also' omitted in Z.

15 Unidentified (cf. Zabīdī, VII. 387). Cf. Haythamī, *Majma*ᶜ, V. 31.

16 *Qūt*, I. 97; Abū Ṭālib al-Makkī, *ᶜIlm al-qulūb*, 217.

17 'in the world' omitted in Z.

18 Ibn ᶜAdī, *al-Kāmil fī ḍuᶜafā' al-rijāl* (Zabīdī, VII. 388).

19 Ṭabarsī, 171.

20 Ibn Māja, Aṭᶜima, 50. See *Muᶜāraḍa*, 17, for an explanation.

21 'on the Day of Arising' omitted in Z.

22 'O Usāma' omitted in Z.

23 Ibn Ḥanbal, *Zuhd* (Zabīdī, VII. 388).

24 Ṭabarsī, 132.

25 Abū Nuᶜaym, *Ḥilya*, II. 370; *Qūt*, I. 95. Cf. Asín, *Logia*, 361–2 for a possible source in Matthew, V. 6–8.

26 Hujwīrī, 324.

27 Abū Nuᶜaym, *Ḥilya*, II. 362; cf. Sakhāwī, 207.

28 Cf. Sakhāwī, 208.

29 *Qūt*, I. 94–5; cf. *Ma'thūr*, II. 374.

30 Ṭabarsī, 168.

31 *al-munāfiq* (Z: *al-kāfir*).

32 Bukhārī, Aṭᶜima, 12; Muslim, Ashriba, 183.

33 Unidentified (cf. Zabīdī, VII. 390).

34 Abū Yaᶜlā, *al-Musnad* (Haythamī, *Majma*ᶜ, V. 31); *Ma'thūr*, I. 216; *Qūt*, I. 97; Ṭabarsī, 171.

35 Unidentified (cf. Zabīdī, VII. 391).

36 al-Ḥārith ibn Abī Usāma, *al-Musnad* (Zabīdī, VII. 391).

37 Ibn Māja, Aṭᶜima, 48; Ibn Ḥanbal, *Musnad*, VI. 42. Z has the version of Muslim (Zuhd, 32), which runs: 'Never did the Prophet (may God bless him and grant him peace) give his family to be sated [...]' etc.

38 Abū Nuᶜaym, *Ḥilya*, III. 346.

39 *Tārīkh Baghdād*, XII. 383; Abū Nuᶜaym, *Ḥilya*, VIII. 292.

40 *al-tā'ibīn* (Z: *al-tābiᶜīn*).

41 Qushayrī, *Risāla*, 91.

42 ᶜAṭṭār, *Tadhkira*, I. 232.

43 ᶜAṭṭār, *Tadhkira*, I. 232.

44 ᶜAṭṭār, *Tadhkira*, I. 253. Other sources give fifteen days (Qushayrī, *Risāla*, 373; Hujwīrī, 201; *Luma*ᶜ, 162), or thirty days (*Muᶜāraḍa*, 34). See Introduction, XXIII.

45 *Qūt*, I. 270; Qushayrī, Risāla, 94.

46 Cf. Ṭabarsī, 171.

47 *Qūt*, I. 95. See above, p. 89.

48 *illā man shā' Allāh* (Z: *niᶜmatᵃⁿ min Allāh*).

49 Abū Nuᶜaym, *Ḥilya*, X. 201; *Muᶜāraḍa*, 23.

50 Z, MA: *bi-ikhmād al-ᶜizz wa-tark al-dhikr* (A: *bi-ikhmāl al-dhikr wa-tark al-ᶜizz*).

51 *al-aghniyā'* (A: *al-qurrā'*, 'the reciters [of the Qur'ān]').

52 'air and' omitted in MA, A.

53 Cf. *Qūt*, I. 95.

54 'of food and drink' omitted in Z.

55 'May God bless you!' omitted in Z.

56 'Rather ... distraction' omitted in Z. Asín (*Logia*, 362-3) suggests that this text may be a remote echo of Matthew, IV. 2,3.

57 'for one night ... result' omitted in Z.

Notes to Exposition 23.2

1 Q. LVIII:11.

2 'to produce ... repressed' omitted in Z.

3 ʿAṭṭār, *Tadhkira*, I. 232.

4 Unidentified (cf. Zabīdī, VII. 394). There is, however, a well-known Tradition which runs, 'You should laugh infrequently, for much laughter deadens the heart' (Tirmidhī, Zuhd, 2; Ibn Māja, Zuhd, 19).

5 Z: 'And he said'.

6 Unidentified (cf. Zabīdī, VII. 395).

7 Unidentified (cf. Zabīdī, VII. 395). There is another *ḥadīth* to the effect that 'There is a tithe for everything, and the tithe of the body is fasting' (Ibn Māja, Ṣiyām, 44).

8 Sahlajī, (ed. Badawī, *Shaṭaḥāt*, 173; tr. Meddeb, 156). Cf. Andrae, 54.

9 'praying' omitted in MA, A.

10 Ṭabarsī, 171.

11 Ibn Ḥanbal, *Musnad*, V. 254; Tirmidhī, Zuhd, 35.

12 'and calamities' omitted in A.

13 'and tribulation'omitted in Z.

14 Q.XII:55.

15 'which has become decrepit' omitted in Z.

16 *Qūt*, I. 96.

17 *aqall* (Z, MA: *awwal*).

18 A Tradition of the Prophet.(Tirmidhī, Īmān, 8; Ibn Māja, Fitan, 12).

19 *Qūt*, I. 98.

20 ʿAṭṭār, *Tadhkira*, I. 231.

21 Cf. Andrae, 53.

22 Q. X:7.

23 Q. XXX:7.

24 'Divine' omitted in A.

25'and the ... stomachs' omitted in MA, A. The account is narrated in ʿAṭṭār, *Tadhkira*, I. 231-2.

26 'it distracts the heart' omitted in Z.

27 Z: 'the Greek'.

28 Z: 'the Iraqi'.

29 Cf. Ibn ʿAdī, *al-Kāmil fī ḍuʿafā' al-rijāl*; Abū Nuʿaym, *al-Ṭibb al-Nabawī* (Zabīdī, VII. 400).

30 Ṭabarsī, 194.

31 *milḥ* (MA, A: *ṭalḥ*: 'plantains').

32 Ṭabarānī, *al-Muʿjam al-Awsaṭ* (Sakhāwī, 381); Quḍāʿī, I. 108.

33 Abū Nuʿaym, *Ḥilya*, VIII. 32; Qushayrī, *Risāla*, 52.

34 Q. XXIV:37.

35 Cf. Ḥākim, I. 416: 'Every man is/shall be in the shade of his charity'.

36 This sentence omitted in Z.

37 Q. XXXIII:72.

38 Z adds, 'assigned for doing good and evil'.

39 'exposing...trials' omitted in Z.

40 Z, MA: *ibghūnī kadhā wa-kadhā wa'tūnī bi-kadhā wa-kadhā* (A: *tabī'unī arḍ kadhā wa-kadhā wa-azīduka kadhā wa-kadhā*).

41 *ḥadīthuhu sukhra* (Z: *khadamatuhu musakhkhara*; MA: *khadamatuhu saḥara*).

42 MA, A: *ahḍimu bihi ṭa'āmī* (Z: *yahḍimu ṭa'āmī*).

43 Ṭayālisī, 171; Abū Ya'lā, *al-Musnad* (Haythamī, *Majma'*, v. 31).

44 *yumsī* (Z: *yamshī*).

45 'so that … faith' omitted in MA, A.

Notes to Exposition 23.3

1 'and distress' omitted in A.

2 'was the custom … and' omitted in Z.

3 *Qūt* (Böwering, 56, 79).

4 'certain' omitted in A.

5 Z adds here: 'which is equivalent in weight to two *riṭls*.'

6 Q. VII:31.

7 'of the Companions' omitted in Z.

8 Ibn Ḥanbal, *Zuhd*, 184; Abū Nu'aym, *Ḥilya*, I. 162.

9 Ḥākim, III. 15.

10 *'anīza* (Z: *ghunayma*).

11 *al-ḥashf* (MA: *al-ḥashīsh*).

12 *al-suwayq* (MA: *al-tamr*).

13 *Qūt*, II. 274; cf. Suyūṭī, *Durar*, 152–3; Andrae, 40.

14 'or more … fifteen' omitted in A.

15 A: 'ibn 'Amr'.

16 Z: 'al-'Uranī'

17 MA adds the conjunction 'and'.

18 Z: 'ibn Sa'īd'.

19 *lā yumkin al-wuṣūl ilayhi illā bi'l-jidd wa'l-mujāhada* (A: *yumkin al-wuṣūl ilayhi bi'l-jidd wa'l-mujāhada)*.

20 Abū Nu'aym, *Ḥilya*, III. 323.

21 Bayhaqī, *Shu'ab al-īmān* (Zabīdī, VII. 410).

22 *tawarrama* (Z: *tazalla'a*).

23 Bukhārī, Tafsīr Sūrat 48, 2 (up to 'swollen').

24 Ibn Ḥanbal, *Musnad*, I. 91, 141.

25 'and sweetmeats' omitted in MA.

26 'the world … for him' omitted in Z.

27 Unidentified (Zabīdī, VII. 412).

28 Wakī', I. 401–2; Abū Nu'aym, *Ḥilya*, VI. 120; Ibn al-Mubārak, 262; Hannād, II. 363; Muḥāsibī, *Masā'il fī a'māl al-qulūb*, 138.

29 Hujwīrī, 191–2; 'Abbādī, *Manāqib*, 86.

30 Daylamī, *Musnad al-firdaws*; Bayhaqī, *Shu'ab al-īmān* (Zabīdī, VII. 413).

31 *tharīd wa-laḥm* (A: *tharīd*

laḥm).

32 Hannād, II. 362.

33 Abū Nuʿaym, *Ḥilya*, VI. 229.

34 MA: *yā aṣfar*.

35 *wa-mashā ḥattā adraknā al-bayt*, which could also mean, 'and walked to the Kaʿba with me.' The entire story is omitted in Z.

36 Abū Nuʿaym, *Ḥilya*, II. 366.

37 Z: 'years'.

38 *mā naqaṣa minnī wa-lā zāda fīkum* (A: *fa-mā zāda fīkum mā naqaṣa minnī, wa-lā naqaṣa minnī mā zāda fīkum*). The tale comes from Qushayrī, *Risāla*, 287.

39 *lubb* (Z, MA: *ṭaʿām*).

40 Abū Nuʿaym, *Ḥilya*, VII. 350.

41 MA: Abū Ḥātim. Z: Abū Ziḥām.

42 Q. LVI:33.

43 'ibn' omitted in A.

44 Q. LXXVI:8.

45 Abū Nuʿaym, *Ḥilya*, VI. 230.

46 Abū Nuʿaym, *Ḥilya*, VI. 229.

47 *baql* (MA, A: *n.ql*, which signifies dried fruit, etc.; see Lane, 3037.)

48 *wazīrī* omitted in Z; present in Qushayrī's version.

49 'in my heart' omitted in A.

50 Qushayrī, *Risāla*, 345.

51 Q. XIV:17.

52 Abū Nuʿaym, *Ḥilya*, VI. 218–9.

53 Qushayrī, *Risāla*, 397.

54 According to Zabīdī (VII. 418), this is a saying of Wahb ibn Munabbih, probably of Judaic origin.

55 Q. XIV:34

56 *Qūt*, I. 252.

57 Z: *al-mutaṭabbib*; MA: *al-Muṭayyab*.

58 Reading *aqwāt* for *awqāt*.

59 'It has been said that' omitted in Z.

60 'which ... him' omitted in Z.

61 Ṭabarānī, *al-Muʿjam al-Awsaṭ* (Zabīdī, VII. 419).

62 In place of 'so that ... latter,' Z has: 'that perhaps he will find it sufficient'.

63 Q. XLVI:20.

64 'rice' omitted in Z.

65 Z: 'he was seen in a dream', and so on in the third person of the passive voice.

66 Q. LXIX:24.

67 This sentence omitted in Z.

Notes to Exposition 23.4

1 Z, MA: *maqṣūd al-akl* (A: *maqṣūd al-ākil*).

2 *akhlāq* (A: *aḥwāl*).

3 Q. VII:31.

4 Bukhārī, Tahajjud, II.

5 Abū Dāūd, Ṣalāt, 69; Tirmidhī, Ṣawm, 34.

6 Cf. Nasā'ī, Ṣiyām, 62.

7 Muslim, Ṣiyām, 169.

8 Cf. above p. 135.

9 *Qūt*, II. 180.

10 Cf. Abū Nuʿaym, *Ḥilya*, II. 370.

11 Qushayrī, *Risāla*, 397.

12 *fī* (A: *min*).

13 *ṭāʿa* (Z: *musāmaḥa*).

14 Bukhārī, Ashriba, 15.

15 Ṭabarsī, 33.

16 Q. XXV:67.

Notes to Exposition 23.5

1 Q. IV:145

2 'and is sincere in it' missing in A.

3 Q. XXVIII:54.

4 *yaqdim ʿalā* (A: *yaqdir ʿalā*).

Notes to Exposition 23.6

1 Q. II:286.

2 *Qūt*, II. 239.

3 Q. CXIII:3.

4 *Qūt*, II. 240

5 *Qūt*, II. 240.

6 *Qūt*, II. 240.

7 A adds *wa-hannī*, for which see Bercher, 'Extrait,' 314.

8 Abū Dāūd, Witr, 32; Tirmidhī, Duʿā', 74; *Qūt*, II. 240. Cited in *Iḥyā'*, I. 291 (*K. al-Adhkār*, bāb 4, anwāʿ al-istiʿādha), (tr. Nakamura, 78).

9 Quḍāʿī, I. 66; Abū Nuʿaym, *Ḥilya*, I. 138.

10 'in company' omitted in Z.

11 Abū Nuʿaym, *Ḥilya*, II. 166.

12 *ḥayyāt* (Z: *bahā'im*). Cf. Bercher, 316.

13 Ṭabarānī, *al-Muʿjam al-Awsaṭ* (Zabīdī, VII. 431); cf. Ṭabarsī, 185.

14 *al-tamattuʿ* (Z: *al-tanʿīm*).

15 *manbaʿ* (A: *saʿa*).

16 *al-ṭuyūr* (MA: *al-ṭunbūr* [a kind of mandoline]).

17 'lutes' omitted in A, and in Bercher's tr., p.317.

18 Bukhārī, Ṣawm, 10.

Notes to Exposition 23.7

1 Unidentified (Zabīdī, VII. 433); the utterance is, however, widely known: cf. Schimmel, *And Muhammad is His Messenger*, 50.

2 Abū Dāūd, Adab, 78.

3 *lam yaqdir ʿalā ḥifẓ farjih* (A and Bercher); (Z, MA: *lam yaqdir ʿalā ḥifẓ dīnih*).

4 Perhaps derived from Matthew, V. 28; cf. Asín, *Logia*, 363.

5 Cf. Asín, *Logia*, 363.

6 Ibn Ḥanbal, *Musnad*, V. 264; cf. Haythamī, *Majmaʿ*, VIII. 63.

7 Bukhārī, Nikāḥ, 17.

8 Muslim, Dhikr, 99.

9 Q. XXIV:99.

10 'to the end of the verse' omitted in Z.

11 Bukhārī, Isti'dhān, 121; Qadar, 9; Muslim, Qadar, 20.

Notes to Breaking the Two Desires

12 Abū Dāūd, Libās, 34; Tirmidhī, Adab, 29.

13 This sentence omitted in Z.

14 Z: 'from fornicating'.

15 Ibn Abi'l-Dunyā, *Dhamm al-malāhī*, cited in Bellamy, 'Sex and Society', 37. Bellamy notes (p.26n) that Robson's edition of this work was based on an incomplete manuscript, and proceeds to use a more complete MS which is not available to the present translator. The modern Cairo edition of Muḥammad ʿAbd al-Qādir ʿAṭā (Dār al-Iʿtiṣām, 1982) is similarly truncated.

16 Ibid, cited in Bellamy, 'Sex and Society', 37.

17 Z: 'Why'.

18 'the rights ... women' omitted in A.

19 Qushayrī, *Risāla*, 475-6.

20 *mālak* (A: *turāthak*).

21 Abū Nuʿaym, *Ḥilya*, II. 166.

22 Abū Nuʿaym, *Ḥilya*, II. 166.

23 Abū Nuʿaym, *Ḥilya*, II. 167-8.

24 Abū Nuʿaym, *Ḥilya*, II. 168-9.

25 'in the eyes of religion' omitted in Z.

26 This sentence omitted in Z.

Notes to Exposition 23.8

1 *Tārīkh Baghdād*, V. 156; XII. 479; XIII. 184. Cf. Sakhāwī, 658; Zabīdī, VII. 439-40.

2 Bukhārī, Adhān, 36; Muslim, Zakāt, 91.

3 'with ... regard to' omitted in A.

4 Q. XII:24; Abū Nuʿaym, *Ḥilya*, II. 190-1.

5 'When ... until' omitted in A.

6 () omitted in A, and in the *Ḥilya*, which inserts it after the word 'tent'.

7 A: *quffāzān* (MA: *ghifārāt*). 'Wearing ... gloves' omitted in Z; present in the *Ḥilya*. Cf. Bercher, 327.

8 Z adds 'at Medina'.

9 Abū Nuʿaym, *Ḥilya*, II. 191.

10 *fa-rāwadtuhā* (Z: *fa-aradtuhā*).

11 'of drought' omitted in A.

12 *thammartu* (A: *nammaytu*).

13 'Take it' omitted in Z.

14 Bukhārī, Buyūʿ, 98.

15 Abū Dāūd, Nikāḥ, 43; Tirmidhī, Adab, 28. Cf. al-Ḥakīm al-Tirmidhī, *Nawādir*, 48-9; Ibn Bābawayh, IV. II.

16 Z: 'Do not look a second time'.

17 Abū Nuʿaym, *Ḥilya*, II. 244.

18 *ʿayn al-jahl* (Z: *ghāyat al-juhd*).

19 Abū Nuʿaym, *Ḥilya*, II. 230.

20 Q. XXII:18.

21 Q. LXX:8,9.

22 *mas͟hg͟hūl* (Z: *mutas͟hāg͟hil*).

23 Q. XL:18–20. 'God ... verity' omitted in A.

24 Q. VI:60.

25 A: "my hope for her".

26 Sarrāj, *Maṣāriᶜ al-ᶜus͟hs͟hāq*, I. 45–8.

27 This entire paragraph omitted in Z.

APPENDIX I

PERSONS CITED IN TEXT
(Excluding prophets)

ʿABD ALLĀH IBN ABĪ WADĀʿA—180. Unidentified.

ʿABD ALLĀH IBN SULAYMĀN—181 Unidentified (cf. Zabīdī, VII. 439).

ʿABD ALLĀH IBN ʿUMAR—9. See 'Ibn ʿUmar'.

ʿABD ALLĀH IBN AL-ZUBAYR ibn al-ʿAwwām (d. 73 [692])—138. The son of a famous Companion of the Prophet, he led a major revolt against Yazīd I following the death of al-Ḥusayn, and was widely recognised as Caliph. (*EI²*, I. 54-5 [H.A.R. Gibb].)

ʿABD AL-MALIK IBN MARWĀN (regn. 65-86 [685-705])—181. The fifth Umayyad caliph, remembered for administrative reforms and a number of successful campaigns against the K͟hārijite rebels and Byzantine encroachment.

ʿABD AL-RAḤMĀN IBN IBRĀHĪM DUḤAYM (d. 245 [859-60])—138. A highly respected traditionist whose *ḥadīt͟hs* appear in the collection of al-Buk͟hārī. An adherent of the legal school of al-Awzāʿī, he was chief judge of Palestine, and also taught in Baghdad and Damascus. (*Tārīk͟h Bag͟hdād*, X. 265-7; *G͟hāya*, I.361; Ziriklī, IV. 64.)

ʿABD AL-RAḤMĀN IBN SAMURA (d. c 50 [670])—11. A Companion of the Prophet, who converted upon the conquest of Mecca, and later participated in the conquest of Iraq and Sijistān, after which he settled at Basra where he transmitted *ḥadīt͟hs* to al-Ḥasan al-Baṣrī. (*Iṣāba*, II. 393; Ṭabarī, *Tārīk͟h*, II. 79; *Mas͟hāhīr*, 45; *Kās͟hif*, II. 149.)

ʿABD AL-RAḤMĀN AL-ṬABĪB—150. A well-known physician resident at Baghdad, who treated Ibn Ḥanbal and Bis͟hr al-Ḥāfī. (*Tārīk͟h Bag͟hdād*, X. 276-8.)

ʿABD AL-WĀḤID IBN ZAYD (d. c 177 [793/4])—115, 148. A companion of al-Ḥasan al-Baṣrī and al-Dārānī chiefly cited for the importance which he attached to solitude. According to Abū Nuʿaym, he was partially paralysed, from which affliction he was released only at the time of prayer. (Abū Nuʿaym, *Ḥilya*, VI. 155-65; *Bidāya*, X. 171; Massignon, *Essai*, 214-5; Vadet, 209.)

ABU'L-ʿABBĀS AL-MAWṢILĪ—57. Unidentified.

ABŪ ʿABD ALLĀH AL-KHAYYĀṬ—72. Unidentified.

ABŪ BAKR IBN AL-JALLĀ'—149. Perhaps a mistake for Abū ʿAbd Allāh ibn al-Jallā', a celebrated Sufi who died in 306 [918]. (Sulamī, 166-9; Hujwīrī, 134-5.)

ABŪ BAKR AL-ṢIDDĪQ ibn Abī Quḥāfa al-Taymī (d. 13 [634])—138. A small businessman of Mecca who personally accompanied the Prophet on his emigration to Medina, Abū Bakr became the Prophet's closest advisor, and after his death became the first caliph. (*EI*², I. 109-11 [W. Montgomery Watt].)

ABU'L-DARDĀ', ʿUwaymir al-Khazrajī (d. 32 [652/3])—8. A celebrated Companion of the Prophet who joined Islam sometime after the battle of Badr, whereupon he is said to have given up commerce in order to occupy himself with worship with the *ahl al-Ṣuffa*. He died in Damascus, where he was buried, and is venerated in particular by the Sufis. (*EI*², I. 113-4 [A. Jeffery]; Abū Nuʿaym, *Ḥilya*, I. 208-27.)

ABŪ DHARR, Jundab ibn Junāda al-Ghifārī (d. c 32 [652/3]) —11, 137. One of the earliest Muslims, his humility and ascetic temperament made him the protagonist of a rich variety of legendary material. He also transmitted a large number of Traditions, of which al-Bukhārī and Muslim include thirty-one between them. (*EI*², I. 114-5 [J. Robson]; Massignon, *Essai*, 158-9; *Istīʿāb*, IV. 62-5.)

ABŪ ḤABĪB ḤAMZA IBN ABĪ ʿABD ALLĀH AL-ʿABBĀDĀNĪ —82. A figure remembered only as the teacher of Sahl al-Tustarī. (Böwering, 48.)

ABŪ ḤĀZIM, Salama ibn Dīnār al-Makhzūmī (d. 140 [757/8]) —146. An ascetic and judge of Medina who became an important figure for the early Sufis. 'Everything which does not bring you to God', he said, 'can only bring you to destruction'. (*GAS*, I. 634-5; *Mashāhīr*, 79; Abū Nuʿaym, *Ḥilya*, III. 229-59.)

ABŪ HURAYRA al-Dawsī al-Yamānī (d. c 58 [677/8])— 9, 109, 110, 112, 140. One of the most prolific narrators of Tradition, and also a model of poverty and the fear of God's chastisement. He is said to have joined Islam during the Khaybar expedition (7/629); after which he became one of the *ahl al-Ṣuffa*. After the Prophet's death he was appointed governor of Baḥrayn by ʿUmar. (Azami, 35-7; *EI²*, I. 129 [J. Robson]; *Iṣāba*, IV. 200-8.)

ABU'L-JAWZĀ', Aws ibn Khālid al-Rabaʿī (d. 83 [702-3]— 138. A respected traditionist of Basra who narrated *ḥadīths* from ʿĀ'isha and Ibn ʿAbbās to Qatāda. He died with Ibn al-Ashʿath at the Battle of al-Jamājim. (Zabīdī, VII. 407; *Maʿārif*, 469; *Ṣifat al-Ṣafwa*, III. 181.)

ABŪ JUḤAYFA, Wahb ibn ʿAbd Allāh al-Suwā'ī (d. 74 [693/4])—11. A Companion of the Prophet who lived at Kūfa, where he related Traditions. (*Kāshif*, III. 215; *Mashāhīr*, 46; Ibn Saʿd, VI. 42; *Tahdhīb al-Tahdhīb*, II. 164-5.)

ABŪ MASʿŪD AL-BADRĪ, ʿUqba ibn ʿAmr al-Khazrajī (d. c 40 [660] or c 60 [679]—9. One of the earliest Medinan converts to Islam, he lived at Kūfa after the conquest of that city. (*Istīʿāb*, IV. 171-2; Ibn Saʿd, VI. 9; *Tahdhīb al-Tahdhīb*, VII. 247-9.)

ABŪ SAʿĪD AL-KHARRĀZ, Aḥmad ibn ʿĪsā (d. 279 [892/3] or 286 [899/900])—16. An important Sufi of Baghdad who, according to Hujwīrī, was 'the first to explain the doctrine of annihilation (*fanā'*) and subsistence (*baqā'*).' He was renowned for the emphasis he placed on *ʿishq*, the passionate love of God, and upon the scrupulous observance of the Law. (Sulamī, 223-8; Hujwīrī, 143; Qushayrī, *Risāla*, 140; *GAS*, I. 646.)

ABŪ SAʿĪD AL-KHUDRĪ, Saʿd ibn Mālik al-Khazrajī (d. c 64 [683/4] or 74 [693/4])—108, 139. A Companion who related a large corpus of *ḥadīths* to Ibn ʿAbbās and Saʿīd ibn al-Musayyab, and was buried at Medina. (*Iṣāba*, II. 32-3; Nawawī, *Tahdhīb*, 723-4.)

ABŪ SULAYMĀN AL-DĀRĀNĪ, ʿAbd al-Raḥmān (d. 205 [820/1] or 215 [830/1])—114, 118, 120, 125, 146, 151, 153, 171. Well-known to the Sufis for his piety and mortification, he left a number of characteristic sayings, such as 'The heart is ruined when fear departs from it even for one moment', and 'The sign of perdition is the drying-up of tears'. (Qushayrī, *Risāla*, I. 96-8; Sulamī, 68-73; Hujwīrī, 112-3; Abū Nuʿaym, *Ḥilya*, IX. 254-80.)

ABŪ ṬĀLIB AL-MAKKĪ, Muḥammad ibn ʿAlī (d. 386 [998/9])—115. A *ḥadīth* scholar, Mālikī jurist, and author of the *Qūt al-qulūb*, one of the most influential works of early Sufism, on which Ghazālī draws very extensively in his *Revival*. He was leader of the Sālimīya group of mystical theologians at Basra. (*EI²* I. 153 [L. Massignon]; Böwering, 25-7.)

ABŪ ʿUTHMĀN, Saʿīd ibn Sallām al-Maghribī (d. 373 [983/4])—15. Born at Qayrawān in present-day Tunisia, this influential Sufi met shaykhs in Egypt, Syria and Mecca. (Sulamī, 505-10; Ṣafadī, xv. 225; *GAS*, I. 665; Ibn al-ʿImād, III. 81; Jāmī, 87.)

ABŪ ʿUTHMĀN AL-ḤĪRĪ, Saʿīd ibn Ismāʿīl (d. 298 [910/11])—71. Born in Rayy, this ascetic saint and pupil of Shāh al-Kirmānī lived most of his life at Nīsābūr, where he followed the *malāmatīya* way. He had a crippled wife, to whom he showed an exemplary kindness. (*Tārīkh Baghdād*, IX. 99-102; Abū Nuʿaym, *Ḥilya*, x. 244-6; Shaʿrānī, I. 74; Hujwīrī, 132-5; Sulamī, 159-65; ʿAfīfī, *al-Malāmatīya*.)

ABŪ YAḤYĀ AL-WARRĀQ—58. Unidentified.

ABŪ YAZĪD AL-BISṬĀMĪ, Ṭayfūr ibn ʿĪsā (d. 261 [874] or 264 [877/8])—119. Al-Junayd is reported as saying that 'Abū Yazīd holds the same rank among us as Gabriel among the angels.' A Sufi of Central Asia famous for his ecstatic and enigmatic utterances (*shaṭaḥāt*). In addition, he was regarded as a reliable Traditionist. (*EI*[2], I. 162-3 [H. Ritter]; Sulamī, 60-7; Hujwīrī, 106-8; *GAS*, I. 645-6.)

AḤMAD— 82. Unidentified.

AḤMAD IBN ABI'L-ḤAWĀRĪ, Abu'l-Ḥasan (d. c 230 [844/5])—146. An early Syrian, or perhaps Kūfan, exponent of Sufism, a disciple of al-Dārānī and a companion of Ibn ʿUyayna. He is said to have thrown away his books and lived the life of a wandering ascetic. (Hujwīrī, 118-9; Qushayrī, *Risāla*, I. 105; Sulamī, 88-92; Ṣafadī, VI. 373; Vadet, 222-3.)

AḤMAD IBN KHALĪFA—147. Unidentified.

AḤMAD IBN SAʿĪD AL-ʿĀBID, ibn Ibrāhīm (d. 243 [857/8]) —189. A *ḥadīth* scholar of Nīsābūr whose *ḥadīths* are used by all the major anthologists except Ibn Māja. He was a pupil of Wakīʿ ibn al-Jarrāḥ. (*Tārīkh Baghdād*, IV. 165-6; Ibn al-ʿImād, II. 102; *Tahdhīb al-Tahdhīb*, I. 30.)

AL-AḤNAF IBN QAYS al-Tamīmī (d. 67 [686/7] or 72 [691/2])—73. An early Muslim who is said to have brought about the conversion of the Arabian tribe of Tamīm. He participated in the conquest of Herāt and Balkh. (Zabīdī, VII. 361; Ibn Saʿd, VII. 66; *EI*[2], I. 303-4 [Ch. Pellat]; *Maʿārif*, 423-5.)

ʿĀ'ISHA bint Abī Bakr (d. 58 [678])—7, 111, 112, 122, 139, 157, 172. The third and most beloved wife of the Prophet. During his final illness he asked his other wives for leave to stay in her house, where he died. After his death she was involved in the revolt of Ṭalḥa and al-Zubayr against the caliph ʿAlī, following which she lived quietly at Medina until she died. She was well-versed in Arab history and in poetry, and some of her verses have been preserved. (*EI*[2], I. 307-8 [W. Montgomery Watt].)

Appendix I

AL-ʿALĀʾ IBN ZIYĀD ibn Maṭar al-ʿAdawī (d. 94 [712/3])—187. An early ascetic of Basra, who remained solitary all his life, only going out to the mosque, or to funerals or to visit the sick. He had a vision in which the world appeared to him in the shape of a misshapen hag wearing fine jewellery. (*Mashāhīr*, 90; Abū Nuʿaym, *Ḥilya*, II. 242-9; *Kāshif*, II. 309; Nawawī, *Tahdhīb*, 540.)

ʿALĪ IBN ABĪ ṬĀLIB (d. 40 [661])—16, 38, 59, 73. The cousin and son-in-law of the Prophet, having married his daughter Fāṭima, he lived a life of austerity and piety. Upon the death of ʿUthmān (35/656) he accepted, with some reluctance, the office of Caliph, which he held for five years disturbed by several rebellions, including that of Muʿāwiya, the governor of Syria. He was assassinated at Kūfa by a member of the extreme Khārijite sect, which repudiated him for having agreed to negotiate with Muʿāwiya. (*EI²*, I. 381-6 [L. Veccia Vaglieri]; *Istīʿāb*, III. 26-67.)

ʿALĪ AL-JURJĀNĪ—125. Unidentified.

ʿALĪ IBN MŪSĀ AL-RIḌĀ, ibn Jaʿfar ibn Muḥammad ibn ʿAlī ibn al-Ḥusayn (d. 203 [818])—71. A devout and learned scholar regarded by the Twelver Shīʿa as their eighth Imām. He taught in the Prophet's mosque at Medina, but is buried at Mashhad in Khurāsān. His mother was a manumitted Nubian slave-woman. (*EI²*, I. 399-400; Shībī, *Ṣila*, 219-26.)

ANAS ibn Mālik ibn al-Naḍr (d. 91-3 [709/10-711/2])—10, 13, 70, 112. A celebrated Companion of the Prophet, he had been presented to the Prophet by his mother at an early age in fulfilment of a vow. After the Prophet's death he participated in the wars of conquest. One hundred and twenty-eight Traditions on his authority are to be found in the collections of al-Bukhārī and Muslim. (*Iṣāba*, I. 84-5; *EI²*, I. 482 [A. J. Wensinck—J. Robson].)

ʿĀṢIM IBN KULAYB (d. 137 [754/5])—140. A devout *ḥadīth* scholar of Kūfa who taught Ibn ʿUyayna and Sufyān al-Thawrī, and who perhaps subscribed to the Murjiʾī doctrinal school. (*Kāshif*, II. 47; *Tābiʿīn*, II. 193; *Mīzān*, II. 356.)

ʿAṬĀʾ AL-SULAMĪ (or 'AL-SALĪMĪ') (d.121 [738/9])—148. An ascetic and traditionist of Basra. (Abū Nuʿaym, *Ḥilya*, VI. 215-27; *Mashāhīr*, 152.)

AL-AWZĀʿĪ, ʿAbd al-Raḥmān ibn ʿAmr (d. 157 [774])—158. The principal Syrian authority on the *Sharīʿa* of his generation, he placed especial emphasis on the 'living tradition' of the Muslim community as an authoritative source of law. His *madhhab* also spread in North Africa and Spain, where it was then replaced by that of Mālik. His tomb near Beirut is still visited. (*EI²*, I. 772-3 [J. Schacht]; *GALS*, I. 308-9; *Fihrist*, 227.)

BAKR IBN ʿABD ALLĀH AL-MAZANĪ (d. 106 [724/5] or 108 [726/7])—116, 188. A 'Follower' of Basra, who, despite his considerable wealth, spent much time teaching and sitting with the poor. A prolific narrator of Tradition, he was known for the importance he attached to the fear of Hell. (*Mashāhīr*, 90; Ṣafadī, x. 207; Abū Nuʿaym, *Ḥilya*, II. 224-32; *Kāshif*, I. 108.)

AL-BARĀ' IBN ʿĀZIB al-Awsī (d. c 72 [691/2])—9. A Companion of the Prophet, who is said to have taken part in all his expeditions save that of Badr, for which he was considered to be too young. Later he was set in charge of the armies which conquered Rayy and Qazwīn. (*EI²*, I. 1025 [K. V. Zetterstéen]; *Iṣāba*, I. 146-7.)

BILĀL ibn Rabāḥ (d. 17-21 [638/9-642/3])—172. Usually held to have been the second adult convert to Islam, Bilāl was born in Mecca into slavery, and was tortured by his master Umayya ibn Khalaf when he refused to renounce his new faith. He was purchased by Abū Bakr, who set him free. He became the Prophet's muezzin at Medina, and later moved to Syria, where he died. (*EI²*, I. 1215 [W. ʿArafat].)

BISHR IBN AL-ḤĀRITH 'al-Ḥāfī' (d. c 227 [841/2])—150. One of the most celebrated figures of early Sufism, he was a companion of Fuḍayl ibn ʿIyāḍ. Many tales of his charismatic and devout life have found their way into the classical works on Sufism. (Qushayrī, *Risāla*, I. 73-7; Hujwīrī, 105-6; *Siyar*, x. 469; Abū Nuʿaym, *Ḥilya*, VIII. 336-60; Sulamī, 33-40; *EI²*, I. 1244-6 [F. Meier]; Dermenghem, 67-78.)

DĀŪD AL-ṬĀ'Ī, ibn Nuṣayr (d. c 165 [781/2])—53, 146, 147. A companion of Ibrāhīm ibn Adham, and an ascetic of whom many anecdotes are told in the early works on Sufism. He placed emphasis on poverty as an aid to the struggle against the lower self, gave all he had to the poor, and is said to have subsisted on a diet of barley bread and water. He was also an outstanding authority on the Law, which he studied under Abū Ḥanīfa. (*Siyar*, VII. 423; *Tārīkh Baghdād*, VIII. 347-55; Qushayrī, *Risāla*, I. 81-4; Abū Nuʿaym, *Ḥilya*, VII. 335-367; *Tahdhīb al-Tahdhīb*, III. 203.)

DHU'L-NŪN al-Miṣrī, Thawbān (d. 245 [859/60])—122. Born in Upper Egypt, he travelled to Mecca and Damascus, and became a leading exponent of Sufism. It is said that he was the first to give a systematic explanation of the *aḥwāl* ('states') and *maqāmāt* ('stations') encountered on the spiritual path. A number of miracles are attributed to him, as well as some fine poetry. (*EI²*, II. 242 [M. Smith]; Sulamī, 23-32; Qushayrī,

Risāla, I. 58-61; Hujwīrī, 100-3; Massignon, *Essai*, 206-13.)

FATḤ AL-MAWṢILĪ, Abū Naṣr ibn Saʿīd (d. 220 [835])—113. A Sufi and well-known ascetic who knew Bis͟hr al-Ḥāfī in Baghdad. (*Tārīk͟h Bag͟hdād*, XII. 381-3; Jāmī, 47-8; Abū Nuʿaym, *Ḥilya*, VIII. 292-4.)

FĀṬIMA (d. 11 [632])—112. The youngest and best-loved of the daughters of the Prophet. He once told her that 'God is angry when you are angry, and glad when you are glad'. In the year 2 she married ʿAlī ibn Abī Ṭālib in the union which was to produce al-Ḥasan and al-Ḥusayn. Her piety made her a figure greatly revered by later generations. (*Iṣāba*, IV. 365-8; *EI*², II. 841-50 [L. Veccia Vaglieri].)

[AL-]FUḌAYL ibn ʿIyāḍ (d. 187 [803/4])—8, 14, 113, 173. Said to have been a converted highwayman, probably of K͟hurāsān, who became a pioneer of early Sufism. He studied *ḥadīt͟h* under Sufyān al-T͟hawrī and Abū Ḥanīfa, and became well-known for his sermons on the worthlessness of the world, which he likened to 'a madhouse, the people in which are lunatics wearing the shackles of desire and sin'. (Hujwīrī, 97-100; Sulamī, 7-12; *Mas͟hāhīr*, 149; *EI*², II. 936 [M. Smith]; *GAS*, I. 636; Dermenghem, 51-66.)

ḤAFṢ AL-ʿĀBID AL-MAṢĪṢĪ—138. Unidentified.

ḤAJJĀJ IBN FURĀFIṢA al-Bāhilī (d. c 140 [757-8])—138. A traditionist who studied under Ibn Sīrīn in Basra and taught Sufyān al-T͟hawrī. (*Kās͟hif*, I. 149; Ṣafadī, XI. 305; *Mīzān*, I. 463.)

ḤAMMĀD IBN ABĪ ḤANĪFA—146. The son of Abū Ḥanīfa (d.150 [767]), who gave his name to one of the four main schools of Sunnī Islamic law. He narrated a number of *ḥadīt͟hs*, but is regarded as an unreliable source. (*GAS*, I. 412; *Mīzān*, I. 590.)

HĀRŪN AL-RAS͟HĪD (regn. 170-193 [786-809])—126. Perhaps the best-known ʿAbbāsid caliph, whose cultured and sumptuous court presided nevertheless over an empire troubled by rebellion and Byzantine encroachment.

AL-ḤASAN al-Baṣrī (d. 110 [728/9])—13, 15, 57, 108, 110, 111, 130, 131, 137. Perhaps the best known personality among the second generation of Muslims, he was born in Medina and took part in the conquest of eastern Iran. He then moved to Basra, where his sanctity and great eloquence attracted great numbers to his circle. He was also a judge and an authority on *ḥadīt͟h*. His tomb at Basra remains an important centre for devout visits. (Hujwīrī, 86-7; Abū Nuʿaym, *Ḥilya*, II. 131-61; ʿAṭṭār [Arberry], 19-26; *EI*², III. 247-8 [H. Ritter].)

ḤĀTIM AL-AṢAMM al-Balkhī (d. 237 [851/2])—69. A disciple of the Khurāsānī Sufi Shaqīq al-Balkhī, he was known as the 'Luqmān of this nation' for his wise sayings. (Hujwīrī, 115; Ṣafadī, xi. 233-4; Sulamī, 80-7; Abū Nuʿaym, *Ḥilya*, viii. 73-84.)

ḤUDHAYFA ibn al-Yamān al-ʿAbasī (d. 36 [656/7])—52. One of the earliest converts to Islam, he became governor of Ctesiphon under ʿUmar. He is particularly revered by the Sufis. He related a considerable number of *ḥadīths*, particularly those relating to eschatology: according to the sources he said that 'the Prophet told me all that would occur from the present until the Day of Judgement'. (*Iṣāba*, i. 316-7; Massignon, *Essai*, 159-61; Nawawī, *Tahdhīb*, 199-201; Abū Nuʿaym, *Ḥilya*, i. 270-83.)

AL-ḤUṢRĪ, ʿAlī ibn Ibrāhīm (d. 371 [981/2])—92. A well-known Sufi of Basra who removed to Baghdad, where he kept the company of al-Shiblī. He was celebrated for his self-discipline and restraint. (*Tārīkh Baghdād*, ii. 340-1; *Bidāya*, ii. 298-9.)

AL-ḤUSAYN IBN MANṢŪR al-Ḥallāj (d. 309 [922])—16. A Sufi of Baghdad known—or notorious—for ecstatic utterances, such as 'I am God', which proceeded from him 'while in the state of annihilation in the Divine Presence'. His eventual execution on heresy charges, which were supported only by a minority of theologians, appears to have been motivated by political considerations. (Massignon, *The Passion of al-Hallāj*.)

IBN ʿABBĀS, ʿAbd Allāh (d.68 [687/8])— 10, 14, 108, 118, 138, 165. A cousin and close companion of the Prophet respected for his piety, and commonly acknowledged as the greatest scholar of the first generation of Muslims, a narrator of *ḥadīth* and the founder of the science of Qur'ānic exegesis. He fought alongside ʿAlī at Ṣiffīn, and died at al-Ṭā'if, where the site of his grave is still visited. (Nawawī, *Tahdhīb*, 351-4; Abū Nuʿaym, *Ḥilya*, i. 314-29; *Mashāhīr*, 9; *Iṣāba*, ii. 322-6; *EI*², i. 40-1 [L. Veccia Vaglieri].)

IBN AṬĀ', Aḥmad b. ʿAbd Allāh (d. 309 [921/2])—14. A Sufi of the Baghdad school, and a companion of al-Junayd. He is said to have written a number of works, but these are now lost. (Sulamī, 260-8.)

IBN MASʿUD, ʿAbd Allāh al-Hudhalī (d. 32-3 [652/3-653/4]) —111. Of Bedouin origin, Ibn Masʿūd is said to have been either the third or the sixth convert to Islam; he became one of the most erudite Companions. He was particularly well versed in the recitation and interpretation of the Qur'ān, and was an expert in matters of law. (*EI*², iii. 873-5 [J.-C. Vadet]; *Iṣāba*, ii. 360-62; *Istīʿāb*, ii. 308-16.)

IBN AL-MUBĀRAK (d. 181 [797/8])—14. An influential saint and scholar of the Law. Originally of Merv in Central Asia, he travelled to study with Mālik ibn Anas in Medina and al-Awzāʿī in Syria before he died in combat against the Byzantines. His works on renunciation and the *jihād* have been published and are still popular. (*GALS*, I. 256; Ṣafadī, XVII. 419-20; Abū Nuʿaym, *Ḥilya*, VIII. 162-91; ʿAṭṭār [Arberry], 124-8.)

IBN SĀLIM, ʿAlī al-Baṣrī (d. 297 [909/10])—127, 152. A disciple of Sahl al-Tustarī, and the founder of the Sālimīya school of mystical theology, which was accused by some authorities of propounding a doctrine of divine anthropomorphism. He was the principal teacher of Abū Ṭālib al-Makkī. (Massignon, *Essai*, 297-30.)

IBN ʿUMAR, ʿAbd Allāh (d. 73 [693/4])—143, 186. A Companion of the Prophet who, at the age of fourteen asked to be permitted to fight at Uḥud, which permission was denied. Possessed of high moral qualities, he commanded universal deference and respect. Although it is said that he was offered the caliphate on three separate occasions, he kept himself aloof from politics and occupied himself instead with study and instruction. (*EI*² I. 53-4 [L. Veccia Vaglieri]; *Iṣāba*, II. 338-41; Abū Nuʿaym, *Ḥilya*, I. 292-314.)

IBN UMM MAKTŪM, ʿAbd Allāh (or ʿAmr) al-Qurashī—174. An early member of the first Muslim community at Mecca, who, although blind, was the Prophet's deputy over Medina during most of the campaigns. (*Iṣāba*, II. 516-7; *Maʿārif*, 290.)

IBRĀHĪM IBN ADHAM (d. 161 [777/8])—70, 128, 138, 144, 158. One of the most prominent early Sufis. According to the traditional account, he was a prince of Balkh in Afghanistan who renounced his kingdom to search for God. It is said that he studied under the great jurist Abū Ḥanīfa. He died during a naval expedition against the Byzantines. (*EI*², III. 985-6 [Russell Jones]; Sulamī, 13-22; Hujwīrī, 103-5; Abū Nuʿaym, *Ḥilya*, VII 367-95, VIII. 3-58.)

IBRĀHĪM AL-KHAWWĀṢ, b. Aḥmad (d. c 290 [903])—61, 90, 138, 160. A Sufi author who taught al-Khuldī. Although he travelled extensively, and visited Mecca, he lived mostly at Rayy, where he lies buried. (*Tārīkh Baghdād*, VI. 7-10; Ṣafadī, V. 303-4; Abū Nuʿaym, *Ḥilya*, X. 325-31.)

IBRĀHĪM AL-TAYMĪ, ibn Yazīd (d. c 93 [711/2])—138. An ascetic of Kūfa and a respected traditionist, who taught al-Aʿmash, and some of whose *ḥadīth* material is employed by al-Bukhārī and Muslim. (Abū Nuʿaym, *Ḥilya*, IV. 210-19; *Mashāhīr*, 101; *Kāshif*, I. 50.)

JAʿFAR IBN MUḤAMMAD ibn ʿAlī ibn al-Ḥusayn, 'al-Ṣādiq' (d. 148 [765])—58, 164. A major authority on law and *ḥadīth*, he taught both Abū

Ḥanīfa and Mālik. His austere and saintly life made him an important ideal for the Sufis, who gathered large numbers of sayings attributed to him. He was regarded as the seventh Imām of the Shī^ca: the Ja^cfarīya sect is named after him. (*EI²*, II. 374-5 [M.G.S. Hodgson]; *Mashāhīr*, 127; Abū Nu^caym, *Ḥilya*, III. 192-206; *Tahdhīb al-Tahdhīb*, II. 104.)

JA^cFAR IBN NUṢAYR al-Khuldī (d. 348 [959/60])—148. (Correct name: Ja^cfar ibn Muḥammad ibn Nuṣayr al-Khuldī.) A major Sufi of Baghdad, a companion of Ruwaym, al-Junayd and al-Nūrī, who spent much of his life engaged in extensive travels. He left a number of aphorisms which are much quoted in the classical works on Sufism. (*GAS*, I. 661; Qushayrī, *Risāla*, I. 178; Hujwīrī, 156-7; *Tārīkh Baghdād*, VII. 226-31; Abū Nu^caym, *Ḥilya*, X. 381.)

JARĪR IBN ^cABD ALLĀH al-Bajalī (d. 51 [671/2])—9. A Companion of the Prophet. Of an aristocratic family, he was renowned for his handsomeness. A number of *ḥadīths* were related by him. (*Mashāhīr*, 44; *Kāshif*, I. 126.)

AL-JUNAYD, Abu'l-Qāsim b. Muḥammad (d. 298 [910/11])—14, 58, 119, 148. The best known of the Sufis of Baghdad. A nephew and disciple of al-Sarī al-Saqaṭī, he vowed that would not teach during the latter's lifetime out of deference to his preceptor; however he received a vision of the Prophet, who told him that 'God shall make your words the salvation of a multitude of mankind'; he then began to teach. His gatherings 'were attended by jurists and philosophers (attracted by his precise reasoning), theologians (drawn by his orthodoxy) and Sufis (for his discoursing upon the Truth)'. In addition, he was an authority on theology and law, in which he followed the school of Abū Thawr. (Sulamī, 141-50; *GAS*, I. 647-50; *EI²*, II. 600 [A.J. Arberry]; A. H. Abdel-Kader, *The Life, Personality and Writings of al-Junayd*.)

KAHMAS b. al-Ḥasan al-Tamīmī (d. 149 [766/7])—113. An ascetic and respected *ḥadīth* scholar of Basra who taught Wakī^c ibn al-Jarrāḥ. (*Kāshif*, III. 10; *Mashāhīr*, 152; *Tābi^cīn*, II. 212; Jāmī, 83-4.)

AL-KATTĀNĪ, Muḥammad b. ^cAlī (d. 322 [933/4])—14. A Baghdad Sufi of the circle of al-Junayd and al-Kharrāz; he spent much of his life in Mecca, where he died. (Sulamī, 386-91; *Tārīkh Baghdād*, III. 74-6; Abū Nu^caym, *Ḥilya*, X. 357-8; ^cAṭṭār (Arberry), 253-6.)

LUQMĀN—13, 119. A sage of pre-Islamic Arabia who figures prominently in Arab legend and proverbs. He is shown in the Qur'ān as a monotheist giving advice to his son. (*EI²*, V. 811-3 [B. Heller—[N. A. Stillman]].)

MĀLIK IBN ḌAYGHAM—146. Although this name is not unknown (cf. Abū Nu^caym, *Ḥilya*, VI. 192), it is probably a mistake for Ḍaygham ibn

Mālik, an ascetic of Basra noted for his profound fear (*khauf*) of God's chastisement. (Munāwī, I. 126; *Ṣifat al-ṣafwa*, III. 270–3.)

MĀLIK IBN DĪNĀR al-Nājī (d.131 [748/9])—59, 74, 113, 158. An ascetic of Basra who made a living by copying the Qur'ān. A companion of al-Ḥasan al-Baṣrī, he was credited with a number of miracles, including the ability to walk on water. (*Mashāhīr*, 90; Hujwīrī, 89–90; *Ghāya*, II. 36; Abū Nuʿaym, *Ḥilya*, II. 357–88.)

MAʿRŪF AL-KARKHĪ, ibn Fīrūz (d.200–1 [815/6–816/7])—158. One of the major early Sufis. His parents are said to have been Christians. He was a major influence on al-Sarī al-Saqaṭī, but also instructed Ibn Ḥanbal in *ḥadīth*. His grave, restored in 1312 AH, is an important focus of the religious life of Baghdad, and many miraculous cures are said to be worked there. (Hujwīrī, 113–5; Sulamī, 74–9; Qushayrī, *Risāla*, I.65–8; Ibn al-Jawzī, *Manāqib Maʿrūf al-Karkhī wa-akhbāruhu*.)

MAYMŪNA bint al-Ḥārith (d. 38 [658/9])—174. A wife of the Prophet. (*Iṣāba*, IV. 389; *Maʿārif*, 137.)

MUḤAMMAD IBN SULAYMĀN AL-HĀSHIMĪ, ibn ʿAlī ibn ʿAbd Allāh ibn ʿAbbās (d. 173 [789/90])—178. One of many men who are said to have been suitors of Rābiʿa al-ʿAdawīya. He was was governor of Basra for a period from AH 145, and narrated a few Traditions of doubtful authority. (*Bidāya*, X. 103, 162–3; ʿUqaylī, IV. 73; Smith, *Rābiʿa*, 10–11; *Mīzān*, III. 572.)

MUḤAMMAD IBN SUWĀR—81. A *ḥadīth* scholar of Basra who followed Sufyān al-Thawrī in *fiqh*. (Böwering, 45–7.)

MUḤAMMAD IBN WĀSIʿ al-Azdī (d. 127 [744/5])—113. An early *ḥadīth* scholar noted for his asceticism. His statement, 'I never saw anything without seeing God therein' was much discussed by later Sufis. He fought under Qutayba ibn Muslim during the conquest of Transoxiana, and later became a judge. (Hujwīrī, 91–2; Abū Nuʿaym, *Ḥilya*, II. 345–57; *Ghāya*, II 274; *Mashāhīr*, 151.)

MŪSĀ AL-ASHAJJ—147. Unidentified.

AL-MUSLIM IBN SAʿĪD—138. Perhaps this is Muslim ibn Saʿīd al-Kilābī, who in 104 became governor of Khurāsān, and defeated the Turks in Farghāna two years later. He was deposed by Khālid al-Qasrī. (*Bidāya*, IX. 229, 234.)

NĀFIʿ, *mawlā* Ibn ʿUmar. (d. 119 [737])—143. An important *ḥadīth* scholar of Medina, who studied under Ibn ʿUmar and Abū Hurayra, and who taught Mālik ibn Anas and al-Layth ibn Saʿd. (*Mashāhīr*, 80; *Kāshif*, III. 174.)

QĀSIM AL-JŪʿĪ, ibn ʿUthmān al-Dimashqī—149. An ascetic and worker of miracles, whose name al-Jūʿī reflects his state of constant hunger. 'The Friends of God,' he is said to have remarked, 'are sated with God's love, and thus feel no hunger.' (Zabīdī, VII. 418; Abū Nuʿaym, *Ḥilya*, IX. 322-4; Munāwī, I. 260-1.)

QAYS IBN ʿĀṢIM al-Tamīmī—73. An intelligent and aristocratic tribal leader who came to the Prophet to accept Islam in the ninth year of the Hegira. After the conquests he settled at Basra. (*Kāshif*, II. 349; *Mashāhīr*, 39; *Tahdhīb al-Tahdhīb*, VIII. 399-400; *Maʿārif*, 301.)

RĀBIʿA AL-ʿADAWĪYA, bint Ismāʿīl (d. 185 [801/2])—178-9. The most famous woman Sufi. It is said that she was stolen as a child and sold into slavery, but was released on account of her piety. She lived for a time in the desert, where she was fed miraculously by God. She later moved to Basra, where she taught Sufyān al-Thawrī and Shaqīq al-Balkhī, emphasising the importance of divine love. She left a number of fine prayers. (M. Smith, *Rābiʿa the Mystic*.)

SAHL IBN ʿABD ALLĀH AL-TUSTARĪ (d. 283 [896/7])— 15, 73, 81, 89, 114, 129, 134, 137, 138, 152, 157. A celebrated Sufi famous for the emphasis he placed on self-discipline and repentance, who was a disciple of Sufyān al-Thawrī, and taught Muḥammad ibn Sālim and al-Ḥallāj. (Böwering; Massignon, *Passion*, I. 69-71; Jāmī, 66-8; Sulamī, 199-205; Ibn al-ʿImād, II. 182.)

SAʿĪD IBN JUBAYR al-Asadī *mawlāhum* (d. 95 [713/4])—173. A legal scholar of the second Muslim generation known for his scrupulousness (*waraʿ*), who studied under Ibn ʿAbbās and Ibn ʿUmar, and whose *ḥadīth* material is used by Bukhārī. He was killed by al-Ḥajjāj, and is buried at Wāsiṭ. (*Tābiʿīn*, I. 147; *Maʿārif*, 445; Ibn Saʿd, VI. 178.)

SAʿĪD IBN AL-MUSAYYIB al-Makhzūmī (d. 93-4 [291/2-292/3])—167, 179, 180. A major genealogist and legal expert of Medina, held by some to have been the most erudite of the second Muslim generation. He refused to marry his devout and learned daughter to the caliph al-Walīd ibn ʿAbd al-Malik, for which he was flogged. (Abū Nuʿaym, *Ḥilya*, II. 161-76; Hujwīrī, 87; *Mashāhīr*, 63.)

ṢĀLIḤ AL-MURRĪ, ibn Bashīr (d. c 172 [788/9])—148. A 'weak' traditionist of Basra who studied under Ibn Sīrīn and Yazīd al-Ruqāshī. Famed for his sermons, he was invited to Baghdad to preach before the caliph al-Mahdī. (Ṣafadī, XVI. 252; *Bidāya*, X. 170; *Ḍuʿafāʾ*, 136; Abū Nuʿaym, *Ḥilya*, VI. 165-77.)

AL-SARĪ AL-SAQAṬĪ, ibn al-Mughallis (d. c 251 [865/6])—62, 125, 149, 159. The maternal uncle of al-Junayd, and one of the first to present Sufism in a systematised fashion. According to Hujwīrī, his conversion to Sufism was instigated by the Baghdad saint Ḥabīb al-Rāʿī, who, upon being given a crust of bread by al-Sarī, said, 'May God reward you!' 'From that time on', al-Saqaṭī later remarked, 'my worldly affairs never prospered again'. He was perhaps the most influential disciple of Maʿrūf al-Karkhī. (*EI*, IV. 171 [L. Massignon]; *Tārīkh Baghdād*, IX. 187-62; J. al-Murābiṭ, *al-Sarī al-Saqaṭī*; Dermenghem, 115-28.)

SHĀH AL-KIRMĀNĪ, ibn Shujāʿ (d. before 300 [913])—15. A Sufi of aristocratic descent and a pupil of al-Nakhshabī, he is said to have left books on Sufism. He was an exponent of *futuwwa*, the mystical virtue of courage and generosity. (Sulamī, 183-5; Hujwīrī, 138; Jāmī, 85-6; Abū Nuʿaym, *Ḥilya*, X. 237-8.)

SHAQĪQ AL-BALKHĪ, al-Azdī (d. 194 [809/10])—113. One of the founders of the Khurāsānī school of Sufism, he was the disciple of the ascetic Ibrāhīm ibn Adham. He was known for his discourses on the imminence of the Last Judgement and the importance of reliance (*tawakkul*) upon God. He was also a noted scholar of the *sharīʿa*. (Qushayrī, *Risāla*, I. 85-7; Abū Nuʿaym, *Ḥilya*, VIII. 58-73; Sulamī, 54-9; Hujwīrī, 111-2.)

AL-SHIBLĪ, ibn Jaḥdar (d. 334 [945/6])—92, 118. Formerly a chamberlain at the Caliph's palace, he converted to Sufism and became a follower of al-Junayd, whose teachings he later communicated to al-Naṣrābādhī. Well-known for his eccentric conduct, and various acts of asceticism and renunciation, it is said that he put salt in his eyes to stay awake for his nocturnal devotions. He was also an authority on the Mālikite school of law. His tomb at Baghdad is still venerated. (Qushayrī, *Risāla*, I. 59-60; Sulamī, 340-55; Hujwīrī, 155-6; *Tārīkh Baghdād*, XIV. 389-97; *EI*, IV. 360-1 [L. Massignon]; Dermenghem, 201-30.)

SUFYĀN —176. See next notice.

SUFYĀN AL-THAWRĪ, ibn Saʿīd (d. 161 [777/8])—57, 152. A traditionist and well-known saint of Kūfa, of whom a great number of anecdotes are recorded. It is said that he was offered high office under the Umayyads but consistently refused. (*Fihrist*, 225; Abū Nuʿaym, *Ḥilya*, VI. 356-93, VII. 3-144; *EI*, IV. 500-2 [M. Plessner].)

SULAYMĀN AL-KHAWWĀṢ (d. before 170 [787])—138. An ascetic of Palestine who studied law under al-Awzāʿī, and was a companion of Ibrāhīm ibn Adham. (Abū Nuʿaym, *Ḥilya*, VIII. 276–7; Ṣafadī, XV 375; *Ṣifat al-Ṣafwa*, IV. 247–8.)

SULAYMĀN IBN YASĀR, Abū Ayyūb al-Madanī (d. c 107 [725])—184. The *mawlā* of the Prophet's wife Maymūna, he is regarded as a reliable transmittor of *ḥadīths*. He was also an authority on the Law, and a noted ascetic. (*Kāshif*, I. 321; *Mashāhīr*, 64; *Tābiʿīn*, I. 157.)

ṬĀWŪS b. Kaysān al-Khawlānī (d. 106 [724/5])—110. An expert on the *Sharīʿa* and the recitation of the Qur'ān, he studied under Ibn ʿAbbās, and was regarded as one of the leading scholars in Mecca of the second Muslim generation. (*Ghāya*, I. 341; *Mashāhīr*, 122; Ibn Saʿd, V 391; Vadet, 237.)

AL-THAWRĪ—158, 176. See 'Sufyān al-Thawrī'.

ʿUMAR ibn al-Khaṭṭāb (regn. 13–23 [634–44])—12, 14, 52, 113, 142, 159. At first an enemy of the Prophet's mission, he became one of its staunchest defenders. His daughter Ḥafṣa married the Prophet after the Emigration. When he succeeded Abū Bakr as caliph, he showed considerable brilliance in the face of the new circumstances which arose as a result of the conquests, regulating the status of minorities, arranging a military pensions system and founding a number of garrison towns (*amṣār*). He was universally respected for his integrity and uncompromising devotion to the faith. (*Iṣāba*, II. 511–2; *Istīʿāb*, II. 450–66; *SEI*, 600–1 [G. Levi della Vida].)

ʿUMAR IBN ʿABD AL-ʿAZĪZ ibn Marwān (regn. 99–101 [717–20])—59. Sometimes called 'the fifth rightly-guided Caliph' for his piety, he was concerned to implement the *Sharīʿa* in a number of neglected areas, such as the equal treatment of converts.

UMM ḤABĪBA, Ramla bint Abī Sufyān (d. c 44 [664])—11. She married the Prophet in the year 4/626, and took part in the emigration to Abyssinia. (*Istīʿāb*, IV. 421–3; Ibn Saʿd, VIII. 68; *Maʿārif*, 136.)

UMM SALAMA, Hind bint Abī Umayya al-Qurashīya (d. c 62 [681/2]—174. A wife of the Prophet, who, like Umm Ḥabība, joined the Abyssinian exodus. (*Iṣāba*, IV. 439–41; *Maʿārif*, 136.)

USĀMA IBN SHARĪK al-Thaʿlabī (d. before 70 [689])—10. A Companion of the Prophet, who later moved to Kūfa, and who was regarded as an authoritative narrator of Tradition. (Ibn Saʿd, VI. 17; *Tahdhīb al-Tahdhīb*, I. 210; *Iṣāba*, I. 46–7.)

USĀMA IBN ZAYD ibn Ḥāritha (d. 54 [673/4])—109. Described by the Prophet as the most beloved of his Companions, he was set in charge of an expedition to Syria, preparations for which began during the

Prophet's final illness. He later removed to Damascus. (*Mashāhīr*, 11; *Kāshif*, I. 57; *Iṣāba*, I. 46.)

ʿUTBA AL-GHULĀM, ibn Abān (d. c 153 [770/1])—144, 147. An ascetic of Basra, where he associated with al-Ḥasan al-Baṣrī. It is said that he received a dream in which he was told that he would gain martyrdom; he later travelled to northern Syria where he was attached to the garrison of a frontier fortress, and shortly afterwards was killed in a cavalry sortie near Aḍana. (*Bidāya*, x. 150; Abū Nuʿaym, *Ḥilya*, VI. 226-38.)

UWAYS AL-QARANĪ, ibn ʿĀmir al-Murādī (d. 37? [657?])— 73. A Yemeni, who although he never met the Prophet, was mentioned and praised by him, and was promised that he would exercise a special intercession for the believers on the Day of Judgement. (Ṣafadī, IX. 456-7; Abū Nuʿaym, *Ḥilya*, II. 79-87; *Mashāhīr*, 100; Ibn Marthad, 71-4; Molé, 81.)

WAHB IBN MUNABBIH (d. c 110 [728/9])—13, 58, 142. A Yemeni sage possibly of Persian extraction, who is said to have prayed all night for forty consecutive years. A number of sermons are ascribed to him, which make considerable use of Jewish and Christian lore. He was made a judge during the reign of ʿUmar II. (*Tahdhīb al-Tahdhīb*, XI. 166; Abū Nuʿaym, *Ḥilya*, IV. 23-82; *Mashāhīr*, 122-3.)

AL-WALĪD (regn. 88-98 [705-15])—181. Umayyad caliph who presided over the conquest of Transoxiana and Sind, and the construction of the Umayyad mosque at Damascus.

AL-WĀSIṬĪ, Muḥammad ibn Mūsā (d. c 320 [932])—15. A Sufi who associated with al-Junayd and al-Nūrī at Baghdad, and who later moved to Merv, where he died. He was also an authority on the *fiqh*. (Qushayrī, *Risāla*, I. 151-2; Sulamī, 302-7.)

WUHAYB IBN AL-WARD al-Makkī (d. c 153 [770/1])—58. A *ḥadīth* scholar who spent his life in mortification and worship, and to whom a number of miracles are attributed. He taught Ibn ʿUyayna and Ibn al-Mubārak, and a few *ḥadīths* are given on his authority by Muslim and al-Tirmidhī. (Abū Nuʿaym, *Ḥilya*, VIII. 140-62; *Mashāhīr*, 148; Massignon, *Essai*, 168; *Kāshif*, III. 216.)

YAḤYĀ IBN MUʿĀDH al-Rāzī (d. 258 [871/2])—13, 14, 57, 113, 141. A Sufi who taught in Central Asia. One of the first to teach Sufism in mosques, he left a number of books and sayings. Despite the emphasis he placed on *rajā'*: the hope for Paradise and for God's forgiveness, he was renowned for his perseverance in worship and his great scrupulousness in matters of religion. (Abū

Nuᶜaym, *Ḥilya*, x. 51–70; Sulamī, 98–104; *GAS*, I. 644; Hujwīrī, 122–3; Massignon, *Essai*, 268–71.)

YAḤYĀ IBN ZIYĀD AL-ḤĀRITHĪ—74. Nephew of the caliph al-Saffāḥ (for whom he wrote panegyrics), he was an obscene poet of Kūfa and was widely regarded as a heretical freethinker (*zindīq*). He died during the caliphate of al-Mahdī. (*Tārīkh Baghdād*, XIV. 106–8; Ziriklī, VII. 145.)

YASĀR IBN ᶜUMAYR—144. A respected narrator of Tradition, perhaps a Companion of the Prophet, who was a *mawlā* of ᶜUmar ibn al-Khaṭṭāb. He resided for the latter part of his life at Kūfa. (Zabīdī, VII. 414; *Tahdhīb al-Tahdhīb*, XI. 377.)

YAZĪD IBN ABĪ SUFYĀN—143–4.

YAZĪD AL-RUQĀSHĪ, ibn Abān (d. c 115 [733/4])—59. A traditionist and judge of Basra who studied under al-Ḥasan al-Baṣrī and taught Ṣāliḥ al-Murrī. One of the 'Weepers', he abandoned his studies to devote himself to worship. (*Kāshif*, III. 240; *Ḍuᶜafā'*, 253; Abū Nuᶜaym, *Ḥilya*, III. 50–5; *Tahdhīb al-Tahdhīb*, XI. 309.)

YŪSUF IBN ASBĀṬ al-Shaybānī (d. 196 [811/2])—73. Dominated by the fear of God and of the Judgement, he influenced Bishr al-Ḥāfī. He also related a number of *ḥadīths* from al-Thawrī. (Abū Nuᶜaym, *Ḥilya*, VIII. 237–53; Zabīdī, x. 343; Vadet, 238.)

ZUHAYR ibn Naᶜīm (?) al-Salūlī (d. after 200 [815])—138. An ascetic and an unreliable traditionist of Basra, who associated with Yazīd al-Ruqāshī. (Zabīdī, VII. 407; *Tahdhīb al-Tahdhīb*, III. 353; *Taᶜjīl*, 139; *Mīzān*, II. 82–3.)

ZULAYKHĀ—58, 184. The wife of Potiphar. According to Muslim legend, she is believed to have obtained a divorce from him, and finally to have married Joseph. (Thackston, *Tales of the Prophets of al-Kisa'i*, 172–180.)

APPENDIX II

Translations from the *Revival* in European languages

Partial renderings are indicated by ★

1 ***al-ʿIlm*** (Knowledge)[1]

a '*The Book of Knowledge*, being a translation with introduction and notes of al-Ghazzali's book of the *Ihya, Kitab al-'Ilm*'. William A. McCall. Unpublished PhD dissertation, Hartford Theological Seminary (Connecticut), 1940.

b *The Book of Knowledge, being a Translation with Notes of the Kitāb al-ʿilm of Al-Ghazzālī's "Iḥyā' ʿUlūm al-Dīn"*. Nabih Amin Faris. Lahore: Sh. Muhammad Ashraf, 1962.‖ Revised ed. Lahore: 1966 and reprints.

2 ***Qawāʿid al-ʿaqā'id*** (Foundations of the Articles of Faith)

a *Die Dogmatik al-Ghazali's, nach den II. Buch seines Hauptwerkes*. H. Bauer. Halle a.S.: Buchdruckerei des Waisenhauses, 1912

b *The Foundations of the Articles of Faith being a Translation with Notes of The Kitāb Qawāʿid al-ʿAqā'id of al-Ghazzālī's "Iḥyā' ʿUlūm al-Dīn"*. Nabih Amin Faris. Lahore: Sh. Muhammad Ashraf, 1963 and reprints.

c ★'Al-Ghazali's Tract on Dogmatic Theology. Edited, Translated, Annotated and Introduced by A.L. Tibawi'. *IQ*, IX (1965) 65–122. [=Bayān III, *Iḥyā'*, I.93–103.] ‖ Issued as separatum by Luzac, 1965.

3 ***Asrār al-ṭahāra*** (The Secrets of Purity)

The Mysteries of Purity: being a translation with notes of the Kitāb Asrār al-Ṭahārah *of Al-Ghazzālī's Iḥyā' ʿUlūm al-Dīn*. Nabih Amin Faris. Lahore: Sh. Muhammad Ashraf, 1966 and reprints.

4 ***Asrār al-ṣalāt*** (The Secrets of the Prayer)

a *Worship in Islam; being a translation with commentary and introduction, of al-Ghazzālī's Book of the Ihyā' on the worship*. Edwin Elliot Calverley. Hartford:

[1] For an alternative and somewhat free translation of these titles see Arberry, *Sufism*, 81–2; also Nakamura, *Ghazali: Invocations and supplications*, xvii–xix.

Hartford Theological Seminary, 1923. Published Madras [etc.]: The Christian Literature Society for India, 1925.‖[repr. with corrections] London: Luzac, 1957. ‖[repr.] Lahore: Sh. Muhammad Ashraf, 1977 and 1981.

b *'Vitalizing of the Religious Sciences. The Mysteries and Essentials of the Worship'. *MW* 14 (1924) 10–22. [Selections from 4a above.]

c **Inner Dimensions of Islamic Worship*. Translated from the Iḥyā' by Muhtar Holland. Pp.19–52 (selected passages). Leicester: The Islamic Foundation, 1983/1403 and reprints.

5 ***Asrār al-zakāt*** (The Secrets of the Zakāt-Tithe)

a *The Mysteries of Almsgiving: A Translation from the Arabic with Notes of the* Kitāb Asrār al-Zakāh *of Al-Ghazzālī's Iḥyā' ʿUlūm al-Dīn*. Nabih Amin Faris. Beirut: The American University in Beirut, 1966. (American University of Beirut Centennial Publications.)

b **Inner Dimensions* (4c above), pp.53–73 (selections).

6 ***Asrār al-ṣawm*** (The Secrets of Fasting)

a *The Mysteries of Fasting, being a Translation with Notes of the Kitāb Asrār al-Ṣawm of Al-Ghazzālī's "Iḥyā' 'Ulūm al-Dīn"*. Nabih Amin Faris. Lahore: Sh. Muhammad Ashraf, 1968 and reprints.

b **Inner Dimensions* (4c above), pp.75–82 (selections).

7 ***Asrār al-ḥajj*** (The Secrets of the Pilgrimage)

a *'The Book on the Secrets of Pilgrimage* (*Kitāb 'Asrār al-Ḥajj*) by 'Abū Ḥāmid Muḥammad al-Ghazālī'. Ibrahim Umar. Unpublished MA dissertation, American University in Cairo, 1975.

b **Inner Dimensions* (4c above), pp.83–120 (selections).

8 ***Ādāb al-tilāwa*** (The Proprieties of Qur'ānic Recitation)

The Recitation and Interpretation of the Qur'an: Al-Ghazālī's Theory. Mohammad Abul Quasem. Bangi, Selangor, Malaysia: National University of Malaysia, 1979.‖ London: Kegan Paul International, 1982 and reprints.

9 ***al-Adhkār wa'l-daʿawāt*** (Invocations and Supplications)

a *Ghazali on Prayer*. Kojiro Nakamura. Tokyo: Institute of Oriental Culture, 1973. ‖ Revised edition entitled *Invocations and Supplications*, Cambridge: Islamic Texts Society, 1990. (Al-Ghazālī Series, 2.)

b **Inner Dimensions* (4c above), pp.129–138 (=Bāb II, Faḍīlat al-ṣalāt ʿalā rasūl Allāh, and Faḍīlat al-istighfār).

c *Temps et prières. Prières et invocations. Extraits de* l'Ihyâ ʿUlum al-Dîn, traduits de l'arabe, présentés et annotés par Pierre Cuperly. Paris: Sindbad, 1990. (Slightly abridged.) 39-99.

10 ***Tartīb al-awrād wa-tafṣīl iḥyā' al-layl*** (The Arrangement of Litanies and Division of the Night Vigil)

a **Inner Dimensions* (4c above), pp.121-8 (=Qiyām al-layl).

b *Temps et prières* (9c above), 101-95.

11 ***Ādāb al-akl*** (The Proprieties of Eating)

Über die guten Sitten beim Essen und Trinken, das ist das 11. Buch von Al-Ghazzālī's Hauptwerk. Übersetzung und Bearbeitung als ein Beitrag zur Geschichte unserer Tischsitten. Hans Kindermann. Leiden: E.J. Brill, 1964.

12 ***Ādāb al-nikāḥ*** (The Proprieties of Marriage)

a *Von der Ehe. Das 12. Buch von al-Gazālī's Hauptwerk,* übersetzt und erläutert von Hans Bauer. Halle a.S.: Max Niemeyer, 1917. (Islamische Ethik, Heft II.)

b *Le Livre des bons usages en matière de mariage. Extrait de l'Ih'ya' 'Ouloûm ed-Dîn, ou: Vivification des Sciences de la foi.* Traduction française annotée par L. Bercher et G.-H. Bousquet. (Bibliothèque de la Faculté de Droit d'Alger, XVII.) Paris, Oxford: Maisonneuve, Thornton, 1953.

c *Marriage and Sexuality in Islam. A translation of al-Ghazālī's Book on the Etiquette of Marriage from the Iḥyā'.* Madelain Farah. Salt Lake City: University of Utah Press, 1984.

13 ***Ādāb al-kasb wa'l-maʿāsh*** (Proprieties of Acquisition and Earning a Livelihood)

14 ***al-Ḥalāl wa'l-ḥarām*** (The Lawful and Unlawful)

a *Erlaubtes und verbotenes Gut. Das 14. Buch von al-Gazāli's Hauptwerk,* übersetzt und erläutert von Hans Bauer. Halle a.S.: Max Niemeyer, 1922. (Islamische Ethik, Heft III.)

b *Le Livre du licite et de l'illicite.* Introduction, traduction et notes par Régis Morelon. Paris: J. Vrin, 1981. (Études Musulmanes, XXV.)

15 ***Ādāb al-ulfa wa'l-ukhuwwa wa'l-ṣuḥba*** (The Proprieties of Friendship, Brotherhood and Companionship)

**On The Duties of Brotherhood.* Translated by Muhtar Holland from the Classical Arabic. (Abridged.) London: The Anchor Press, 1975. || (repr.)

Woodstock, N.Y.: The Overlook Press, 1979. ‖ (repr.) Leicester: The Islamic Foundation, 1980/1400 and reprints.

16 ***Ādāb al-ʿuzla*** (The Proprieties of Seclusion)

17 ***Ādāb al-safar*** (The Proprieties of Travelling)

18 ***Ādāb al-samāʿ wa'l-wajd*** (The Proprieties of Audition and Ecstasy)

'Emotional Religion in Islām as affected by Music and Singing. Being a Translation of a Book of the *Iḥyā' ʿUlūm ad-Dīn* of al-Ghazzālī, with Analysis, Annotation and Appendices'. Duncan B. Macdonald. *JRAS* 1901, 195–252, 705–48; 1902, 1–28.

19 ***al-Amr bi'l-maʿrūf wa'l-nahy ʿan al-munkar*** (Enjoining good and forbidding evil)

*'Le Livre de l'obligation d'ordonner le bien et d'interdire le mal selon Al-Ghazali (*Kitab al-amr bi-l-maʿruf wa-n-nahy ʿani-l-munkar*)'. Léon Bercher. *IBLA* 18 (1955), 53–91, 313–21. ‖ Issued as separatum by the Publications de l'Institut des Belles Lettres Arabes, Tunis, 1961. [Selected passages.]

20 ***Ādāb al-maʿīsha wa-akhlāq al-nubuwwa*** (Proprieties of Living and the Virtues of Prophethood)

Book XX *of Al-Ghazālī's Iḥyā' ʿUlūm al-Dīn*. L. Zolondek. Leiden: E.J. Brill, 1963.

21 ***Sharḥ ʿajā'ib al-qalb*** (Expounding the Wonders of the Heart)

a 'The religious psychology of Al-Ghazzali; a translation of his book of the Ihya on the explanation of the wonders of the heart; with introduction and notes.' Skellie, Walter J. Unpublished dissertation, Hartford Theological Seminary (Connecticut), 1938.

b *'Texte d'al-Ghazâli, traduit de l'arabe et annoté'. Gardet, L. *Révue Thomiste* 1938, 569–78. [French translation with notes of selected passages.]

c 'Die Wunder des Herzens. Ein Beitrag zur Religionspsychologie des Islams. Aus al Gazzalis Werk Ihya ulum ad-din, übertragen und mit kommentar und Glossar versehen.' Eckman, Karl Friedrich. Unpublished PhD dissertation, Mainz Univ. 1958.

d **Mystique Musulmane* by G.-C. Anawati and Louis Gardet (Paris: J. Vrin, 1961), annexe II, pp. 272–9. [French translation with notes of 'Bayān al-farq bayn al-ilhām wa'l-taʿallum'.]

e *Freedom and Fulfillment* by R.J. McCarthy (Boston: Twayne, 1980). (Library of Classical Arabic Literature, IV.) Pp.363–382. [Bayāns 1, 2, 3, 4, 8.]

22 ***Riyāḍat al-nafs wa-tahdhīb al-akhlāq wa-muʿālajat amrāḍ al-qalb*** (Disciplining the Soul, Refining the Character, and Curing the Sicknesses of the Heart)

Al-Ghazālī. Spiritual Discipline. Translated, with an Introduction and Notes, by T.J. Winter. pp.1-101. Cambridge: Islamic Texts Society, 1994. (Al-Ghazālī Series 3.)

23 ***Kasr al-shahwatayn*** (*Breaking the Two Desires*)

a *'Extrait du livre XXIII du Kitab Ihya...(Chapitre de la Concupiscence charnelle).' L. Bercher. *Hespéris*, 40 (1953) 313-31. [French translation of Bayāns 6, 7, 8.]

b *Al-Ghazālī. Spiritual Discipline.* Translated, with an Introduction and Notes, by T.J. Winter. pp. 105-191. Cambridge: Islamic Texts Society, 1994. (Al-Ghazālī Series 3.)

24 ***Āfāt al-lisān*** (Defects of the Tongue)

25 ***Dhamm al-ghaḍab wa'l-ḥiqd wa'l-ḥasad*** (Condemnation of Anger, Rancour and Envy)

26 ***Dhamm al-dunyā*** (Condemnation of the World)

**The Concept of Man in Islam in the Writings of Al-Ghazali.* Ali Issa Uthman. Appendix, pp.197-213 [='Bayān ḥaqīqat al-dunyā'.] Cairo: Dar al-Maaref, 1960.

27 ***Dhamm al-bukhl wa-dhamm ḥubb al-māl*** (Condemnation of Avarice, and Condemnation of the Love of Wealth)

28 ***Dhamm al-jāh wa'l-riyā'*** (Condemnation of Status and Ostentation)

29 ***Dhamm al-kibr wa'l-ʿujb*** (Condemnation of Pride and Conceit)

30 ***Dhamm al-ghurūr*** (Condemnation of Self-Delusion)

31 ***al-Tawba*** (Penitence)

a *'Al-Ghazali on Penitence'. C.G. Naish. *MW* 16 (1926), 6-18.[Very brief excerpts from various sections.]

b Gramlich, Richard. *Muḥammad al-Ġazzālīs Lehre von den Stufen zur Gottesliebe. Die Bücher 31-36 seines Haupwerkes eingeleitet, Übersetzt und kommentiert.* Wiesbaden: Franz Steiner, 1984. (Freiburger Islamstudien, x.) A. 'Die Umkehr'. 21-135.

c Stern, M.S. *Al-Ghazzali on Repentance.* New Delhi: Sterling Publishers, 1990.

32 ***al-Ṣabr wa'l-shukr*** (Steadfastness and Thanksgiving)

Gramlich (31b above): B. 'Die Geduld und die Dankbarkeit'. 139–293.

33 ***al-Khawf wa'l-rajā'*** (Fear and Hope)

a *Al-Ghazali's Book of Fear and Hope.* William McKane. Leiden: E.J. Brill, 1962.

b Gramlich (31b above): C. 'Die Hoffnung und die Furcht'. 297–394.

34 ***al-Faqr wa'l-zuhd*** (Poverty and Abstinence)

Gramlich (31b above): D. 'Die Armut und der Verzicht'. 397–511.

35 ***al-Tawḥīd wa'l-tawakkul*** (The Unity of God, and Reliance upon Him)

a *Al-Ġazzālīs Buch vom Gottvertrauen. Das 35. Buch des Iḥyā' ʿulūm al-dīn. Übersetzt und mit Einleitung und Anmerkungen versehen.* H. Wehr. (Islamische Ethik, Heft IV.) Halle.a.S: Max Niemeyer,1940.

b *'L'Abandon à Dieu (tawakkul), presentation et traduction d'un texte d'Al-Ghazzâli'. *IBLA* 13 (1950), 37–48. [Selected passages.]

c Gramlich (31b above): E. 'Der Einheitsglaube und das Gottvertrauen'. 515–628.

36 ***al-Maḥabba wa'l-shawq wa'l-uns wa'l-riḍā*** (Love, longing, intimacy and contentment)

a *Al-Ghazzalis Boek der Liefde.* H.H. Dingemanns. Leiden: E.J. Brill, 1938.

b *'Livre de l'amour, du désir dans l'absence, de l'intimité dans la présence et du contentement.' Hamoui, S.G.[Brief selections] in *Rythm du Monde* 3 (1948), 22–33.

c Gramlich (31b above): F. 'Die Gottesliebe, die Sehnsucht nach Gott, die Vertrautheit und die Zufriedenheit'. 631–767.

d *Al Ghazali. Revivification des sciences de la religion. Traduction et notes.* A. Moussali. Algiers: Entreprise Nationale du Livre, 1985.

e *Al-Ġazālī. Livre de l'amour, du désir ardent, de l'intimité et du parfait contentement.* Introduction, traduction et notes par M.-L.Siauve. Préface de Roger Arnaldez. Paris: J. Vrin, 1986. (Études Musulmanes, XXIX.)

f *'L'Amour de Dieu pour lui-même chez al-Ġazālī. Analyse et traduction du *bayān* 10, L.36 de *l'Iḥyā' ʿUlūm ad-Dīn.'* A. Regourd. *Arabica* 39 (1992) 151–82.

37 ***al-Niyya wa'l-ṣidq wa'l-ikhlāṣ*** (Intention, Truthfulness and Sincerity)

Über Intention, reine Absicht und Wahrhaftigkeit: das 37. Buch von Al-Ġazālī's Hauptwerk; übersetzt und erläuetrt [sic] von H. Bauer. (Islamische Ethik, Heft 1.) Halle a.S.: Max Niemeyer, 1916.

38 ***al-Murāqaba wa'l-muḥāsaba*** (Holding Vigil and Self-Examination)

39 ***al-Tafakkur*** (Meditation)

Al-Ghazālī. Il libro della Meditazione (Kitāb al-Tafakkur) dall'Iḥyā' 'ulūm ad-dīn. Celentano, Giuseppe. Trieste: Società Italiana Testi Islamici, 1988.

40 ***Dhikr al-mawt wa-mā baʿdahu*** (The Remembrance of Death and What Comes After)

Al-Ghazālī. The Remembrance of Death and the Afterlife. Translated, with an Introduction and Notes by T.J. Winter. Cambridge: Islamic Texts Society, 1989. (Al-Ghazālī Series, 1.)

★

Asín Palacios, M. *La Espiritualidad de Algazel y su Sentido Cristiano.* (Madrid and Granada, 1934-41) contains an extensive Spanish synopsis of the *Iḥyā'*.

Bousquet, G.H. *Ih'ya ʿouloûm ad-dîn, ou vivification des sciences de la foi* (Paris, 1955) is a French synopsis of the entire *Iḥyā'*.

Hell, J. *Von Mohammed bis Ghazâlî. Quellentexte aus dem Arabischen Übersetzt und eingeleitet* (Jena, 1915) contains selected passages in translation on pp.81-138.

Vaglieri, Laura Veccia, and Rubinacci, Roberto. *Scritti Scelti di al-Ghazālī.* (Turin, 1970.) Translated passages from the *Iḥyā'* on pages 149-560.

A Russian translation of several important sections is: V.V. Naumkin, *Voskrezhenie nauk o vere.* Moscow: Izdatel'stvo "Nauka", 1980. (Pamyatniki' Pis'menosti Vostoka, 47.) (English 'summary' on pp.370-376.)

APPENDIX III

THE WONDERS OF THE HEART

The religious psychology developed in Ghazālī's *Revival* is rich with Platonic and Aristotelian elements, and these are particularly well-developed in Book XXI of the work, entitled *The Wonders of the Heart*, in which Ghazālī outlines the pneumatological doctrines on which his ethical and spiritual method is founded. As this book immediately precedes the two books translated here, and forms a preface to the entire third Quarter of the *Revival*, it would seem useful to provide a brief synopsis of its contents, both to supply a context for the present translation, and because of its intrinsic interest.[1]

1 *An Exposition of the Meaning of Soul* (nafs), *Spirit* (rūḥ), *Heart* (qalb), *and Intellect* (ʿaql).

Ghazālī identifies two senses in which each of these terms are used:

I Soul (*Nafs*)

(i) The principle which unites the irascible and appetitive faculties, the 'soul which constantly enjoins evil' (*al-nafs al-ammāra bi'l-sū'*). This is the normal Sufi usage of the term. (ii) Man's soul and essence (*dhāt*), referred to as *ammāra bi'l-sū'*, *lawwāma*, or *muṭma'inna*, depending on its state in relation to God.[2]

II Spirit (*Rūḥ*)

(i) A subtle body originating in the cavity of the physical heart, which spreads through the body via the arteries, just as light from a lantern fills a room. (ii) The subtle thing which knows and perceives, referred to by God in the verse *They ask you concerning the spirit. Say, the Spirit is of the command of my Lord.* (Q.XVII:87)

III Heart (*Qalb*)
(i) The pine-shaped piece of flesh in the body, which contains a cavity filled with blood, which is the locus of the Spirit. (ii) In the *Iḥyā'*, however, the word is employed in its second sense: a spiritual, divine subtlety (*laṭīfa*) connected to the physical heart, which is the reality of man, which perceives, knows and intuits.

IV Intelligence (*ʿAql*)
(i) Knowledge; (ii) The second definition of 'heart', above.

The above eight can be reduced to five principles: the corporeal heart, the corporeal spirit, the 'soul which constantly enjoins evil', knowledge, and the subtle thing which perceives and knows (*qalb* ii). This fifth principle incorporates the other four.

2 *An Exposition of the Soldiers of the Heart.*[3]

The heart has two types of soldiers. One type is visible, comprising the bodily members which follow the instructions of the heart. The other is invisible, comprising ideas and perceptions. The 'soldiers' can also be divided according to three other categories: (i) *irāda* (the will), which instigates, such as appetite (*shahwa*) and anger (*ghaḍab*); (ii) *qudra* (power), which includes sinews and muscles, which are the actual means by which the members are made to move; (iii) *al-ʿilm wa'l-idrāk* (knowledge and perception), which provide information acquired through the five external senses of hearing, sight, smell, taste and touch, and also the five internal senses, located in the brain, which are imagination (*takhayyul*), the sensus communis (*ḥiss mushtarak*) (which coordinates information received through the various faculties),[4] thought (*tafakkur*), remembrance (*tadhakkur*), and memory (*ḥifẓ*).

3 *An Exposition of some Examples of the Heart and its Internal Soldiers.*

The armies of the appetitive and irascible faculties may be submissive to the spirit, thereby assisting it towards salvation, or rebellious, thus driving it to perdition. To discipline and make use of these armies it must call on other soldiers, which are knowledge, wisdom and thought.

Example One. The spirit in the body is like a king in a city. The members and capacities are like craftsmen and labourers. The intellect is like a sincere, wise minister, while anger is like a chief of police, who controls the appetite, which, in turn, is a base slave who brings food and supplies to the city. Although the slave presents himself as a sincere adviser, he constantly opposes the minister: he is in reality a saboteur. The city prospers when, thanks to the efforts of the chief of police, the slave is rehabilitated, and is forced to submit to the minister.

Example Two. The body is like a city and the percipient intellect is like a king; the exterior and interior senses are the king's soldiers, while the members are his subjects. The 'soul which constantly enjoins evil' is the enemy, determined to overmaster the king and subvert the population. The consequent warfare is 'the greater *jihād*'.[5]

Example Three. The intellect is a horseman on a hunt. His appetite is like a horse, and his anger, his dog. If he is skilled, his horse well-trained (a symbol for mastery of the desire for food and sex), and his dog disciplined, he will be successful in the chase.

4 *An Exposition of the Special Property of Man's Heart.*

Man is distinguished from the animals in that he not only possesses desire, anger and sense-perception, but also the divine gift of the intellect: knowledge, and the will to act upon it in a way which contradicts the appetite. In youth, reason is only a potential in the primordial disposition (*fiṭra*), which is realised upon the learning of first principles, and then through experience. Acquisition of the highest knowledge—of God—which is of innumerable degrees, comes about either through learning, or directly through divine inspiration (*ilhām*). Man can prepare his heart for this inspiration by purifying it.

5 *An Exposition of the Overall Attributes of the Heart, and Examples thereof.*

Four qualities exist in every heart: predatory (*sabuʿīya*), animal (*bahīmīya*), satanic (*shayṭānīya*) and divine (*rabbānīya*). The first of these is the faculty of anger, the second is appetite for food, sex, and so forth, the third is the faculty which justifies the turning of the capacity of discernment to evil ends, while the fourth, being in part a divine mystery, must use its intelligence and insight to uncover the wiles of the satanic quality, and to submit the appetite to the irascible faculty. When man achieves this, an equilibrium, or justice, results. The implications of this for ethics are spelt out: the predatory quality engenders such vices as wastefulness, boasting, pride, and lust for oppression; the animal quality produces hypocrisy, slander, greed, and shamelessness; the satanic quality, having successfully encouraged the soul to obey the first two, produces guile, deceit, fraud, and so on.[6] But should the divine element triumph, and subdue all of these, then the virtues will appear. When man controls his predatory quality and sets it within its proper limits, he acquires such virtues as courage, generosity, self-control, patience, forgiveness and dignity. When the animal faculty is controlled, virtues such as chastity, contentment, modesty and helpfulness ensue.

The heart is a mirror which may be polished by stuggling against the appetites, and working to acquire good character traits, and holding to actions such as the remembrance of God, 'until the true nature of that matter which is sought in religion is revealed in it.' Bad influences, by contrast, are like smoke which clouds over the heart's mirror until it is entirely veiled from God, which is the 'heart's rust' mentioned in the Qur'an.[7]

6 *An Exposition of the Heart's Similitude, particularly in Relation to the Knowledges.*

The heart, as the seat of knowledge, is like a mirror which reflects the specific nature of things. Intelligibles are forms reflected in it, while the intelligence is its actual reflection in the mirror.

Although man's heart alone is capable of knowing all realities, various obstacles may impede this: (i) The mirror may be unfinished due to youth; (ii) It may be veiled by sins; (iii) Worldly distractions may turn it away from God; (iv) It may be tarnished by the imitative acceptance (*taqlīd*) of dogma;[8] (v) Ignorance.

There are three levels of knowledge: (i) the faith of the ordinary people (*ʿawāmm*), which is gained through imitative acceptance from people believed to be truthful; (ii) the faith of the theologians (*mutakallimūn*), which contains an element of proof; (iii) the faith of the saints (*ṣiddīqūn*), who, through 'witnessing' (*mushāhada*), experience God at first hand, and whose knowledge is hence beyond doubt. These three levels can be compared to hearing that a man is in a house, then hearing his voice and hence deducing his presence, and, finally, seeing him face-to-face.

UNIVERSITY OF WINCHESTER
LIBRARY

7 *An Exposition of the State of the Heart in relation to the Divisions of Intellectual, Religious, Worldly and Otherworldly Knowledges.*

The knowledges which may be reflected in the heart are of two categories: intellectual and religious. The former are subdivided into necessary and acquired knowledges, while religious knowledge, being that which is learnt through prophets, and without which the heart cannot be perfected, is subdivided into (i) knowledges received on authority (*taqlīd*), and (ii) those granted directly by God to the Prophets and saints.

The intellectual sciences are like foods, while the religious sciences are like medicines. Although some have claimed that the two are incompatible, and have hence renounced religion, they are in fact in harmony. Apparent discrepancies between them are to be attributed to insufficient knowledge, for both are intricate, and few indeed are the men who have mastered both.

8 *An Exposition of the Difference between Inspiration and Learning, and between the Sufi Method of Unveiling Truth and that of the Philosophers and Theologians.*

There are knowledges which appear in the heart only under certain conditions, either through inspiration (for the saints and prophets), or inductive reasoning (for the scholars). The five obstacles mentioned in Exposition Six form a veil between the heart and the Well-preserved Tablet (*al-lawḥ al-maḥfūẓ*), which is where God has inscribed everything which He has decreed from Creation until the Judgement. This veil may be removed by hand, or by a wind, which causes the heart to behold something of what the Tablet contains. Often this happens during sleep, but it may happen when the seeker is awake, either as a transient 'shaft of lightning', or—but this is exceedingly rare—as a permanent condition. For this reason the Sufis have not been concerned only with book-learning, but have instead sought to reach this state where the veil is lifted, by means of self-discipline, the wiping-away of vile attributes, the severing of all ties, and earnestly directing themselves to God. As this goal draws near, the seeker should isolate himself for a while, far from all distractions, and recall (*dhikr*) God within himself. If his determination is sincere, collected and strong, gleams of the Truth may appear in his heart, and these may then be followed by others of different kinds, coming at increasingly short intervals. The variety of such stations is beyond reckoning, but all are granted after a process of self-purification and diligent polishing of the heart.

The philosophers and theologians (*al-nuẓẓār*) do not deny this way, but they consider it extremely difficult to pursue, since it is rigorous and slow, and may, if pursued to excess, be harmful to the body. Similarly, if the spiritual voyager is not well-versed in scholarly learning he may be veiled by a false imagining which he will never be able to shake off.

9 *An Exposition of the Difference between the two Positions shown by a Tangible Example.*

The heart is like a pool filled either from rivers or from underground springs. The first represent knowledge derived by means of deduction from the evidence of the world, while the second is the inner, spiritual knowledge.

One side of a portico was once decorated by Byzantine craftsmen, while the other was decorated by craftsmen from China. Between the two sides a veil was suspended. The Byzantines painted and carved their side, while the Chinese merely polished their side so that it became a mirror. When the veil was removed, the mirror reflected the work of the Byzantines with added brilliance. The Byzantines, then, resemble the scholars, while the Chinese are like the Sufis.

10 *An Exposition of Religious Texts testifying to the Correctness of the Sufis' Method in Acquiring Knowledge, not by Learning or from the Customary Method.*

To experience only a small amount of inspiration is to know the validity of this method. But for those who have not attained this, there are numerous proof-texts. For instance, the Qur'an has spoken of *He whose heart God opens to Islam, so that he has a light from his Lord.*[9] And the Prophet used to pray, 'O Lord! Give me light in my heart!' Further, the reality of the Sufi method is proved by the experience of dreams in which future events are revealed.

11 *An Exposition of Satan's Mastery of the Heart through Insinuations (*waswasa*); the Meaning of Insinuation, and the Cause of its Subdual.*

It has been seen that the heart is affected by information brought by the five senses, and by internal faculties such as imagination, appetite, anger, and character traits. The most important influence, however, comes from those random thoughts, promptings and ideas which are projected by the devil into the mind, and distract or confuse it: these are termed *khawāṭir.*[10] To ward these off, man should engage in remembrance (*dhikr*) of God, and continue with the process of self-discipline and inner purification.

12 *An Exposition detailing Satan's Entrances into the Heart.*

The heart is like a castle, and man must guard its entrances against the enemy, who is the devil. The main entrances are: (i) irascibility and desire; (ii) envy and greed; (iii) Eating one's fill, for this increases the other desires, causes illness, and reduces one's receptivity to wisdom and desire for worship; (iv) Love of self-adornment, whether in clothes, furnishings or residence; (v) Coveting what others own and control, and hence flattering and deceiving them; (vi) Haste, which, according to the Prophet, 'comes from Satan'; (vii) Money, property, and all other kinds of wealth in excess of one's needs, for wealth creates its own concerns which will distract the heart; (viii) Avarice and fear of poverty, which destroy the heart's serene conviction that God will provide; (ix) Fanatical attachment to schools of thought and sects (*ahwā'*), hatred of rival doctrines, and delight in criticising them; (x) studying advanced theological doctrines for which one is not prepared, and hence falling into false beliefs about God; (xi) Harbouring a low opinion of other Muslims, which leads to self-satisfaction and backbiting.

The heart must be purified of all these evil traits before *dhikr* can be effective; otherwise the *dhikr* will itself be a form of *khawāṭir* with no real influence. Even when these traits are removed, it is necessary to cure oneself of *ghafla* (heedlessness and distraction). If one does not, one will be like a patient who derives little benefit from a medicine because he takes it when his stomach is full of food.

There are many devils, each with his own name, who cast *khawāṭir* into the heart on specific occasions: ritual ablution, the canonical Prayer, visiting the marketplace, dealing with one's family, and so on. When they appear, they take the form of base animals such as dogs, frogs and pigs.

13 *An Exposition of the Heart's Insinuations, Concerns, Whisperings and Intentions for which Man is taken to Task, and those in which Man is Forgiven.*

The Prophet said: 'The people of my community are forgiven the discourse of their souls, insofar as they do not mention it or act upon it.' There are four stages between thought and act: (i) an involuntary suggestion; (ii) the inclination of the nature; (iii) reasoned judgement; (iv) determination. The first two involve no moral responsibility, while the second two are to be judged according to the underlying intention.

14 *An Exposition of Whether it is Conceivable that Insinuations should Cease Entirely during the Remembrance of God, or not.*

The Sufis have given five possible answers to this. (i) Insinuation does cease entirely; (ii) It still exists, but has no effect on the heart, since the heart is distracted from it by the *dhikr*; (iii) Its whisperings are heard, but weakly and from afar; (iv) *dhikr* and *waswasa* follow each other in quick succession, so that the distinction between them is blurred; (v) The two exist simultaneously in the heart, which has an ability to focus on two activities at once; this is the view of al-Muḥāsibī. The correct view, however, is that all of these can occur, depending on circumstance.

There are three types of insinuation. (i) The devil may use an argument which seems to contain some truth, for instance: 'Enjoy yourself now; there is surely time for righteousness in future years'; or 'You pray so much; you must surely be beloved of God'; (ii) He may incite a passion in the soul, which one may or may not know to be sinful; (iii) He may make suggestions which are not sinful, but merely distract the heart, such as reminding him of worldly affairs during the canonical prayer. This is the hardest type to remove; and it was thus that the Prophet said, 'Whoever prays two *rakʿas* without his *nafs* speaking to him of any worldly affair, shall have all his former sins forgiven.'

15 *An Exposition of the Speed with which the Heart Changes, and a Categorisation of Hearts on the basis of Change and Stability.*

The heart, being the battleground of angelic and satanic impulses, is like a target struck from all directions, and hence moves and changes rapidly. God has said: *And We change* (nuqallib) *their hearts and perceptions.*[11] There are three kinds of hearts in this respect. (i) The pious heart which self-discipline has purified of evil character traits, and which thus receives good suggestions from the higher world. Safe from the insinuations of Satan, it is the heart referred to in God's word, *Truly, in the remembrance of God do hearts find rest.*[12] (ii) The sinful heart filled with passion and evil character traits. Here the devil's suggestions are actually supported by the intellect, which has been habituated to following its whims. This may extend to all aspects of the soul, or only express itself in specific weaknesses, such as anger or greed. (iii) Most men, however, have the third kind, where the devil's whisperings, supported by the *nafs*, are countered by the voice of faith and the intellect. Victory will be decided by the relative predominance of character traits in the heart.

Notes to Appendix III

1 It is hoped that a complete translation of this work will appear in due course as part of the present series; a partial translation by the late R. McCarthy having already appeared: R.J. McCarthy (*Freedom and Fulfillment*, 363-82). For other translations see Appendix II. In the present epitome I have been assisted by the summary included in the PhD thesis of Walter Skellie, pp.LIV-LXXI.

2 For these three terms see above, XXVIII.

3 The word *junūd*, soldiers, is probably an echo of the *ḥadīth*: 'Spirits are mobilised soldiers,' although it was used in Ghazālī's sense by the Brethren of Purity. (*Rasā'il*, I. 311; Wensinck i.385.) Cf. Ghazālī, *Maqṣad*, 70, for a further use of the term.

4 See Corbin, *Avicenna*, 301n; Goichon, *Lexique*, no.150, pp.70-1; also her translation of Ibn Sīnā's *K. al-Ishārāt*, 317-8 (note 5), where the origin of the term in Aristotle's *De Anima* is outlined.

5 For this *ḥadīth*, see p.LXIII above.

6 The complete list is to be found on p.10 of the Arabic; and should be compared with the inventory on pp.20-22 below.

7 Q. LXXXIII:14. For the heart as 'mirror', see e.g. van Ess, *Gedankenwelt*, 65-6; Schimmel, *Mystical Dimensions*, 171.

8 See above, p.85c.

9 Q. XXXIX:22.

10 See above, LXVII.

11 Q. VI:110.

12 Q. XIII:28.

BIBLIOGRAPHY

Includes all works cited, with the exception of articles from the *Encyclopedia of Islam*.

ʿAbbādī, Quṭb al-Dīn Manṣūr, al-. *Manāqib al-Ṣūfīya*. Ed. Muḥammad Dānish-Pazhūh and Īraj Afshār. Tehran, 1362 (AH solar)/1984.

Abdelkader, A.H. *The Life, Personality and Writings of al-Junayd*. London, 1962.

Abū Ghudda, ʿAbd al-Fattāḥ. *al-ʿUlamāʾ al-ʿuzzāb*. Beirut, 1982.

Abū Zahra, Muḥammad. *Muḥāḍarāt fī ʿaqd al-zawāj wa-āthārih*. Cairo, 1958.

ʿAfīfī, Abu'l-ʿAlā. *al-Malāmatīya wa'l-ṣūfīya wa-ahl al-futuwwa*. Cairo, 1945.

Afnan, S. *Greek Philosophical Terms and their Arabic and Persian Equivalents*. Cambridge, 1956.

ʿAjlūnī, Ismāʿīl b. Muḥammad. *Kashf al-khafāʾ*. Beirut. 1399/1979.

Ājurrī, Muḥammad b. al-Ḥusayn, al-. *K. al-Sharīʿa*. Partial ed. by M. H. al-Fiqī. Cairo, 1369/1950.

Akaltun, Nevzat. *Islam Fıkhı ve Hukukuna Ait 1099 Fetva*. Ankara, 1974.

Al-Wohaibi, Abdullah. *The Northern Hijaz in the Writings of the Arab Geographers 800-1150*. Beirut, 1973.

Alonso, M. 'Influencia de Algazel en el mundo latino'. *Al-Andalus*, XXIII (1958), 371-80.

ʿĀmirī, Abu'l-Ḥasan, al-. *al-Saʿāda wa'l-isʿād*. Presented by M. Minovi. Wiesbaden/Tehran, 1957.

Anawati, G. *Mu'allafāt Ibn Sīnā*. Cairo, 1950.

Anawati, G.and Gardet, L. *Mystique musulmane. Aspects et tendances. Expériences et techniques*. 4th ed. Paris, 1986.

Andrae, T. *In the Garden of Myrtles. Studies in Early Islamic Mysticism*. Albany (New York), 1984.

Anṣārī Harawī, ʿAbd Allāh. *Manāzil al-sāʾirīn*. Ed. Revān Ferhādī. Tehran, 1355 solar.

Antes, Peter. *Prophetenwunder im der Ašʿariya bis al-Ġazālī (Algazel)*. Freiburg im Breisgau, 1970.

Arberry, A.J. *The Book of Truthfulness*. Oxford, 1937. [Ed. and trans. of the *K. al-Ṣidq* of al-Kharrāz.]

——*The Doctrine of the Ṣūfīs*. Cambridge 1935, repr. Cambridge 1979. [Trans. of the *Taʿarruf* of al-Kalābādhī.]

——*Revelation and Reason in Islam*. London, 1957.

——*Muslim Saints and Mystics. Episodes from the Tadhkirat al Auliya' ("Memorial of the Saints") by Farid al-Din Attar*. London, 1979.

——*Sufism: An Account of the Mystics of Islam*. London, 1950.

——'The Nicomachean Ethics in Arabic'. *BSOAS* 17 (1955), 1-17.

Arbesmann, A. 'Fasting and Prophecy in Pagan and Christian Antiquity'. *Traditio* VII (1949-51), 1-71.

Aristotle. *Nicomachean Ethics*. Tr. H. Rackham. Cambridge, Massachusetts and London, 1934, repr. 1982. (Loeb Classical Library, no. 73.)

Arkoun, Mohammed. *Contribution à l'étude de l'humanisme arabe au* IVe/Xe *siècle: Miskawayh philosophe et historien*. Paris, 1970.

——*Essais sur la pensée islamique*. Paris, 1984.

——*Traité d'Éthique*. Traduction française avec introduction et notes du Tahdib al-ahlāk de Miskawayh. Damascus, 1969.

Arnaldez, R. 'Les grands traits de la pensée et de l'oeuvre de Ghazâlî', in *Ghazâlî, la raison et le miracle*. Table rond UNESCO 9-10 décembre 1985. Paris, 1987. Pp.3-10.

——*Jésus fils de Marie prophéte de l'Islam*. Paris, 1980.

Asad, Muhammad. *The Message of the Qur'ān*. Gibraltar, 1980.

Ash[c]arī, Abu'l-Ḥasan, al-. *Maqālāt al-Islāmīyīn wa'khtilāf al-muṣallīn*. Ed. H. Ritter. Istanbul, 1929-30.

Asín Palacios, M. *La Espiritualidad de Algazel y su sentido Cristiano*. Madrid & Granada, 1934-1941.

——*Algazel, Dogmática, Moral y Ascética*. Saragossa, 1901.

——*Logia et Agrapha Domini Jesu, apud Moslemicos Scriptores, Asceticos Praesertim, usitata*. Paris, 1916.

——*La Escatología Musulmana en la Divina Comedia*. 2nd.(extended) ed. Granada, 1943.

[c]Aṭṭār, Farīd al-Dīn. *Tadhkirat al-awliyā'*. Ed. R. Nicholson. 1905-7.

Azami, M.M. *Studies in Early Hadith Literature*. Indianapolis, 1978.

[c]Azzām, Muḥammad al-Muṣṭafā. *'al-Irāda'*. *Al-Murīd* 1 (Safar -Rabī[c] 1, 1410/Sept. - Oct. 1989), 5-10.

Badawī, [c]Abd al-Raḥmān. *Mu'allafāt al-Ghazālī*. Cairo, 1380/1961.

——*La transmission de la philosophie grecque au monde arabe*. Paris, 1987.

——*Plotinus apud arabes. Theologia Aristoteles et fragmenta quæ supersunt*. Cairo, 1955.

——*Quelques figures et thèmes de la philosophie islamique*. Paris, 1979.

——*Shaṭaḥāt al-ṣūfīya*, I: Abū Yazīd al-Bisṭāmī. Cairo, 1949.

Badawi, Mostafa, al-. *The Book of Assistance*. Dorton (UK), 1989.

Baer, Gabriel. 'Women and *waqf*: an analysis of the Istanbul *tahrīr* of 1546.' In Warburg and Gilbar (eds.), *Studies in Islamic Society, Contributions in memory of Gabriel Baer*. Haifa, 1984. Pp.9-27.

Baghdādī, Muḥammad b. Muḥammad, al-. (=al-Shaykh al-Mufīd.) *al-Ikhtiṣāṣ*. Najaf, 1390/1971.

Baghdādī, al-Khaṭīb, al-. See under 'Khaṭīb al-Baghdādī, al-.'

Bagley, F.R.C. *Ghazālī's Book of Counsel for Kings* (Naṣīḥat al-mulūk). London, 1964. [English translation with notes of Ghazālī's *al-Tibr al-masbūk fī naṣīḥat al-mulūk*.]

Balkhī, Shaqīq al-. *Ādāb al-ʿibādāt*. Ed. P. Nwyia in *Trois oeuvres inédites de Mystiques musulmans*. Second ed. Beirut, 1982.

Basyūnī, Ibrāhīm. *Nash'at al-taṣawwuf al-Islāmī*. Cairo, 1969.

Bauer, H. 'Zum Titel und zur Abfassung von Ghazālī's *Iḥyā*''. *Der Islam*, 4 (1913), 159-60.

Bayḍāwī, ʿAbd Allāh b. ʿUmar, al-. *Anwār al-tanzīl wa-asrār al-ta'wīl*. Istanbul 1329 AH.

Bayhaqī, Aḥmad b. al-Ḥusayn, al-. *al-Iʿtiqād wa'l-hidāya ilā sabīl al-rashād*.Ed. K. al-Ḥūt. Beirut, 1403/1983.

——*K. al-Asmā' wa'l-ṣifāt*. Beirut 1405/1985.

Bell, J.N. *Love Theory in Later Ḥanbalite Islam*. Albany (New York), 1979.

——'Al-Sarrāj's *Maṣāriʿ al-ʿushshāq*: A Ḥanbalite Work?' *JAOS* 99 (1979), 235-48.

Bell, R. *The Qur'an Translated, With a Critical Re-arrangement of the Surahs*. Edinburgh, 1938.

Bellamy, J. 'Sex and Society in Islamic Popular Literature'. Pp.23-42 of Afaf Lutfi Al-Sayyid Marsot (ed.), *Society and the Sexes in Medieval Islam*. Malibu, 1979.

Bercher, Léon. 'Extrait du Livre XXIII du Kitāb Iḥyā' 'Ulūm ad-Dīn d'al-Gazālī.' *Hespéris* XL (1953), 313-331.

Bergsträsser, G. *Ḥunain ibn Isḥāq, Über die syrischen und arabischen Galen-Übersetzungen*. Leipzig, 1925.

——*Ḥunain ibn Isḥāq und seine Schule*. Leiden, 1913.

——*Neue Materialen zu Ḥunain ibn Isḥāq's Galen-Bibliographie*. Leipzig, 1932.

Berman, L.V. 'A Note on the Added Seventh Book of the Nicomachean Ethics in Arabic'. *JAOS* 82 (1962), pp.555-6.

Bilādī, ʿĀtiq b. Ghayth, al-. *Maʿālim Makka al-tārīkhīya wa'l-atharīya*. 2nd ed. Mecca,1403/1983.

Boisard, M. *L'Humanisme de l'Islam*. 3rd edition. Paris, 1979.

Bousquet, G.H. *La Morale de l'Islam et son ethique sexuelle*. Paris, 1953.

Bouyges, M. *Essai de chronologie des oeuvres de al-Ghazālī (Algazel)*. Ed. and revised by M. Allard. Beirut, 1959.

Böwering, Gerhard. *The Mystical Vision of Existence in Classical Islam. The Qur'ānic Hermeneutics of the Ṣūfī Sahl al-Tustarī (d.283/896)*. Berlin and New York, 1980.

Bravmann, M.M. *The Spiritual Background of Early Islam. Studies in Ancient Arab Concepts*. Leiden, 1972.

Brockelmann, C. *Geschichte der arabischen Litteratur*. 2nd. ed. Leiden, 1943-1949; *Supplement*, Leiden, 1937-1942.

Brown, P. *The Body and Society. Men, Women and Sexual Renunciation in Early Christianity*. London, 1990.

Brundage, James A. 'Prostitution, Miscegenation and Sexual Purity in the First Crusade.' In Peter Edbury (ed.), *Crusade and Settlement*. Cardiff, 1985. Pp.57-65.

Bukhārī, Muḥammad b. Ismāʿīl, al-. *al-Jāmiʿ al-Ṣaḥīḥ*. Cairo, 1309 AH.

——*al-Adab al-Mufrad*. Cairo, 1340 AH.

Bulliet, R.W. *The Patricians of Nishapur*. Cambridge (Mass), 1972.

Bürgel, J. Christoph. *'Adab* und *Iʿtidāl* in ar-Ruhāwī's *Adab aṭ-Ṭabīb*. Studie zur Bedeutungsgeschichte zweier Begriffe'. *ZDMG* 117 (1967), pp.90-102.

Calverley, E.E. 'Doctrines of the Soul (*nafs* and *rūḥ*) in Islam'. *MW* 33 (1943), pp.254-264.

Celentano, Giuseppe. *Due Scritti Medici di Al-Kindī*. Naples, 1979.

Chehata, C. 'L'ikhtilāf et la conception musulmane du droit'. In *L'ambivalence dans la culture arabe*. Paris, 1967. Pp.258-70.

Chishti, S.K.K. 'Female Spirituality in Islam'. In S.H.Nasr (ed.), *Islamic Spirituality: Foundations*. London, 1987. Pp.199-219.

Chittick, William C. *The Sufi Path of Knowledge*. Albany (New York), 1989.

——'The Theological Roots of Peace and War According to Islam'. *IQ* 34 (1410/1990), 145-63.

Cooper, J. (tr.) *The Commentary on the Qur'ān by Abū Jaʿfar Muḥammad b. Jarīr al-Ṭabarī. Being an abridged translation of* Jāmiʿ al-bayān ʿan ta'wīl āy al-Qur'ān. Oxford, 1987.

Coomaraswamy, A.K. *Coomaraswamy 2: Selected Papers*. Ed. R. Lipsey. Princeton, 1977.

Corbin, H. *Avicenna and the Visionary Recital*. Princeton, 1960, repr. 1988.

Cragg, K. *The Dome and the Rock. Jerusalem Studies in Islam*. London, 1964.

Çubukcu, İbrahim Agâh. *Gazzalî ve Şüphecilik*. Ankara, 1963 (?).

Cuperly, P. *Ghazali. Temps et prières. Prières et invocations. Extraits de* l'Ihyâ' ʿulum al-Dîn. Paris, 1990. [French trans. of Books 9 and 10 from the *Iḥyā'*.]

Daniels, N. *Islam and the West. The Making of an Image*. Edinburgh, 1960.

Dar, B.A. 'Ethical Teachings of the Qur'ān'. In M.M. Sherif (ed.), *A History of Muslim Philosophy*, I. 155-78. Wiesbaden, 1963.

Dāraquṭnī, ʿAlī b. ʿUmar, al-. *al-Sunan*. Cairo, n.d.

——*Dhikr asmā' al-Tābiʿīn*. Ed. Būrān al-Ḍannāwī and Kamāl al-Ḥūt.

Beirut, 1406/1985.
Dārimī, Abū Muḥammad, al-. *al-Sunan*. Cawnpore, 1293 AH.
Dawwānī, Jalāl al-Dīn, al-. *Akhlāq-i Jalālī*. Lucknow, 1283 /1866.
Daylamī, Abū Shujāʿ Shīrawayhi, al-. *al-Firdaws bi-ma'thūr al-khiṭāb*. Ed. al-Saʿīd Zaghlūl. Beirut, 1406/1986.
Dermenghem, E. *Vies des saints musulmans*. (Édition définitive). Paris, 1983.
Dhahabī, Muḥammad b. Aḥmad, al-. *Siyar aʿlām al-nubalā'*. Ed. Shuʿayb al-Arnā'ūṭ et al. Beirut, 1401- AH.
——*al-ʿIbar fī khabar man ghabar*. Ed. Ṣalāḥ al-Dīn al-Munajjid. Kuweit, 1960-6.
—— *al-Kāshif fī maʿrifa man lahu riwāya fi'l-kutub al-sitta*. Beirut, 1403/1983.
——*Mīzān al-iʿtidāl fī naqd al-rijāl*. Ed. ʿAlī al-Bijāwī. Cairo,n.d.
——*Tadhkirat al-ḥuffāẓ*. Hyderabad, 1315/1897.
Dols, Michael W. *Medieval Islamic Medicine. Ibn Riḍwān's Treatise 'On the Prevention of Bodily Ills in Egypt.'* Berkeley (California), 1984.
Dozy, R. *Supplément aux dictionnaires arabes*. Leiden,1881; repr. Beirut, 1968.
Dunlop, D.M. 'The Nichomachean Ethics in Arabic, Books I-VI'. *Oriens*, 1962, 18-34.
——'Observations on the Medieval Arabic Version of Aristotle's Nicomachean Ethics.' In *Oriente e occidente nel medioevo: filosofia e scienzie*. Rome,1971. Pp.229-50.
——'The Manuscript Taimur Pasha 290 Aḫlāq and the Summa Alexandrinorum.' *Arabica* 21 (1974), 252-63.
Dunyā, Sulaymān. *al-Ḥaqīqa fī naẓr al-Ghazālī*. Cairo, 1965.
Encyclopaedia of Islam, The. Ed. by M. Houtsma et al. Leiden, 1927. New edition, ed. by J.H. Kramers, H.A.R. Gibb et al. Leiden, 1954-.
Endress, G. *The Works of Yaḥyā ibn ʿAdī*. Wiesbaden,1977.
Ess, Josef von. *Die Gedankenwelt des Ḥārit al-Muḥāsibī, anhand von Übersetzungen aus seinen Schriften dargestellt und erläutert*. Bonn, 1961.
Fakhry, M. 'The Platonism of Miskawayh and its implications for his ethics'. *SI* 42 (1975), 39-57.
al-Fārābī. *Fuṣūl al-madanī*. Ed. and trans. D.M. Dunlop. Cambridge, 1961.
——*al-Tanbīh ʿalā sabīl al-saʿāda*. Hyderabad, 1346 AH.
al-Fārūqī, I. 'On the Ethics of the Brethren of Purity'. *MW* 50 (1960), 109-21, 193-8, 252-8; 51 (1961), 18-24.
Farah, Madelein. *Marriage and sexuality in Islam*. Salt Lake City, 1984. [Translation of Book 12 of the *Iḥyā'*.]
Fazul-ul-Karim, Al-Haj Maulana. *Imam Gazzali's Ihya Ulum-id-din*. Lahore, n.d. [English translation of the *Iḥyā'*.]
Fortenbaugh, W.W. *Aristotle on Emotion*. London, 1975.

Fuchs, E. *Sexual Desire and Love. Origins and History of the Christian Ethic of Sexuality and Marriage*. Cambridge and New York, 1983.

Gardet, L. *La Pensée Religieuse d'Avicenne (Ibn Sīnā)*. Paris, 1951.

——*La Connaissance Mystique chez Ibn Sīnā et ses présupposés philosophiques*. (Mémorial Avicenne, II.) Cairo, 1952.

——'La mention du Nom divin, *dhikr*, dans la mystique musulmane'. *RT*, 52 (1952), 542-676; 53 (1953), 197-216.

Gardet, L, and Anawati, M.-M. *Introduction à la théologie musulmane. Essai de théologie comparée*. Paris, 1970.

Gauthier, L. *Antécédents gréco-arabes de la psychophysique*. Beirut, 1938.

Gauthier, R.A. *La Morale d'Aristote*. Paris, 1963.

Ghazālī, Abū Ḥāmid Muḥammad b. Muḥammad, al-. *Tahāfut al-falāsifa*. Ed. M. Bouyges. Beirut, 1927.

——*Maqāṣid al-falāsifa*. Cairo, 1331.

——*Ayyuhā al-walad*. Ed. and intro. by ʿAlī al-Qaradāghī. Cairo, 1405/1985.

——*Bidāya al-hidāya*. Ed. Muḥammad al-Khusht. Cairo, 1985.

——*Miʿyār al-ʿilm fī fann al-manṭiq*. Cairo, 1329.

——*al-Mustaṣfā min ʿilm al-uṣūl*. Cairo, 1353/1937.

——*Iḥyā' ʿulūm al-dīn*. Cairo, 1347 AH.

——*Faḍā'iḥ al-Bāṭinīya*. Ed. ʿAbd al-Raḥmān Badawī, Cairo, 1964.

——*Fayṣal al-tafriqa bayn al-Islām wa'l-zandaqa*. Ed. Sulaymān Dunyā. Cairo, 1961.

——*al-Iqtiṣād fi'l-iʿtiqād*. Ed. M. Abu'l-ʿAlā.Cairo, 1972.

——*al-Maqṣad al-asnā fī sharḥ maʿānī asmā' Allāh al-husnā*. Ed. Fadlou Shehadi. Beirut, 1971.

——*al-Munqidh min al-ḍalāl wa'l-mūṣil ilā dhi'l- ʿizza wa'l-jalāl*.[Ar. ed. and French trans. by Farid Jabre.] Beirut, 1959.

——*Iljām al-ʿawāmm ʿan ʿilm al-kalām*. Ed. M. Abu'l-ʿAlā, in *al-Quṣūr al-ʿawālī min rasā'il al-Imām al-Ghazālī*. Cairo, 1390/1970.

——*al-Wajīz*. Cairo, 1317 AH.

——*Mishkāt al-anwār*. Ed. Abu'l-ʿAlā ʿAfīfī. Cairo, 1964.

——[pseudo?] *Mīzān al-ʿamal*. Ed. M. Abu'l-ʿAlā. Cairo, 1973.

Gimaret, D. *Les noms divins en Islam. Exégèse lexicographique et théologique*. Paris, 1988.

Goichon, A.-M. *Ibn Sina (Avicenne). Livre des directives et remarques*. Beirut and Paris, 1951. [French tr. of the *K. al-Ishārāt wa'l-tanbīhāt* of Ibn Sīnā.]

——*Introduction à Avicenne. Son Épître des définitions. Traduction avec notes*. Paris, 1933.

Goldziher, Ignaz. *Muslim Studies*. Tr. C.R. Barber and S.M. Stern. London,

1967, 1971.
——*Streitschrift des Gazālī gegen die Bāṭinijja-Sekte*. Leiden, 1956.
——'Matth. VII.5 in der muhammedanischen Literatur'. *ZDMG* XXXI (1877), 765-7.
Gould, J. *The Development of Plato's Ethics*. Cambridge, 1955.
Gramlich, R. *Die Gaben der Erkenntwisse des ʿUmar as-Suhrawardī*. Wiesbaden, 1978. [German transl. and introd. of the *ʿAwārif al-maʿārif* of al-Suhrawardī.]
——*Muḥammad al-Ġazzālīs Lehre von den Stufen zur Gottesliebe*. Wiesbaden, 1984. [German transl. and introd. of Books 31-36 of the *Iḥyā'*.]
——*Das Sendschreiben Al-Qušayrīs über das Sufitum*. Wiesbaden, 1989. [German transl. and introd. of al-Qushayrī's *Risāla*.]
Graziani, J. 'Ibn Jazlah's Eleventh Century Tabulated Medical Compendium, *Taqwīm al-Abdān*.' PhD dissertation, University of California, Los Angeles, 1973.
Guillaume, A. *The Life of Muḥammad. A Translation of Ibn Isḥāq's Sīrat Rasūl Allāh*. London, 1955.
Hachem, Hikmat. *Critère de l'action (Mīzān al-a'mal): traite d'éthique psychologique et mystique*. Paris, 1945. [French translation and study of the *Mīzān al-ʿamal* attributed to al-Ghazālī.]
Ḥaddād, ʿAbd Allāh b. ʿAlawī, al-. *Madīḥa nabawīya balīgha*. Cairo (?), n.d.
Ḥākim al-Nīsābūrī, al-. *al-Mustadrak ʿalā al-Ṣaḥīḥayn*. Hyderabad, 1334-42 AH.
Ḥakīm al-Tirmidhī, al-. *Nawādir al-uṣūl fī maʿrifat aḥādīth al-Rasūl*. Istanbul, 1293 AH.
——*al-Riyāḍa*, published with *Adab al-nafs* of the same author. Ed. A.J. Arberry. Cairo, 1366/1947.
——*al-Masā'il al-maknūna*. Ed. Muḥammad al-Juyūshī. Cairo, 1400/1980.
——*al-Amthāl*. Beirut and Damascus, n.d.
——*Bayān al-farq bayn al-ṣadr wa'l-qalb wa'l-fu'ād wa'l-lubb*. Ed. N. Heer. Cairo, 1958.
Hanley, T. 'St. Thomas' Use of Al-Ghazali's *Maqasid al-Falasifa*'. *Medieval Studies* XLIV (1982), pp.243-270.
Ḥalīmī, al-Ḥusayn b. al-Ḥasan, al-. *al-Minhāj fī shuʿab al-īmān*. Ed. Ḥ.M. Fawda. Beirut, 1399/1979.
Hardie, W.F.R. *Aristotle's ethical theory*. Oxford, 1968.
——'Aristotle's Doctrine that Virtue is a 'Mean''. In J. Barnes, M. Schofield and R. Sorabji (eds.), *Articles on Aristotle*. 2. Ethics and Politics. London, 1977. Pp.33-46.
Haythamī, ʿAlī b. Abī Bakr, al-. *Majmaʿ al-zawā'id wa-manbaʿ al-fawā'id*. Cairo, 1352 AH.

——*Mawārid al-ẓam'ān ilā zawā'id Ibn Ḥibbān*. Cairo, n.d.

——*Kashf al-astār ʿan zawā'id al-Bazzār*. Ed. Ḥ. al Aʿẓamī. Beirut, 1404/1984.

Ḥillī, Warrām b. Abī Firās, al-. *Tanbīh al-khawāṭir wa-nuzhat al-nawāẓir*. Najaf, 1389/1969.

Holmes, Urban Tignor. 'Life among the Europeans in Palestine and Syria'. In Setton et al. (ed.), *A History of the Crusades*, volume IV (Madison, Wisconsin, 1977), 3-35.

Horten, M. *Die Philosophie des Islam in ihren Beziehungen zu den philosophischen Weltanschauungen des westlichen Orients*. Munich, 1924.

Hourani, George F. *Reason and tradition in Islamic ethics*. Cambridge, 1985.

Hutchinson, S. 'The Issue of the Ḥijāb in Classical and Modern Muslim Scholarship.' London University PhD thesis, 1987.

Ibn ʿAbd al-Barr, Yūsuf. *al-Istīʿāb fī maʿrifat al-Aṣḥāb*. With *al-Iṣāba* of Ibn Ḥajar. Cairo, 1358-9 AH.

Ibn Abī ʿĀṣim, Abū Bakr ʿAmr. *al-Sunna*. Ed. M.N. al-Albānī. Beirut, 1400/1980.

——*K. al-Zuhd*. Ed. A.A. al-Aʿẓamī. Beirut, 1405/1985.

Ibn Abi'l-Dunyā, ʿAbd Allāh b. Muḥammad. *Makārim al-akhlāq*. Ed. and introd. by J.A. Bellamy. Wiesbaden, 1973.

——*Muḥāsabat al-nafs wa'l-izrā' ʿalayhā*. Beirut, n.d.

——*Dhamm al-malāhī*. (I) Ed. and trans. James Robson in *Tracts on Listening to Music*. London, 1938. (II) Ed. Muḥammad ʿAbd al-Qādir ʿAṭā. Cairo, 1987.

——*al-Ḥilm*. Ed. Majdī al-Sayyid Ibrāhīm. Cairo, 1986 (?).

Ibn Abī Shayba. *al-Muṣannaf*. Bombay, 1386-1390 AH.

Ibn ʿAdī, Yaḥyā. *Tahdhīb al-akhlāq*. In N. al-Takrītī, *Yaḥyā ibn ʿAdī*. Beirut/Paris 1978, pp.67-157.

Ibn ʿArabī, Muḥyī al-Dīn. *Fuṣūṣ al-ḥikam*. Ed. A. ʿAfīfī. Cairo, 1365/1946.

——*al-Futūḥāt al-Makkīya*. Cairo, 1293 AH.

Ibn ʿAsākir, ʿAlī b. al-Ḥusayn. *Tabyīn kadhib al-muftarī fīmā nusiba ilā al-imām Abi'l-Ḥasan al-Ashʿarī*. Damascus, 1347 AH.

Ibn ʿAyād, Aḥmad b. Muḥammad. *al-Mafākhir al-ʿAlīya fī al-ma'āthir al-Shādhilīya*. Cairo, 1384/1964.

Ibn Bābawayh, al-Ḥusayn. *Man lā yaḥḍuruhu al-faqīh*. Beirut, 1401/1981.

Ibn al-Daybaʿ, ʿAbd al-Raḥmān b. ʿAlī. *Tamyīz al-ṭayyib min al-khabīth fīmā yadūru ʿalā alsinat al-nās min al-ḥadīth*. Cairo, 1382/1962.

Ibn Fātik, Mubashshir. *Mukhtār al-ḥikam wa-maḥāsin al-kilam*. Ed. ʿAbd al-Raḥmān Badawī. Madrid, 1958.

Ibn Ḥajar al-ʿAsqalānī, *Fatḥ al-Bārī sharḥ Ṣaḥīḥ al-Bukhārī*.Cairo, 1344 AH.

——*al-Maṭālib al-ʿĀliya bi-zawā'id al-Masānīd al-Thamāniya*.Ed. Ḥ. al-

Aʿẓamī. Kuwait, 1393/1973.
——*al-Iṣāba fī tamyīz al-Ṣaḥāba*. Cairo, 1358–9 AH.
——*Tahdhīb al-Tahdhīb*. Hyderabad, 1326 AH.
——*Taʿjīl al-manfaʿa bi-zawā'id rijāl al-a'immat al-arbaʿa*. Hyderabad, 1324 AH.
——*Lisān al-mīzān*. Hyderabad, n.d.
Ibn Ḥanbal, Aḥmad b. Muḥammad. *al-Musnad*. Cairo, 1313 AH.
——*K. al-Zuhd*. Beirut, 1403/1983.
Ibn al-Ḥashshā'. *Mufīd al-ʿulūm wa-mubīd al-humūm wa-huwa tafsīr al-alfāẓ al-ṭibbīya wa'l-lughawīya al-wāqiʿa fī 'l-kitāb al-Manṣūrī li'l-Rāzī*. Ed. G.S. Colin and H.P.J. Renaud. Rabat, 1941.
Ibn Ḥibbān, Muḥammad, al-Bustī. *Mashāhīr ʿulamā' al-amṣār*. Ed. M. Fleischhammer. Cairo, 1959.
Ibn Ḥunayn, Isḥāq. *al-Akhlāq*. Ed. and introd. by ʿAbd al-Raḥmān Badawī. Kuweit, 1979. [Arabic translation of the *Nicomachean Ethics* of Aristotle.]
Ibn al-ʿImād al-Ḥanbalī. *Shadharāt al-dhahab*. Cairo, 1351 AH.
Ibn al-Jarrāḥ, Wakīʿ. *al-Zuhd*. Ed. ʿAbd al-Raḥmān al-Faryawā'ī. Medina, 1404/1984.
Ibn al-Jawzī. *al-ʿIlal al-Mutanāhiya fī'l-aḥādīth al-wāhiya*. Beirut, 1399/1979.
——*Talbīs Iblīs*. Cairo, 1352 AH.
——*Manāqib Maʿrūf al-Karkhī wa-akhbāruhu*. Ed. A. al-Jabbūrī. Beirut, 1406/1985.
——*Ṣifat al-ṣafwa*. Hyderabad, 1355 AH.
——*al-Ṭibb al-Rūḥānī*. Cairo, 1929.
Ibn al-Jazarī, Shams al-Dīn Muḥammad. *Ghāyat al-nihāya fī ṭabaqāt al-Qurrā'*. Ed. G. Bergsträsser and O. Pretzl. Cairo, 1352/1933.
Ibn Kathīr, Ismāʿīl b. ʿUmar. *al-Bidāya wa'l-nihāya*. Cairo, 1351 AH.
Ibn Khallikān, Aḥmad b. Muḥammad. *Wafayāt al-aʿyān wa'anbā' abnā' al-zamān*. Ed. F. Wüstenfeld. Göttingen, 1835.
Ibn Māja al-Qazwīnī. *al-Sunan*. Delhi, 1333 AH.
Ibn Marthad, ʿAlqama. *Zuhd al-thamāniya min al-Tābiʿīn*. Ed. ʿAbd al-Raḥmān al-Faryawā'ī. Medina, 1404 AH.
Ibn al-Mubārak, ʿAbd Allāh. *al-Zuhd wa'l-raqā'iq*, including the *riwāya* of Nuʿaym b. Ḥammād (with separate pagination). Ed. Ḥabīb al-Raḥmān al-Aʿẓamī. Malegaon (India), 1385/1966.
Ibn al-Nadīm, Muḥammad. *al-Fihrist*. Ed. G. Flügel. Leipzig, 1871–2.
Ibn Qutayba, ʿAbd Allāh b. Muslim. *ʿUyūn al-akhbār*. Ed. A. al-ʿAdawī. Cairo, 1343–8/1925–30.
——*al-Maʿārif*. Ed. Tharwat ʿUkāsha. Cairo, 1960.
Ibn Saʿd. *al-Ṭabaqāt al-kabīr*. Ed. E. Sachau et al. Leiden, 1322–47/1905–28.

Ibn al-Sarī, Hannād. *al-Zuhd*. Ed. ʿAbd al-Raḥmān al-Faryawā'ī. Kuweit, 1406/1985.

Ibn Sīnā. *al-Shifā'*. Partial ed. by F. Rahman as *Avicenna's De Anima (Arabic text). Being the psychological part of Kitāb al-Shifā'*. Oxford, 1960.

——*al-Qānūn fi'l-ṭibb*. Ed. Jibrān Jabbūr. Beirut, 1972.

——*Fi'l-akhlāq wa'l-infiʿālāt al-nafsānīya*. Pp.19-29 of *Mémorial Avicenne* IV, Miscellanea. Contributions de M. Louis Massignon, Mme Denise Remondon et M.G. Vajda. Cairo, 1954.

——*Fī ʿilm al-akhlāq*. In *Tisʿ Rasā'il fi'l-ḥikma wa'l-ṭabīʿīyāt*. Cairo, 1326/1908.

——*Risāla fī amr al-hindibā. Un court résumé de l'article d'Avicenne sur la chicorée*. Ed. A. Süheyl Ünver. Istanbul, n.d.

——*Risāla fī māhiyat al-ʿishq*. Ed. and Turkish translation by Ahmed Ateş (Ibn Sina, *Risaleler*, 3, Istanbul Üniversitesi Edebiyat Fakültesi yayınları, 552). Istanbul, 1953.

——*al-Ishārāt wa'l-tanbīhāt*. With commentary of Naṣīr al-Dīn al-Ṭūsī. Ed. Sulaymān Dunyā. Cairo, 1958.

Ibn al-Sunnī, Abū Bakr. *ʿAmal al-yawm wa'l-layla*. Ed.ʿAbd Allāh Ḥajjāj. Cairo, 1982.

Ikhwān al-Ṣafā. *Rasā'il*. Beirut, 1376/1957.

Iṣfahānī, Abū Nuʿaym, al-. *Ḥilyat al-awliyā' wa-ṭabaqāt al-aṣfiyā'*. Cairo, 1351-7/1932-8.

Iṣṭakhrī, Abū Isḥāq, al-. *Masālik al-mamālik*. Ed. M.J. de Goeje. Leiden, 1870.

Ivanow, W. *A Guide to Ismaili Literature*. London, 1933.

ʿIyāḍ al-Yaḥṣubī (al-Qāḍī), *al-Shifā' bi-taʿrīf ḥuqūq al-Muṣṭafā*. Damascus n.d.

Jabre, F. 'La biographie et l'oeuvre de Ghazālī réconsidérées à la lumière des Ṭabaqāt de Sobkī'. *MIDEO* I (1954), pp.73-102.

——*La notion de certitude chez Ghazali*. Beirut, 1958.

——*La notion de la maʿrifa chez Ghazali*. Beirut,1958.

——*Essai sur le lexique de Ghazali. Contribution à l'étude de la terminologie de Ghazali dans ses principaux ouvrages à l'exception du Tahāfut*. Beirut, 1970.

Jadaane, F. *L'influence du stoïcisme sur la pensée musulmane*. Beirut, 1968.

Jaeger, W. *Aristotle. Fundamentals of the History of his Development*. Tr. Richard Robinson. Oxford, 1934.

——'Aristotle's Use of Medicine as Model of Method in his Ethics'. *Journal of Hellenic Studies* 77 (1957),54-61, 491-509.

Jāmī, ʿAbd al-Raḥmān b. Aḥmad. *Nafaḥāt al-uns min ḥaḍarāt al-quds*. Ed. Mahdī Tawḥīdīpūr. Tehran, 1336 solar / 1957.

Jayūshī, Muḥammad al-. *al-Ḥakīm al-Tirmidhī. Dirāsa li-āthārihī wa-afkārihī*.

Cairo, 1401/1980 (?).

Jazīrī, ʿAbd al-Raḥmān, al-. *al-Fiqh ʿalā al madhāhib al-arbaʿa*. Cairo, 1970.

Jennings, R.C. 'Women in early 17th century Ottoman judicial records—The Sharia court of Anatolian Kayseri'. *JESHO* XVIII (1975), 53-114

Johns, A.H. 'David and Bathsheba. A Case Study in the Exegesis of Qur'anic Storytelling'. *MIDEO* 19 (1989), 225-66.

Jomier, Jacques. 'Jésus tel que Ghazālī le présente dans 'al-Ihyā''. *MIDEO* 18 (1988), 44-82.

Jurjānī, ʿAlī al-. *al-Taʿrīfāt*. Ed. G. Flügel. Leipzig, 1845.

Juwaynī, Abu'l-Maʿālī al-. *al-Irshād ilā qawāṭiʿ al-adilla fī uṣūl al-iʿtiqād*. Ed. Muḥammad Mūsā and ʿAlī ʿAbd al-Ḥamīd. Cairo, 1950.

Kably, Mohammed. 'Satan dans *l'Iḥyā'* d'Al-Ghazālī'. *Hespéris-Tamuda* v (1964), 5-37.

Kaḥḥāla, ʿUmar Riḍā. *Muʿjam al-mu'allifīn*. Damascus, 1377/1957.

Kalābādhī, Abū Bakr Muḥammad b. Isḥāq, al-. *al-Taʿarruf li-madhhab ahl al-Taṣawwuf*. Ed. A.J.Arberry. Cairo, 1352/1933.

Kamali, Hashim M. *Principles of Islamic Jurisprudence*. Cambridge, 1991.

——'Divorce and Women's Rights: Some Muslim Interpretations of S. 2:228'. *MW* LXXIV (1984), 85-99.

Kenny, A. 'Aristotle on Happiness'. In J. Barnes, M.Schofield and R. Sorabji (eds.), *Articles on Aristotle. 2. Ethics and Politics*. London, 1977. Pp.25-32.

Khadduri, M. *al-Shāfi'ī's Risāla. Treatise on the Foundations of Islamic Jurisprudence*. Repr. Cambridge, 1987.

Kharā'iṭī, Muḥammad b. Jaʿfar, al-. *Makārim al-akhlāq wa-maʿālīhā*. Ed. ʿAbd Allāh ibn Ḥajjāj. Cairo, 1980.

Kharrāz, Abū Saʿīd al-. *K. al-Ṣidq*. Ed. and trans. A. Arberry. Oxford, 1937.

——*Rasā'il*. Ed. Qāsim al-Sāmarrā'ī. Baghdad, 1387/1967.

Khaṭīb al-Baghdādī, al-. *Tārīkh Baghdād*. Cairo, 1349.

Khawam, René R. *Nuits de noces, ou comment humer le doux brouvage de la magie licite*. Paris, 1972. [Tr. of a treatise by al-Suyūṭī.]

Kindermann, Hans. *Über die guten Sitten beim Essen und Trinken das ist das 11. Buch von Al-Ghazzālī's Hauptwerk*. Leiden, 1960. [German trans. of Book 11 of the *Iḥyā'*.]

Kindī, Yaʿqūb b. Isḥāq, al-. *Fi'l-falsafa al-ūlā*. In *Rasā'il al-Kindī al-falsafiya*, ed. M. Abū Rīda (Cairo, 1369/1950), I. 97-162.

——*Fī ḥudūd al-ashyā' wa-rusūmihā*. In *Rasā'il*, I. 163-80.

——*al-Qawl fi'l-nafs*. In *Rasā'il*, I. 272-80.

——*K. al-Jawāhir al-Khamsa*. In *Rasā'il*, II. 8-32.

——*Fi'l-ḥīla li-dafʿ al-aḥzān*. Ed. H. Ritter and R. Walzer, in 'Studi su al-Kindi II, uno scrittomorale inedito di al-Kindi.' *Memorie delle Reale*

Academia Nazionale dei Lincei. Ser. VI. vol. VIII, fasc. I (1938) pp.1-38.
——*K. al-Bāh*. In Celentano, *Due Scritti*.

Kraus, P. 'Plotin chez les Arabes' *Bulletin de l'Institut égyptien*, 23(1941) 263-95.

——'The Book of Ethics by Galen'. *Bulletin of the Faculty of Arts of the University of Egypt*. v.i (1937), 1-51.

Kraye, Jill, Ryan, W.F., and Schmitt, C.B. [eds.] *Pseudo-Aristotle in the Middle Ages. The* Theology *and Other Texts*. London, 1986.

Küng, H. 'Christianity and World Religions: The Dialogue with Islam as One Model'. *MW* LXXVII (1987), 80-95.

Lane, E. *An Arabic-English Lexicon*. London, 1863-1893.

Laqqānī, ʿAbd al-Salām, al-. *Irshād al-murīd ilā maqām al-tawḥīd*. Printed at margin of *al-Ḥāshiya* of Muḥammad al-Amīr. Cairo, 1373/1953.

Laoust, Henri. *La politique de Gazālī*. Paris, 1970.

——*Essai sur les doctrines sociales et politiques de Taḳī-d-Dīn Aḥmad B. Taymīya*. Cairo, 1939.

Laraoui, Abdallah. *Islam et modernité*. Paris, 1986.

Lazarus-Yafeh, H. *Studies in Al-Ghazzālī*. Jerusalem, 1975.

Leewen, A.P. van. 'Essai de Bibliographie sur Al Ghazzali'. *IBLA* (1958), 221-7.

Le Strange, G. *Lands of the Eastern Caliphate*. Cambridge, 1905.

Levey, Martin. *Early Arabic Pharmacology. An Introduction based on Ancient and Medieval Sources*. Leiden, 1973.

Levey, Martin, and al-Khaledy, Noury. *The Medical Formulary of Al-Samarqandī and the Relation of Early Arabic Simples to Those Found in the Indigenous Medicine of the Near East and India*. Philadelphia, 1967.

Lings, Martin. *Muhammad. His life based on the earliest sources*. London, 1983.

——*Symbol and Archetype. A study of the meaning of existence*. Cambridge, 1991.

Lobato, Chantal. 'Femmes afghanes, femmes musulmanes'. In O. Mongin and O. Roy (eds.), *Islam, le grand malentendu*. Paris, 1987. Pp.170-3.

Lyall, Sir Charles. 'The meaning of the words *'ala hubbihi* in Qur. II.172'. *JRAS* (1914), 158-163.

Lyons, M.C. 'A Greek Ethical Treatise'. *Oriens*, 13-14 (1960-1), 35-57.

Macdonald, D.B. 'The Life of al-Ghazzālī'. *JAOS* 20 (1899) pp.70-133.

Madelung, W. *Religious Trends in Early Islamic Iran*. Albany (New York), 1988.

—— 'Ar-Rāġib al-Iṣfahānī und die Ethik al-Ġazalis'. In R.Gramlich (ed.), *Islamwissenchaftliche Abhandlungen*, Wiesbaden, 1974.

Maghribī, al-Ḥusayn b. ʿAlī, al-. *K. Fi'l-siyāsa*. Ed. Sāmī al-Dahhān. Damascus, 1367/1948.

Maḥfūẓ, Ḥusayn ʿAlī. *Muʿjam al-mūsīqā al-ʿarabīya*. Baghdad, 1964.

Makdisi, George. 'Al-Ghazâlî, disciple de Shâfiʿî en droit et en théologie.' In *Ghazâlî, la raison et le miracle*. Table rond UNESCO 9-10 décembre 1985. Paris, 1987. Pp.45-55.

——'The Sunnī Revival.' In D.S. Richards (ed.), *Islamic Civilisation 950-1150*. Oxford, 1973. Pp. 155-163.

Makkī, Abū Ṭālib, al-. *Qūt al-qulūb fī muʿāmalat al-Maḥbūb wa-waṣf ṭarīq al-murīd ilā maqām al-tawḥīd*. Cairo, 1310 AH.

——*ʿIlm al-qulūb*. Ed. ʿAbd al-Qādir ʿAṭā'. Cairo, n.d.

Mala, S. Babs. 'The Sufi convent and its social significance in the medieval period of Islam'. *IC* 51 (1977), 31-52.

Mālik b. Anas. *Al-Muwaṭṭa'*. Cairo, 1383/1964.

Mallet, Dominique. *Farabi. Deux traités philosophiques: l'harmonie entre les opinions des deux sages, le divin Platon et Aristote, et de la Religion*. Damascus, 1989.

Massignon, L. *Essai sur les origines du lexique technique de la mystique musulmane*. 2nd. ed. Paris, 1954.

——*The Passion of al-Hallāj. Mystic and Martyr of Islam*. Translated by Herbert Mason. Princeton, 1982.

Maʿṣūmī, M. Ṣaghīr Ḥasan. *Imām Rāzī's ʿIlm al akhlāq*. New Delhi, 1981. [English translation with notes of Fakhr al-Dīn al-Rāzī's *K. al-Nafs wa'l-rūḥ wa-sharḥ quwāhumā*.]

Mattock, J.N. 'A Translation of the Arabic Epitome of Galen's Book Περὶ Ἠθῶν.' In *Islamic Philosophy and the Classical Tradition*. Ed. S.M. Stern, Albert Hourani and Vivian Brown. Oxford, 1972. pp.235-260.

Māwardī, ʿAlī b. Muḥammad. *Adab al-dunyā wa'l-dīn*. Ed. ʿAbd Allāh Abū Zīna. Cairo, 1979.

Maydānī, Aḥmad b. Muḥammad, al-. *Majmaʿ al-amthāl*. Ed. Muḥammad ʿAbd al-Ḥamīd. Cairo, 1374/1955.

McCarthy, R.J. *Freedom and Fulfillment. An Annotated Translation of al-Ghazālī's* al-Munqidh min al-Ḍalāl *and other Relevant Works of Al-Ghazālī*. Boston, 1980.

Meddeb, Abdelwahab. *Les dits de Bistami (shatahât)*. Paris, 1989. [French trans. of Sahlajī's *al-Nūr*.]

Meier, Fritz. 'The Problem of Nature in the Esoteric Monism of Islam', in J. Campbell (ed.), *Spirit and Nature. Papers from the Eranos-Yearbooks*. I. Princeton, 1954. pp.149-203.

Meyerhof, Max. *Alî aṭ-Ṭabarî's "Paradise of Wisdom", one of the oldest Arabic Compendiums of Medicine*. Bruges, 1931.

Michon, Jean-Louis. *Le Soufi Marocain Aḥmad ibn ʿAjība (1746-1809) et son* Miʿrāj. *Glossaire de la mystique musulmane*. Paris, 1973.

Milson, Menahem. *A Sufi Rule for Novices. K. Adab al-murīdīn of Abu'l-Najib al-Suhrawardi*. [Abridged translation with notes.] Harvard, 1975.

Miskawayh, Aḥmad b. Muḥammad [b.]. *al-Ḥikma al-Khālida. Jāvidān khirad*. Ed. ʿAbd al-Raḥmān Badawī. Cairo, 1952.

——*Tahdhīb al-akhlāq*. Ed. Constantine K. Zurayk. Beirut, 1967.

Mohaghegh, M. 'Notes on the "Spiritual Physic" of Al-Rāzī'. *SI* XXVI (1967), pp.5-22.

Molé, Marijan. *Les mystiques musulmans*. Paris 1965.

Morelon, R. *Le livre du licite et de l'illicite. Kitāb al-ḥalāl wa'l-ḥarām*. Paris, 1981. [French tr. and introd. of book 14 of the *Iḥyā'*.]

Mufīd, al-Shaykh, al-. See 'al-Baghdādī'.

Muḥāsibī, al-Ḥārith, al-. *al-Riʿāya li-ḥuqūq Allāh*. Ed. M. Smith. London, 1940.

——*al-Masā'il fi'l-zuhd wa-ghayrih*. In *al-Masā'il fī aʿmāl al-qulūb wa'l-jawāriḥ wa'l-makāsib wa'l-ʿaql*. Ed. ʿAbd al-Qādir ʿAṭā. Cairo, 1969. Pp.41-88.

——*al-Makāsib*. In *al-Masā'il* (see above), pp.171-234.

——*Muʿātabat al-nafs*. Ed. Muḥammad ʿAṭā. Cairo, 1986.

——*Ādāb al-nufūs*. Ed. ʿAbd al-Qādir ʿAṭā. Cairo, 1984.

——*al-Qaṣd wa'l-rujūʿ ila'Llāh*. Ed. ʿAbd al-Qādir ʿAṭā. Cairo, 1980.

Munāwī, ʿAbd al-Ra'ūf, al-. *al-Kawākib al-durrīya fī tarājim al-Sāda al-Ṣūfīya*. Cairo, 1357/1938.

Mundhirī, Zakī al-Dīn, al-. *al-Targhīb wa'l-tarhīb*. Ed. Muṣṭafā ʿImāra. Beirut, 1406.

Murābiṭ, J. al-. *al-Sarī al-Saqaṭī*. Beirut, 1398 AH.

Murata, Sachiko. 'Masculine-Feminine Complementarity in the Spiritual Psychology of Islam'. *IQ* 33 (1989), 165-87.

——'The Angels'. In S.H. Nasr (ed.), *Islamic Spirituality, Foundations*. London, 1987. Pp.324-44.

Musallam, B.F. *Sex and society in Islam. Birth control before the nineteenth century*. Cambridge, 1983.

Musurillo, H. 'The Problem of Ascetical Fasting in the Greek Patristic Writers'. *Traditio* XII (1956), 1-64.

Nader, A. *Le système philosophique des Mu'tazila*. Beirut, 1956.

Nakamura, K. *Ghazali on prayer*. 2nd ed. Cambridge, 1990. [English tr. with introd. of the *Kitāb al-adhkār wa'l-daʿawāt* from the *Iḥyā'*.]

Nasafī, ʿAbd Allāh b. Aḥmad, al-. *Madārik al-tanzīl wa ḥaqā'iq al-ta'wīl* Cairo, 1343 AH.

Nasā'ī, Aḥmad b. Shuʿayb, al-. *al-Ḍuʿafā' wa'l-matrūkīn*. Ed. B. al-Ḍannāwī and K. al-Ḥūt. Beirut, 1405/1985.

Nasir, Jamal. *The Islamic Law of Personal Status*. London, 1986.

Nawawī, Muḥyi'l-Dīn Yaḥyā, al-. *al-Minhāj fī Sharḥ Ṣaḥīḥ Muslim ibn al-*

Ḥajjāj. Cairo, 1347 AH.

——*Tahdhīb al-asmā' wa'l-lughāt*. Ed. F. Wüstenfeld. Göttingen, 1842-7.

——*Sharḥ al-arbaʿīn al-Nawawīya*. With notes by Muḥammad Rashīd Riḍā. Cairo, n.d.

Netton, Ian. *Muslim Neoplatonists. An introduction to the thought of the Brethren of Purity (Ikhwān al Ṣafā)*. London, 1982.

Nwyia, P. *Exégèse coranique et langage mystique*.Beirut, 1970.

——(ed.) *Trois oeuvres inédites de mystiques musulmans. Šaqīq al-Balḫī, Ibn ʿAṭā, Niffarī*. Beirut, 1973.

Nicholson, R.A. *The Kashf al-maḥjúb, the oldest Persian treatise on Sufiism*. Leiden and London, 1911. [Tr. with introd. of the *Kashf al-Maḥjūb* of al-Jullābī al-Hujwīrī.]

——*Studies in Islamic Mysticism*. Cambridge, 1921, repr. 1978.

Obermann, J. *Der Philosophische und Religiöse Subjektivismus Gazzālīs*. Leipzig, 1921.

Parmaksızoğlu, İ. 'Kemal Paşa-Zâde'. *Islam Ansiklopedisi*, VI. 562-7.

Pellat, C. *Le Milieu basrien et la formation de Ġāḥiẓ*. Paris, 1953.

Peters, F.E. *Aristoteles Orientalis*. Leiden, 1968.

——*Aristotle and the Arabs. The Aristotelian Tradition in Islam*. New York and London, 1968.

Pickthall, M.M. *The Meaning of the Glorious Koran*. London, 1934.

Pinès, Shlomo. 'Quelques notes sur les rapports de l'*Iḥyâ' ʿulūm al-dîn* d'al-Ghazâlî avec la pensée d'Ibn Sînâ', in *Ghazâlî, la raison et le miracle*. Table rond UNESCO 9-10 Décembre 1985. Paris, 1987. Pp.11-16.

Plato. *The Republic*. Tr. P. Shorey. Cambridge (Mass.) and London, (vol.I) 1937, repr. 1982; (vol.II) 1935, repr. 1987. (Loeb Classical Library nos. 237, 276.)

Plessner, M. *Der Oikonomikoc des Neupythagoreers 'Bryson' und sein Einfluss auf die islamische Wissenschaft*. Edition und Übersetzung der erhalttenen Versionen, nebst einer Geschichte der Ökonomik im Islam mit Quellenproben in text und Übersetzung.Heidelberg, 1928.

Poggi, Vicenzo M. *Un Classico della Spiritualità Musulmana. Saggio monografico sul "Munqiḏ" di al-Gazālī*. Rome, 1967.

Pouzet, L. *Une Herméneutique de la tradition islamique. Le Commentaire des Arbaʿūn al-Nawawīya de Muḥyī al-Dīn Yaḥyā al-Nawawī*. Beirut, 1982.

Pretzl, Otto. *Die Streitschrift des Gazâlî gegen die Ibâḥiya*. Munich, 1933. [Edition and German translation of *al-Radd ʿalā al-Ibāḥīya* attributed to Ghazālī.]

Qazwīnī, ʿUmar b. ʿAbd al-Raḥmān, al-. *Mukhtaṣar Shuʿab al-īmān*. Cairo, 1355 AH.

Quasem, Muhammad Abul. *The Ethics of al-Ghazali: a Composite Ethics in*

Islam. Malaysia, 1975.

——'Al-Ghazālī's Theory of Good Character'. *IC* LI (1977), 229–39.

Quḍāʿī, Muḥammad b. Salāma, al-. *Musnad al-Shihāb*. Beirut, 1405/1985.

Qushayrī, Abu'l-Qāsim, al-. *al-Risāla fī ʿilm al-taṣawwuf*. Ed. ʿAbd al-Ḥalīm Maḥmūd and Maḥmūd ibn al-Sharīf. Cairo, 1385/1966.

——*K. ʿIbārāt al-ṣūfīya wa-maʿānīhā*. In Qāsim al-Sāmarrāʾī (ed.), *Arbaʿ rasāʾil fī'l-taṣawwuf*. Baghdad, 1389/1969.

——*Risāla Tartīb al-sulūk*. In Muḥammad Ḥasan (ed.), *al-Rasāʾil al-Qushayrīya*. Pakistan, 1964.

al-Rāghib al-Iṣfahānī. *al-Dharīʿa ilā makārim al-sharīʿa*. Beirut, 1400/1980.

Rahman, F. *Avicenna's Psychology*. London, 1952.

Rāzī, Fakhr al-Dīn, al-. *Jāmiʿ al-ʿulūm*. Bombay, 1323 AH.

Rāzī, Muḥammad b. Zakarīyāʾ al-. *al-Ṭibb al-Rūḥānī*. In *Rasāʾil Falsafīya* [*Opera Philosophica, fragmentaque quæ supersunt*], pp.1–96. Ed. Paul Kraus. Cairo, 1939.

Renard, J. 'al-Jihād al-Akbar: Notes on a Theme in Islamic Spirituality.' *MW* LXXVII (1988), 225–42.

Rhys Davids, T. 'Does Al-Ghazzali Use an Indian Metaphor?' *JRAS* (1911), 200–1.

Ritter, H. *Das Meer der Seele*. Leiden, 1955.

Robson, James. *Mishkat al-Masabih*. English translation with explanatory notes. Lahore: 1970. [Translation of the *Mishkāt al-maṣābīḥ* of al-Tabrīzī.]

Rodinson, Maxime. 'Récherches sur les documents arabes relatifs à la cuisine.' *Révue des Études Islamiques*, (1949), 95–165.

Rosenthal, Franz. 'Child psychology in Islam.' *IC*, 26(1952), 1–22.

——*The Classical Heritage in Islam*. London, 1975.

——'On the knowledge of Plato's Philosophy in the Islamic World'. *IC* XIV (1940), 387–422.

——'Sources for the Role of Sex in Medieval Muslim Society'. Pp.3–22 of Marsot (ed), *Society and the Sexes in Medieval Islam*. Malibu, 1979.

Ṣafadī, Ṣalāḥ al-Dīn Khalīl b. Aybak, al-. *al-Wāfī bi'l-wafayāt*. Ed. H. Ritter et al.. Wiesbaden, 1962– .

Sakhāwī, Muḥammad b. ʿAbd al-Raḥmān, al-. *al-Maqāṣid al-Ḥasana fī bayān kathīrⁱⁿ min al-aḥādīth al-mushtahira ʿala'l-alsina*. Ed. and introd. by Muḥammad al-Khusht. Beirut, 1405/1985.

Salazar, Patricia. 'The role of women in the transmission of hadith in the early centuries of Islam.' London University MA thesis, 1989.

Salīm, Muḥammad Ibrāhīm. *Ṭabāʾiʿ al-nisāʾ wa-mā jāʾa fīhā min ʿajāʾib wa-gharāʾib wa-akhbār wa-asrār*. Cairo, 1985.

Saljūqī, Ṣalāḥ al-Dīn al-. *Athar al-Imām al-Ghazālī fī'l-akhlāq*. In *Abū Ḥāmid al-Ghazālī fī al-dhikrā al-mi'awīya al-tāsiʿa li-mīlādih*, Cairo, 1962, pp.69–82.

Sarrāj, Abū Naṣr ʿAbdallāh b. ʿAlī, al-. *al-Lumaʿ fi'l-taṣawwuf.* Edited for the first time, with critical notes, abstract of contents, glossary and indices, by Reynold Alleyne Nicholson. London,1914, repr. 1963. (Gibb Memorial Series XXII.)

Sarrāj, Jaʿfar b. Aḥmad, al-. *Maṣāriʿ al-ʿushshāq*. Beirut, 1378/1958.

Schammas, Yusuf Easa. 'al-Ghazali's *The Ascent of the Divine Through the Path of Self-knowledge (Maʿārij al-quds fī Madārij Maʿrifat al-Nafs)* being a psychological approach to theology, translated and annotated with an introduction and glossary index.' Hartford Theological Seminary dissertation, 1958.

Schimmel, Annemarie. *Mystical dimensions of Islam*. Chapel Hill (North Carolina, USA), 1975.

——*And Muhammad is his Messenger.* Chapel Hill (North Carolina, USA), 1985.

——*The Triumphal Sun.* A Study of the Works of Jalāloddin Rumi. London, 1980.

——'Eros - Heavenly and not so heavenly - in Sufi literature and life'. In Afaf Lutfi al-Sayyid Marsot (ed.), *Society and the Sexes in Medieval Islam* (Malibu, 1979), 120–41.

Schleifer, Aliah. 'A Modified Phenomenological Approach to the Concept and Person of Maryam in Islam'. PhD thesis, University of Exeter, 1991.

Schuon, F. *Sufism: Veil and Quintessence*. Bloomington,1981.

Sezgin, F. *Geschichte des arabischen Schrifttums*. Leiden, 1967– .

Shaʿrāni, ʿAbd al-Wahhāb, al-. *Lawāqiḥ al-anwār fī ṭabaqāt al-akhyār*. Cairo, 1343/1925.

Sherif, M.A. *Ghazali's Theory of Virtue*. Albany (New York), 1975.

Shībī, Kāmil Muṣṭafā. *al-Ṣila bayn al-taṣawwuf wa'l-tashayyuʿ*. 2nd ed. Cairo, 1969.

Shorter Encyclopaedia of Islam, The. Ed. H.A.R. Gibb and J.H. Kramers. Leiden, 1974.

Shukri, M.A.M. 'Abū Ṭālib al-Makkī and his Qūt al-Qulūb.' *IS* 28 (1989), 161–70.

Siddiqi, M.Z. *Ḥadīth Literature*. 2nd ed. Cambridge, 1993.

Siggel, A. *Das Buch der Gifte des Čābir ibn Ḥayyān. Übersetzt und erläutert.* Wiesbaden, 1958.

Sijistānī, Abū Dāūd, al-. *al-Sunan*. Cairo, 1369–70/1950–51.

Skellie, Walter James. 'The religious psychology of Al-Ghazzālī.' PhD thesis, Hartford Seminary (USA),1938. [Trans. with intro. of Book 21 from the *Iḥyā'*.]

Smith, J. 'The Experience of Muslim Women: Considerations of Power and Authority.' Pp.89–112 of Y. Haddad, B.Haines, and E. Findly (eds.), *The Islamic Impact*. Syracuse (USA), 1984.

Smith, Jane, and Haddad, Y. *The Islamic Understanding of Death and Resurrection*. Albany (New York), 1981.

——'The Virgin Mary in Islamic Tradition and Commentary'. *MW* LXXIX (1989), pp.161–87.

Smith, M. *Al-Ghazālī the Mystic*. London, 1944.

——*Rābiʿa the Mystic and Her Fellow Saints in Islam*. Cambridge, 1928.

——*An Early Mystic of Baghdad. A study of the life and teachings of Ḥārith b. Asad al-Muḥāsibī*. London, 1935.

——'The Forerunner of al-Ghazālī (al-Muḥāsibī)'. *JRAS* (1936) pp.65–78.

Steinschneider, M. *Die arabischen Übersetzungen aus dem Grieschischen*. Graz, 1960.

Subkī, Tāj al-Dīn, al-. *Ṭabaqāt al-Shāfiʿīya al-Kubrā*. Cairo, 1324.

Suhrawardī, ʿUmar. *ʿAwārif al-maʿārif*. Cairo, 1358/1939.

Sulamī, Abū ʿAbd al-Raḥmān, al-. *Jawāmiʿ ādāb al-Ṣūfīya*, printed together with his *ʿUyūb al-nafs wa-mudāwātuhā*. Ed.& introduced by E. Kohlberg. Jerusalem, 1976.

——*Ṭabaqāt al-Ṣūfīya*. Ed. J. Pedersen. Leiden, 1960.

——*Risāla al-malāmatīya*. Ed. Abu'l-ʿAlā ʿAfīfī. Cairo, 1942.

Sunar, Cavit. *Ibn Miskeveyh ve Yunan'da ve Islâm'da Ahlâk Görüşleri*. Ankara, 1980.

Suyūṭī, Jalāl al-Dīn, al-. *al-Durar al-muntathira fī'l-aḥādīth al-mushtahira*. Ed. K. M. al-Mīs. Beirut, 1404/1984.

——*al-Mujtabā min Sunan al-Nasā'ī*. Cairo, 1383–4/1964–5.

——*al-Īḍāḥ fī ʿilm al-nikāḥ*. Cairo, n.d.

Ṭabarānī, Sulaymān b. Aḥmad, al-. *al-Muʿjam al-Ṣaghīr*. Cairo, 1388 AH.

Ṭabarī, Ibn Jarīr, al-. *Jāmiʿ al-bayān fī ta'wīl āī al-Qur'ān*. Cairo, 1323–9 AH.

Ṭabarī, ʿAlī, al-. *Firdaws al-ḥikma*. In Meyerhof, above.

Taftāzānī, Abu'l-Wafā', al-. 'Thalātha mabādi' fī ʿilm al-akhlāq.' *Minbar al-islām*, Jumādā I, 1410, pp.42–44.

Ṭaḥāwī, Aḥmad b. Muḥammad, al-. *Mushkil al-āthār*. Hyderabad, 1333 AH.

al-Takriti, Naji. *Yahya ibn 'Adi. A Critical Edition and Study of his Tahdhib al-akhlaq*. Beirut/Paris, 1978.

Talas, Asad. *L'Enseignement chez les Arabes: La Madrasa Nizamiyya et son histoire*. Paris, 1939.

Ṭayālisī, Muḥammad b. Jaʿfar, al-. *al-Musnad*. Hyderabad, 1321 AH.

Temkin, Owsei. *Galenism: Rise and Decline of a Medical Philosophy*. Ithaca and London, 1973.

——'On Galen's Pneumatology'. *Gesnerus* 8 (1951), 180–9.

Tritton, A.S. *Materials on Muslim Education in the Middle Ages*. London, 1957.

——*'Man, nafs, rūḥ, ʿaql'*. *BSOAS* XXXIV (1971), pp.491–95.

——*'Maʿārij al-quds'*, *BSOAS* XXII (1959), 353.

Tunç, Cihad. *Sahl ibn ʿAbdallāh at-Tustarī und die Sālimīya*. Bonn, 1970.

Tustarī, Sahl b. ʿAbdallāh. *K. al-Muʿāraḍa wa'l-radd ʿalā ahl al-firaq wa-ahl al-daʿāwī fī al-aḥwāl min kalām Sahl*. In Tunç, op. cit.

Umaruddin, Muhammad. *The Ethical Philosophy of al-Ghazzali*. Lahore, 1970, repr. 1982.

ʿUqaylī, Muḥammad b. ʿAmr, al-. *al-Ḍuʿafā' al-Kabīr*. Ed. A. Qalʿajī. Beirut, 1404/1984.

Uthman, Ali Issa. *The Concept of Man in Islam in the Writings of Al-Ghazali*. Cairo, 1960.

Vacca, Virginia. *Il Libro dei Doni (Kitāb laṭā'if al minan wa'l-akhlāq), Passi scelti, tradotti e annotati*. Naples, 1972. [Tr. of a work by al-S̲h̲aʿrānī.]

Vadet, Jean-Claude. *Le traité d'amour mystique d'al-Daylamī*. Geneva and Paris, 1980. [French trans. of the *K. ʿAṭf al-alif al-ma'lūf ʿala'l-lām al-maʿṭūf*.]

Vaglieri, Laura Veccia, and Rubinacci, Roberto. *Scritti Scelti di al-G̲h̲azālī*. Turin, 1970.

Vajda, G. *'Le ma'āriǧ al-quds fī madāriǧ ma'rifat al-nafs* attribué à al-Gazālī et les écrits d'Ibn Sīnā.' *Israel Oriental Studies*, 2 (1972), 470–3.

Van den Bergh, S. *Averroes' Tahafut al-Tahafut (The Incoherence of the Incoherence)*. London, 1969. [Translation of Ibn Rus̲h̲d's *Tahāfut al-tahāfut*.]

Von Grunebaum, G. 'Concept and function of reason in Islamic ethics'. *Oriens* XV (1962), 1–17.

Walzer, R. *Greek into Arabic*. Oxford, 1962.

Watt, W. Montgomery. *Muslim Intellectual: A Study of al-G̲h̲azālī*. Edinburgh, 1963.

——*Islamic Philosophy and Theology*. 2nd ed. Edinburgh,1985.

——'A Forgery in al-Ghazālī's Mishkāt?' *JRAS* (1949), 5–22.

——'The Authenticity of the Works Ascribed to Al-Ghazālī'. *JRAS* (1952), pp.24–45.

Wensinck, A.J. *La pensée de Ghazzālī*. Paris, 1940.

Wensinck, A.J. et al.. *Concordance et indices de la tradition musulmane*. Leiden, 1936–1969.

Wickens, G.M. *The Nasirean Ethics by Naṣīr al-Dīn Ṭūsī*. London 1964. [Translation of the *Ak̲h̲lāq-i Naṣīrī*.]

Wilkinson, L.P. *Classical Attitudes to Modern Issues*. London, 1979.

Winter, T.J. *Al-G̲h̲azālī. The Remembrance of death and the afterlife.*

Cambridge, 1989. [Trans. of book 40 of the *Iḥyā'*.]

Wolfson, H.A. *The Philosophy of the Kalam*. Harvard and London, 1976.

Yāqūt al-Ḥamawī. *Muʿjam al-buldān*. Ed. F. Wüstenfeld. Leipzig, 1866.

Yakan, Fatḥī. *al-Islām wa'l-jins*. Beirut, 1392/1972.

Zabīdī, al-Murtaḍā, al-. *Itḥāf al-sādat al-muttaqīn bi-sharḥ asrār Iḥyā' ʿulūm al-dīn*. Cairo, 1311 AH.

Zamakhsharī, Jār Allāh, al-. *al-Fā'iq fī gharīb al-ḥadīth*. Ed. ʿAlī al-Bijāwī and Muḥammad Ibrāhīm. Cairo, 1945-8.

Ziadeh, F.J. 'Integrity (*ʿAdālah*) in Classical Islamic Law'. In N. Heer (ed.), *Islamic Law and Jurisprudence*. Seattle and London, 1990. Pp.73-93.

Zimmermann, F.W. 'The Origins of the so-called *Theology of Aristotle*'. In Kraye et al., *Pseudo-Aristotle,* pp.110-240.

Zirikli, Khayr al-Dīn, al-. *Al-Aʿlām*. (4th ed.) Beirut, 1972.

INDEX TO QUR'ĀNIC QUOTATIONS

SŪRA	VERSE	PAGE
I. *al-Fātiḥa*	6	50, 156
II. *al-Baqara*	45	32
	269	19
	286	165
III. *Āl ʿImrān*	134	28
IV. *al-Nisā'*	69	95, 55
	145	162
VI. *al-Anʿām*	60	190
VII. *al-Aʿrāf*	22	106
	31	136, 156
	142	116
	199	7
	200	94
	201	94
VIII. *al-Anfāl*	2	68
	3	68
	4	68
IX. *al-Tawba*	24	47
	31	29
	112	67
XI. *Hūd*	88	101
	112	50
X. *Yūnus*	7	63, 65, 126
XII. *Yūsuf*	24	184
	90	58
XIV. *Ibrāhīm*	17	148–50
	34	149
XVI. *al-Naḥl*	33	38
XVII. *al-Isrā'*	29	29
XIX. *Maryam*	52	116
	72	49
XX. *ṬāHā*	121	104
XXII. *al-Ḥajj*	18	189

Sūra	Verse	Page
XXIII. *al-Mu'minūn*	1–10	67
XXIV. *al-Nūr*	35	89
	37	129
	99	174
XXV. *al-Furqān*	63	68
	67	29, 160
XXVI. *al-Shuʿarā'*	89	29
XXVIII. *al-Qaṣaṣ*	54	163
XXX. *al-Rūm*	7	126
XXXIII. *al-Aḥzāb*	72	129
XXXVI. *YāSīn*	9	38, 85
XXXVIII. *Ṣād*	71	17
XL. *al-Mu'min*	18	190
	19	190
	20	190
XLII. *al-Shūrā*	20	83, 85
XLVIII. *al-Fatḥ*	29	23, 28
XLIX. *al-Ḥujurāt*	3	56
	14	14
	15	23
LI. *al-Dhāriyāt*	56	46
LVI. *al-Wāqiʿa*	33	147
LVII. *al-Ḥadīd*	20	63
LVIII. *al-Mujādala*	11	55, 118
LXIX. *al-Ḥāqqa*	24	153
LXVI. *al-Taḥrīm*	6	75
LXVIII. *al-Qalam*	4	7, 70
LXX. *al-Maʿārij*	8	190
	9	190
LXXIII. *al-Muzzammil*	1	91
LXXIV. *al-Muddaththir*	1	91
LXXVI. *al-Insān*	8	147
LXXIX. *al-Nāziʿāt*	41	45, 56
	42	45, 56
LXXXVII. *al-Aʿlā*	16	100
	17	100
	18	100
	19	100
XCI. *al-Shams*	9	5
	10	5

XCIX. *al-Zilzāl*	8	38
	9	38
CIV. *al-Humaza*	5	5
	6	5
CXIII. *al-Falaq*	3	166

GENERAL INDEX

Abdāl, 89, 90, 98, 114
ʿAbbādān, 82
ʿAbd Allāh ibn Abī Wadāʿa, 180
ʿAbd Allāh ibn ʿAmr, XXXVI, 155A
ʿAbd Allāh ibn Sulaymān, 181
ʿAbd Allāh ibn ʿUmar, 9, 124E, 143, 152, 160, 186
ʿAbd Allāh ibn al-Zubayr, 138
ʿAbd al-Malik ibn Marwān, 181
ʿAbd al-Raḥmān ibn Ibrāhīm Duḥaym, 138
ʿAbd al-Raḥmān ibn Samura, 11
ʿAbd al-Raḥmān al-Ṭabīb, 150
ʿAbd al-Wāḥid ibn Zayd, 115, 148
Abraham, XX, 100, 112A
abrār, 89B
Abu'l-ʿAbbās al-Mawṣilī, 57
Abū ʿAbd Allāh al-Khayyāṭ, 72
Abū ʿAlī al-Daqqāq, LXXVII
Abū Bakr, 4B, 138
Abū Bakr ibn al-Jallā', 149
Abu'l-Dardā', 8
Abū Dharr, 11, 137
Abū Ḥabīb Ḥamza ibn Abī ʿAbd Allāh al-ʿAbbādānī, 82
Abū Ḥāzim, 146
Abū Hurayra, 9, 109, 110, 112, 140
Abu'l-Jawzā', 138
Abū Juḥayfa, 111
Abū Masʿūd al-Badrī, 9
Abū Nuwās, 77A
Abū Saʿīd al-Kharrāz, 16
Abū Saʿīd al-Khudrī, 108, 139
Abū Sulaymān al-Dārānī, XXIII, XLIII, 114, 118, 119, 120, 125, 126, 146, 151, 153, 171
Abū Ṭālib al-Makkī, 115
Abū ʿUthmān al-Maghribī, 15
Abū ʿUthmān al-Ḥīrī, 71
Abū Yaḥyā al-Warrāq, 58
Abū Yazīd al-Bisṭāmī, XCI, 93A, 97A, 119
al-Abwā', 184
Adam, XXIV, XXXV, LXXVIII, 106
aḥdāth, 175a
Aḥmad ibn Abi'l-Ḥawārī, 146
Aḥmad ibn Khalīfa, 147
Aḥmad ibn Saʿīd al-ʿĀbid, 189
al-Aḥnaf ibn Qays, 73
ʿĀ'isha, 7, 111, 112, 122, 139, 140, 157, 172
akhlāq, defined, XXI; LIV; mutability of, LX, LXXXIX, 24–30; and passim
afterlife (*ākhira*), XX
ahl al-bayt, XXXIX
ahl al-ṣuffa, 137
Aḥmad, 82
al-ʿAlā' ibn Ziyād, 187
ʿAlī ibn Abī Ṭālib, 16, 38, 59, 65, 73
ʿAlī al-Jurjānī, 125
ʿAlī ibn Mūsā al-Riḍā, 71
amāna, 130
Anas, 10, 11, 12, 13, 70, 112

angels, XXXV, 110, 142, 149
anger, 28, 43, 234, 236, 240; see also 'irascible faculty'
animals, LXXVIII, 47, 122, 149, 156, 241
animal symbolism, XXIX, 25, 64, 168, 169, 235
Antioch, 61
aphrodisiacs, 167
appetitive soul/faculty, LIII, 19, 31, 234-5
arrogance (*ṣalaf*), 21
asceticism (*zuhd*), XV, XXII, XXIII, XXIV, XXVI, XXVII, XXXI, LXXXVII, 93A; and passim
ᶜĀṣim ibn Kulayb, 140
Asín Palacios, Miguel, LXXVIII
Aristotle, XLIV, XLVII, LI, LII, LVI, LVII, LX, LXIV, LXXXIX; *Nicomachean Ethics*, LIII, LVI, LXI, 19B
Ashᶜab, XLII
Ashᶜarism, XXVII, XLVI, LXVI, 37, 61A
aspirancy (*irāda*), LXV, 83-101, 176
astrology, LIV
ᶜAṭā' al-Sulamī, 148
Augustine, XXXV
avarice, 29, 48, 241
Avicenna, see Ibn Sīnā
awtād, 89B
al-Awzāᶜī, 158

backbiting, 69, 123, 241
Bakr ibn ᶜAbd Allāh al-Mazanī, 116, 188
balā', ibtilā', 121
al-Barā' ibn ᶜĀzib, 9
baṣīra, XCI, 16
Baṣra, XXIV, 81, 146, 153, 178
basṭ, 158B
Bathsheba, 173
al-Bayhaqī, XXXIV
Beatific Vision (*ru'ya*), XXXVI
begging, 41, 128C, 143
bidᶜa, XLVII, XLIX, 94, 122
Bilāl, 172
Bishr ibn al-Ḥārith al-Ḥāfī, XXIV, XXX, XXXI, 150, 158
al-Bisṭāmī, XCI, 93A, 97A, 119
blanquette, 150
brain, 234
Brethren of Purity (Ikhwān al-Ṣafā), LIV-LV
Bryson, LVII, LXIV
al-Būṣīrī, XCII
Byzantines, 239

Calligraphy, 35
carob, 150
charity, 129, 131, 143
Children, LVI-LVII, LXIV, 31, 42, 75-82, 118, 171
Chinese, 239
Christianity, XXIII, XXIV, XXIX, XXXV, XXXVII, XLI, XLV, XLVI, LII, LXXV, 127B, 135, 138
clemency, 21
clothing, 60, 77, 78, 240
compassion, 126
conceit (*badhkh*), 21
contentedness with one's lot (*qināᶜa*), 22, 129, 237
contraception, LXXXIII
courage (*shujāᶜa*), 19, 21, 22, 23, 44, 236
cowardice (*jubn* or *jazaᶜ*), 20, 21, 44
Crates, 44C
cunning, 21
cupidity, 20, 22

General Index

ḍalāl, XIX
al-Daqqāq, LXXVII
al-Dārānī, XXIII, XLIII, 114, 118, 119, 120, 125, 126, 146, 151, 153, 171
Dāūd al-Ṭā'ī, 53, 146, 147
David, XXXI, 56, 173
deception, 21, 241
death, 124
Delilah, LXXXI
dhāt, 233
dhawq, LXVI, 120
dhilla, 21
Dhu'l-Nūn al-Miṣrī, XXVI, XXXII, 122, 162
dignity (*waqār*), 21
Diogenes, XLIV
Dionysios, 44A
discretion (*ḥusn al-tadbīr*), 21
divorce, LXXIX
dreams, 11, 99A, 176, 238, 240
drinking, 90, 109, 115

endives, 150
endurance (*iḥtimāl*), 21
envy (*ḥasad*), 22, 107, 240
Epictetus, LXXXVIII
equilibrium (*i*ᶜ*tidāl*), XLV, LII, LVII, LIX, LXI, LXIX, 19, 20, 22, 28, 30, 39, 48, 139-140, 154-60, 167, 236
erotic literature, LXXXIII
eudaimonia, LII
excellence of discernment (*jawdat al-dhihn*), 21
extravagance (*tabdhīr*), 22, 29, 139

Faḍā'iḥ al-Bāṭiniyya (of Ghazālī), LXXII
Fall of man, LXXVIII, 106
faqīh al-nafs, 36
al-Fārābī, XLIX, LV, LXI
fasting, XXX-XXXI, 43, 126, 128, 134, 135, 138, 140, 170, 172
Fatḥ al-Mawṣilī, 113
Fāṭima, XXXIX, 112
fear (*khawf*), XX, XXII, XXV, XXVII, XXVII
firāsa, 96
filial piety, XXI
fiṭra, XXXV, 18, 26, 38, 81, 236
foolishness (*ḥamq*), 21
forgiveness, 73-4, 237
fornication, 123, 172, 173, 174, 183, 186
flattery (*malq*), 22, 52, 241
al-Fuḍayl ibn ᶜIyāḍ, 8, 14, 113, 173

Gabriel, 168
Galen, XLIV, XLVII, LI, LIII, LVI, LIX, LX, LXII, 17A, 76A
gambling, 33
gardens, XXXVI
generosity (*sakhā'*), 22, 32, 48, 236
ghaḍḍ al-baṣar, XLII
gharīb, *ḥadīth*, 168
ghassāq, 121
ghurūr, XXVI, 42A, 97, 100, 129
ghusl, 125A
gnosis (*ma*ᶜ*rifa*), 46, 47, 93A, 119, 120, 158, 162, 172
greatness of soul, 21
greed/gluttony, 22, 43, 69, 76, 106-164, 236, 240
Greeks, XLIV, XLV, LIII, LXIV, 22A, 126, 175A; Arabic translation of Greek works, XLVI-XLVII, LIII
Gregory of Nyssa, XXXV
guests, 68

ḥabb al-rashād, 127A
ḥadīth al-nafs, see '*khawāṭir*'

Ḥafṣ al-ʿĀbid al-Maṣīṣī, 138
ḥajj, 184
al-Ḥajjāj ibn Furāfiṣa, 138
al-Ḥakīm al-Tirmidhī, LXIII, XC
ḥalāl food, 93A, 133
al-halīlaj al-aswad, 126
Ḥammād ibn Abī Ḥanīfa, 146
Ḥanbalism, XXVII, XLVI, XLVIII
harīsa, 168
al-Ḥārith al-Muḥāsibī, XXVI, XLVIII, LXII, LXV, LXXV, 133A, 242
Hārūn al-Rashīd, 126
al-Ḥasan al-Baṣrī, XXIV, XXV, XXXIII, LVI, 13, 15, 57, 82B, 108, 110, 111, 130, 131, 137
hātif, 148
Ḥātim al-Aṣamm, 69
hawā, XIX, XXVIII, XXXI, 59A
ḥayā', 13, 22, 69, 124E, 237
ḥays, 157
heart (*qalb*), XVIII, XIX, LXII, 29, 35, 38, 40, 53, 81, 82A, 90, 93, 98, 118, 119, 126, 128, 234-244; mirror of, 89, 244, 237, 239
heaven, XXXVI-XXXVII, LXX, 11B, 13, 119
heedlessness, 21, 84, 99, 241
hell, 49
Hermeticism, LIV
hindibā, 150
Hippocrates, LXI
al-ḥiss al-mushtarak, 234
Homer, LVI
homosexuality, LXXI, 34, 174-6
honey, 159
hope (*rajā'*), XX, XXII, XXIV, XXV, XXVII; *amal*, 69
houris, XXXVI, 119
hudā, XVIII
Ḥudhayfa, 52
al-Hujwīrī, XXXI, LXXXII
humours (*akhlāṭ*), LIV, LXI, 39, 126
hunger (*jūʿ*), XXX-XXXI, 88, 89, 108-133
al-Ḥuṣarī, 92
al-Ḥusayn ibn Manṣūr (al-Ḥallāj), 16
hypocrisy, 52, 67, 69, 111, 137, 162, 236

Ibāḥa, 87C, 95A
Ibn ʿAbbās, 10, 14, 108, 118, 138, 165
Ibn ʿAjība, LXXXIII
Ibn ʿArabī, XXXV, XLI, LXXXI, XCII
Ibn ʿAṭā', 14
Ibn Fātik, LXXXIV
Ibn Ḥajar, LXXXII
Ibn Ḥanbal, XLVIII
Ibn Jamāʿa, LXXXIII
Ibn al-Jawzī, XLIV, 44C
Ibn Khafīf, XLIII
Ibn Masʿūd, III
Ibn al-Mubārak, 14
Ibn Rushd, LXXII
Ibn Sālim, 127, 152
Ibn Sīnā, XLIV, XLIX, LV-LVI, LXIV
Ibn Taymiya, LXXXII
Ibn Umm Maktūm, 174
Ibrāhīm ibn Adham, XXIII, 70, 128, 138, 144, 158
Ibrāhīm al-Khawwāṣ, XXIX, 61, 90, 138, 160
Ibrāhīm al-Taymī, 138
iḥtilām, 124
Iḥyā' ʿUlūm al-Dīn, LI, LXV, LXXVI, 4A
Ijmāʿ, LXXXII
ikhlāṣ, 162
Ikhwān al-Ṣafā, LIV-LV
ilhām, LXVII, 236, 238

illness, 115, 121
imagination (*takhayyul*), 234
īmān, XVIII, XXIV, XXVII, 9, 55, 67, 83, 84, 111, 118, 237
Imru'l-Qays, 77A
India, 44, 126
indifference, 20
inexperience (*ghimāra*), 21
insanity, 21
intellect, 19, 28, 31, 118, 234, 236, 243
intention, XXV
intimacy (*uns*), XXVII, 172
intrepidity (*najda*), 21
ʿIrāq, 126–7
irascible soul/faculty, LIII, 19, 20, 31, 234–5
iṣābat al-ẓann, 21
isfīdhbāja, 150
Isḥāq ibn Ḥunayn, LIII
ʿ*ishq* (passion), XLIV, LXX, 168, 183
ʿ*iṣma* (prophetic inerrancy), LXVII, 88A
Ismāʿīlism, LIV
istiqāma, 50
istishāṭa, 21
īthār, XXXIII
iʿtikāf, LXXVI

Jabal al-Likām, 61
Jaʿfar ibn Muḥammad al-Ṣādiq, 58, 164
Jaʿfar ibn Nuṣayr, 148
jāh, 85
janāba, 125a
Jarīr ibn ʿAbd Allāh, 9
Jesus, 31, 54, 56, 89, 110, 112A, 116, 138, 173
Jews, 127B, 142, 173, 188
Jezebel, LXXXI
jihād, XX, LXIII, 56, 97, 108, 235
John, 31, 173
Joseph, XIX, LXXXI, 4B, 58, 121, 184, 186
Judaism, XLVI
al-Junayd, XXVIII, LXI, 14, 45A, 58, 99A, 119, 148
jurbuza, 20A
al-Jurjānī, LXXXIX, 17A
justice, 20, 21, 22, 236; see also 'equilibrium'
al-Juwaynī, XLVIII, LXXXVI

Kaʿba, 185AB
Kahmas, 113
kalām, 237
Kamāl Pasha-zāde, LXXXIII
karāmāt, 97
al-Kattānī, 14
kaẓm al-ghayẓ, 21
Khārijism, XXIII, XXVII, 37A
khalīfa, LIV, LXXXVII
khalwa, LXVII, 90
khasāsa, 21
khawāṭir, LXVII, XCII, 240, 241, 242
al-Khiḍr, 145
al-Kindī, XLIV, XLVI, LIV, LVI
knowledge, 55, 236, 238
Kūfa, 189
kufr, XVIII
Küng, Hans, LXXIX

langour (*khūr*), 20
Laraoui, Abdallah, 27A
laughter, 118
al-lawḥ al-maḥfūẓ, 238
leprosy, 111, 127A
Likām, Mount, 61
Lings, Martin, LXXXI
love (*maḥabba, ḥubb*), of God, XXIV, XXVII, 33, 47, 60; of the world, XXV, LXXV, 33, 47, 61,

79, 91, 100; of the Prophet, 47; of women, XLIV, 165-191
lubb, albāb, XVII-III
Luqmān, XX, 13, 113, 119

*Ma*ᶜ*ārij al-Quds* (attributed to Ghazālī), LXXXVIII
mahāna, 21
malakūt, 138
malāma, 162A
malice (*shamāta*), 22
Mālik ibn Ḍaygham, 146
Mālik ibn Dīnār, XXIII, 59, 74, 113, 146, 158
Maqāmāt, XXVI-XXVII
Maqāṣid al-Falāsifa (of Ghazālī), LXXII
al-Maqṣad al-Asnā (of Ghazālī), XXXIV
*Ma*ᶜ*rifa*, 46, 47, 93A, 119, 120, 158, 162, 172
Marriage, XXIV, XXXVI, XXXVIII, XLIII, LXX, 11, 60, 169-70, 171-82
Maᶜrūf al-Karkhī, XXXIII, 158
Mary, XXXIX
Massignon, L., XVI-II, XXIII
al-Māwardī, LVII
al-Mawṣilī, 57
Maymūna, 174
mean, see 'equilibrium'
meat, 151
Mecca, XXIX, 144, 185-6
medicine, 126, 127; medical analogy in ethics, LII, LXI, 5, 35, 39, 48, 117
Medina, 143, 184
Meditation (*fikr*), XVII, XXX, 60, 69, 94B, 108, 235
memory, 235
Michael, 149
miracles, 97A
Miskawayh, LV, LVI-LVII, LIX, LX, LXI, LXII, LXIV, 17A
*Mīzān al-*ᶜ*amal* (attributed to Ghazālī), LXXXVIII
monks, 135, 138-9
Moses, XVII, 100, 112A, 116, 145, 166
mosques, 125, 126
mothers, 181
Muḥammad the Prophet, as moral exemplar, XX-XXII, 14, 22 and passim; life of, XXIX, XCI, 91; mother of, 184; and sexuality, XXXVI, XLII, LXXXV, 171; descendents of, XXXIX; intercession of, 61a
Muḥammad ibn Sulaymān al-Hāshimī, 178
Muḥammad ibn Suwār, 81
Muḥammad ibn ᶜUmar, 138
Muḥammad ibn Wāsiᶜ, 113
muḥāsaba, XXVI, XXVII, LVII, LXII
al-Muḥāsibī, XXVI, , XLVIII, LXII, LXV, LXXV, 133A, 242
mukāshafa (unveiling), LXVI, LXVII, 4B, 89, 98, 138, 139, 237, 238, 239
munājāt, 120, 126
al-Munqidh min al-ḍalāl (of Ghazālī), XLVIII
muqarrabūn, 74
*muraqqa*ᶜ*āt*, 42
murāqaba, XXVII
murīd, LXV, LXXVII, 41, 172
mursal Tradition, 111
muruwwa, 10
Mūsā ibn al-Ashajj, 147
music, 115D
al-Muslim ibn Saᶜīd, 138
Muᶜtazilism, XXVII, XLVI, 37

muzhir, 115
myrobalan, 126

Nāfiᶜ, 143
Najrān, 70
nasturtium cress, 127
al-Nawawī, LXXXII, LXXXIII
naẓar, LXX, 123, 172, 187-8
Neoplatonism, XLVII, LII-LIII, LIV, LVI
Nīsābūr, 72
Noah, 112A
nobility (*karam*), 14, 21
nuqabā', 89B

obscenity (*waqāḥa*), 22
Orientalism, XVII
Origen, LXXVIII
Original sin, XXV, LXXVIII
orthodoxy, XXVII, XLI, LXXV
ostentation (*riyā'*), 22, 162, 164
Ottoman society, LXXX
oxymel, 150

Pali, XCI
parents, XXI, 186
Philo, XLVI
Philoponus, XLVI
philosophy, XV, XLV-LVIII, LIX, LXXII, 238, 239
pigeons, 34
Plato, XLIV, XLVII, LI, LXI
Platonism, XXXIV, LV, LVII; Platonic virtues, LIX
Plotinus, LII, LIV, LXXXIV, 124E
pomegranates, 128
Porphyry, LII, LIII, LVI, LXXXIV
Proclus, LXXXIV
prayer, XXXI, XXXVI, XXXVIII, LXVII, 10, 32, 45A, 57, 67, 80A, 116, 119, 124, 125, 140, 152, 241
pride (*takabbur*), 21, 41, 97, 100, 163, 236
Posidonius of Rhodes, LXXXVI
Pythagorean thought, LIV, LVI, LVII, LXIV

qabḍ, 158
al-Qārānī, 138
qarīḥa, 118
Qāsim al-Jūᶜī, 149
Qays ibn ᶜĀṣim, 73
quinces, 150
Qur'ān, LXXII, 87, 125A; and ethics, XVII-XXII, LVI, LXIII; recitation of, 111, 116, 152
Quraysh, 70
al-Qushayrī, XXXIV, 82A, 130A
quṭb, 89B

Rābiᶜa al-ᶜAdawīya, LXXX, 178-9
raḥma, XVIII, XXIV
Ramaḍān, XXIX, XXX-XXXI
rational soul/faculty, LIII, 19, 31
al-Rāzī, Muḥammad ibn Zakarīya, XLIV, LIV, LXII
recklessness (*tahawwur*), 20
remembrance (*dhikr*), XXX, LXVII, 60, 63, 64, 92, 93, 96, 119, 129, 135, 239, 240, 241, 242; *dhikr al-qalb*, 93
repentance (*tawba*), XX, 38, 67, 87
resurrection, XVIII, XXXV, 62, 63, 108, 114, 121, 129, 190
al-Riḍā, 71
riḍā, XXVII, XXXIII
riyāḍa, XXVIII, XXIX, LVI, LVII, 32, 115, 133-153
al-Rūdhbārī, 92A

saᶜāda, LXXXVI
ṣabr, XXXI, 22

St Augustine, 124E
St John Chrysostom, XXIII
Sahl al-Tustarī, XXIII, XXXI, XXXII, XLIII, LXIV, XCII, 15, 73, 81, 89, 97A, 114, 129, 134, 137, 138, 152, 157, 161A
Sa'īd ibn Jubayr, 173
Sa'īd ibn al-Musayyib, 167, 179, 180
sakanjubīn, 150A
Ṣāliḥ al-Murrī, 148
Salmān al-Fārisī, 52
salt, 128
[al-]Sarī al-Saqaṭī, 62, 125, 149, 159
Satan, XIX, XLII, LXVII, 88, 89, 94, 107, 111, 166, 236, 240
al-Sawād, 126
Scales (*mīzān*), 7, 9
scopophilia, 123, 172, 187-8
scrupulousness (*wara'*), 22, 90, 133, 158
senses, 234
sensus communis, 234
sexual relations, desire, XXXI, XXXV-XLV, LXX, 432, 107, 122, 123, 151, 165-191
Shāfi'ī law, XVI, XLVII, LVIII, LXXIV, 50B
Shāh al-Kirmānī, XXXII, 15
shahāma, 21
shāhid, 175A
Shaqīq al-Balkhī, 113, 144
al-Sha'rānī, LXXXIII, XCI
Sha'wāna, XL
shawq, XXVII
Shaykh (spiritual master), LX, LXI, LXII, XCI, 29, 41, 51, 54, 88, 92, 95, 156, 160
al-Shiblī, 44C, 92, 118
shirk, XIX, 161
Shī'ism, XXIII, XXVII
ṣiddīq, 4, 60, 74, 123, 133A, 134, 138, 141, 156, 163, 183, 237
ṣighar al-nafs, 21
sikbāj, 144
silence (*ṣamt*), XXX, 59, 68, 88, 89, 90
Sinai, XVII
ṣirāṭ, 49
sleepnessness (*sahr*), XXXII, 88, 89, 90, 114, 123-5
Socrates, LXXXI
solitude, XXIX-XXX, LXVII, 65, 69, 88, 89
Solomon, 173
soul (*nafs*), passional, XIX-XX, XXVI, XXVII, XXX, , XXXI, 16, 18, 34-5, 39, 45, 233 and passim; faults in, 51-4; *ammāra bi'l-sū'*, XXVIII, 233, 235; *lawwāma*, XXVIII, 233; *muṭma'inna*, XXVIII, 233; Platonic division of, LI, LIII, LV, LIX, 19A, 22; Ibn Sīnā on, LVI; in Neoplatonism, LV; subdual of, XXXI, LII, LXIII and passim.
subḥān Allāh, 93, 152
Sufyān al-Thawrī, XXX, XXXIII, 57, 152, 158, 176
Sulaymān al-Khawwāṣ, 138
Sulaymān ibn Yasār, 184-6
sulūk, 84
sunna, 139
al-Suyūṭī, LXXXIII
spirit (*rūḥ*), XXVIII, LVI, LXXVI, 16, 93A, 233-4, 235
spite, 22
steadfastness (*thabāt*), 21
Stoicism, LI, LIV, LVII, LX, LXXIV, LXXXVII
stupidity (*balah*), 20, 21
swindling, 21

Tahāfut al-falāsifa, LXXII
tahajjud, 124, 140
taqlīd, LXIII, LXVI, 85, 132, 158, 237, 238
'tasting' (*dhawq*) LXVI, 120
tawāḍuᶜ, XXXIII
tawakkul, XX, 44C
Ṭāwūs, 110
tawḥīd, 4B
temperance (*ᶜiffa*), 20, 21, 22
Tertullian, XXXV
thaqābat al-ra'y, 21
al-Thawrī, 138
Theology of Aristotle, XLVII
al-Tifāshī, LXXXIII
tolerance (*musāmaḥᶜa*), 22
Torah, 111, 114
al-Ṭūsī, Naṣīr al-Dīn, XC, 77A
Tustar, 82
al-Tustarī, see 'Sahl'
tyranny (*jūr*), 20

Uḥud, 70
ᶜulamā', 47, 84
ᶜUmar ibn ᶜAbd al-ᶜAzīz, 59
ᶜUmar ibn al-Khaṭṭāb, 12, 14, 52, 113, 135, 142, 143, 159, 160
Umayyads, XXIII, 181D
Umm Ḥabība, 11
Umm Salama, 174
uns, XXVII, 172
unveiling (*mukāshafa*), LXVI, LXVII, 4B, 89, 98, 138, 139, 237, 238, 239
Usāma ibn Sharīk, 10
Usāma ibn Zayd, 109, 110
ᶜUtba al-Ghulām, 144, 147, 148
Uways al-Qaranī, 73
vainglory, 21
veil, XXXVIII
vices, XXX
virginity, celibacy, XXIII, XXXV, XLII–XLIII, 172

Wahb ibn Munabbih, 13, 58, 142
al-Walīd ibn ᶜAbd al-Malik, 181
waraᶜ, 22
al-Wāsiṭī, XXXIII, 15
waswās, LXVII, 115, 240, 242; and see '*khawāṭir*'
wird, 58
wisdom (*ḥikma*), 19, 20, 21, 22, 23, 46, 68, 119, 126
wit, 22
witr prayer, 124
witnessing (*mushāhada*), LXVI, 237
women, XXXVII–XXXVIII, 12, 177
wool, 108, 110
world (*dunyā*), XX, XXV, 62, 63 and passim.
Wuhayb ibn al-Ward, 58

Yaḥyā ibn ᶜAdī, XLIV, LV, LVI
Yaḥyā ibn Muᶜādh al-Rāzī, XXIV, XXV, 13, 14, 57, 113, 141
Yaḥyā ibn Ziyād al-Ḥārithī, 74
Yasār ibn ᶜUmayr, 144
Yazīd ibn Abī Sufyān, 143–4
Yazīd al-Ruqāshī, 59
Yūsuf ibn Asbāṭ, 73

al-Zabīdī, 44C
zaqqūm, 121
zāwiya, 92
zakāt, 118
Zoroastrian, 39, 72
Zuhayr, 138
Zulaykhā, LXXX, 58, 184